Lecture Notes in Computer Science 11812

More information about this series at http://www.springer.com/series/7408

Christophe Gaston · Nikolai Kosmatov ·
Pascale Le Gall (Eds.)

Testing Software and Systems

31st IFIP WG 6.1 International Conference, ICTSS 2019
Paris, France, October 15–17, 2019
Proceedings

Springer

Editors
Christophe Gaston (iD)
CEA List
Gif-sur-Yvette, France

Nikolai Kosmatov (iD)
CEA List
Gif-sur-Yvette, France

Pascale Le Gall (iD)
CentraleSupélec
Gif-sur-Yvette, France

ISSN 0302-9743   ISSN 1611-3349   (electronic)
Lecture Notes in Computer Science
ISBN 978-3-030-31279-4   ISBN 978-3-030-31280-0   (eBook)
https://doi.org/10.1007/978-3-030-31280-0

LNCS Sublibrary: SL2 – Programming and Software Engineering

This Springer imprint is published by the registered company Springer Nature Switzerland AG
The registered company address is: Gewerbestrasse 11, 6330 Cham, Switzerland

Preface

This volume contains the proceedings of the 31st IFIP International Conference on Testing Software and Systems (ICTSS 2019). ICTSS has become a traditional event of the WG 6.1 of the International Federation for Information Processing (IFIP). This year the acronym of the conference evolved to IFIP-ICTSS 2019 to reinforce the connection with IFIP. The conference was held in Paris, France, during October 15–17, 2019.

ICTSS is a series of international conferences addressing conceptual, theoretical, and practical problems of testing software systems, including communication protocols, services, distributed platforms, middleware, embedded and cyber-physical systems, and security infrastructures. It is a forum for researchers, developers, testers, and users from industry to review, discuss, and learn about new approaches, concepts, theories, methodologies, tools, and experiences in the field of testing of software and systems.

This year, IFIP-ICTSS 2019 received 30 submissions. Each paper was reviewed in a single-blind process by three reviewers and discussed by the Program Committee. After a careful selection process, the Program Committee accepted 14 regular papers, 3 short papers, and 1 industrial paper. Papers cover a large range of subjects such as test-case generation, testing in relation with artificial intelligence, proof and verification techniques, security, performance, as well as empirical studies.

The program also featured two invited talks. The first keynote "Intelligence Testing of Autonomous Software Systems" was given by Arnaud Gotlieb (Simula Lab, Norway). The second keynote "Testing Human-Centric Cyber-Physical Systems" was given by Mauro Pezzè (USI – Università della Svizzera italiana, Switzerland). We thank them for accepting to give an invited presentation at IFIP-ICTSS 2019.

This year, IFIP-ICTSS 2019 was co-located with the MTV2 2019 workshop. This annual workshop gathers the French testing community participating in the MTV2 (Methods of Testing for Verification and Validation) working group of the French network on Software Engineering and Programming (GDR GPL) of CNRS. We hope that this co-location encourages interactions and exchanges between the international and the French community interested in testing.

We would like to thank the Steering Committee for their advice and support in the organization of the conference. Many thanks to the Program Committee members, as well as to the additional reviewers, for their careful reviews and participation in the discussions during the paper selection. The process of reviewing and selecting the papers was significantly simplified through the use of EasyChair. We would also like to thank IFIP for their continuous support of the conference series, as well as Springer for having published this volume.

We kindly thank the Organizing Committee for their help in local organization of the event, and in particular Natalia Kushik and Sylvie Vignes for their support in the preparation of the conference at Télécom ParisTech.

Finally, we are very grateful to the sponsors of the conference: the List institute of CEA Tech, CentraleSupélec, Télécom ParisTech, the French network on Software Engineering and Programming (GDR GPL) of CNRS, and University of Paris-Saclay. Their support strongly contributed to the success of this event.

On behalf of the ICTSS organizers, we hope that you find the proceedings useful, interesting, and challenging.

July 2019

Nikolai Kosmatov
Christophe Gaston
Pascale Le Gall

Organization

Program Committee

Rui Abreu	INESC-ID/IST, University of Lisbon, Portugal
Bernhard K. Aichernig	TU Graz, Austria
Harald Altinger	Audi Electronics Venture GmbH, Germany
Gregor Bochmann	University of Ottawa, Canada
Ana R. Cavalli	Institut Mines-Télécom/Télécom SudParis, France
David Clark	University College London, UK
Pedro Delgado-Pérez	Universidad de Cádiz, Spain
Khaled El-Fakih	American University of Sharjah, UAE
Ylies Falcone	Grenoble Alpes University, France
Angelo Gargantini	University of Bergamo, Italy
Christophe Gaston (Co-chair)	CEA List, France
Arnaud Gotlieb	SIMULA Research Laboratory, Norway
Juergen Grossmann	Fraunhofer, Germany
Roland Groz	Grenoble INP, France
Rob Hierons	The University of Sheffield, UK
Teruo Higashino	Osaka University, Japan
Jie-Hong Roland Jiang	National Taiwan University, Taiwan
Thierry Jéron	Inria, France
Ferhat Khendek	Concordia University, Canada
Nikolai Kosmatov (Co-chair)	CEA List, France
Moez Krichen	REDCAD Research Unit, Tunisia
Natalia Kushik	Institut Mines-Télécom/Télécom SudParis, France
Pascale Le Gall (Co-chair)	CentraleSupélec, France
Luis Llana	Universidad Complutense de Madrid, Spain
Delphine Longuet	University Paris Saclay, France
Jorge Lopez	Institut Mines-Télécom/Télécom SudParis, France
Radu Mateescu	Inria, France
Inmaculada Medina-Bulo	University of Cadiz, Spain
Mercedes Merayo	Universidad Complutense de Madrid, Spain
Manuel Núñez	Universidad Complutense de Madrid, Spain
Mike Papadakis	University of Luxembourg, Luxembourg
Jan Peleska	University of Bremen, Germany
Antoine Rollet	University of Bordeaux, France
Sébastien Salva	University Clermont Auvergne, France
Sergio Segura	University of Seville, Spain
Hasan Sozer	Ozyegin University, Turkey

Daniel Sundmark	Mälardalen University, Sweden
Kenji Suzuki	Kennisbron Co., Ltd, Japan
Masaki Suzuki	KDDI Research, Inc., Japan
Andreas Ulrich	Siemens AG, Germany
Helene Waeselynck	CNRS, France
Burkhart Wolff	University Paris-Saclay, France
Franz Wotawa	Technische Universität Graz, Austria
Hüsnü Yenigün	Sabanci University, Turkey
Nina Yevtushenko	Tomsk State University, Russia
Fatiha Zaidi	University Paris-Saclay, France

Additional Reviewers

Ahuja, Mohit
Bombarda, Andrea
Collet, Mathieu
Lee, Nian-Ze
Mallouli, Wissam
Nguyen, Huu Nghia
Radavelli, Marco
Segovia, Mariana
Tappler, Martin

Keynotes

Intelligence Testing of Autonomous Software Systems

Arnaud Gotlieb

Simula Research Laboratory, Fornebu, Norway

Abstract. Autonomous Software Systems (ASS) are systems able to plan and execute complex functions with limited human intervention, i.e., systems with self-decision capabilities. They usually complement humans capacity to deal with unexpected events such as faults or hazards and take decisions based on vast amounts of uncertain data. Testing ASS is highly challenging as their requirements in terms of safety, performance, robustness, and reliability evolve with their level of autonomy. My talk will address the challenges of testing ASS and will present some cases where Artificial Intelligence techniques have been successful in deploying automated testing methods.

Testing Human-Centric Cyber-Physical Systems

Mauro Pezzè

USI - Università della Svizzera Italiana, Lugano, Switzerland

Abstract. Human-centric cyber-physical systems are systems where software, devices, and people seamlessly and endlessly interact with evolving goals, requirements, and constraints. They are increasingly pervading our life, and span from simple mobile and Web applications, like recommendation systems and virtual shops, to complex evolving systems, like autonomous vehicles and smart cities. In this talk, I will give a broad and visionary view of the emerging issues and opportunities in the verification of human-centric cyber-physical systems. I will introduce the main features and survey the main open challenges of testing human-centric cyber-physical systems. I will discuss scope and limitation of the most recent research results in software testing; I will overview the ongoing partial but promising rescarch activities in our USI-Star and UniMiB-LTA laboratories, and I will propose my vision of the most challenging open research issues.

Contents

Testing and Verification Techniques

Security and Performance Testing

Industrial Applications

Test and Artificial Intelligence

Learning a Behavior Model of Hybrid Systems Through Combining Model-Based Testing and Machine Learning

Bernhard K. Aichernig, Roderick Bloem, Masoud Ebrahimi, Martin Horn, Franz Pernkopf, Wolfgang Roth, Astrid Rupp, Martin Tappler[✉], and Markus Tranninger

Graz University of Technology, Graz, Austria
{aichernig,martin.tappler}@ist.tugraz.at,
{roderick.bloem,masoud.ebrahimi}@iaik.tugraz.at
{martin.horn,pernkopf,roth,markus.tranninger}@tugraz.at
astrid.rupp@fprimezero.com

Abstract. Models play an essential role in the design process of cyber-physical systems. They form the basis for simulation and analysis and help in identifying design problems as early as possible. However, the construction of models that comprise physical and digital behavior is challenging. Therefore, there is considerable interest in learning such hybrid behavior by means of machine learning which requires sufficient and representative training data covering the behavior of the physical system adequately. In this work, we exploit a combination of automata learning and model-based testing to generate sufficient training data fully automatically.

Experimental results on a platooning scenario show that recurrent neural networks learned with this data achieved significantly better results compared to models learned from randomly generated data. In particular, the classification error for crash detection is reduced by a factor of five and a similar F1-score is obtained with up to three orders of magnitude fewer training samples.

Keywords: Hybrid systems · Behavior modeling · Automata learning · Model-Based Testing · Machine learning · Autonomous vehicle · Platooning

1 Introduction

In Cyber Physical Systems (CPSs), embedded computers and networks control physical processes. Most often, CPSs interact with their surroundings based on the context and the (history of) external events through an analog interface.

© IFIP International Federation for Information Processing 2019
Published by Springer Nature Switzerland AG 2019
C. Gaston et al. (Eds.): ICTSS 2019, LNCS 11812, pp. 3–21, 2019.
https://doi.org/10.1007/978-3-030-31280-0_1

We use the term hybrid system to refer to such reactive systems that intermix discrete and continuous components [23]. Since hybrid systems are dominating safety-critical areas, safety assurances are of utmost importance. However, we know that most verification problems for hybrid systems are undecidable [14].

Therefore, models and model-based simulation play an essential role in the design process of such systems. They help in identifying design problems as early as possible and facilitate integration testing with model-in-the-loop techniques. However, the construction of hybrid models that comprise physical and digital behavior is challenging. Modeling such systems with reasonable fidelity requires expertise in several areas, including control engineering, software engineering and sensor networks [9].

Therefore, we see a growing interest in learning such cyber-physical behavior with the help of machine learning. Examples include helicopter dynamics [29], the physical layer of communication protocols [26], standard continuous control problems [11], and industrial process control [35].

However, in general, machine learning requires a large and representative set of training data. Moreover, for the simulation of safety-critical features, rare side-conditions need to be sufficiently covered. Given the large state-space of hybrid systems, it is difficult to gather a good training set that captures all critical behavior. Neither nominal samples from operation nor randomly generated data will be sufficient. Here, advanced test-case generation methods can help to derive a well-designed training set with adequate coverage.

In this paper, we combine automata learning and Model-Based Testing (MBT) to derive an adequate training set, and then use machine learning to learn a behavior model from a black-box hybrid system. We can use the learned behavior model for multiple purposes such as monitoring run-time behavior. Furthermore, it could be used as a surrogate of a complex and heavy-weight simulation model to efficiently analyze safety-critical behavior offline [33]. Figure 1 depicts the overall execution flow of our proposed setting. Given a black-box hybrid system, we learn automata as discrete abstractions of the system. Next, we investigate the learned automata for critical behaviors.

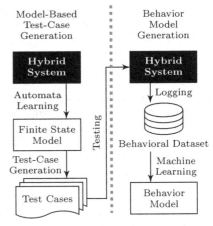

Fig. 1. Learning a behavior model of a black-box hybrid system.

Once behaviors of interest are discovered, we use Model-Based Testing (MBT) to drive the hybrid system towards these behaviors and determine its observable actions in a continuous domain. This process results in a behavioral dataset with high coverage of the hybrid system's behavior including rare conditions. Finally, we train a Recurrent Neural Network (RNN) model that generalizes the behav-

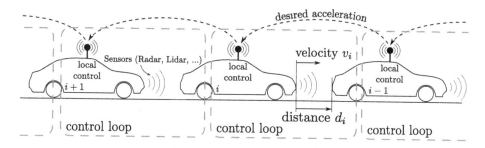

Fig. 2. Platooning as distributed control scenario. Adapted from a figure in [10].

ioral dataset. For evaluation, we compared four different testing approaches, by generating datasets via testing, learning RNN models from the data and computing various performance measures for detecting critical behaviors in unforeseen situations. Experimental results show that RNNs learned with data generated via MBT achieved significantly better performance compared to models learned from randomly generated data. In particular, the classification error is reduced by a factor of five and a similar F1-score is accomplished with up to three orders of magnitude fewer training samples.

Motivating Example. Throughout the paper we illustrate our approach utilizing a platooning scenario, implemented in a testbed in the Automated Driving Lab at Graz University of Technology (see also https://www.tugraz.at/institute/irt/research/automated-driving-lab/). Platooning of vehicles is a complex distributed control scenario, see Fig. 2. Local control algorithms of each participant are responsible for reliable velocity and distance control. The vehicles continuously sense their environments, e.g. the distance to the vehicle ahead and may use discrete, i.e. event triggered, communication to communicate desired accelerations along the platoon [10]. Besides individual vehicle stability, the most crucial goal in controller design is to guarantee so-called string stability of the platoon [28]. This stability concept basically demands that errors in position or velocity do not propagate along the vehicle string which otherwise might cause accidents or traffic jams upstream. Controllers for different platooning scenarios and spacing policies are available, e. g., constant time headway spacing [28] or constant distance spacing with or without communication [31].

Available controller designs are legitimated by rigorous mathematical stability proofs as an important theoretical foundation. In real applications it is often hard to fulfill every single modeling assumption of the underlying proofs, e. g., perfect sensing or communication. However, these additional uncertainties can often be captured in fine-grained simulation models. This motivates MBT of vehicle platooning control algorithms by the approach presented in this paper. Also, the learned behavior model can be used to detect undesired behavior during run-time. In [10], a hybrid system formulation of a platooning scenario is presented based on control theoretic considerations. In this contribution we aim to determine targeted behavior of such models with as few assumptions as possible by combining MBT and machine learning. As a first step, we consider two vehicles of the platoon, the leader and its first follower, in this paper, but the general approach can be extended to more vehicles.

Outline. This paper has the following structure. Section 2 summarizes automata learning and MBT. Section 3 explains how to learn an automaton from a black-box hybrid system, then use it to target interesting behavior of the hybrid system such that we create a behavioral dataset that can be used for machine learning purposes. Section 4 discusses the results gained by applying our approach to a real-world platooning scenario. Section 5 covers related work. Section 6 concludes and discusses future research directions.

2 Preliminaries

Definition 1 (Mealy Machine). *A Mealy machine is a tuple* $\langle I, O, Q, q_0, \delta, \lambda \rangle$ *where* Q *is a nonempty set of states,* q_0 *is the initial state,* $\delta : Q \times I \to Q$ *is a state-transition function and* $\lambda : Q \times I \to O$ *is an output function.*

We write $q \xrightarrow{i/o} q'$ if $q' = \delta(q, i)$ and $o = \lambda(q, i)$. We extend δ as usual to δ^* for input sequences π_i, i.e., $\delta^*(q, \pi_i)$ is the state reached after executing π_i in q.

Definition 2 (Observation). *An observation* π *over input/output alphabet* I *and* O *is a pair* $\langle \pi_i, \pi_o \rangle \in I^* \times O^*$ *s.t.* $|\pi_i| = |\pi_o|$. *Given a Mealy machine* $\mathcal{M}$, *the set of observations of* $\mathcal{M}$ *from state* q *denoted by* $obs_\mathcal{M}(q)$ *are*

$$obs_\mathcal{M}(q) = \left\{ \langle \pi_i, \pi_o \rangle \in I^* \times O^* \,\middle|\, \exists q' : q \xrightarrow{\pi_i/\pi_o} {}^* q' \right\}, \text{ where } \xrightarrow{\pi_i/\pi_o} {}^* \text{ is the tran-}$$

sitive and reflexive closure of the combined transition-and-output function to sequences which implies $|\pi_i| = |\pi_o|$. *From this point forward,* $obs_\mathcal{M} = obs_\mathcal{M}(q_0)$. *Two Mealy machines* $\mathcal{M}_1$ *and* $\mathcal{M}_2$ *are observation equivalent, denoted* $\mathcal{M}_1 \approx \mathcal{M}_2$, *if* $obs_{\mathcal{M}_1} = obs_{\mathcal{M}_2}$.

2.1 Active Automata Learning

In her semimal paper, Angluin [5] presented L*, an algorithm for learning a deterministic finite automaton (DFA) accepting an unknown regular language L from a minimally adequate teacher (MAT). Many other active learning algorithms also use the MAT model [16]. An MAT generally needs to be able to answer two types of queries: *membership* and *equivalence* queries. In DFA learning, the learner asks membership queries, checking inclusion of words in the language L. Once gained enough information, the learner builds a hypothesis automaton $\mathcal{H}$ and asks an equivalence query, checking whether $\mathcal{H}$ accepts exactly L. The MAT either responds with *yes*, meaning that learning was successful. Otherwise it responds with a counterexample to equivalence, i.e., a word in the symmetric difference between L and the language accepted by $\mathcal{H}$. If provided with a counterexample, the learner integrates it into its knowledge and starts a new round of learning by issuing membership queries, which is again concluded by a new equivalence query. L* is adapted to learn Mealy machines by Shahbaz and Groz [32]. The basic principle remains the same, but *output queries* replace membership queries asking for outputs produced in response to input sequences. The goal in this adapted L* algorithm, is to learn a Mealy machine that is observation equivalent to a black-box system under learning (SUL).

Abstraction. L* is only affordable for small alphabets; hence, Aarts et al. [1] suggested to abstract away the concrete domain of the data, by forming equivalence classes in the alphabets. This is usually done by a mapper placed in between the learner and the SUL; see Fig. 3. Practically, mappers are state-full components transducing symbols back and forth between abstract and concrete alphabets using constraints defined over different ranges of concrete values. Since the input and output space of control systems is generally large or of unbounded size, we also apply abstraction by using a mapper.

The mapper communicates with the SUL via the concrete alphabet and with the learner via the abstract alphabet. In the setting shown in Fig. 3, the learner behaves like the L* algorithm by Shahbaz and Groz [32], but the teacher answers to the queries by interacting with the SUL through the mapper.

Learning and Model-Based Testing. Teachers are usually implemented via testing to learn models of black-box systems, The teacher in Fig. 3 wraps the SUL, uses a mapper for abstraction and includes a Model-Based Testing (MBT) component. Output queries typically reset the SUL, execute a sequence of inputs and collect the produced outputs, i.e., they perform a single test of the SUL. Equivalence queries are often approximated via MBT [3]. For that, an MBT compo-

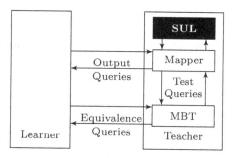

Fig. 3. Abstract automata learning [37].

nent derives test cases (test queries) from the hypothesis model, which are executed to find discrepancies between the SUL and the learned hypothesis, i.e., to find counterexamples to equivalence.

Various MBT techniques have been applied in active automata learning, like the W-METHOD [8,38], or the PARTIAL W-METHOD [13], which are also implemented in LearnLib [18]. These techniques attempt to prove conformance relative to some bound on the SUL states. However, these approaches require a large number of tests. Given the limited testing time available in practice, it is usually necessary to aim at "finding counterexamples fast" [17]. Therefore, randomized testing has recently shown to be successful in the context of automata learning, such as a randomized conformance testing technique [34] and fault-coverage-based testing [4]. We apply a variation of the latter, which combines transition coverage as test selection criterion with randomization.

While active automata learning relies on MBT to implement equivalence queries, it also enables MBT, by learning models that serve as basis for testing [3,16]. Automata learning can be seen as collecting and incrementally refining information about a SUL through testing. This process is often combined with formal verification of requirements, both at runtime and also offline using learned models. This combination has been pioneered by Peled et al. [27] and called black-box checking. More generally, approaches that use automata learning for testing are also referred to as Learning-Based Testing (LBT) [25].

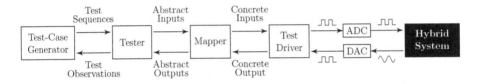

Fig. 4. Components involved in the testing process

3   Methodology

Our goal is to learn a behavior model capturing the targeted behavior of a hybrid SUL. The model's response to a trajectory of input variables, (e. g., sensor information), shall conform to the SUL's response with high accuracy and precision. As in discrete systems, purely random generation of input trajectories is unlikely to exercise the SUL's state space adequately. Consequently, models learned from random traces cannot accurately capture the SUL's behavior. Therefore, we propose to apply automata learning followed by MBT to collect system traces while using a machine learning method (i. e., Recurrent Neural Networks) for model learning. Figure 1 shows a generalized version of our approach.

Our trace-generation approach does not require any knowledge, like random sampling, but may benefit from domain knowledge and specified requirements. For instance, we do not explore states any further, which already violate safety requirements. In the following, we will first discuss the testing process. This includes interaction with the SUL, abstraction, automata learning and test-case generation. Then, we discuss learning a behavior model in the form of a Recurrent Neural Network with training data collected by executing tests.

Back to Motivating Example. We learn a behavior model for our platooning scenario in three steps: (1) automata learning exploring a discretized platooning control system to capture the state space structure in learned models, (2) MBT exploring the state space of the learned model directed towards targeted behavior while collecting non-discrete system traces. In step (3), we generalize from those trace by learning a Recurrent Neural Network.

3.1 Testing Process

We apply various test-case generation methods, with the same underlying abstraction and execution framework. Figure 4 depicts the components implementing the testing process.

- **Test-Case Generator:** the test-case generator creates abstract test cases. These test-cases are generated offline as sequences of abstract inputs.
- **Tester:** the tester takes an input sequence and passes it to the mapper. Feedback from test-case execution is forwarded to the test-case generator.
- **Mapper:** the mapper maps each abstract input to a concrete input variable valuation and a duration, defining how long the input should be applied. Concrete output variable valuations observed during testing are mapped to abstract outputs. Each test sequence produces an abstract output sequence which is returned to the tester.
- **Test Driver & Hybrid System:** The test driver interacts with the hybrid system by setting input variables and sampling output variable values.

3.1.1 System Interface and Sampling

We assume a system interface comprising two sets of real-valued variables: input variables U and observable output variables Y, with U further partitioned into controllable variables U_C and uncontrollable, observable input variables U_E affected by the environment. We denote all observable variables by $Obs = Y \cup U_E$. Additionally, we assume the ability to *reset* the SUL, as all test runs for trace generation need to start from a unique initial state. During testing, we change the controllable variables U_C and observe the evolution of variable valuations at fixed sampling intervals of length t_s.

Back to Motivating Example. We implemented our platooning SUL in MathWorks Simulink®. The implementation actually models a platoon of remote-controlled trucks used in our testbed at the Automated Driving Lab, therefore the acceleration values and distance have been downsized. The SUL interface comprises: $U_C = \{acc\}$, $Y = \{d, v_l, v_f\}$, and $U_E = \{\Delta\}$. The leader acceleration 'acc' is the single controllable input with values ranging from $-1.5 m/s^2$ to $1.5 m/s^2$, the distance between leader and first follower is 'd', and 'v_l' and 'v_f' are the velocities of the leader and the follower, respectively; finally 'Δ' denotes the angle between the leader and the x-axis in a fixed coordinate systems given in radians, i. e., it represents the orientation of the leader that changes while driving along the road. We sampled values of these variables at fixed discrete time steps, which are $t_s = 250$ ms apart.

3.1.2 Abstraction

We discretize variable valuations for testing via the mapper. With that we effectively abstract the hybrid system such that a Mealy machine over an abstract alphabet can model it. Each abstract input is mapped to a concrete valuation for U_C and a duration specifying how long the valuation shall be applied, thus U_C only takes values from a finite set. As abstract inputs are mapped to uniquely defined concrete inputs, this form of abstraction does not introduce non-determinism. In contrast, values of observable variables Obs are not restricted to a finite set. Therefore, we group concrete valuations of Obs and assign an abstract output label to each group.

The mapper also defines a set of labels $Violations$ containing abstract outputs that signal violations of assumptions or safety requirements. In the abstraction to a Mealy machine, these outputs lead to trap states from which the model does not transit away. Such a policy prunes the abstract state space.

A mapper has five components: (1) an abstract input alphabet I, (2) a corresponding concretization function γ, (3) an abstraction function α mapping concrete output values to (4) an abstract output alphabet O, and (5) the set $Violations$. During testing, it performs the following two actions:

- **Input Concretization:** the mapper maps an abstract symbol $i \in I$ to a pair $\gamma(i) = (\nu, d)$, where ν is a valuation of U_C and $d \in \mathbb{N}$ defining time steps, for how long U_C is set according to ν. This pair is passed to the test driver.
- **Output Abstraction:** the mapper receives concrete valuations ν of Obs from the test driver and maps them to an abstract output symbol $o = \alpha(\nu)$ in O that is passed to the tester. If $o \in Violations$, then the mapper stores o in its state and maps all subsequent concrete outputs to o until it is reset.

The mapper state needs to be reset before every test-case execution. Repeating the same symbol $o \in Violations$, if we have seen it once, creates trap states to prune the abstract state space. Furthermore, the implementation of the mapper contains a cache, returning abstract output sequences without SUL interaction.

Back to Motivating Example. We tested the SUL with an alphabet I of six abstract inputs: *fast-acc*, *slow-acc*, *const*, *const$_l$*, *brake* and *hard-brake*, concretized by $\gamma(\textit{fast-acc}) = (acc \mapsto 1.5m/s^2, 2)$, $\gamma(\textit{slow-acc}) = (acc \mapsto 0.7m/s^2, 2)$, $\gamma(\textit{const}) = (acc \mapsto 0m/s^2, 2)$, $\gamma(\textit{const}_l) = (acc \mapsto 0m/s^2, 8)$, $\gamma(\textit{brake}) = (acc \mapsto -0.7m/s^2, 2)$, and $\gamma(\textit{hard-brake}) = (acc \mapsto -1.5m/s^2, 2)$. Thus, each input takes two time steps, except for *const$_l$*, which represents prolonged driving at constant speed.

The output abstraction depends on the distance d and the leader velocity v_l. If v_l is negative, we map to the abstract output *reverse*. Otherwise, we partition d into 7 ranges with one abstract output per range, e. g., the range $(-\infty, 0.43m)$ (length of a remote-controlled truck) is mapped to *crash*. We assume that platoons do not drive in reverse. Therefore, we include *reverse* in $Violations$, such that once we observe *reverse*, we ignore the subsequent behavior. We also added *crash* to $Violations$, as we are only interested in the behavior leading to a crash.

3.1.3   Test-Case Execution

The concrete test execution is implemented by a test driver. It basically generates step-function-shaped inputs signals for input variables and samples output variable values. For each concrete input (ν_j, d_j) applied at time t_j (starting at

$t_1 = 0ms$), the test driver sets U_C according to ν_j for $d_j \cdot t_s$ milliseconds and samples the values ν'_j of observable variables $Y \cup U_E$ at time $t_j + d_j \cdot t_s - t_s/2$. It then proceeds to time $t_{j+1} = t_j + d_j \cdot t_s$ to perform the next input if there is any. In that way, the test driver creates a sequence of sampled output variable values ν'_j, one for each concrete input. This sequence is passed to the mapper for output abstraction.

3.1.4   Viewing Hybrid Systems as Mealy Machines

Our test-case execution samples exactly one output value for each input, $t_s/2$ milliseconds before the next input, which ensures that there is an output for each input, such that input and output sequences have the same length. Given an abstract input sequence π_i our test-case execution produces an output sequence π_o of the same length. In slight abuse of notation, we denote this relationship by $\lambda_h(\pi_i) = \pi_o$. Hence, we view the hybrid system under test on an abstract level as a Mealy machine $\mathcal{H}_m$ with $obs_{\mathcal{H}_m} = \{\langle \pi_i, \lambda_h(\pi_i)\rangle | \pi_i \in I^*\}$.

3.1.5   Learning Automata of Motivating Example

We applied the active automata learning algorithm by Kearns and Vazirani (KV) [19], implemented by LearnLib [18], in combination with the *transition-coverage* testing strategy described in previous work [4]. We have chosen the KV algorithm, as it requires fewer output queries to generate a new hypothesis model than, e.g., L* [5], such that more equivalence queries are performed. As a result, we can guide testing during equivalence queries more often. The Transition-Coverage Based Testing (TCBT) strategy is discussed below in Sect. 3.1.6.

Here, our goal is not to learn an accurate model, but to explore the SUL's state space systematically through automata learning. The learned hypothesis models basically keep track of what has already been tested. Automata learning operates in rounds, alternating between series of output queries and equivalence queries. We stop this process once we performed the maximum number of tests N_{autl}, which includes both output queries and test queries implementing equivalence queries. Due to the large state space of the analyzed platooning SUL, it was infeasable to learn a complete model, hence we stopped learning when reaching the bound N_{autl}, even though further tests could have revealed discrepancies.

Back to Motivating Example. The learned automata also provided insights into the behavior of the platooning SUL. A manual analysis revealed that collisions are more likely to occur, if trucks drive at constant speed for several time steps. Since we aimed at testing and analyzing the SUL with respect to dangerous situations, we created the additional abstract $const_l$ input, which initially was not part of the set of abstract inputs.

During active automata learning we executed approximately $N_{\mathrm{autl}} 260000$ concrete tests on the platooning SUL in 841 learning rounds, producing 2841 collisions. In the last round, we generated a hypothesis Mealy machine with 6011 states that we use for model-based testing. Generally, N_{autl} should be chosen as large as possible given the available time budget for testing, as a larger N_{autl} leads to more accurate abstract models.

3.1.6 Test-Case Generation

In the following, we describe random test-case generation for Mealy machines, which serves as a baseline. Then, we describe three different approaches to model-based test-case generation. Note that our testing goal is to explore the system's state space and to generate system traces with high coverage, with the intention of learning a neural network. Therefore, we generate a fixed number of test cases N_{train} and do not impose conditions on outputs other than those defined by the set *Violations* in the mapper.

3.1.6.1 Random Testing. Our random testing strategy generates input sequences with a length chosen uniformly at random between 1 and the maximum length l_{max}. Inputs in the sequence are also chosen uniformly at random from I.

3.1.6.2 Learning-Based Testing. The LBT strategy performs automata learning as described in Sect. 3.1.5. It produces exactly those tests executed during automata learning and therefore sets N_{autl} to N_{train}. While this strategy systematically explores the abstract state space of the SUL, it also generates very simple tests during the early rounds of learning, which are not helpful for learning a behavior model in Sect. 3.2.

3.1.6.3 Transition-Coverage Based Testing. The Transition-Coverage Based Testing (TCBT) strategy uses a learned model of the SUL as basis. Basically, we learn a model, fix that model and then generate N_{train} test sequences with the *transition-coverage* testing strategy discussed in [4]. We use it, as it performed well in automata learning and it scales to large automata. The intuition behind it is that the combination of variability through randomization and coverage-guided testing is well-suited in a black-box setting as in automata learning.

Test-case generation from a Mealy machine $\mathcal{M}$ with this strategy is split into two phases, a generation phase and a selection phase. The generation phase generates a large number of tests by performing random walks through $\mathcal{M}$. In the selection phase, n tests are selected to optimize the coverage of the transitions of $\mathcal{M}$. Since the n required to cover all transitions may be much lower than N_{train}, we performed several rounds, alternating between generation and selection until we selected and executed N_{train} test cases.

3.1.6.4 Output-Directed Testing. Our Output-Directed Testing strategy also combines random walks with coverage-guided testing, but aims at covering a given abstract output '*label*'. Therefore, it is based on a learned Mealy machine of the SUL. A set consisting of N_{train} tests is generated by Algorithm 1. All tests consist of a random '*prefix*' that leads to a random source state q_r, an '*interfix*' leading to a randomly chosen destination state q_r' and a '*suffix*' from q_r' to the '*label*'. The suffix explicitly targets a specific output, the interfix aims to increase the coverall SUL coverage and the random prefix introduces variability.

Algorithm 1. Output-Directed test-case generator

Input: $\mathcal{M} = \langle I, O, Q, q_0, \delta, \lambda \rangle$, $label \in O$, N_{train}
Output: TestCases : a set of test cases directed to '$label \in O$'
1: TestCases $\leftarrow \emptyset$
2: **while** $|\text{TestCases}| < N_{train}$ **do**
3:    $rand\text{-}len \leftarrow$ RANDOMINTEGER
4:    $prefix \leftarrow$ RANDOMSEQUENCE$(I, rand\text{-}len)$
5:    $q_r \leftarrow \delta^*(q_0, prefix)$
6:    $q_r' \leftarrow$ RANDOMSTATE(Q)
7:    $interfix \leftarrow$ PATHTOSTATE(q_r, q_r') ▷ input sequence to q_r'
8:    **if** $interfix \neq \bot$ **then**   ▷ check if path to state exists
9:      $suffix \leftarrow$ PATHTOLABEL$(q_r, label)$ ▷ input sequence to $label$
10:     **if** $suffix \neq \bot$ **then**   ▷ check if path to label exists
11:       TestCases $\leftarrow$ TestCases $\cup \{prefix \cdot interfix \cdot suffix\}$
12: **return** TestCases

Back to Motivating Example. In our platooning scenario, we aim at covering behavior relevant to collisions, thus we generally set $label = crash$ and refer to the corresponding test strategy also as Crash-Directed Testing.

3.2 Learning a Recurrent Neural Network Behavior Model

In our scenario, we are given length T sequences of vectors $\mathbf{X} = (\mathbf{x}_1, \ldots, \mathbf{x}_T)$ with $\mathbf{x}_i \in \mathbb{R}^{d_x}$ representing the inputs to the hybrid system, and the task is to predict corresponding length T sequences of target vectors $\mathbf{T} = (\mathbf{t}_1, \ldots, \mathbf{t}_T)$ with $\mathbf{t}_i \in \mathbb{R}^{d_y}$ representing the outputs of the hybrid system. Recurrent Neural Networks (RNNs) are a popular choice for modelling these kinds of problems.

Given a set of N training input/output sequence pairs $\mathcal{D} = \{(\mathbf{X}_n, \mathbf{T}_n)\}_{n=1}^N$, the task of machine learning is to find suitable model parameters such that the output sequences $\{\mathbf{Y}_n\}_{n=1}^N$ computed by the RNN for input sequences $\{\mathbf{X}_n\}_{n=1}^N$ closely match their corresponding target sequences $\{\mathbf{T}_n\}_{n=1}^N$, and, more importantly, generalize well to sequences that are not part of the training set $\mathcal{D}$, i.e., the RNN produces accurate results on unseen data. To obtain suitable RNN parameters, we typically minimize a loss function describing the misfit between predictions $\mathbf{Y}$ and ground truth targets $\mathbf{T}$. Here, we achieve this through a minimization procedure known as stochastic gradient descent which works efficiently. For details on RNN learning, we refer to the extended version of this paper [2].

Back to Motivating Example. In our platooning scenario, the inputs $\mathbf{x}_i \in \mathbb{R}^2$ at time step i to the hybrid system comprise the input variables U from Sect. 3.1.1, i.e., the acceleration value acc and the orientation Δ of the leader car in radians. We preprocess the orientation Δ and transform it to $\Delta' = \Delta_i - \Delta_{i-1}$, the angular difference of orientation in radians of consecutive time steps to get rid of discontinuities when these values are constrained to a fixed interval of length 2π. The outputs $\mathbf{y}_i \in \mathbb{R}^3$ at time step i of the hybrid system comprise the values of observable output variables Y from Sect. 3.1.1, i.e., the velocity of the leader v_l and the first follower v_f, respectively, as well as the distance d between the leader and the first follower.

Note that RNNs are not constrained to sequences of a fixed length T. However, training with fixed-length sequences is more efficient as it allows full parallelization through GPU computations. Hence, during test-case execution, we pad sequences at the end with concrete inputs ($acc \mapsto 0, 1$), i. e., the leader drives at constant speed at the end of every test. In rare cases the collected test data showed awkward behavior that needed to be truncated at some time step, e. g., when the leader's velocity v_l became negative. We padded the affected sequences at the beginning by copying the initial state where all cars have zero velocity. We used this padding procedure to obtain fixed-length sequences with $T = 256$.

In our experiments we use RNNs with one hidden layer of 100 neurons. Since plain RNNs are well-known to lack the ability to model long-term dependencies, we use long short-term memory (LSTM) cells for the hidden layers [15]. To evaluate the generated training sequences, we train models for several values of training set sizes N_{train}. We used ADAM [20] implemented in Keras [7] with a learning rate $\eta = 10^{-3}$ to perform stochastic gradient descent for 500 epochs. The number of training sequences per mini-batch is set to $\min(N_{\text{train}}/100, 500)$. Each experiment is performed ten times using different random initial parameters and we report the average performance measures over these ten runs.

4 Experimental Evaluations

4.1 Predicting Crashes with RNNs

We aim to predict whether a sequence of input values results in a crash, i.e., we are dealing with a binary classification problem. A sequence is predicted as positive, i.e., the sequence contains a crash, if at any time step the leader-follower distance d gets below $0.43m$ which is the length of a remote-controlled truck.

For the evaluation, we generated validation sequences with the Output-Directed Testing strategy. This strategy produces crashes more frequently than the other testing strategies which is useful to keep the class imbalance between crash and non-crash sequences in the validation set minimal. We emphasize that these validation sequences do not overlap with the training sequences that were used to train the LSTM-RNN with Output-Directed Testing sequences. The validation set[1] contains $N_{\text{val}} = 86800$ sequences out of which 17092 (19.7%) result in a crash.

For the reported scores of our binary classification task we first define the following convenient values:

True Positive (TP): #{ positive sequences predicted as positive }
False Positive (FP): #{ negative sequences predicted as positive }
True Negative (TN): #{ negative sequences predicted as negative }
False Negative (FN): #{ positive sequences predicted as negative }

---

[1] This set is usually called test set in the context of machine learning, but here we adopt the term validation set to avoid confusion with model-based testing.

We report the following four measures: (1) the classification error (CE) in %, (2) the true positive rate (TPR), (3) the positive predictive value (PPV), and (4) the F1-score (F1). These scores are defined as

$$CE = \frac{FP + FN}{N_{val}} \times 100 \qquad\qquad TPR = \frac{TP}{TP + FN}$$

$$PPV = \frac{TP}{TP + FP} \qquad\qquad F1 = \frac{2TP}{2TP + FP + FN}$$

The TPR and the PPV suffer from the unfavorable property that they result in unreasonably high values if the LSTM-RNN simply classifies all sequences either as positive or negative. The F1-score is essentially the harmonic mean of the TPR and the PPV so that these odd cases are ruled out. Note that while for the CE a smaller value indicates a better performance, for the other scores TPR, PPV, and F1 a higher score, i. e., closer to 1, indicates a better performance.

The average results and the standard deviations over ten runs for these scores are shown in Fig. 5. The LSTM-RNNs trained with sequences from Random Testing and LBT perform poorly on all scores especially if the number of training sequences N_{train} is small. Notably, we found that sequences generated by LBT during early rounds of automata learning are short and do not contain a lot of variability, explaining the poor performance of LBT for low N_{train}.

We can observe in Fig. 5b that Random Testing and LBT perform poorly at detecting crashes when they actually occur. Especially the performance drop of LBT at $N_{train} = 10000$ and of Random Testing at $N_{train} = 100000$ indicate that additional training sequences do not necessarily improve the capability to detect crashes as crashes in these sequences still appear to be outliers.

Training LSTM-RNNs with TCBT and Output-Directed Testing outperforms Random Testing and LBT for all training set sizes N_{train}, where the results slightly favor Output-Directed Testing. The advantage of TCBT and Output-Directed Testing becomes evident when comparing the training set size N_{train} required to achieve the performance that Random Testing achieves using the maximum of $N_{train} = 200000$ sequences. The CE of Random Testing at $N_{train} = 200000$ is 7.23% which LBT outperforms at $N_{train} = 100000$ with 6.36%, TCBT outperforms at $N_{train} = 1000$ with 6.16%, and Output-Directed Testing outperforms at $N_{train} = 500$ with 5.22%. Comparing LBT and Output-Directed Testing, Output-Directed Testing outperforms the 2.77% CE of LBT at $N_{train} = 200000$ with only $N_{train} = 5000$ sequences to achieve a 2.55% CE.

The F1-score is improved similarly: Random Testing with $N_{train} = 200000$ achieves 0.809, while TCBT achieves 0.830 using only $N_{train} = 1000$ sequences, and Output-Directed Testing achieves 0.865 using only $N_{train} = 500$ sequences. Comparing LBT and Output-Directed Testing, LBT achieves 0.929 at $N_{train} = 200000$ whereas Output-Directed Testing requires only $N_{train} = 5000$ to achieve a F1-score of 0.936. In total, the sample size efficiency of TCBT and Output-Directed Testing is two to three orders of magnitudes larger than for Random Testing and LBT.

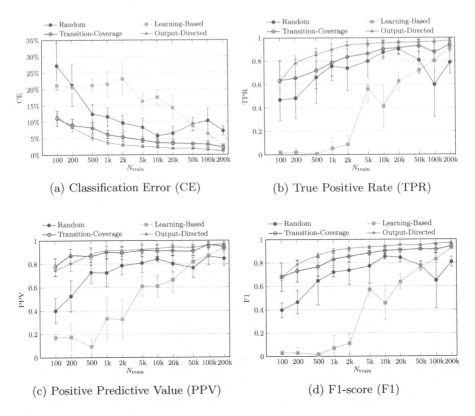

(a) Classification Error (CE)   (b) True Positive Rate (TPR)

(c) Positive Predictive Value (PPV)   (d) F1-score (F1)

Fig. 5. Performance measures for all testing strategies over changing N_{train}.

4.2   Evaluation of the Detected Crash Times

In the next experiment, we evaluate the accuracy of the crash prediction time. The predicted crash time is the earliest time step at which d drops below the threshold of $0.43m$, and the crash detection time error is the absolute difference between the ground truth crash time and the predicted crash time. Please note that the crash detection time error is only meaningful for true positive sequences.

Figure 6 shows CDF plots describing how the crash detection time error distributes over the true positive sequences. It is desired that the CDF exhibits a steep increase at the beginning which implies that most of the crashes are detected close to the ground truth crash time. The CDF value at crash detection time error 0 indicates the percentage of sequences whose crash is detected without error at the correct time step.

As expected the results get better for larger training sizes N_{train}. Random Testing and LBT exhibit large errors and only relatively few sequences are classified without error. For Random Testing, less than 30% of the crashes in the true positive sequences are classified correctly using the maximum of $N_{\text{train}} = 200000$ sequences. On the other side, TCBT requires only $N_{\text{train}} = 20000$ sequences to

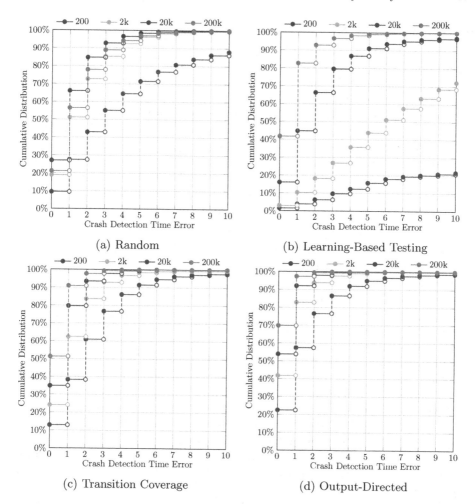

Fig. 6. CDF plots for the difference between true crash time and predicted crash time for sequences that are correctly classified as resulting in a crash. Results are shown for all testing strategies and several training dataset sizes N_{train}.

classify 34.9% correctly, and Output-Directed Testing requires only $N_{\text{train}} = 2000$ to classify 41.8% correctly. Combining the results from Fig. 6 with the TPR shown in Fig. 5b strengthens the crash prediction quality even more: While TCBT and Output-Directed Testing do not only achieve a higher TPR, they also predict the crashes more accurately. Furthermore, TCBT and Output-Directed Testing classify 90.9% and 97.3% of the sequences with at most one time step error using the maximum of $N_{\text{train}} = 200000$ sequences, respectively.

5   Related Work

Verifying Platooning Strategies. Meinke [24] used LBT to analyze vehicle platooning systems with respect to qualitative safety properties, like collisions. While the automata learning setup is similar to our approach, he aimed (1) to show how well a multi-core implementation of LBT method scales, and (2) how problem size and other factors affect scalability. Fermi et al. [12] applied rule inference methods to validate collision avoidance in platooning. More specifically, they used decision trees as classifiers for safe and unsafe platooning conditions, and they suggested three approaches to minimize the number of false negatives. Rashid et al. [30] modelled a generalized platoon controller formally in higher-order logic. They proved satisfaction of stability constraints in HOL LIGHT and showed how stability theorems can be used to develop runtime monitors.

System Identification and Safety Assurance. Determining models by using input-output data is known as *system identification* in the control systems community [21]. Such models can be useful for simulation, controller design or diagnosis purposes. Recently, progress towards system identification techniques for hybrid systems based on the classical methods presented e.g. in the book of Ljung [21] has been made, see [39] and the references therein. In [39], single-input single-output models are considered. Furthermore, the contribution focuses on so-called piece-wise affine ARX models. We believe that the presented hybrid automata learning techniques could essentially contribute to this research field by relaxing some of the modeling assumptions.

If the model parameters and the switching mechanism is known, the problem reduces to a hybrid state estimation problem [22,36]. Such estimators or observers are used in various problems, i.e. closed loop control, parameter estimation or diagnosis. However, the traditional methods often assume accurate and exact models. These models are mostly derived based on first principles [22], which is often not feasible in complex scenarios. This shows the advantage of our learning-based approach especially in cases without detailed model knowledge.

6   Future Work and Conclusion

We successfully combined abstract automata learning, MBT, and machine learning to learn a behavior model from observations of a hybrid system. Given a black-box hybrid system, we learn an abstract automaton capturing its discretized state-space; then, we use MBT to target a behavior of interest. This results in test suites with high coverage of the targeted behavior from which we generate a behavioral dataset. LSTM-RNNs are used to learn behavior models from the behavioral dataset. Advantages of our approach are demonstrated on a real-world case study; i.e., a platooning scenario. Experimental evaluations show that LSTM-RNNs learned with model-based data generation achieved significantly better results compared to models learned from randomly generated data, e.g., reducing the classification error by a factor of five, or achieving a relatively similar F1-score with up to three orders of magnitude fewer training samples than random testing. This is accomplished through systematic testing (i.e., automata learning, and MBT) of a black-box hybrid system without requiring a priori knowledge on its dynamics.

Motivated by the promising results shown in Sect. 4, we plan to carry out further case studies. For future research, we target runtime verification and runtime enforcement of safety properties for hybrid systems. To this end, we conjecture that a predictive behavior model enables effective runtime monitoring, which allows us to issue warnings or to intervene in case of likely safety violations. Adaptations of the presented approach are also potential targets for future research, e.g. automata learning and test-based trace generation could be interleaved in an iterative process.

Acknowledgment. This work is supported by the TU Graz LEAD project "Dependable Internet of Things in Adverse Environments". It is also partially supported by ECSEL Joint Undertaking under Grant No.: 692455.

References

1. Aarts, F., Heidarian, F., Kuppens, H., Olsen, P., Vaandrager, F.: Automata learning through counterexample guided abstraction refinement. In: Giannakopoulou, D., Méry, D. (eds.) FM 2012. LNCS, vol. 7436, pp. 10–27. Springer, Heidelberg (2012). https://doi.org/10.1007/978-3-642-32759-9_4
2. Aichernig, B.K., et al.: Learning a behavior model of hybrid systems through combining model-based testing and machine learning (full version). CoRR abs/1907.04708 (2019). http://arxiv.org/abs/1907.04708
3. Aichernig, B.K., Mostowski, W., Mousavi, M.R., Tappler, M., Taromirad, M.: Model learning and model-based testing. In: Bennaceur et al. [6], pp. 74–100. https://doi.org/10.1007/978-3-319-96562-8_3
4. Aichernig, B.K., Tappler, M.: Efficient active automata learning via mutation testing. J. Autom. Reason. (2018). https://doi.org/10.1007/s10817-018-9486-0
5. Angluin, D.: Learning regular sets from queries and counterexamples. Inf. Comput. **75**(2), 87–106 (1987)
6. Bennaceur, A., Hähnle, R., Meinke, K. (eds.): Machine Learning for Dynamic Software Analysis: Potentials and Limits. LNCS, vol. 11026. Springer, Cham (2018). https://doi.org/10.1007/978-3-319-96562-8
7. Chollet, F., et al.: Keras (2015). https://keras.io
8. Chow, T.S.: Testing software design modeled by finite-state machines. IEEE Trans. Softw. Eng. **4**(3), 178–187 (1978). https://doi.org/10.1109/TSE.1978.231496
9. Derler, P., Lee, E.A., Sangiovanni-Vincentelli, A.L.: Modeling cyber-physical systems. Proc. IEEE **100**(1), 13–28 (2012). https://doi.org/10.1109/JPROC.2011.2160929
10. Dolk, V.S., Ploeg, J., Heemels, W.P.M.H.: Event-triggered control for string-stable vehicle platooning. IEEE Trans. Intell. Transp. Syst. **18**(12), 3486–3500 (2017). https://doi.org/10.1109/TITS.2017.2738446
11. Duan, Y., Chen, X., Houthooft, R., Schulman, J., Abbeel, P.: Benchmarking deep reinforcement learning for continuous control. In: Balcan, M., Weinberger, K.Q. (eds.) ICML 2016. JMLR Workshop and Conference Proceedings, vol. 48, pp. 1329–1338. JMLR.org (2016). http://jmlr.org/proceedings/papers/v48/duan16.html

12. Fermi, A., Mongelli, M., Muselli, M., Ferrari, E.: Identification of safety regions in vehicle platooning via machine learning. In: WFCS (2018)
13. Fujiwara, S., von Bochmann, G., Khendek, F., Amalou, M., Ghedamsi, A.: Test selection based on finite state models. IEEE Trans. Softw. Eng. **17**(6), 591–603 (1991). https://doi.org/10.1109/32.87284
14. Henzinger, T.A.: The theory of hybrid automata. In: LICS (1996)
15. Hochreiter, S., Schmidhuber, J.: Long short-term memory. Neural Comput. **9**(8), 1735–1780 (1997)
16. Howar, F., Steffen, B.: Active automata learning in practice. In: Bennaceur, A., Hähnle, R., Meinke, K. (eds.) Machine Learning for Dynamic Software Analysis: Potentials and Limits. LNCS, vol. 11026, pp. 123–148. Springer, Cham (2018). https://doi.org/10.1007/978-3-319-96562-8_5
17. Howar, F., Steffen, B., Merten, M.: From ZULU to RERS. In: Margaria, T., Steffen, B. (eds.) ISoLA 2010. LNCS, vol. 6415, pp. 687–704. Springer, Heidelberg (2010). https://doi.org/10.1007/978-3-642-16558-0_55
18. Isberner, M., Howar, F., Steffen, B.: The open-source LearnLib. In: Kroening, D., Păsăreanu, C.S. (eds.) CAV 2015. LNCS, vol. 9206, pp. 487–495. Springer, Cham (2015). https://doi.org/10.1007/978-3-319-21690-4_32
19. Kearns, M.J., Vazirani, U.V.: An Introduction to Computational Learning Theory. MIT Press, Cambridge, (1994)
20. Kingma, D., Ba, J.: Adam: a method for stochastic optimization. In: International Conference on Learning Representations (ICLR) (2015). arXiv:1412.6980
21. Ljung, L.: System Identification: Theory for the User. PTR Prentice Hall Information and System Sciences Series. Prentice Hall, New Jersey (1999)
22. Lv, C., Liu, Y., Hu, X., Guo, H., Cao, D., Wang, F.: Simultaneous observation of hybrid states for cyber-physical systems: a case study of electric vehicle powertrain. IEEE Trans. Cybern. **48**(8), 2357–2367 (2018). https://doi.org/10.1109/TCYB.2017.2738003
23. Manna, Z., Pnueli, A.: Verifying hybrid systems. In: Hybrid Systems (1992)
24. Meinke, K.: Learning-based testing of cyber-physical systems-of-systems: a platooning study. In: Reinecke, P., Di Marco, A. (eds.) EPEW 2017. LNCS, vol. 10497, pp. 135–151. Springer, Cham (2017). https://doi.org/10.1007/978-3-319-66583-2_9
25. Meinke, K.: Learning-based testing: recent progress and future prospects. In: Bennaceur et al. [6], pp. 53–73. https://doi.org/10.1007/978-3-319-96562-8_2
26. O'Shea, T.J., Hoydis, J.: An introduction to deep learning for the physical layer. IEEE Trans. Cogn. Commun. Netw. **3**(4), 563–575 (2017). https://doi.org/10.1109/TCCN.2017.2758370
27. Peled, D.A., Vardi, M.Y., Yannakakis, M.: Black box checking. J. Autom. Lang. Comb. **7**(2), 225–246 (2002). https://doi.org/10.25596/jalc-2002-225
28. Ploeg, J., Shukla, D.P., van de Wouw, N., Nijmeijer, H.: Controller synthesis for string stability of vehicle platoons. IEEE Trans. Intell. Transp. Syst. **15**(2), 854–865 (2014). https://doi.org/10.1109/TITS.2013.2291493
29. Punjani, A., Abbeel, P.: Deep learning helicopter dynamics models. In: IEEE International Conference on Robotics and Automation, ICRA 2015, Seattle, WA, USA, 26–30 May 2015, pp. 3223–3230. IEEE (2015). https://doi.org/10.1109/ICRA.2015.7139643
30. Rashid, A., Siddique, U., Hasan, O.: Formal verification of platoon control strategies. In: Johnsen, E.B., Schaefer, I. (eds.) SEFM 2018. LNCS, vol. 10886, pp. 223–238. Springer, Cham (2018). https://doi.org/10.1007/978-3-319-92970-5_14

31. Rupp, A., Steinberger, M., Horn, M.: Sliding mode based platooning with non-zero initial spacing errors. IEEE Control Syst. Lett. **1**(2), 274–279 (2017). https://doi.org/10.1109/LCSYS.2017.2714978
32. Shahbaz, M., Groz, R.: Inferring Mealy machines. In: Cavalcanti, A., Dams, D.R. (eds.) FM 2009. LNCS, vol. 5850, pp. 207–222. Springer, Heidelberg (2009). https://doi.org/10.1007/978-3-642-05089-3_14
33. Simpson, T., Booker, A., Ghosh, D., Giunta, A., Koch, P., Yang, R.J.: Approximation methods in multidisciplinary analysis and optimization: a panel discussion. Struct. Multidiscip. Optim. **27**(5), 302–313 (2004). https://doi.org/10.1007/s00158-004-0389-9
34. Smeenk, W., Moerman, J., Vaandrager, F., Jansen, D.N.: Applying automata learning to embedded control software. In: Butler, M., Conchon, S., Zaïdi, F. (eds.) ICFEM 2015. LNCS, vol. 9407, pp. 67–83. Springer, Cham (2015). https://doi.org/10.1007/978-3-319-25423-4_5
35. Spielberg, S., Gopaluni, R.B., Loewen, P.D.: Deep reinforcement learning approaches for process control. In: 2017 6th International Symposium on Advanced Control of Industrial Processes (AdCONIP), pp. 201–206 (2017)
36. Tanwani, A., Shim, H., Liberzon, D.: Observability for switched linear systems: characterization and observer design. IEEE Trans. Autom. Control **58**(4), 891–904 (2013). https://doi.org/10.1109/tac.2012.2224257
37. Vaandrager, F.W.: Model learning. Commun. ACM **60**(2), 86–95 (2017)
38. Vasilevskii, M.P.: Failure diagnosis of automata. Cybernetics **9**(4), 653–665 (1973). https://doi.org/10.1007/BF01068590
39. Vidal, R., Ma, Y., Sastry, S.S.: Hybrid system identification. Generalized Principal Component Analysis. IAM, vol. 40, pp. 431–451. Springer, New York (2016). https://doi.org/10.1007/978-0-387-87811-9_12

Regular Expression Learning with Evolutionary Testing and Repair

Paolo Arcaini[1]($\boxtimes$) (ID), Angelo Gargantini[2] (ID), and Elvinia Riccobene[3] (ID)

[1] National Institute of Informatics, Tokyo, Japan
arcaini@nii.ac.jp
[2] University of Bergamo, Bergamo, Italy
angelo.gargantini@unibg.it
[3] Dipartimento di Informatica, Università degli Studi di Milano, Milan, Italy
elvinia.riccobene@unimi.it

Abstract. Regular expressions are widely used to describe and document regular languages, and to identify a set of (valid) strings. Often they are not available or known, and they must be learned or inferred. Classical approaches like L* make strong assumptions that normally do not hold. More feasible are testing approaches in which it is possible only to generate strings and check them with the underlying system acting as *oracle*. In this paper, we devise a method that starting from an initial guess of the regular expression, it repeatedly generates and feeds strings to the system to check whether they are accepted or not, and it tries to repair consistently the alleged solution. Our approach is based on an evolutionary algorithm in which both the population of possible solutions and the set of strings co-evolve. Mutation is used for the population evolution in order to produce the offspring. We run a set of experiments showing that the string generation policy is effective and that the evolutionary approach outperforms existing techniques for regular expression repair.

Keywords: Regular expression · Mutation testing · Software repair · Evolutionary approach

1 Introduction

Regular expression (regexps) are widely used to describe regular languages and to identify a set of (valid) strings. However, in some cases they are not available. Consider, for example, a method that accepts strings in an unknown format or a service that validates some inputs according to some rules only partially documented. In such cases, the user may have a good candidate regexp C for

P. Arcaini is supported by ERATO HASUO Metamathematics for Systems Design Project (No. JPMJER1603), JST. Funding Reference number: 10.13039/501100009024 ERATO.

C. Gaston et al. (Eds.): ICTSS 2019, LNCS 11812, pp. 22–40, 2019.
https://doi.org/10.1007/978-3-030-31280-0_2

these inputs but still (s)he wants to check if C is correct and, in case it is not, (s)he wants to *learn* or *infer* the correct regexp representing the language of the System Under Learning (*SUL*) starting from C. Having a formal representation or model of the *SUL* input format, enables several engineering activities like verification and validation, test-case generation, and documentation.

Consider, for example, a web service that accepts a time t presumably in HH:MM format and converts t into different time zones (if t is in the correct format). The user formulates an initial guess about the time format, e.g., [0-2][0-3]:[0-5][0-9], but still one wants to test if the initial guess is correct and, in case some faults are found, to repair it and learn the correct regexp.

Classical approaches like the L* algorithm [2], solve this problem by querying the *SUL* for checking string acceptance and equivalence of the alleged solution. However, L* is based on several strong assumptions (e.g., the possibility to check equivalence of regexps) that rarely hold in practice. Indeed, in general, there is no way for a tester to know whether a regexp is equivalent to the language accepted by the *SUL*, and the only information (s)he can gather is the acceptance of a given string. In the example above, the server code may not be accessible, or may not be using any regexp internally. The only available action is calling the time server with a string at a time and see whether it is accepted or not. The general problem we tackle here is to build a model of some unknown regular language based only on sets of positive and negative classifications [9].

Under the weaker assumption of performing only acceptance queries, synthesizing or repairing a regexp with a symbolic method like L* becomes unpractical. For this reason, evolutionary algorithms have been widely used in this ambit [6,16]. They take a given data set *DS* (strings and their evaluation) and build the regexp that gives the largest number of right evaluations of the strings in *DS*. Genetic programming and operations like crossover and genetic mutations are used in [6], while in [16] mutation operators similar to those we use in this paper are employed. These mutation operators try to mimic possible faults done by programmers [4].

Another assumption regards strings construction. In *passive* learning methods [7], the set of strings together with their labels is given before the inference method is started; in *active* learning [8,10], strings are assumed to be continuously generated, and most of these methods like [8] aim at synthesizing a regexp from scratch.

We presented an approach based on active testing and mutation in [3]. In that work, we assumed that a human user is used as oracle, so we severely limited the number of strings to be evaluated. In case of an automatic oracle, this limitation can be partially relaxed, as calling the oracle to properly label strings is not very expensive (however, a constraint over the maximum number of queries one can execute may still exist).

In this work, we propose an evolutionary approach that aims at learning a regexp modeling the set of strings accepted by the *SUL*. The following assumptions make this active learning approach different from existing methods:

- The user has an initial guess of the regexp (s)he wants to learn. In this way, (s)he can provide the learning algorithm with some domain knowledge about the structure of the language of the *SUL*. Furthermore, this allows our technique to consider more possibly good solutions, as it does not have to consider very wrong solutions at the beginning. The more accurate the guess, the more likely should our process be to converge to a right solution.
- Strings are continuously generated and fed to the *SUL* that acts as oracle and gives an almost immediate answer (no user is involved, differently from [3]). In this way, the population of possible solutions co-evolves with the test suite.

Upon building the initial population on the base of an initially guessed regexp, the process iterates through a sequence of steps, and at each iteration:

- it generates *meaningful strings*, that show the differences among the solutions in the population. Specifically, it generates strings able to *distinguish* pairs of members of the population and invokes the *SUL* for assessing the classifications of these strings;
- for each member of the population, a *fitness* value is computed in terms of generated strings it evaluates correctly;
- some members of the current population are selected as parents of the population of the next iteration;
- the new population is obtained by mutation of the parents, using suitable operators.

As the fitness is subject to change over time and may be very unstable (at least at the beginning), it is not suitable to be used as termination condition. Therefore, we decided to stop the process after a given timeout decided by the user.

Experiments show that, under the assumption that the initial guess of the user is reasonable, the approach, on average, is able to completely repair (i.e., find a regexp capturing the *SUL* language) 81.3% of the initial regexps and improve 99.8% of them. Also in the case in which the initial guess of the user is not very good, 25.4% of initial regexps are totally repaired, and 83.5% improved.

Paper Structure. Section 2 provides basic definitions on regexps and their mutation operators. Section 3 presents our evolutionary method for learning a regexp modeling the language of the *SUL*. Section 4 describes the experiments we did to evaluate the approach, both on an existing web service and on some benchmarks. Finally, Sect. 5 reviews some related work, and Sect. 6 concludes the paper.

2 Background

We focus on regular expressions from formal automata theory, i.e., only regular expressions that describe regular languages. The proposed approach is indeed based on the use of the finite automaton accepting the language described by a regular expression.

Definition 1 (Regular expression). *A regular expression (*regexp*), defined over an alphabet Σ, can be recursively defined as follows. (i) The empty string ϵ and each symbol in Σ is a regular expression; (ii) if $r_1 \ldots r_n$ are regular expressions, then $op(r_1, \ldots, r_n)$ is a regular expression where op is a valid operator (see below). The regexp r accepts a set of* words $\mathcal{L}(r) \subseteq \Sigma^*$ *(i.e., a language).*

We also use r as predicate: $r(s)$ if $s \in \mathcal{L}(r)$, and $\neg r(s)$ otherwise.

As Σ we support the Unicode alphabet (UTF-16); the supported operators op are union, concatenation, intersection, repeat, complement, character range, and wildcards (e.g., any char or any string).

Acceptance can be computed by converting r into an automaton $\mathcal{R}$, and checking whether $\mathcal{R}$ accepts the string. In this paper, we use the library dk.brics.-automaton [19] to transform a regexp r into an automaton $\mathcal{R}$ and perform standard operations on it.

For our purposes, we give the notion of a string distinguishing two languages.

Definition 2 (Distinguishing string). *Given two languages $\mathcal{L}_1$ and $\mathcal{L}_2$, a string s is* distinguishing *if it is a word of their symmetric difference $\mathcal{L}_1 \oplus \mathcal{L}_2 = \mathcal{L}_1 \setminus \mathcal{L}_2 \cup \mathcal{L}_2 \setminus \mathcal{L}_1$.*

We define a function $\texttt{genDs}(r_1, r_2)$ that returns a distinguishing string between the languages of two regexps r_1 and r_2. $\texttt{genDs}$ builds two automata for r_1 and r_2, makes the symmetric difference (using union, intersection, and complement of automata) and returns a string accepted by the difference. If r_1 and r_2 are equivalent, it returns $\texttt{null}$.

2.1   Conformance Faults

In this section, we describe how to compare the language characterized by a developed regexp with the language accepted by the *SUL*. We suppose to have a reference *oracle* that represents the language of the *SUL*. Formally:

Definition 3 (Oracle). *An* oracle *sul is a predicate saying whether a string is accepted or not. We identify with $\mathcal{L}(SUL)$ the set of strings accepted by the SUL.*

The oracle can be queried and it must say whether a string belongs to $\mathcal{L}(SUL)$ or not, i.e., whether it must be accepted or rejected. Usually, the oracle is a software procedure that can be called and that checks whether a given string should be accepted or not. The oracle may use a regexp and some string matching code in order to evaluate strings, but this internal mechanism is unknown during the process.

A correct regexp is indistinguishable from its oracle (i.e., they share the same language), while a faulty one wrongly accepts or wrongly rejects some strings.

Definition 4 (Conformance Fault). *A regexp r (allegedly representing the language of SUL) contains a* conformance fault *if and only if $\exists s \in \Sigma^* : r(s) \neq sul(s)$, i.e., there is a string s which is wrongly evaluated by r with respect to its reference oracle sul.*

A fault shows that the user specified the regexp r wrongly, maybe misunderstanding the semantics·of the regexp notation or the SUL documentation. In this case, r must be repaired in order to learn the correct regexp describing the language accepted by SUL.

Finding all conformance faults would require to test all the strings in Σ^*, which is unfeasible. Therefore, the first problem is how to select strings to be used as tests. Randomly is an option that we will explore in the experiments, but we propose an alternative method based on distinguishing strings. The second problem is what to do when a fault has been found and how to repair a faulty regexp. In the following, we try to answer these two questions by proposing a *testing and repair* approach.

Theorem 1. *Let r_1 and r_2 be two regexps that are not equivalent, and s a distinguishing string returned by* genDs(r_1, r_2), *then either r_1 or r_2 will contain a conformance fault.*

To check which of the two regexps contains a fault, we can test s with the oracle and see which one wrongly evaluates s. If we find that r_1 is faulty, we can say that r_2 fits better to the oracle than r_1 with the string s, and r_2 should be preferred to r_1.

Note that even if r_2 fits better than r_1 with s, on other strings r_1 may fit better than r_2 and r_2 may still contain other conformance faults. For this reason, it is important to keep track of the generated strings in the whole test suite.

How to choose suitable r_1 and r_2? In this paper, we assume that r_1 and r_2 belong to the population of possible solutions, which evolves over time. Moreover, following a fault-based approach, we claim that the syntactical faults that are more likely done by developers are those described by fault classes. If such assumption holds, possible solutions should be generated using a mutation approach as explained in the following.

2.2   Mutation

Our approach is based on the idea that regexps can be repaired by slightly modifying them. In the process, we try to remove faults by applying *mutation operators*. A mutation operator is a function that, given a regexp r, returns a list of regexps (called *mutants*) obtained by mutating r (possibly removing the fault); a mutation *slightly* modifies the regexp r under the assumption that the programmer has defined r close to the correct version (competent programmer hypothesis [20]).

We use the fault classes and related mutation operators proposed in [4]; for example, some operators change metachars in chars (and the other way round), change quantifiers, modify/add character classes, etc. In the following, given a regexp r, we identify with mut(r) the set of its mutants.

3   Proposed Approach

We here explain the technique that users can apply in order to discover the regexp describing the language accepted by a SUL.

In our approach, they specify a regexp r_i representing their initial guess. Starting from this, they want to validate r_i and possibly automatically modify it in order to find a regexp r_f that correctly captures the language of the *SUL*. In order to learn the correct regexp, we propose an approach based on evolutionary algorithms [11]: it can be understood as an optimization problem in which different solutions (*population*) are modified by random changes (by *mutation*) and their quality is checked by an objective (*fitness*) function. The process consists in the following phases:

1. **Initial population.** Initially, starting from the user's regexp r_i, a *population* P of candidate solutions is created.
2. Then, the following steps are repeatedly executed:
   (a) **Evaluation.** Each member of the population P is evaluated using a given *fitness function*.
   (b) **Termination.** A termination condition is checked to decide whether to start the next iteration or to terminate. If the termination condition holds, the candidate with the best *fitness value* is returned as final regexp r_f.
   (c) **Selection.** Some members of P are selected as parents (collected in the multi-set PAR) of the next generation.
   (d) **Evolution.** Parents PAR are mutated to obtain the *offspring* to be used as population in the next iteration.

In the following, we describe each step in details.

Initial Population. The size M of the population is a parameter of the evolutionary algorithm. In our approach, we set M to $H \cdot |operators(r_i)|$, where *operators* is a function returning the operators of a regexp, and H a parameter of our approach. In the experiments, we set $H=100$. The initial population contains r_i and M-1 mutants randomly taken from $\mathtt{mut}(r_i)$.

Evaluation. In this step, the quality of the candidates in P is evaluated using a *fitness function* being the objective of our search. Usually, the fitness function is *complete* as it precisely identifies when a candidate is totally correct. In our approach, instead, the fitness function is only *partial*; indeed, to learn the regular language accepted by the *SUL*, we can only rely on the knowledge of the *SUL* evaluation of a finite set of strings. We therefore define the fitness function as follows.

Definition 5 (Fitness function). *Given a regexp r and two sets A and R of strings accepted and rejected by the SUL, the* fitness value *of r is defined as:*

$$fitness(r, A, R) = \frac{|\{s \in A \mid r(s)\}| + |\{s \in R \mid \neg r(s)\}|}{|A \cup R|}$$

Note that the fitness value depends on strings that are known to be accepted and rejected by the *SUL* (contained in A and R). Since the possible strings are infinite, finding meaningful strings to be used for fitness computation is extremely important. Since the fitness function is used to evaluate and rank

Algorithm 1. Evaluation step: Test generation and fitness update

Require: P: population
Require: sul: oracle of the SUL
1: $A \leftarrow \emptyset$: strings **A**ccepted by the oracle
2: $R \leftarrow \emptyset$: strings **R**ejected by the oracle
3: STARTGENTIMEOUT()
4: **for each** $p_i, p_j \in P$ **do**
5:   **if** $genTimeout$ **then**
6:     **return**
7:   **end if**
8:   **if** $\exists s \in (A \cup R) : p_i(s) \neq p_j(s)$ **then**
9:     **continue**
10:   **end if**
11:   $ds \leftarrow \text{genDs}(p_i, p_j)$
12:   **if** $ds \neq \text{null}$ **then**
13:     $sulEv \leftarrow sul(ds)$
14:     **if** $sulEv$ **then**
15:       $A \leftarrow A \cup \{ds\}$
16:     **else**
17:       $R \leftarrow R \cup \{ds\}$
18:     **end if**
19:     UPDATEFITNESS($P, ds, sulEv$)
20:   **end if**
21: **end for**

regexps contained in P, we try to generate strings able to show the differences among the different candidates. Thanks to Theorem 1, if such strings are generated as those distinguishing regexps of the population P, the fitness value can better differentiate the elements in P. Moreover, A and R should not be too small, in order to avoid a too partial fitness evaluation. At each iteration, we therefore enlarge the sets A and R by generating new strings, using the procedure described in Algorithm 1. The approach tries to generate a distinguishing string for each pair of members p_i and p_j of the population, as follows:

1. Since generating strings for each pair of candidates could be computationally too expensive, we fix a timeout $genTimeout$ after which the test generation for the current generation terminates (line 6).
2. If the timeout does not occur, the algorithm first checks whether there is already a string able to distinguish the two regexps (line 8) and, if so, it continues with the next pair of regexps (line 9).
3. Otherwise, a string ds is generated using function genDs that picks a string from the symmetric difference of the languages of two regexps [4] (line 11).
4. If the two regexps are equivalent, no string is produced; otherwise, ds is submitted to the oracle sul of the SUL and its evaluation recorded in $sulEv$ (line 13).
5. According to the string evaluation, ds is added either to A or R (lines 15 and 17).
6. Finally, the fitness of each member of the population is updated by considering the new string ds with its correct evaluation $sulEv$ (line 19).

Note that, as new strings are generated in each iteration, the fitness value of a candidate may change in different evolutions.

This phase corresponds to the *testing* part of our approach, in which strings are generated to be used as tests, and collected in A and R representing the test suite.

Termination Condition. In this step, the process decides whether to terminate or continue with another iteration. For this, different termination conditions can be specified. A classical termination condition is usually related to the fitness function (when it reaches 1 or a given threshold). In our context, however, the fitness function is partial as it only considers a finite subset of all the possible strings that can be evaluated; it is therefore not particularly suitable as termination condition. The only reasonable termination condition that we can impose is related to the computation time: after a given *timeout*, we terminate the process. The timeout represents the effort that the user can spend in learning the language accepted by *SUL*.

When the process terminates, the member of the population P with the highest fitness is returned as final regexp r_f.[1]

Selection. In this step, starting from population P, a multiset of *parents* PAR of size p is built, being p a parameter of the evolutionary process. Different selection strategies have been proposed in literature, as *truncation*, *roulette wheel*, and *rank* [11]. We here use the *truncation* selection that selects the first $n = \lceil K \cdot |P| \rceil$ members of the population with the highest fitness value, where K is a parameter specifying a percentage of the population; in the experiments, we use $K=5\%$. Then, the first n elements are added to PAR as many times as necessary to reach the size p.

Evolution. In this step, the population (called *offspring*) for the next generation is built starting from the parents in PAR. In order to build the offspring, we mutate all the regexps r in PAR using function mut, as defined in Sect. 2.2. We set an upper bound M to the new population size. If the mutation operators generate at most M mutants, we take all of them as the new population; otherwise, we randomly select M of them.

The mutation operators applied by mut [4] resemble the edit operations a user would make on the initial regexp r_i to repair it. If r_i is not too faulty, the mutation operators should be sufficient to repair it; the assumption that the user has defined a software artefact (in this case, a regexp) close to the correct one is know in literature as *competent programmer hypothesis* [20].

This is the *repair* part of the approach, that possibly removes syntactical faults.

4   Experiments

To validate our approach, we need to select some *SULs* that we can query and a set of regexps to be used as initial guesses r_i. We have performed two types of experiments. In the first one, the *SUL* is a real web service for which we want to learn a regexp representing the language the *SUL* accepts. This type of experiment is useful to assess the viability of our approach, but suffers from several limitations discussed below. In the second type of experiments, we have simulated a *SUL* in a controlled environment and this has allowed us to better estimate the effectiveness of our method.

---

[1] If there is more than one regexp with the highest fitness, the process randomly selects one.

Table 1. regexps used as r_i in the experiment with the real web service

Id	Expression	Length	# oper.
r_i^1	[0-9]{4}-(1[0-2]—0[1-9])-(3[01]—0[1-9]—[12][0-9])T(2[0-3]—[01][0-9]):([0-5][0-9]):([0-5][0-9])(\.[0-9]+)?(Z)?	109	45
r_i^2	(-?([1-9][0-9]*)?[0-9]{4})-(1[0-2]—0[1-9])-(3[01]—0[1-9]—[12][0-9])T(2[0-3]—[01][0-9]):([0-5][0-9]):([0-5][0-9])(.[0-9]+)?(Z)?	126	54
r_i^3	([0-9]{4})-?(1[0-2]—0[1-9])-?(3[01]—0[1-9]—[12][0-9])(2[0-3]—[01][0-9]):?([0-5][0-9]):?([0-5][0-9])	99	41
r_i^4	(2[0-3]—[01][0-9]):([0-5][0-9]):([0-5][0-9])(\.[0-9]+)?(Z—[+-](2[0-3]—[01][0-9]):[0-5][0-9]))?	93	37
r_i^5	([0-9]{4}(((\-)?((00[1-9]—0[1-9][0-9]—[1-2][0-9][0-9]—3[0-5][0-9]—36[0-6]))?—((\-)?(1[0-2]—0[1-9]))?—((\-)?(1[0-2]—0[1-9])(\-)?(0[1-9]—[12][0-9]—3[01]))?—((\-)?W(0[1-9]—[1-4][0-9]5[0-3]))?—((\-)?W(0[1-9]—[1-4][0-9]5[0-3])(\-)?[1-7])?)?)	235	90

The process has been implemented in Java using Watchmaker [26] as evolutionary framework. Experiments have been executed on a Linux machine, Intel(R) Core(TM) i7, 16 GB RAM. Code, benchmarks, and results are available online at https://github.com/fmselab/evo_regexp_learn.

4.1 Learning the Language of a Real Web Service

In this experiment, we want to discover the format of dates and times accepted by the API services of the timeanddate.com web site. That site offers, among other services, a time API service that does time zone conversions. When the user calls that service, (s)he must provide the date and time in ISO format (as it is claimed on the web site) and the service will convert from one time zone to another one. The conversion can be obtained by calling a web service like
https://api.xmltime.com/converttime?fromid=750&toid=146
&iso=DATETIME;version=2&accesskey=KEY&expires=TIMESTAMP
&signature=SIGNATURE.
If {DATETIME} is in the wrong format (or the query is incorrect), the web service returns an error code, otherwise it returns a json message with the conversion of {DATETIME}.

We have performed the experiment with 5 initial regexps (see Table 1) we found on the Internet representing possible ISO dates and times[2] and called our approach to test and repair them w.r.t. the web service. We executed the approach with 7 combinations of its two parameters, the total *timeout* (used in the termination phase) and the timeout *genTimeout* on string generation (see Algorithm 1 and Sect. 3). Table 2a reports, for each setting, the results in terms of average number of generated strings, average number of generations, and average final fitness. As expected, increasing the total timeout allows testing more strings against the *SUL*. Moreover, for a given total timeout, increasing *genTimeout* allows generating more strings, but decreases the number of generations. The final fitness of the returned final regexp r_f is always almost 1. However, in this case, even when the fitness is 1, the only assurance that we have is that r_f evaluates correctly all the generated strings; we cannot be sure that the final

---

[2] The ISO 8601 format does not come with an official regexp and it is regularly updated, so several versions exist.

Table 2. Results of the experiment with the real web service

(a) Aggregated by approach setting

TO (s) total	gen	avg # str	avg # gen	avg fitness of r_f
180	10	835.4	7.2	0.99
180	30	1272.8	3.6	0.99
300	30	1478.6	6.4	0.99
300	60	2114	3.8	0.99
600	30	1831.2	11.6	1
600	60	2769.6	7	0.99
600	120	3445.6	3.8	1

(b) Aggregated by r_i (average)

r_i id	# str	# gen	# failures in r_i	fitness of r_f
r_i^1	1914.0	7	115.4	0.99
r_i^2	1975.7	6.4	195.7	0.98
r_i^3	2450.6	6.1	219.9	1
r_i^4	2662.9	7.4	161.2	1
r_i^5	816.3	4	106.2	0.99

regexp r_f actually represents the language accepted by the service since we do not have access to the server internals.

Table 2b reports the results aggregated by r_i (average across the approach settings) with also the average number of strings wrongly evaluated by r_i. We observe that the highest number of strings is generated for r_i^3 and r_i^4, while the lowest number is generated for r_i^5. This is probably related to the size of r_i (length and number of operators in Table 1): bigger regexps as r_5 produce big populations requiring more time in the evolution phase (during mutation) and in the fitness update during the evaluation phase. We observe that all the initial guesses of regexps were wrong, as proved by the number of generated strings that are evaluated differently by the initial regexp r_i and by the SUL.

When starting from r_i^3 and r_i^4, the process always terminates with a regexp r_f having final fitness 1. In these cases, the final regexp evaluates correctly all the generated tests. However, as said before, since we do not know exactly the language of the SUL, it is impossible to check if the final regexps are completely correct (even when their fitness is 1). For this reason, we perform the experiments described in Sect. 4.2 with a known SUL language.

4.2 Controlled Experiment

In this experiment, we assume that the SUL itself is defined by a regexp r_{SUL}, unknown to the user, but available to us. In this way, we can measure the quality of the final regexp r_f w.r.t. the initial regexp r_i, by comparing both of them to the correct regexp r_{SUL} representing the SUL.

We have taken as SULs 20 different matching tasks (e.g., email addresses, credit cards, social security numbers, zip codes, Roman numbers, etc.) from two websites [24,25]. For each task, we have taken a regexp as r_{SUL} and another regexp developed for the same matching task as initial regexp r_i. We have randomly chosen the two regexps (r_i and r_{SUL}) in a way that they are never equivalent (i.e., a repair is necessary) and moreover, they are also syntactically quite different (i.e., the repair is not trivial and the competent programmer hypothesis may not hold).

The initial regexps r_i are between 17 and 279 chars long (60.65 on average) and have between 7 and 112 operators (26.25 on average). All the regexps operators are considered, as shown in the results reported online.

In order to evaluate our approach, we introduce a measure of the reduction of conformance faults in the final regexp r_f. In order to check whether the final regexp r_f captures the regular language described by the SUL, we check the equivalence between r_f and r_{SUL}. For non-totally repaired regexps, we need to count the number of conformance faults. We use the measure F_r that counts the number of strings that a regexp r does not evaluate correctly (i.e., wrongly accepts or wrongly rejects). Since the number of such strings is possibly infinite, we have to consider only strings of length up to n. The number of faults of a regexp r is defined as follows, where $\mathcal{L}^n(r_x) = \mathcal{L}(r_x) \cap (\bigcup_{i=0}^{n} \Sigma^i)$:

$$F_r^n = |\mathcal{L}^n(r) \oplus \mathcal{L}^n(r_{SUL})|$$

In order to know whether the repaired regexp r_f is better than the initial regexp r_i, we compute $\Delta F = F_{r_f}^n - F_{r_i}^n$ with a fixed n. In the experiments, we set $n = 100$ to restrict the evaluation to the strings of length n up to 100. If $\Delta F < 0$ or the final regexp r_f is totally repaired, the process has *improved* the original regexp; if $\Delta F = 0$, the process did not remove any conformance fault (or removed and introduced faults equally); otherwise, $\Delta F > 0$ means that the process has *worsened* the regexp by introducing more faults.

To better evaluate the approach, we measure the fault reduction (FR) as percentage change of the number of faults between the final and initial regexps r_f and r_i:

$$FR = \frac{F_{r_f}^n - F_{r_i}^n}{F_{r_i}^n} * 100$$

As done in the experiment with the real SUL (see Sect. 4.1), we performed a series of experiments by varying the two main parameters of the proposed approach, the total *timeout* and the timeout *genTimeout* on string generation; in total, we experimented with 7 combinations of these two parameters. We executed 10 runs of each experiment, and all the reported data are the averages of the 10 runs. In all the experiments, we fix the parameters of the evolutionary algorithm as follows: in the selection phase, we use truncation with $K = 5\%$, and as multiplicative factor H for the population size we use 100. Table 3a reports the experimental results in terms of percentage of completely repaired (*Rep*) regexps, percentage of improved (*Imp*) regexps (i.e., for which the number of faults decreased), percentage of worsened (*Wor*) regexps (i.e., for which the number of faults increased), average fault reduction (FR) among the regexps, average number of generated strings, and average number of generations of the evolutionary algorithm. The execution time corresponds to the total timeout (*TO total*).

In the following, we analyse the results using different research questions.

RQ1 Is the proposed process able to learn the regular language of the SUL? What is the improvement in terms of fault reduction?

Table 3. Bench

(a) Results

TO (s) total	gen	Rep (%)	Impr (%)	Wor (%)	avg FR	avg # str	avg # gen
180	10	25	85	0	-53.9	1075.2	14.9
180	30	23.5	81.5	3.5	-26	1202.8	8.1
300	30	25.5	85	0	-53.6	1343.8	12.4
300	60	24	82	3	-37	1415	10.1
600	30	28.5	85	0	-54	1471.7	21.2
600	60	28	83.5	1.5	-44.3	1577.7	15.9
600	120	23	82.5	2.5	-35.8	1603.1	13.5
AVG		25.4	83.5	1.5	-43.5	1384.2	13.7

(b) Results using random strings

TO (s) total	gen	Rep (%)	Impr (%)	Wor (%)	avg FR	avg # str	avg # gen
180	10	0.5	16.5	82.5	1.9e+296	49964.2	6.6
180	30	0	22.5	73	9.6e+288	81408.9	3.1
300	30	0	16.5	79.5	3.8e+296	114560.6	4.5
300	60	0	24	72	9.6e+288	162314.8	2.8
600	30	0	16.5	82.5	1.9e+296	133290.6	6.8
600	60	0	26	71.5	1.3e+294	176726.8	4.3
600	120	0	18.5	77	3.8e+296	250812.2	2.9
AVG		0.1	20.2	76.9	1.6e+296	138439.7	4.4

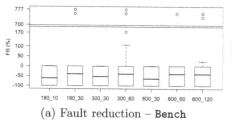

(a) Fault reduction – Bench

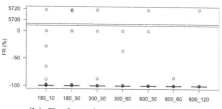

(b) Fault reduction – MutBench

Fig. 1. Fault reduction

First of all, we are interested in checking whether the proposed approach is able to learn the regular language of the *SUL*. From Table 3a, we observe that, with any setting, we are always able to completely repair around 25.4% of the regexps, and improve around 83.5%. With some settings, the process can also worsen the regexp (maximum 3.5%). However, on average, the number of faults is always decreased; Fig. 1a shows the distribution of the fault reduction among the regexps for each setting. We notice that the process worsens some regexps when the timeout for string generation (*TO gen*) is higher; it seems that generating too many strings for one generation is not beneficial and it is more productive to spend time in evaluating new generations.

RQ2 Is using distinguishing strings effective?

We are here interested in investigating if using distinguishing strings generated among the mutants is effective. In order to do this, in Algorithm 1, instead of generating distinguishing strings, we generate random strings. The maximum number of strings that can be generated (if the timeout does not occur) is still $C_2^{|P|}$. Table 3b reports the results by using random strings. We observe that the approach is almost never able to totally repair the regexp: it at most improves 26% of the benchmarks, and it always worsens at least 71.5% of them. We can also observe that, since the test generation is fast, many more strings are generated (from 1 to 2 orders of magnitude more); however, their fault-detecting capability is much lower than that of the distinguishing strings. This confirms that targeting conformance faults among mutants in the search is effective.

RQ3 How many distinguishing strings are generated? How long does the SUL take to evaluate them?

Differently from [3], we assume that calling the SUL (acting as oracle) is not very expensive and, so, there is not urgency to limit the number of string evaluations. However, in some settings (e.g., database query), calling the SUL may have a non-negligible cost. We here try to assess such cost. In the experiments (see Table 3a), we at most generate 1603 strings with one setting having the highest timeout of 600 secs (10 min). If we assume that invoking the SUL for a single input is expensive and takes 1 sec (we used such delay between two queries in the experiment of Sect. 4.1 to wait for the service response and to avoid queries were interpreted as DoS attacks), the evaluation of the strings takes 26.7 min; therefore, in this case, the total time would be 36.7 min.

RQ4 How are the results if the competent programmer hypothesis hold?

Benchmark set **Bench** has been built by taking regexps pairs r_i and r_{SUL} that are very different from each other (the average Levenshtein distance between the initial regexp r_i and the oracle r_{SUL} is 36.65). However, fault-based approaches usually assume the *competent programmer hypothesis*, stating that the user defined a regexp close to the correct one (different for one or few syntactic faults).

Therefore, we want to assess the process effectiveness under the assumption of the competent programmer hypothesis. We built another benchmark set, **MutBench**, as follows. We took each oracle regexp r_{SUL} of **Bench** and we randomly mutated it introducing n faults (with $n = 1, \ldots, 3$), obtaining three faulty versions of the oracle. In this way, **MutBench** contains 60 pairs of regexps. The regexps are between 38 and 277 characters long (111.7 on average) and contain between 5 and 59 operators (26.82 on average). Then, we have experimented with our approach using **MutBench**; Table 4a reports the aggregated results for the experiments. Regarding RQ1, we observe that the results are much better than the benchmark **Bench**. Any timeout configuration is able to totally repair at least 78.5% of the regexps, and all of them improve more than 99.5% of the regexps. Figure 1b reports detailed results of fault reduction.

Table 4. `MutBench`

(a) Results

TO (s) total	gen	Rep (%)	Impr (%)	Wor (%)	avg FR	avg # str	avg # gen
180	10	79.8	99.7	0.3	-87.5	797.5	1010.3
180	30	78.7	99.7	0.3	-80.3	871.9	4177.6
300	30	79.8	99.5	0.5	-79.7	974.5	1446
300	60	78.5	100	0	-99.7	1042.6	3373.9
600	30	86	99.8	0.2	-90.1	1130.9	10843.4
600	60	83.7	100	0	-99.9	1128.7	7667.9
600	120	82.3	99.8	0.2	-90.3	1191.8	7578.8
AVG		81.3	99.8	0.2	-89.6	1019.7	5156.8

(b) Results using random strings

TO (s) total	gen	Rep (%)	Impr (%)	Wor (%)	avg FR	avg # str	avg # gen
180	10	0.3	35.3	62.5	1.9e+294	41721	6.4
180	30	0.2	31.8	62.8	9.4e+293	70417	3.1
300	30	0.5	34.2	64.3	6.3e+293	92685.4	4.6
300	60	0.2	33.8	61.5	3.1e+293	126599	2.9
600	30	0.8	35.5	63.7	1.6e+294	121126	7
600	60	0.2	33.7	64	7.1e+292	158346	4.5
600	120	0.5	31.5	63.7	6.2e+293	191531.7	2.9
AVG		0.4	33.7	63.2	8.6e+293	114632.3	4.5

We also evaluated the approach using randomly generated strings on `MutBench`, and the results are reported in Table 4b. Results are slightly better with benchmark `MutBench` than with `Bench` (compare the results in Table 3b), but still almost no regexp is repaired and at most only 35.5% of the regexps are improved.

RQ5 Does the proposed approach improve the state of the art?

A related approach that just relies on *interactive* string evaluation of the *SUL* is the one we presented in [3] (from now on, called IA). IA is quite different from the current *evolutionary* approach (from now on, called EA), as it does not have a population of candidates, but a single candidate; when a mutant *better* than the current candidate is found, the candidate is changed; the repairing process stops when no better mutant is found. Four policies are proposed for choosing the new candidate (*Greedy, MultiDSs, Breadth*, and *Collecting*). The only similarity with EA is that candidates are generated by mutation and fault-detecting strings are used as tests.

We applied IA to the benchmarks `Bench` and `MutBench`, using the setting *Breadth* that in [3] showed, on average, the best performance in terms of fault reduction. Table 5 shows the results for the two benchmarks. We observe that for `MutBench` (i.e., if the competent programmer hypothesis holds), IA has a good performance, similar to the one of EA (cfr. with Table 4a); however, EA with the best setting can completely repair 9% more regexps. For `Bench`, EA has an even better performance (cfr. with Table 3a); it totally repairs from 4% to 9.5% more regexps, improves from 16% to 19.5% more regexps, and worsens (in the worst case) almost the same number of regexps. IA is meant for interactive testing with a user and, therefore, it tries to generate not too many strings; for this reason, it always produces fewer strings and takes less time than EA.

Table 5. Results of a state-of-the-art approach IA [3]

Benchmark	Rep (%)	Impr (%)	Wor (%)	Avg *FR* (%)	Avg # str	Avg time (s)
`Bench`	19	65.5	3	6e+283	636.8	61.5
`MutBench`	77	97.3	0	-96	447.2	140.6

We checked if the results are statistically significant by performing the Wilcoxon signed-rank test[3] between the results of EA and IA. Regarding totally repaired (Rep) and improved (Impr) regexps, EA is significantly better, while there is no significant difference for worsen regexps (Wor) and fault reduction (*FR*). As expected, EA is worse in terms of number of generated strings (# str), as IA is designed to generate few strings.

---

[3] We checked that the distributions are not normal with the non-parametric Shapiro-Wilk test.

We conclude that a conservative approach as IA should be used if there are constraints on time and number of strings (usually, when the oracle is the user), while our approach EA should be used when the oracle can be called several times (as our *SUL*).

RQ6 How does our approach compare with L*?

The classical algorithm for learning regexps is L*. L* starts from the strong assumption of having the possibility to check the equivalence of a regexp w.r.t. the *SUL*. This assumption is unpractical so there exist several attempts to use L* in combination with approximate equivalent checkers. These methods are generally based on conformance testing methods: some tests are generated from the current hypothesis and executed over the *SUL* and, if they are all equally accepted or rejected by using membership queries, then the hypothesis is considered equivalent to the *SUL*. Conformance checking can be expensive though, since methods like the W-method, Wp-method, or UIO-method require an exponential number of tests, although they can provide some guarantees (e.g., assuming the target system has at most N additional states). Other approximate methods randomly generate a maximum number of tests but they cannot guarantee correctness. To study the feasibility of using L* with an approximate equivalent checker, we have executed L* using LearnLib [14,23] over the regexps of Bench. For each oracle regexp r_{SUL} in Bench, we have tried to learn it using L* with different equivalence checkers: different versions of the random equivalence checker (between 10 and 10^6 tests of length between 10 and 10^2) and three versions of the W-method (with exploration depth from 1 to 3); we restrict the alphabet to the readable range of ASCII, because using Unicode would make L* unusable. Table 6 reports results for 6 versions of the random method and all the 3 versions of the W-method. It shows the percentage of times that L* is better/worst than the best setting of EA (600-30 in Table 3a) in terms of final number of faults in the final regexp r_f; moreover, it reports the average number of strings (i.e., tests) and average execution time across the benchmarks. We observe that increasing the number of tests and their length in the random method does not improve the learning capability of L*; the W-method does improve the learning capability by increasing the exploration depth, but at the expenses of an exponential number of tests.

Table 6. L* results (R-n-m: random method with m tests of length up to n. W-n: W-method with exploration depth n)

Eq. checker	Comparison with EA		avg	avg	Eq. checker	Comparison with EA		avg	avg
	better (%)	worse (%)	# str	time (s)		better (%)	worse (%)	# str	time (s)
R-10-10^2	35	61.75	200.75	0.01	W-1	35	61.75	53491.45	0.17
R-10-10^4	35	61.75	10100.75	0.02	W-2	37	58.50	6.47×10^6	15.55
R-10-10^6	34.75	62.25	1042574.6	1.93	W-3	38	56.25	1.93×10^8	2668.81
R-10^2-10^2	35	61.75	200.75	0					
R-10^2-10^4	35	61.75	10100.75	0.16	EA 600–30			1471.7	600
R-10^2-10^6	34.75	62.25	1076471.6	16.72					

5   Related Work

A first set of related works regards the use of the L* algorithm [2] and its variants for specification mining which shares many similarities with regexp learning. In the L* algorithm, a *Student* tries to learn an unknown regular automaton S by posing two types of queries to a *teacher*. In a *membership query*, the student gives a string t and the teacher tells whether it is accepted by S or not. In a *conjecture query*, the student provides a regular automaton S' and the teacher answers *yes* if S' corresponds to S, or with a *wrong* string t (as our distinguishing string) otherwise. L* can be used also to learn a black-box system SUL by replacing the ability of the teacher to test conjectures by a random sampling. This works only under the strong assumptions that the Student *gets an approximately correct hypothesis with high probability and the problem of testing a conjecture against randomly drawn strings is sufficiently tractable* [2]. Lee and Yannakakis [15] showed how to use L* for conformance testing, to check if an FSM I implements a specification S with n states, and to repair I if a fault has been found. Nevertheless, serious practical limitations (like the number of states and the types of faults) are associated with such experiments (see [15] for a complete discussion). A more recent survey on automata learning can be found in [13], and a survey on the usage of model learning for testing can be found in [1].

For these reasons, genetic and evolutionary algorithms for regular expression learning are preferred instead. They are mainly used for automatically synthesizing a regular expression from sets of accepted/rejected strings. Bartoli and al. [7] propose a passive approach for synthesizing a regular expression automatically, based only on examples of the desired behavior, i.e., strings described by the language and of strings not described by the language. The approach is improved in [8] by proposing an active learning approach aimed at minimizing the user annotation effort: the user annotates only one desired extraction and then merely answers extraction queries generated by the system. Differently from them, we do not start from scratch by generating the initial population, and we do not use predefined set of accepted/rejected strings.

Another approach for regexp synthesis from a set of labeled strings is ReLIE [16]. It is a passive learning algorithm that, given an initial regexp and a set of labeled strings, tries to learn the correct regexp. It performs some regexp transformations (a kind of mutation); however, it is not an evolutionary algorithm, as it exploits a greedy hill climbing search that chooses, at every iteration, the regexp with the highest fitness value.

We share some ideas with our previous work [3]. Mutation operators and use of automata is in common with that paper. However, in [3] we did not use an evolutionary algorithm, but a greedy approach very similar to [16]. Moreover, we assumed that the oracle is the user and the approach was meant to be interactive. For this reason, we tried to generate very few strings. In RQ5, we demonstrate that the current evolutionary approach is much more efficient in repairing regexps. We believe that a population-based evolutionary algorithm is able to reduce the risk of being stuck in local optimum since possible solutions are continuously evaluated and generated.

The idea of co-evolving the population of solutions together with the tests is not new; e.g., the approach in [28] evolves software artefacts and test cases in tandem.

Our approach has some similarities with *automatic software repair* [5, 18, 21, 22, 27] and automatic repair of specifications [12].

6   Conclusions and Future Work

In the paper, we proposed an evolutionary approach to learn the regexp modeling the unknown language accepted by a given system. The user gives an initial guess of a regexp, and the approach tries to learn the correct regexp by evolving a population of possible solutions obtained by mutation. The fitness function is based on the strings a candidate evaluates correctly. The testing strings evolve together with the population: at each evolution step, they are built as those strings able to distinguish the population members. Experiments have been done on a case study of a real web service, and on some benchmarks. Results show that the approach, on average, is able to completely repair 81.3% of the initial regexps and improve 99.8% of them. Even if the initial guess of the user is not accurate, 25.4% of initial regexps are totally repaired, and 83.5% improved.

In the evaluation, we used a given setting for the parameters of the evolutionary approach. As future work, we plan to use a tool as irace [17] to find the best setting.

Our approach could be adapted for regexp synthesis (but not passive) as well, e.g., by taking as r_i the first random string that is accepted by the *SUL*. Although the experiments suggest that starting from a very faulty regexp makes finding the correct solution very hard, we are interested to experiment also with this use of our technique.

We plan to improve the fitness in several directions: considering readability, weighting differently false negative and false positive, and making the fitness more sensitive to minor improvements by introducing a measure of *partial acceptance*.

References

1. Aichernig, B.K., Mostowski, W., Mousavi, M.R., Tappler, M., Taromirad, M.: Model learning and model-based testing. In: Bennaceur, A., Hähnle, R., Meinke, K. (eds.) Machine Learning for Dynamic Software Analysis: Potentials and Limits. LNCS, vol. 11026, pp. 74–100. Springer, Cham (2018). https://doi.org/10.1007/978-3-319-96562-8_3

2. Angluin, D.: Learning regular sets from queries and counterexamples. Inf. Comput. **75**(2), 87–106 (1987). https://doi.org/10.1016/0890-5401(87)90052-6

3. Arcaini, P., Gargantini, A., Riccobene, E.: Interactive testing and repairing of regular expressions. In: Medina-Bulo, I., Merayo, M.G., Hierons, R. (eds.) ICTSS 2018. LNCS, vol. 11146, pp. 1–16. Springer, Cham (2018). https://doi.org/10.1007/978-3-319-99927-2_1

4. Arcaini, P., Gargantini, A., Riccobene, E.: Fault-based test generation for regular expressions by mutation. Softw. Test. Verif. Reliab. **29**(1–2), e1664 (2019). https://doi.org/10.1002/stvr.1664
5. Arcuri, A.: Evolutionary repair of faulty software. Appl. Soft Comput. **11**(4), 3494–3514 (2011). https://doi.org/10.1016/j.asoc.2011.01.023
6. Bartoli, A., Davanzo, G., De Lorenzo, A., Medvet, E., Sorio, E.: Automatic synthesis of regular expressions from examples. Computer **47**(12), 72–80 (2014). https://doi.org/10.1109/MC.2014.344
7. Bartoli, A., De Lorenzo, A., Medvet, E., Tarlao, F.: Inference of regular expressions for text extraction from examples. IEEE Trans. Knowl. Data Eng. **28**(5), 1217–1230 (2016). https://doi.org/10.1109/TKDE.2016.2515587
8. Bartoli, A., De Lorenzo, A., Medvet, E., Tarlao, F.: Active learning of regular expressions for entity extraction. IEEE Trans. Cybern. **48**(3), 1067–1080 (2018). https://doi.org/10.1109/tcyb.2017.2680466
9. Bergadano, F., Gunetti, D.: Inductive Logic Programming: From Machine Learning to Software Engineering. MIT Press, Cambridge (1995)
10. Bongard, J., Lipson, H.: Active coevolutionary learning of deterministic finite automata. J. Mach. Learn. Res. **6**, 28 (2005). 00076
11. Eiben, A.E., Smith, J.E.: Introduction to Evolutionary Computing. Springer, Heidelberg (2003). https://doi.org/10.1007/978-3-662-05094-1
12. Henard, C., Papadakis, M., Perrouin, G., Klein, J., Le Traon, Y.: Towards automated testing and fixing of re-engineered feature models. In: Proceedings of the 2013 International Conference on Software Engineering, ICSE 2013, pp. 1245–1248. IEEE Press, Piscataway (2013). https://doi.org/10.1109/ICSE.2013.6606689
13. Howar, F., Steffen, B.: Active automata learning in practice. In: Bennaceur, A., Hähnle, R., Meinke, K. (eds.) Machine Learning for Dynamic Software Analysis: Potentials and Limits. LNCS, vol. 11026, pp. 123–148. Springer, Cham (2018). https://doi.org/10.1007/978-3-319-96562-8_5
14. Isberner, M., Howar, F., Steffen, B.: The open-source LearnLib. In: Kroening, D., Păsăreanu, C.S. (eds.) CAV 2015. LNCS, vol. 9206, pp. 487–495. Springer, Cham (2015). https://doi.org/10.1007/978-3-319-21690-4_32
15. Lee, D., Yannakakis, M.: Principles and methods of testing finite state machines-a survey. Proc. IEEE **84**(8), 1090–1123 (1996). https://doi.org/10.1109/5.533956
16. Li, Y., Krishnamurthy, R., Raghavan, S., Vaithyanathan, S., Jagadish, H.V.: Regular expression learning for information extraction. In: Proceedings of the Conference on Empirical Methods in Natural Language Processing, EMNLP 2008, pp. 21–30. Association for Computational Linguistics, Stroudsburg (2008)
17. López-Ibáñez, M., Dubois-Lacoste, J., Cáceres, L.P., Birattari, M., Stützle, T.: The irace package: iterated racing for automatic algorithm configuration. Oper. Res. Perspect. **3**, 43–58 (2016). https://doi.org/10.1016/j.orp.2016.09.002
18. Martinez, M., Monperrus, M.: Mining software repair models for reasoning on the search space of automated program fixing. Empirical Softw. Eng. **20**(1), 176–205 (2015). https://doi.org/10.1007/s10664-013-9282-8
19. Møller, A.: dk.brics.automaton - finite-state automata and regular expressions for Java (2010). http://www.brics.dk/automaton/
20. Papadakis, M., Kintis, M., Zhang, J., Jia, Y., Le Traon, Y., Harman, M.: Mutation testing advances: an analysis and survey. In: Advances in Computers. Advances in Computers. Elsevier (2018). https://doi.org/10.1016/bs.adcom.2018.03.015
21. Pei, Y., Furia, C.A., Nordio, M., Wei, Y., Meyer, B., Zeller, A.: Automated fixing of programs with contracts. IEEE Trans. Softw. Eng. **40**(5), 427–449 (2014). https://doi.org/10.1109/TSE.2014.2312918

22. Petke, J., Haraldsson, S.O., Harman, M., Langdon, W.B., White, D.R., Woodward, J.R.: Genetic improvement of software: a comprehensive survey. IEEE Trans. Evol. Comput. **22**(3), 415–432 (2018). https://doi.org/10.1109/tevc.2017.2693219

23. Raffelt, H., Steffen, B., Berg, T., Margaria, T.: LearnLib: a framework for extrapolating behavioral models. Int. J. Softw. Tools Technol. Transf. **11**(5), 393–407 (2009). https://doi.org/10.1007/s10009-009-0111-8

24. Regexlib.com. http://www.regexlib.com. Accessed 24 May 2019

25. Regular-expressions.info. http://www.regular-expressions.info/. Accessed 24 May 2019

26. Watchmaker. https://watchmaker.uncommons.org/. Accessed 24 May 2019

27. Weimer, W., Forrest, S., Le Goues, C., Nguyen, T.: Automatic program repair with evolutionary computation. Commun. ACM **53**(5), 109–116 (2010). https://doi.org/10.1145/1735223.1735249

28. Wilkerson, J.L., Tauritz, D.: Coevolutionary automated software correction. In: Proceedings of the 12th Annual Conference on Genetic and Evolutionary Computation - GECCO 2010. ACM Press (2010). https://doi.org/10.1145/1830483.1830739

Testing Chatbots Using Metamorphic Relations

Josip Bozic$^{(\boxtimes)}$ and Franz Wotawa

Institute of Software Technology, Graz University of Technology,
8010 Graz, Austria
{jbozic,wotawa}@ist.tugraz.at

Abstract. Modern-day demands for services often require an availability on a 24/7 basis as well as online accessibility around the globe. For this sake, personalized software systems, called chatbots, are applied. Chatbots offer services, goods or information in natural language. These programs respond to the user in real-time and offer an intuitive and simple interface to interact with. Advantages like these makes them increasingly popular. Chatbots can even act as substitutes for humans for specific purposes. Since the chatbot market is growing, chatbots might outperform and replace classical web applications in the future. For this reason, ensuring correct functionality of chatbots is of high and increasing importance. However, since different implementations and user behavior result in unpredictable results, the chatbot's output is difficult to predict and classify as well. In fact, testing of chatbots represents a challenge because of the unavailability of a test oracle. In this paper, we introduce a metamorphic testing approach for chatbots. In general, metamorphic testing can be applied to situations where no expected values are available. In addition, we discuss how to obtain test cases for chatbots, i.e. sequences of interactions with a chatbot, in an according manner. We demonstrate our approach using a hotel booking system and discuss first experimental results.

Keywords: Metamorphic testing · Functional testing · Chatbots

1 Introduction

Virtual assistants are programs that realize the communication with a user in natural language. These programs, called chatbots [13], offer the advantage to resemble a natural and intuitive way of interaction. Usually, these programs comprehend information from a certain domain. In such way, the chatbot provides specific information in an often entertaining and anonymous manner [5]. Natural language interfaces (NLI) handle the communication between chatbot and user. On the side of the chatbots, this is usually implemented either by a set of rules or by means of natural networks. Here pre-specified patterns define boundaries of possible user interaction [20,24]. Since several studies predict the rise of the chatbot market in the future, addressing the functionality of these

© IFIP International Federation for Information Processing 2019
Published by Springer Nature Switzerland AG 2019
C. Gaston et al. (Eds.): ICTSS 2019, LNCS 11812, pp. 41–55, 2019.
https://doi.org/10.1007/978-3-030-31280-0_3

systems becomes essential [2]. Until now, only a few testing approaches exist that check the correctness of chatbots (e.g. [4, 22, 23]).

Since the behavior of a chatbot might be difficult to predict, traditional testing approaches might not always provide an optimal solution. In testing, it's common practice to rely on test oracles in order to obtain test verdicts. However, problems may arise due to non-testable programs or because of the high amount of manual effort needed to draw a test conclusion. Difficulties with test oracles have been initially pointed to by Weyuker [25]. The author addressed the issue when test oracles are not available during testing. This can be due to multiple reasons, like high costs or complexity of implementations or the domain.

Driven by the same motivation, the concept of *metamorphic testing* (MT) has been introduced by Chen et al. [7]. In MT, the output of a system is not checked against an expected value but a *metamorphic relation* (MR). These describe a relation between the input data and the corresponding output. New test cases are inferred from previous ones according to the specified MRs. These inferred test cases are meant to detect errors that the former ones failed to do. MT is not meant only to detect errors in cases where no expected values are defined, but helps to reveal errors in the production phase as well. In addition to that, MT does not depend on a specific testing strategy; thus, it can be combined with other test selection approaches (see Sect. 4).

In this paper, we introduce a metamorphic testing approach for chatbots. The approach is defined by terms of MT and checks the functionality of a chatbot in an automated manner. Basically, the motivation of our approach is to guarantee functional correctness of a system under the absence of expected data. We provide the theoretical background and elaborate the implementation on a chatbot from the tourism industry. To our knowledge, this is the first adaptation of MT for testing of chatbots.

The remainder of the paper is structured as follows: Sect. 2 introduces metamorphic testing and its adaptation to testing of chatbots. Then, Sect. 2.1 describes the underlying test generation. Section 2.2 discusses the test execution as well as the underlying algorithm of the approach. The implementation is evaluated in Sect. 3, whereas related work is enumerated in Sect. 4. Finally, Sect. 5 concludes the work.

2   Metamorphic Testing for Chatbots

The bulk of this paper addresses two major fields: Metamorphic testing and one concrete manifestation of AI systems, namely chatbots. In our previous work in [4] we introduced a functional testing approach for chatbots, where the expected values were known in advance. The chatbot, a hotel booking system, is checked whether valid reservations are processed correctly. However, due to unpredictive behavior of such systems, MT addresses situations where only sparse or no knowledge exist about a system.

First, let's denote the basic principles of MT, as initially described in [7] and [17]. In contrast to other testing techniques, the basic principle for test generation differs in MT.

Definition 1. *Let f be an implemented function of a program P. R_f defines a property that must be valid for all inputs $x_1, x_2, ..., x_n$ over f, and the corresponding outputs $f(x_1), f(x_2), ..., f(x_n)$. The relation R_f represents a metamorphic relation (MR) over the input-output pairs, thus $R_f((x_1, f(x_1)), (x_2, f(x_2)), ..., (x_n, f(x_n)))$, where $n > 1$.*

Since no expected test value is available, properties have to be defined that must hold for all test inputs against a program, regardless of their value. However, conditions can be specified as part of a MR that put restrictions on test cases [17]. A metamorphic relation can represent any suitable type of relation, such as equalities, properties, constraints etc. The function of MR is twofold: (1) it serves as a guideline for generation of test inputs from existing data, and (2) acts as an output relation, which is checked after the test execution. In such way, MR replaces the test oracle by comparing the input-output pairs from test cases. We call this comparison a *metamorphic check* (MC). A metamorphic check fails in case that the input-output pair satisfies a metamorphic relation.

Definition 2. *An initial source test case x_1 that does not trigger an error or vulnerability in P, is a successful test case. A follow-up test case x_2 is inferred from x_1 according to a selection criteria, as specified by R_f. The pair of the source and follow-up test case can be defined as a metamorphic test case.*

Usually, the source test case represents a random value or is derived from partial knowledge about the domain of P. All new test cases are derived from the successful test cases. For the source test case x_1 and its output $f(x_1)$, new test cases will be generated based on the input-output pair $(x_1, f(x_1))$. During test execution, the applied MRs must hold for input-output pairs of both, source and the follow-up, test cases. If the MR does not hold for a certain metamorphic test case [17], then we conclude that a fault or inconsistency is detected in P.

In general, three tasks constitute a MT-based approach, regardless of the domain:

1. Definition of metamorphic relations
2. Test generation
3. Test execution

In the following sections, we will address each of the challenges individually. For all three cases, the adaptation of MT for chatbots has to be addressed in detail.

2.1   Metamorphic Test Generation

We describe our MT approach for testing of chatbots and evaluate it on a real example. The tested chatbot is a hotel booking system that was introduced in [4]. In this paper, we will omit technical details about the implementation but provide a few details about its functionality. The agent is implemented in Dialogflow [1] and communicates with the user by sending and receiving messages in natural language. Since the goal of the chatbot is to make a hotel booking, the chatbot demands some information in order to finalize a reservation. On the side of the chatbot, this information is hard coded in form of eight mandatory parameters. During communication, the chatbot will ask the user to provide this information. Also, we assume that the chatbot comprises the natural processing and necessary data. A typical communication flow, initiated by the user, does look as follows.

```
I want to book a room in Vienna.
- Do you want a hotel, hostel or apartment?
book a hotel
- Which one do you prefer?
Fairmont
- When do you want to start your stay?
I want to check-in today.
- How many adults?
1 adult
- How many children?
2 children
- How many nights?
1 night
- How many stars do you prefer?
i want 5 stars
- Let me sum up! Location: Vienna, Name: Fairmont, Check-In:
  2019-05-20, Accommodation: hotel, People: 1 adults, 2 children,
  Nights: 1, Stars: 5 stars
```

In case that the user does not provide a specific information, the chatbot will continue to ask for clarification. Thus, no reservation will be made. On the other hand, the behavior of the user can be unpredictable to a certain degree as well. For example, the user can make an inquiry by rephrasing sentences or providing multiple information in one message. This fact will play a role in the test generation process. The chatbot is expected to recognize different types of input utterances. In fact, the chatbot understands additional messages (like exit or abort), but in our example, we ignore such situations. However, regardless of the user input, the chatbot demands information about the following parameters.

```
$location, $venue-type, $venue-title, $checkin-date, $adult,
$child, $night, $star
```

In our previous work, we tested whether the chatbot makes a valid reservation. However, in this paper, the functionality is tested from another perspective. From the starting point of view, the chatbot is unpredictable for the user. However, the user is unpredictable in front of the chatbot as well. In fact, we assume that the user initially knows the information that she or he intends to submit. Also, the intention of the user is to make a valid reservation with this information. That is, the information in a reservation must not deviate from the provided values. Additionally, according to practice in MT, we assume that some information about the domain is known in advance. One sequence of messages from the point of the user is considered to be one test case. We suppose that the input values for the source test case are denoted as I_s, whereas the follow-up values are given as I_f. Also, their outputs are defined as O_s and O_f, respectively. The obtained output serves as an indicator for the test verdict. The output differs for individual inquiries and available information. For example, different numerical inputs will result in different registration information. The type of responses, however, will remain the same.

As can be seen Table 1, I_s consists of eight actions that will be submitted as individual requests. The individual actions themselves comprise several terms and numerical values that are considered keywords. As will be described below, these play an important role for further test generation. After every request, the chatbot is programmed to give a corresponding response. During testing, we record all responses for every submitted action. On the right side of the table the chatbot's mandatory parameters are enumerated. The chatbot processes the individual actions and, if possible, assigns provided values to their parameter.

Table 1. Source test case

#	Action	Parameter
0:	I want to book a room in Vienna	`$location`
1:	book a hotel	`$venue-type`
2:	Fairmont	`$venue-title`
3:	I want to check-in today	`$checkin-date`
4:	1 adults	`$adult`
5:	2 children	`$child`
6:	1 night	`$night`
7:	i want 5 stars	`$star`

Now, we define the following properties of the chatbot as MRs. As already mentioned, these relations must be valid for test inputs and outputs. The source test case from Table 1 encompasses sentences in natural language. However, several keywords are emphasized that will be addressed by the MRs. The MRs focus on input generation for chatbots, as follows:

MR1: Replace keywords with synonyms: In order to infer I_f from I_s, they keywords are replaced by synonyms. Although, for every follow-up test case, keywords are changed in only one action. The obtained O_s serves as a reference that is compared to the obtained O_f. When applying synonyms, we expect the same behavior from the chatbot, thus $O_s = O_f$ must be valid.

MR2: Change numerical values: This relation instructs to change numerical values for individual actions. The outputs of O_s and O_f should be equal, with the exception of the numerals from the final reservation.

MR3: Omit words: This relation demands that keywords are omitted, thus providing insufficient information. The chatbot should recognize the difference, thus resulting in different responses. MR3 is valid in case that $O_s \neq O_f$ for every I_f.

MR4: Replace keywords with unrelated terms: This relation is similar to MR1 but instead of synonyms, keywords are exchanged with unrelated terms. Therefore, the corresponding outputs must never resemble each other. Therefore, the expected outputs equal $O_s \neq O_f$.

MR5: Change order of actions: The order of actions in I_s is changed in the follow-up test case I_f. Since the tester does not know about the SUT's behavior, the obtained outputs are expected to differ, thus $O_s \neq O_f$. (Although, a valid reservation might still be accomplished accidentally by a valid random combination.)

For every MR, a grammar is constructed that provides the building blocks for test generation. For example, the grammar for MR1 is defined in the standard Backus-Naur form (BNF).

```
<sentence>::= I want to <book> a <room> in <place>
<book>::= book | order | take | prefer
<room>::= room | place | hotel | hostel | apartment
<place>::= Vienna | Prague | Madrid
<accomodation>::= hotel | hostel | apartment
<venue>::= Sacher | Fairmont | Elmhurst
<days>::= in two days | yesterday | tomorrow | today
<adults>::= <number> <guests>
<guests>::= guests | people | humans | adults
<youngling>::= <number> <children>
<children>::= children | kids
<nights>::= <number> <sleep>
<sleep>::= nights | days
<rating>::= <number> <points>
<points>::= stars | ratings
<number>::= 1 | 2 | 3 | 4 | 5
```

Formal grammars are defined by finite sets of terminal and nonterminal symbols. In the above example, nonterminal symbols resemble keywords in our approach, whereas terminals represent concrete values. The expression, i.e. a sequence of symbols, guides the generation of an action by assigning concrete values according to MR. Some terminals in the grammar are set manually by checking the supported library from Dialogflow. In order to generate meaningful inputs, we use a modified version of Grammar Solver [3]. The implementation applies MRs and traverses through the BNF structure, thereby constructing new user inputs. In fact, this process can be subtracted as a mutation process. MRs proscribe unique mutations to individual actions, thus generating modified, i.e. follow-up, test cases. So, the final shape of a follow-up test cases is determined by the mutation operation and the source test case.

Table 2. Follow-up test case for MR4

#	Action
0:	I want to book a room in nowhere
1:	book a hotel
2:	Fairmont
3:	I want to check-in today.
4:	1 adults
5:	2 children
6:	1 night
7:	i want 5 stars

For example, the follow-up test case I_f in Table 2 depicts the case where MR4 is applied to I_s from Table 1. In fact, every inferred test case will differ from its original by adding one change. In such way, we want to check how minimal changes affect the overall testing result. We obtain a diverse test case by applying mutations to just one initial test. By doing so, our intention is to obtain tests that are able to lead to states during execution that are not covered by the implementation or the specification. After the mutations from all MRs have been applied to the source test case, we initiate the execution process.

2.2   Metamorphic Test Execution

After the individual MRs have been specified, the test generation process can begin. The algorithm, **BotMorph**, as shown in Algorithm 1, implements our entire test generation and execution approach. The process starts with the initial source test case, I_s, from Table 1. Its individual actions are manually defined and represent a sequence that ultimately leads to a specific reservation. I_s is executed and the chatbot's source output, O_s, is recorded. This represents an important step that substitutes the test oracle: The comparison of O_s to the result from the follow-up test case, O_f, will determine the test verdict.

Then, the MRs are applied in optional order to derive follow-up test cases. The new test case is executed against the SUT and the output is recorded. From the technical point of view, obtained values from Grammar Solver are assigned to HTTP requests and submitted to the chatbot system on the fly. In return, its HTTP responses are processed and handled accordingly. The MR checks are done after the final O_f of a test case is received. If no vulnerability is triggered, i.e. if the MC fails, then the test case is added to the list of successful tests V. Otherwise, in case that an issue has been detected, the test will be disregarded. The process continues until all MRs have been applied and checked. Afterwards, the same process is restarted but with new source tests from the successful ones.

In theory, the process can continue until every symbol has occurred for every combination of values for all MRs. It remains the task of the tester to define the termination condition.

Algorithm 1. BotMorph – Metamorphic test generation and execution algorithm for chatbots

Input: Program P, set of metamorphic relations $MR = \{\mathtt{mr}_1, \ldots, \mathtt{mr}_n\}$, source test case $I_s = \{\mathtt{a}_1, \ldots, \mathtt{a}_n\}$, grammar G and a function $\Phi = (MR, I_s, G) \mapsto I_f$ that infers follow-up test cases.

Output: Metamorphic test set $TS = \{\mathtt{I}_{f1}, \ldots, \mathtt{I}_{fi}\}$ where each $I_{fi} = \{\mathtt{a}_0, \ldots, \mathtt{a}_n\}$ and a list with source test cases $V = \{\mathtt{v}_1, \ldots, \mathtt{v}_n\}$.

```
1:  TS = ∅
2:  O_s = exec(I_s, P)
3:  V = V ∪ {(I_s, O_s)}
4:  for v ∈ V do
5:      while MR.hasNext() do
6:          I_f = generate(Φ, mr_n, G, I_s)              ▷ Generate test case
7:          TS = TS ∪ {I_f}
8:          for I_f ∈ TS do
9:              res(I_f) = FAIL
10:             O_f = exec(I_f, P)                        ▷ Execute test case
11:             if check((I_s, O_s), (I_f, O_f), mr_n) fails then   ▷ Execute MC
12:                 res(I_f) = PASS
13:                 V = V ∪ {(I_f, O_f)}                  ▷ Save successful test case
14:             else
15:                 res(I_f) = FAIL
16:             end if
17:         end for
18:     end while
19: end for
```

3 Evaluation

For the evaluation we generated several test sets from the initial test case. The source test case I_s serves as the starting point for all inferred I_f's. The defined MRs serve as test guidelines as well as the basis for conducted metamorphic checks. We execute the procedure from M1 in a descending order. Since the individual actions from I_s differ from each other, the MRs will cause different results with regard to number and shape of test cases. For example, a_0 contains three keywords, whereas a_1 comprehends just one. When applying MR1, synonyms will be created for every keyword separately (with the exception of the check-in date). For example, in case of a_0, the mutation is applied only for one keyword at the time. Thus, the number of resulting follow-up's is multiplied by each keyword and the grammar values. On the other hand, a_1 will provide only one follow-up test case per mutation. Also, each MR is applied individually on just one action, so the new test case differs only in one change from its original (the exception being MR5). In such way we want to observe the testing behaviour by adding just small changes.

In total, we generated 104 test cases that were submitted against the booking chatbot. Table 3 depicts all results that have been achieved.

Table 3. Results for metamorphic test cases

MR	#total	#pass	#fail
MR1	60	56	4
MR2	16	16	0
MR3	10	5	5
MR4	10	5	5
MR5	8	8	0

Since the SUT behaves different for each input, we will analyse the results with regard to every MR.

MR1: We added several synonyms for keywords and encountered a few discrepancies with Dialogflow. The initial booking request action was successful in all cases. Thus, the chatbot was able to recognize the intent and finalize the reservation even when the client reformulates the request. A failing test case was encountered with a_{4-6} and a_8, where synonyms like "guests" instead of "adults", "kids" instead of "children" and "ratings" could not be recognized by the chatbot.

MR2: This MR is unique among the relations because it affects only actions with numerical values. That is, only four out of eight inputs are addressed by the mutation. It can be concluded that changing the number in an action does not cause any failures. The chatbot succeeds with generating a reservation with different values. Therefore, all tests have been successful.

MR3: Omitting words causes a lot of confusion in the chatbot. Initiating a reservation with a_0 is possible even without the explicit mentioning of "book" or "room". However, if no city name is provided, the client cannot proceed further. We conclude that the explicit statement of a city name at the beginning of the communication is mandatory. Also, if no accommodation type, check-in dates and stars are provided, then the reservation fails. The chatbot keeps insisting for the information and ignores further user requests. For actions with numerals, we kept the numbers but omitted the words to their right. Interestingly, a valid information is made when providing just numerals without "adults", "children" or "nights". It seems that the chatbot assumes that a client always provides information in a strict order. Thus, it assigns the information to parameters without further clarification. However, this seems not to be the case when "stars" is omitted.

MR4: Replacing keywords with nonrelated terms triggered strange behaviour on side of the chatbot. For example, formulating a_0 into "I want to exchange a pod in nowhere" (three follow-up test cases, one for every keyword) resulted in a valid registration! If we compare the behaviour to MR3, the chatbot seems to accept every value for city name as a valid one. This is an important implementation flaw in the chatbot. Actions a_{2-4} are processed as expected by the SUT. On the other hand, "alien" and "kobolds" seem to be a valid substitute for "adults" and "children" in a_5 and a_6, for unknown reasons. However, a_7 and a_8 have been rejected, as demanded by the relation.

MR5: This MR is unique since it requests a reordering of actions in a test case. This means that concrete values will not differ between I_s and I_f. We adapted a randomized approach that resulted in eight test cases with different sequences of actions. As expected, every O_f from SUT differs from O_s. The chatbot's response depends on the first user inquiry. Usually the SUT keeps asking for a certain information and remains in a specific queue. If the requested information is received in the meanwhile, then it switches to another queue. Also, if the chatbot encountered unexpected input (from its point of view), then unexpected responses were sent. This included an empty text or unrelated sentences (e.g. "Talk to you soon!").

Since we applied MT for functional testing purposes, our intention was not to exploit a SUT. Since a tester does not know about the inner workings of a SUT and its available information, some guessing is needed. The tester can assume that some keywords will be understood by the chatbot, others can be completely avoided. In our approach, unintended behaviour indicates that (1) an implementation flaw or oversight or (2) insufficient information on side of the Dialogflow implementation. Actually, here both observations affirm known advantages of MT, namely the detection of verification and validation defects, respectively [8]. In the first case, we can assume that the chatbot did behave to its implementation or incomplete specification. However, it failed to cover cases, which it should be able to understand. Also, the assignment of information to a specific parameter without clear indication can be considered a drawback as well. Finalizing a reservation with unsuitable data (e.g. fictional city names or substitutes) is even worse.

On the other hand, the chatbot's permanent insistence on a specific information at a certain point during the conversation indicates that a strict order must be followed. As already proven in [4], the hotel booking chatbot insists that the first and last inquiries must be of a specific type. The sequence of other information is optional.

```
$location
$venue-type
$venue-title
$checkin-date
$adult
$child
$night
$star
```

The approach in that work demonstrated that the chatbot concluded reservations even with missing information in a nonintuitive manner. This means that the chatbot does something it should not. The same observation was proven when testing against MR3. On the other hand, MT detected that the SUT does not what it should do (e.g. with MR1). Also, meaningless input is wrongly associated with an intent with MR4. We assume that the reason why unrelated terms are still "understood" is due to the fact that the chatbot follows its strict order and ignores other information ("stars" being an exception). The recognition of terms depends upon the pre-specified entries in the chatbot's entity database. A different set of values and intents would likely result in different behaviour of the system. Interestingly, some natural language input does disturb the chatbot as well. Adding a "I want to" to mandatory information does not match the chatbot's intent. It seems that the SUT follows a minimalistic approach.

In general, we conclude that the use of metamorphic test cases succeeds to trigger defects in natural language systems. In addition to that, it provides some clarification about possible reasons with regard to diverse inputs. Also, it uncovers clues about inner workings of the chatbot by relying on a small set of metamorphic relations. For all these reasons, we consider the presented approach as a good starting concept for further actions.

4   Related Work

Research that correlates with our work includes metamorphic testing and chatbot testing. Works that focus on the first topic are often conducted on industrial and online applications. Also, these approaches often interact with external implementations and resources. On the other hand, literature that focuses on testing of chatbots, is sparse. To our knowledge, no work deals with the adaptation of MT to chatbots.

4.1   Metamorphic Testing

MT was introduced in [7] and the idea was elaborated on several examples of numerical problems. Comprehensive surveys about papers that deal with MT can be found in [17] and [8].

The preliminary work that addressed oracle-free programs is discussed in [25]. Here the notion of *pseudo-oracles* is used, i.e. external programs that substitute a real test oracle. Additional programs are implemented and tests are run against both the original and the substitute program. If the results match, then the results of the original program are considered to be valid.

In [18] and [16] the authors elaborate a MT-based approach for testing of *feature models* (FM) and *variability models* (VM). Such models encompass the definition of specific products by means of features or configurations, respectively. MRs are defined between models and their inferred products, and a test generator. New models are generated from previous ones by adding mandatory features. In this way, many models and valid configurations can be generated automatically.

[26] addresses testing of implementations that use ML classification algorithms. The authors derive MRs for the individual algorithms and test a real-world ML application framework. Individual MRs define properties that are

necessary to be valid for a classifier algorithm. Finally, they claim that their MT-based approach can be used against any SUT that uses ML. This work is evaluated further in [15].

In [28] a MT-based framework is proposed for testing of autonomous driving systems that rely on Deep Neural Networks (DNN). Another work that elaborates MT for testing of autonomous systems is given in [29]. Here MT relies on deep learning models and comes in combination with fuzzing. The authors evaluate their approach on the mission-critical LiDAR Obstacle Perception system, with promising results.

Additional adaptations of MT to AI systems that include autonomous systems and DNN are elaborated in [12] and [21], respectively. Also, [10] discusses the use of MT for debugging of ML applications.

The authors of [9] address the applicability of MT to cybersecurity. In this approach, MRs are defined in order to test for web failures. Several real-world obfuscators have been tested by using a small test suite. The conducted evaluation indicates that several bugs were found.

Additionally, [19] applies MT to test Web Application Programming Interfaces (APIs).

[6] discusses an implementation of MR for testing of event sequences for business processes. The approach, MTES, defines metamorphic relations for fault-detection purposes. The authors conclude that more diverse inputs result in higher detection capabilities.

Also, works exist that address MT for machine translators (e.g. [27]). A MR applies translations to different sentences and checks for semantic (dis)similarity between languages. Inputs are generated that are meant to be homologous in different languages. The authors discuss the quality of translators and their translation errors. In contrast to our work, they validate the produced inputs from the translator and ignore the SUT that processes these inputs.

4.2   Testing of Chatbots

In contrast to the plentiful number of MT-related papers, only a few papers address testing of chatbots.

For example, [23] introduces PARADISE, a system that deals with the evaluation of conversational systems. Different dialogue strategies are compared and checked against a performance function. In this way, the correctness of an answer is determined. However, in our work, we concentrate on the user's side without having an insight in expected results.

[22] that deals with testing of conversational systems with regard to functionality. A testing system emulates a user that interacts with the chatbot. A large amount of pre-defined user inputs is submitted to the chatbot in an automated manner. The tested system itself, CognIA, represents a financial advisor. During exhaustive communication, specific metrics are used that validate the chatbot's responses with regard to submitted inputs.

In our previous work [4], we introduced an approach for functional testing of a hotel booking chatbot. We applied AI planning for generation of test cases and compared the chatbot's output to an expected result in an automated manner.

Techniques that resemble our test case generation technique are given in [14] and [11]. They discuss a technique for conversational input generation for chatbots. The idea behind the proposed technique is to change valid user inputs by paraphrasing them. Different techniques are used for this sake in order to retrieve a divergent input from the original one. The changes encompass lexical substitutions, as well as non-native preposition errors and native colloquial phrasing, respectively. An external source is used for retrieving original synonyms. Finally, the resulting framework tests the robustness of the system by checking on the input variations. The evaluations, based on a chatbot and a flight booking system, indicate that several weaknesses have been encountered. The obtained results indicate that the SUT does not always recognize an intent when words are replaced with synonyms. Consequently, it might be claimed that our results from MR1 complement the observations from their approach. However, the reasons for these observations should be investigated in more detail. On the other hand, the main difference represents the fact that their technique relies on known expected values. This stands in stark contrast to a MT-based approach. In our case, the use of multiple MRs yield more insight into the inner workings of the SUT.

5   Conclusion and Future Work

In this paper, we addressed an emerging issue in software testing, namely testing of AI systems. The nature of such systems often impedes a straight-forward approach. Especially systems that communicate in natural language might become more important in the future. Because of that, testing of these systems becomes an essential task to ensure correct functionality. In this paper we introduced a metamorphic testing approach for testing of chatbots. Instead of models of existing systems, it relies on metamorphic relations. Since the output of an AI system is difficult to predict, the approach introduces metamorphic checks instead of traditional test oracles. We presented a program that combines metamorphic test case generation and execution for functional testing of chatbots. In the aftermath, the approach is successfully evaluated on a chatbot system from the tourism industry.

The obtained results indicate that the metamorphic approach is able to detect unexpected behaviour in a system. Although the chatbot did succeed to ensure functionality in some cases, other test cases triggered situations, which the SUT failed to handle correctly. Consequently, the reasons for these issues must be addressed separately.

Finally, we claim that our approach can be used for functional testing of chatbots. In addition to that, metamorphic testing can be used for testing of non-functional properties as well. Precisely, MT-based approaches can be applied under circumstances where expected behaviour is difficult or impossible to determine. In the future, we plan to extend our approach by improving the test generation. MRs can be easily added to the existing ones. Thus, a more diverse test suite will be obtained. Also, using the MT approach against other chatbot systems remains an open challenge. Eventually, it would be interesting to compare the MT-based approach to other chatbot testing techniques and tools.

Acknowledgement. The research presented in the paper has been funded in part by the Cooperation Programme Interreg V-A Slovenia-Austria under the project AS-IT-IC (Austrian-Slovenian Intelligent Tourist Information Center). We thank our colleague Oliver A. Tazl, who helped us with the implementation of the SUT in [4], which was used in this work. In addition to that, we want to thank the anonymous reviewers for their constructive feedback, which we addressed in the paper.

References

1. Dialogflow. https://dialogflow.com/. Accessed 11 Dec 2018
2. Gartner Top Strategic Predictions for 2018 and Beyond. https://www.gartner.com/smarterwithgartner/gartner-top-strategic-predictions-for-2018-and-beyond/. Accessed 07 May 2018
3. Grammar-solver. https://github.com/bd21/Grammar-Solver. Accessed 13 July 2018
4. Bozic, J., Tazl, O.A., Wotawa, F.: Chatbot testing using AI planning. In: Proceedings of the International Conference on Artificial Intelligence Testing (AITest) (2019)
5. Brandtzæg, P.B., Følstad, A.: Why people use chatbots. In: Proceedings of the 4th International Conference on Internet Science (INSCI 2017) (2017)
6. Chen, J., Wang, Y., Guo, Y., Jiang, M.: A metamorphic testing approach for event sequences. PLoS ONE **14**(2), e0212476 (2019)
7. Chen, T.Y., Cheung, S.C., Yiu, S.M.: Metamorphic testing: a new approach for generating next test cases. Technical report HKUST-CS98-01, Department of Computer Science, Hong Kong University of Science and Technology, Hong Kong (1998)
8. Chen, T.Y., et al.: Metamorphic testing: a review of challenges and opportunities. ACM Comput. Surv. (CSUR) **51**(1), 4 (2018)
9. Chen, T.Y., et al.: Metamorphic testing for cybersecurity. Computer **49**(6), 48–55 (2016)
10. Dwarakanath, A., et al.: Identifying implementation bugs in machine learning based image classifiers using metamorphic testing. In: Proceedings of the 27th ACM SIGSOFT International Symposium on Software Testing and Analysis (ISSTA 2018) (2018)
11. Guichard, J., Ruane, E., Smith, R., Bean, D., Ventresque, A.: Assessing the robustness of conversational agents using paraphrases. IEEE, University College Dublin (2019)
12. Lindvall, M., Porter, A., Magnusson, G., Schulze, C.: Metamorphic model-based testing of autonomous systems. In: Proceedings of the 2nd International Workshop on Metamorphic Testing (MET 2017) (2017)
13. Mauldin, M.L.: ChatterBots, TinyMuds and the turing test: entering the loebner prize competition. In: AAAI 1994 Proceedings of the Twelfth National Conference on Artificial Intelligence, vol. 1, pp. 16–21 (1994)

14. Ruane, E., Faure, T., Smith, R., Bean, D., Carson-Berndsen, J., Ventresque, A.: BoTest: a framework to test the quality of conversational agents using divergent input examples. In: Proceedings of the 23rd International Conference on Intelligent User Interfaces Companion (IUI 2018 Companion) (2018)
15. Saha, P., Kanewala, U.: Fault detection effectiveness of metamorphic relations developed for testing supervised classifiers. In: Proceedings of the International Conference on Artificial Intelligence Testing (AITest) (2019)
16. Segura, S., Durán, A., Sánchez, A.B., Le Berre, D., Lonca, E., Ruiz-Cortés, A.: Automated metamorphic testing of variability analysis tools. Softw. Test. Verif. Reliab. **25**(2), 138–163 (2015)
17. Segura, S., Fraser, G., Sánchez, A.B., Ruiz-Cortés, A.: A survey on metamorphic testing. IEEE Trans. Softw. Eng. **42**(9), 805–824 (2016)
18. Segura, S., Hierons, R.M., Benavides, D., Ruiz-Cortés, A.: Automated test data generation on the analyses of feature models: a metamorphic testing approach. In: Proceedings of the 2010 Third International Conference on Software Testing, Verification and Validation (2010)
19. Segura, S., Parejo, J.A., Troya, J., Ruiz-Cortés, A.: Metamorphic testing of RESTful web APIs. IEEE Trans. Softw. Eng. **44**(11), 1083–1099 (2018)
20. Shawar, B.A., Atwell, E.: Using corpora in machine-learning chatbot systems. Int. J. Corpus Linguist. **10**, 489–516 (2005)
21. Tian, Y., Pei, K., Jana, S., Ray, B.: DeepTest: automated testing of deep-neural-network-driven autonomous cars. In: Proceedings of the 40th International Conference on Software Engineering (2018)
22. Vasconcelos, M., Candello, H., Pinhanez, C., dos Santos, T.: Bottester: testing conversational systems with simulated users. In: Proceedings of the XVI Brazilian Symposium on Human Factors in Computing Systems (IHC 2017) (2017)
23. Walker, M.A., Litman, D.J., Kamm, C.A., Abella, A.: PARADISE: a framework for evaluating spoken dialogue agents. In: Proceedings of the 35th Annual General Meeting of the Association for Computational Linguistics, ACL/EACL 1997 (1997)
24. Wallace, R.S.: The elements of AIML style. In: ALICE A.I. Foundation (2003)
25. Weyuker, E.: On testing non-testable programs. Comput. J. **25**(4), 465–470 (1982)
26. Xie, X., Ho, J.W.K., Murphy, C., Kaiser, G., Xu, B., Chen, T.Y.: Testing and validating machine learning classifiers by metamorphic testing. J. Syst. Softw. **84**(4), 544–558 (2011)
27. Yan, B., Yecies, B., Zhou, Z.Q.: Metamorphic relations for data validation: a case study of translated text messages. In: Proceedings of the 4th International Workshop on Metamorphic Testing (MET 2019) (2019)
28. Zhang, M., Zhang, Y., Zhang, L., Liu, C., Khurshid, S.: DeepRoad: GAN-based metamorphic testing and input validation framework for autonomous driving systems. In: Proceedings of the 33rd ACM/IEEE International Conference on Automated Software Engineering (ASE 2018) (2018)
29. Zhou, Z.Q., Sun, L.: Metamorphic testing of driverless cars. Commun. ACM **62**(3), 61–67 (2019)

Generating Biased Dataset for Metamorphic Testing of Machine Learning Programs

Shin Nakajima[1]($\boxtimes$) and Tsong Yueh Chen[2]

[1] National Institute of Informatics, Tokyo, Japan
nkjm@nii.ac.jp
[2] Swinburne University of Technology, Melbourne, Australia

Abstract. Although both positive and negative testing are important for assuring quality of programs, generating a variety of test inputs for such testing purposes is difficult for machine learning software. This paper studies why it is difficult, and then proposes a new method of generating datasets that are test inputs to machine learning programs. The proposed idea is demonstrated with a case study of classifying hand-written numbers.

1 Introduction

Machine learning such as deep neural networks (DNN) [4] is applied to advanced services of extreme reliability such as auto-pilot cars. However, quality assurance of DNN-based programs is more difficult than conventional software systems, because the programs are categorized as *untestable* [12]. Thus, Metamorphic Testing (MT) framework [1] has been used as a standard practice for testing of machine learning programs [2].

Because machine learning programs work on collections of data (datasets) to derive useful information, generating a wide variety of datasets systematically is key to effective testing. Most existing works [7,9,15–17] make use of application characteristics and serve for specific test targets.

This paper proposes a systematic follow-up dataset generation method. The method is formulated as an optimization problem referring only to trained learning models without accessing to any application specific information. We conjecture that the method is applicable to a wide variety of neural network learning models [4,5]. The paper also discusses how the proposed method is related to *distortion degrees* in trained learning models, which may open a new research direction of the machine learning software quality.

2 Machine Learning Software

We explain a basic idea of machine learning problems with the case of neural network (NN) supervised learning method [5]. Assume that a learning model

© IFIP International Federation for Information Processing 2019
Published by Springer Nature Switzerland AG 2019
C. Gaston et al. (Eds.): ICTSS 2019, LNCS 11812, pp. 56–64, 2019.
https://doi.org/10.1007/978-3-030-31280-0_4

$y(W; x)$ is given as a multi-dimensional non-linear function, differentiable with respect to both learning parameters W and input data x. Learning aims at obtaining a set of parameter values W^* by solving a numerical optimization problem. Below, a training dataset LS is expressed as $\{\langle x^n, t^n \rangle\}$.

$$W^* = \underset{W}{argmin}\ \mathcal{E}(W; LS), \quad \mathcal{E}(W; LS) = \frac{1}{N}\sum_{n=1}^{N} \ell(y(W;\ x^n),\ t^n)$$

The function $\ell(\_, \_)$ denotes distances to represent how much a calculated output $y(W; x^n)$ differs from an expected supervisor tag value t^n. The machine learning problem is to search for learning parameter values to minimize the mean of ℓ under ρ_{em} of the empirical distribution of the training dataset LS.

Let $\mathcal{F}_L(X)$ be a function to calculate W^*, that is a program to solve the above optimization problem with its input dataset X. $\mathcal{F}_L(X)$ is a faithful implementation of a machine learning method [5]. Another function, $\mathcal{F}_I(x)$, calculates prediction or inference results of incoming data x. Its functional behavior depends on W^* or $y(W^*; x)$. Quality assurance of machine learning software involves two different programs [8]. Although this paper focuses on testing of $\mathcal{F}_L$, data generated with the proposed method can be input to $\mathcal{F}_I$ as well.

3   Dataset Diversity in Testing

Software testing is a systematic method to provide quality assurance of programs, and is sometimes viewed from two different perspectives. *Positive testing* focuses on ensuring that a program does what it is supposed to do for normal input satisfying the preconditions. *Negative testing* ensures that the program does not do what it is not supposed to do even when the input is unexpected or violates the preconditions.

We raise a question here how we consider preconditions for machine learning programs. $\mathcal{F}_L$ accepts a training dataset LS and calculates learning parameter values W^*. Alternatively, $\mathcal{F}_L$ is regarded to synthesize W^* from a piece of specification information that LS implicitly has. Although it is related to *specifications*, LS is just a collection of concrete data, and can not be a checkable condition.

A dataset X is a sample by statistics, and its elements are theoretically viewed to be generated *independently and identically distributed* according to a probabilistic distribution ρ; $X = \{d \mid d \sim_{i.i.d.} \rho\}$ (written as $X \sim_{i.i.d.} \rho$ in this paper). If X does not satisfy the relation $X \sim_{i.i.d.} \rho$, X is not a faithful representative of ρ. The situation is a sample selection bias [11] and consequently considered as a specification error [6].

In machine learning, we know only an empirical distribution ρ_{em} of LS, which is believed to be an approximation of a hypothetical distribution ρ. We assume that there are M $(M > 0)$ LS_js, each of which is of a different empirical distribution ρ_j, but collectively satisfies a relationship, $(\cup_{j=1}^{M} LS_j) \sim_{i.i.d.} \rho$. Such a ρ defines a group of input, and hense can be interpreted as a precondition. Some of LS_js are free from sample selection bias ($LS_j \sim_{i.i.d.} \rho$); they form a group of datasets LSS_P. The others LS_k, each of which is still a sample of ρ, are biased and written here as $LS_k \sim_{\neg i.i.d.} \rho$; they form LSS_N. We consider all datasets in LSS_P satisfying the precondition, and all datasets in LSS_N not satisfying it. Then, $LSS_P \cap LSS_N = \phi$. Furthermore, all of them serve the same machine learning task, because they are related to the ρ. The datasets in $LSS_P \cup LSS_N$ show different nature, and thus embed the *dataset diversity* [9].

Note that a randomly generated dataset does not have any relationship with ρ and thus is not appropriate even for negative testing.

4   Generating Distorted Dataset

We generate biased or distorted datasets algorithmically from LS of ρ_{em}. The method is based on the L-BFGS [13], explained below.

Given a dataset LS of $\{\langle x^n, t^n \rangle\}$, $W^* = \mathcal{F}_L(LS)$. An adversarial example is a solution of an optimization problem; $x^A = \underset{x}{argmin}\, A_\lambda(W^*; x_S, t_T, x)$, where

$$A_\lambda(W^*; x_S, t_T, x) = \ell(y(W^*; x), t_T) + \lambda \cdot \ell(x, x_S),$$

with a hyper-parameter λ. Such a data x^A is visually close to a seed x_S for human eyes, but actually adds faint noises so as to induce miss-inference such that $\mathcal{F}_I(x^A) = t_T$; we assume here $\langle x_S, t_T \rangle \notin LS$.

Our method uses this optimization problem, in which a seed x_S is x^n and its target label t_T is t^n. Let x^{n*} be a solution of $\underset{x}{argmin}\, A_\lambda(W^*; x^n, t^n, x)$ for $\langle x^n, t^n \rangle \in LS$. The method basically obtains a new data x^{n*} such that x^n is augmented with *noises*. Because the predicted label is not changed, x^{n*} is not adversarial, but may be *distorted* from the seed x^n. When λ is very small, the distortion from x^n is large. If λ is appropriate, x^{n*} can be close to x^n. By applying the method to all the elements in LS, a new dataset $\{\langle x^{n*}, t^n \rangle\}$ is obtained. Now, let $LS^{(K)}$ be $\{\langle x^n, t^n \rangle\}$. We define $T_\lambda(LS^{(K)})$ to generate a new dataset $LS^{(K+1)}$;

$$LS^{(K+1)} = T_\lambda(LS^{(K)}) \equiv \{ \langle \underset{x}{argmin}\, A_\lambda(\mathcal{F}_L(LS^{(K)}); x^n, t^n, x),\ t^n \rangle \}.$$

Because W^* used in A_λ is derived from a training dataset $LS^{(0)}$ of $\{\langle x^n, t^n \rangle\}$, the solution x^{n*} of the optimization problem can be x^n as a special case with appropriately chosen λ values. $LS^{(1)}$, a result of $T_\lambda(LS^{(0)})$, is not much different from $LS^{(0)}$ and may refer to the same machine learning task as $LS^{(0)}$ does. Contrarily, if we choose some small λ values or we apply the function T_λ repeatedly, the deviation of x^{n*} from x^n can be large, and $LS^{(K)}$ is mostly not *i.i.d.*. We can obtain datasets in either LSS_P or LSS_N automatically.

5   A Case Study

5.1   Machine Learning Classifier for MNIST

MNIST dataset is a standard problem of classifying handwritten numbers. It consists of a training dataset LS of 60,000 vectors, and a testing dataset TS

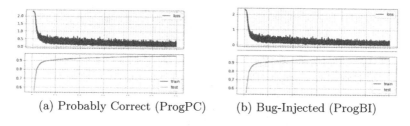

(a) Probably Correct (ProgPC)   (b) Bug-Injected (ProgBI)

Fig. 1. Loss and accuracy: MNIST dataset

of 10,000. Both LS and TS are randomly selected from a pool of vector data, and thus are considered to follow the same empirical distribution. The machine learning task is to classify an input vector data into one of ten categories from 0 to 9. An input data is presented as a sheet of 28×28 pixels, each representing gray scales. Pixel values comprise handwritten strokes, and a number appears as a specific pattern of these pixels.

In the experiments, the learning model is a classical neural network with a hidden layer and an output layer. Activation function for neurons in the hidden layer is $ReLU$; its output is linear to positive input values and a constant zero for negatives. The activation function of the output layer is $softmax$; it is a probability distribution over a variable with n values; $n = 10$ in this case.

We prepared two learning programs $\mathcal{F}_L^{PC}$ and $\mathcal{F}_L^{BI}$. The former is a probably correct implementation of NN learning algorithms, and the latter is its bug-injected version. We conducted two experiments in parallel, one using $\mathcal{F}_L^{PC}$ and the other with $\mathcal{F}_L^{BI}$, and made comparisons. Their behavior in the learning process is shown in Fig. 1. The graphs in Fig. 1(b) are mostly similar to those in Fig. 1(a). Note that the graphs in Fig. 1(b) are the results of a bug-injected program. We cannot conclude that the learning program is free from faults just looking at loss and accuracy graphs [9].

5.2 Metamorphic Testing with Distorted Dataset

We will see how we conduct testing of MNIST machine learning programs with distorted datasets.

A Quick Review of Metamorphic Testing. Metamorphic testing [1] is a property-based testing technique. Let $f(x)$ be a test target. For N input data $x^{(n)}$ ($N{\geq}2$ and $1{\leq}n{\leq}N$) and N execution results $f(x^{(n)})$, a $2N$ relation $\mathcal{R}(x^{(1)}, \ldots, x^{(N)}, f(x^{(1)}), \ldots, f(x^{(N)}))$ is a metamorphic relation (MR) [2]. If the MR is violated for a particular combination of inputs, then we consider that the program $f(x)$ may contain some faults.

MR, employed in various literature, takes a form simpler than the above. It consists of two sub-relations: an input sub-relation T which only involves source and follow-up inputs in the form of a mapping, and an output sub-relation which involves only the outputs of the source and follow-up inputs. Given a source

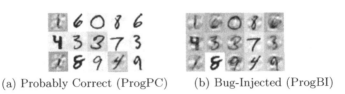

(a) Probably Correct (ProgPC)   (b) Bug-Injected (ProgBI)

Fig. 2. Distorted data

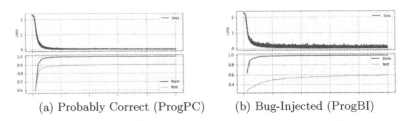

(a) Probably Correct (ProgPC)   (b) Bug-Injected (ProgBI)

Fig. 3. Loss and accuracy: distorted dataset

data x, the translation function T generates a follow-up data $T(x)$. An MR, $Rel_T(f(x), f(T(x)))$, is violated if f is not correct with respect to its functional specifications.

When test targets are machine learning programs, the function T must work not on a single discrete data, but on a dataset so as to build up the dataset diversity [9]. Finding appropriate Rel_T together with such a T is key in conducting the metamorphic testing.

Follow-Up Dataset. We generated distorted datasets; $LS^{(1)} = T_\lambda(LS^{(0)})$ where $LS^{(0)}$ is the original MNIST training dataset. The formula takes the form of the translation function T, which works on a dataset $LS^{(0)}$. Thus, T_λ in Sect. 4 can be considered as a function to generate a follow-up dataset.

Figure 2 shows a fragment of $LS_C^{(1)}$ where C is either PC or BI. All the data are not so clear as those of the original MNIST dataset $LS^{(0)}$ and thus are considered as distorted. Furthermore, for human eyes, Fig. 2(b) is unclear as compared with Fig. 2(a). It implies that $LS_{BI}^{(1)}$ is more distorted than $LS_{PC}^{(1)}$.

Metamorphic Relations. In Fig. 3, the two accuracy graphs for the MNIST testing dataset TS show different behavior. This indicates that the ProgBI case is less accurate than the ProgPC case; the accuracy of the ProgPC case (Fig. 3(a)) is about 90%, while the ProcBI case (Fig. 3(b)) is about 60%. The distorted follow-up data are thus useful in that the accuracy graphs show some discrepancy.

Comparing Figs. 1 and 3, we notice some differences in the accuracy graphs for TS. Note that Fig. 1 are monitored results of $\mathcal{F}_L^C(LS^{(0)})$ where $LS^{(0)}$ is the original MNIST training dataset, and that Fig. 3 are those of $\mathcal{F}_L^C(LS^{(1)})$ where $LS^{(1)} = T_\lambda(LS^{(0)})$. For the case of ProgBI, the accuracy graph for the

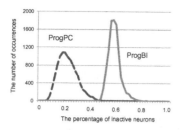

Fig. 4. Frequencies of inactive neurons

MNIST testing dataset TS reaches nearly 100% (Fig. 1(b)), while the accuracy in Fig. 3(b) is about 60%. For the case of ProgPC, the accuracy in Fig. 1(a) is nearly 100% as well. The graph in Fig. 3(a) shows that the accuracy is about 90%, which is still not so bad.

Therefore, we define a metamorphic relation such that it compares the two resultant accuracies, one calculated with the learning model trained against $LS^{(0)}$ and another for the case of $LS^{(1)}$. If the difference is larger than a given threshold, we conclude that the test is failed. Particularly, for this case study, we may choose 0.2 as the threshold so that the MR is violated for ProgBI.

5.3   Degrees of Distortion

We think that a certain degree of distortion in trained learning models W^* must account for distorted datasets, since the generation method in Sect. 4 refers to trained learning models of $\mathcal{F}_L$. We now have a question what metrics are suitable for the degrees of distortion in the trained learning models. We will study below *neuron coverage* [10] whether it is appropriate.

Neuron Coverages and Distorion. A neuron is said to be *activated* if its output signal *out* is larger than a given threshold when a set of input signals in_j is presented; $out = \sigma(\sum w_j \times in_j)$. The weight values w_js constitute the trained learning model W^*. *Activated Neurons* refer to a set of neurons to have values larger than a given threshold when a vector data $\boldsymbol{a}$ is input as in $\boldsymbol{y}(W^*; \boldsymbol{a})$. *Neuron coverage (NC)* is defined in terms of the size of the two sets; $NC = |Activated\ Neurons|/|Total\ Neurons|$.

We focus on the neurons in the hidden layer of our NN learning model. As its activation function is *ReLU*, we choose 0 as the threshold. Figure 4 is a graph to show the numbers of input vectors in the distorted dataset leading to $(1 - NC)$ neurons (i.e. inactive neurons).

As observed in Fig. 4, the graph for the case of ProgPC shows that the ratio of inactive neurons is almost 20%; i.e. 80% of neurons in the hidden layer are activated for the classification results. However, the ProgBI graph shows that about 60% of them are inactive and do not contribute to the results. This difference in the ratios of inactive neurons implies that the trained learning model W^*_{BI} of ProgBI is more distorted than W^*_{PC} of ProgPC.

| (a) 6 mixed with 4 | (b) 4 mixed with 6 |

Fig. 5. Mixing two numbers

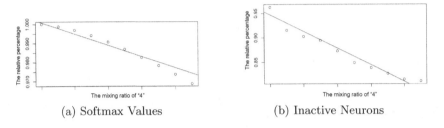

| (a) Softmax Values | (b) Inactive Neurons |

Fig. 6. Metrics for mixed numbers: 6 mixed with 4

Mixing Data and Neuron Coverages. We extend the proposed dataset generation method to synthesize a new vector data by mixing two data. B_λ mixes x_S with x_M to generate a new data x^* such that its tag is t_S.

$$B_\lambda(W^*; x_S, t_S, x_M, x) = \ell(y(W^*; x), t_S) + \lambda_S \cdot \ell(x, x_S) + \lambda_M \cdot \ell(x, x_M),$$

where $\lambda_S + \lambda_M = \lambda$ (a constant). Figure 5 shows two series of number data with a variety of λ_S and λ_M combinations. The leftmost image in Fig. 5(a) is the case where $\lambda_{S=6} = \lambda$ and the rightmost one is that $\lambda_{S=6} = 0$. We see, in Fig. 5(a), the images change their shapes of 6 to seemingly 4, and reach an adversarial example case; the rightmost one is visually seen as 4 but the inferred tag is 6.

Figure 6 shows two graphs that are calculated for the case of Fig. 5(a). Figure 6(a) is a graph to show the ratio of softmax values of the output signal of the anticipated supervisor tag 6. The graph values are normalized with respect to the softmax value of the leftmost one. As all the values are nearly 1.0, we can say that $\mathcal{F}_I$ shows a good prediction performance, although the softmax value at the rightmost is slightly smaller, about 3% less, than that the leftmost.

Figure 6(b) is a graph to show the ratio of inactive neurons. The value at the rightmost one is about 15% less than that at the leftmost. In other word, about 15% more neurons are activated to infer in the adversarial example case. This may imply that adversarial examples activate neurons that are *inactive* for normal data.

6 Related Work and Discussion

DeepRoad [16] adopts an approach with Generative Adversarial Networks (GAN) [3] to synthesize various weather conditions as driving scenes. GAN is formulated as a two-player zero-sum game. Given a dataset whose empirical distribution is ρ^{DS}, its Nash equilibrium, solved with Mixed Integer Linear Programing (MILP), results in a DNN-based generative model to emit new data to satisfy the relation $x \sim_{i.i.d.} \rho^{DS}$. Thus, such new data preserve characteristics of the original machine learning problem. Consequently, we regard the GAN-based approach as a method to enlarge coverage of test scenes within what is anticipated at the training time.

Machine Teaching [18] is an inverse problem of machine learning, and is a methodology to obtain a dataset to optimally derive a *given* trained learning model. The method is formalized as a two-level optimization problem, which is generally difficult to solve. We regard the machine teaching as a method to generate unanticipated dataset. Obtained datasets can be used in negative testing.

Our method uses an optimization problem with one objective function for generating datasets that are not far from what is anticipated, but probably are biased to build up the dataset diversity.

Last, reconciling learning algorithms with biased training dataset has been one of the major concerns in machine learning research [11]. The view therein is that biased distribution is what to be avoided. Contrarily, this paper makes use of such biased datasets to conduct either positive or negative testing.

7   Concluding Remarks

The proposed dataset generation method employs the L-BFGS [13], but the other methods on adversarial input generation (e.g. [14]) can be adapted as well. Since our study only involves the MNIST dataset with a simple NN learning model, studies on various DNN learning models, such as CNN, are desirable. In addition, further studies are needed to see whether the neuron coverage [10] is effective as a metric for the distortion degrees.

Acknowledgment. The work is supported partially by JSPS KAKENHI Grant Number JP18H03224, and is partially based on results in a project commissioned by the NEDO.

References

1. Chen, T.Y., Chung, S.C., Yiu, S.M.: Metamorphic Testing - A New Approach for Generating Next Test Cases, HKUST-CS98-01, The Hong Kong University of Science and Technology (1998)
2. Chen, T.Y., et al.: Metamorphic testing: a review of challenges and opportunities. ACM Comput. Surv. **51**(1), 1–27 (2018). Article No. 4
3. Goodfellow, I., et al.: Generative adversarial nets. In: Advances NIPS 2014, pp. 2672–2680 (2014)
4. Goodfellow, I., Bengio, Y., Courville, A.: Deep learning. The MIT Press, Cambridge (2016)
5. Haykin, S.: Neural Networks and Learning Machines, 3rd edn. Pearson India (2016)
6. Heckman, J.J.: Selection bias as a specification error. Econometrica **47**(1), 153–161 (1979)
7. Nakajima, S., Bui, H.N.: Dataset coverage for testing machine learning computer programs. In: Proceedings of the 23rd APSEC, pp. 297–304 (2016)

8. Nakajima, S.: Quality assurance of machine learning software. In: Proceedings GCCE 2018, pp. 601–604 (2018)
9. Nakajima, S.: Dataset diversity for metamorphic testing of machine learning software. In: Duan, Z., Liu, S., Tian, C., Nagoya, F. (eds.) SOFL+MSVL 2018. LNCS, vol. 11392, pp. 21–38. Springer, Cham (2019). https://doi.org/10.1007/978-3-030-13651-2_2
10. Pei, K., Cao, Y., Yang, J., Jana, S.: DeepXplore: automated whitebox testing of deep learning systems. In: Proceedings of the 26th SOSP, pp. 1–18 (2017)
11. Quinonero-Candela, J., Sugiyama, M., Schwaighofer, A., Lawrence, N.D. (eds.): Dataset Shift in Machine Learning. The MIT Press, Cambridge (2009)
12. Segura, S., Towey, D., Zhou, Z.Q., Chen, T.Y.: Metamorphic testing: testing the untestable. IEEE Softw. (in press)
13. Szegedy, C., et al.: Intriguing properties of neural networks. In: Proceedings of the ICLR 2014 (2014)
14. Warde-Farley, D., Goodfellow, I.: Adversarial perturbations of deep neural networks. In: Perturbation, Optimization and Statistics, pp. 1–32. The MIT Press, Cambridge (2016)
15. Xie, X., Ho, J.W.K., Murphy, C., Kaiser, G., Xu, B., Chen, T.Y.: Testing and validating machine learning classifiers by metamorphic testing. J. Syst. Softw. 84(4), 544–558 (2011)
16. Zhang, M., Zhang, Y., Zhang, L., Liu, C., Khurshid, S.: DeepRoad: GAN-based metamorphic testing and input validation framework for autonomous driving systems. In: Proceedings of the 33rd ASE, pp. 132–142 (2018)
17. Zhou, Z.Q., Sun, L.: Metamorphic testing of driverless cars. Comm. ACM 62(3), 61–67 (2019)
18. Zhu, X.: Machine teaching: an inverse problem to machine learning and an approach toward optimal education. In: Proceedings of the 29th AAAI, pp. 4083–4087 (2015)

Test Case Generation

Combining Model Refinement and Test Generation for Conformance Testing of the IEEE PHD Protocol Using Abstract State Machines

Andrea Bombarda[1(✉)], Silvia Bonfanti[1], Angelo Gargantini[1], Marco Radavelli[1], Feng Duan[2], and Yu Lei[2]

[1] Department of Management, Information and Production Engineering, University of Bergamo, Bergamo, Italy
{andrea.bombarda,silvia.bonfanti,angelo.gargantini, marco.radavelli}@unibg.it
[2] Department of Computer Science and Engineering, University of Texas at Arlington, Arlington, TX, USA
feng.duan@mavs.uta.edu, ylei@cse.uta.edu

Abstract. In this paper we propose a new approach to conformance testing based on Abstract State Machine (ASM) model refinement. It consists in generating test sequences from ASM models and checking the conformance between code and models in multiple iterations. This process is applied at different models, starting from the more abstract model to the one that is very close to the code. The process consists of the following steps: (1) model the system as an Abstract State Machine, (2) generate test sequences based on the ASM model, (3) compute the code coverage using generated tests, (4) if the coverage is low refine the Abstract State Machine and return to step 2. We have applied the proposed approach to Antidote, an open-source implementation of IEEE 11073-20601 Personal Health Device (PHD) protocol which allows personal healthcare devices to exchange data with other devices such as small computers and smartphones.

1 Introduction

The model-based testing (MBT) process consists in reuse the specification for testing purposes. It is one of the main applications of formal methods and it offers several advantages over classical testing procedures. Test cases are derived from models and subsequently used to test the code. In the classical MBT approach, the model is abstract, still it should contain enough details in order to test all the desired aspects of the SUT (system under test). The designer should spend a good amount of time to validate the model before it can be used for test generation and conformance testing [5,11,17,19]. In case a conformance fault is found, the system (or sometimes the model) should be modified. If no

© IFIP International Federation for Information Processing 2019
Published by Springer Nature Switzerland AG 2019
C. Gaston et al. (Eds.): ICTSS 2019, LNCS 11812, pp. 67–85, 2019.
https://doi.org/10.1007/978-3-030-31280-0_5

error is found, the designer has the confidence that the SUT conforms to its specification. MBT does not suffer from the weaknesses of code testing based on coverage criteria, like inability to detect missing logic [23]. On the other hand, this classical MBT approach has several drawbacks we try to address in this paper: (a) Before starting the testing, a considerable effort should be spent in order to have a correct and complete model. So testing can start only later in the SUT life cycle. (b) Focusing only on the specification level may leave some critical implementation parts uncovered; for instance, if the specification misses some critical cases which instead are considered in the code, with MBT they will not be tested. (c) In case no fault is found, it may not be clear if the testing activity has been sufficient or not. In general, if one still has some resources to spend on testing, there is no guidance in which directions these resources should be spent.

In this paper we propose an iterative approach which is based on the use of Abstract State Machines (ASM) and combines conformance testing [15,25, 28,30] with the refinement methodology [8] guided by code coverage. Initially the designer models the system at a high level with a first ASM. This model must be validated in a classical way (by simulation and property verification, for example). Starting from this ASM model, tests are generated and executed on the real system. A coverage report is provided with information about which parts of code are not covered by the model. Based on this information, the developer refines the initial ASM model by adding details about the not covered parts of the real system code. The process is iteratively executed until good coverage is reached. This process tries to mix a *black box* approach where tests are generated from the specifications and a *white box* approach where code is instrumented and coverage information collected in order to understand where the models must be refined. We emphasize that models are not modified arbitrarily, but they must be refined as defined by the ASM refinement [8].

The approach we propose in this paper makes use of Abstract State Machines, but it can be applied to any formal method that supports refinement and test-case generation.

The paper is structured as follows. In Sect. 2 we introduce the Abstract State Machines, its supporting tool Asmeta, the refinement of ASMs and the IEEE 11073-20601 protocol used in our case study. Our approach of combining testing and model refinement is explained in Sect. 3 and its application to the case study is presented in Sect. 4. The evaluation of the results and a comparison with other techniques (mainly combinatorial testing) are presented in Sect. 5.

2   Background

This work is based on the use of Abstract State Machines (ASMs) [14], which are an extension of Finite State Machines (FSMs) in which unstructured control states are replaced by states with arbitrarily complex data. They are presented in this section along with the case study of the IEEE 11073-20601 protocol [1], which is a core component in the standards family of IEEE 11073 Personal Health Data (PHD).

2.1   ASM and the Asmeta Framework

ASM *states* are mathematical structures, i.e., domains of objects with functions and predicates defined on them, and the transition from one state s_i to another state s_{i+1} is obtained by firing *transition rules* (see Fig. 1). Functions are classified as *static* (never change during any run of the machine) or *dynamic* (may change as a consequence of agent actions or *updates*). Dynamic functions are distinguished between *monitored* (only read by the machine and modified by the environment) and *controlled* (read in the current state and updated by the machine in the next state).

Fig. 1. An ASM run with a sequences of states and state-transitions (steps)

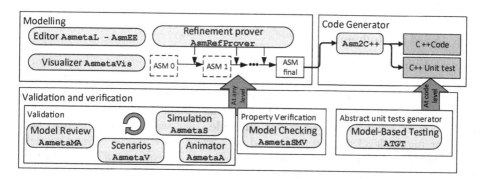

Fig. 2. The ASM development process powered by the `Asmeta` framework

The ASM method can facilitate the entire life cycle of software development, i.e., from modeling to code generation. Figure 2 shows the development process based on ASMs supported by the `Asmeta` (ASM mETAmodeling) framework[1] [9] which provides a set of tools to help the developer in various activities:

- **modeling**: the system is modeled using the language `AsmetaL`. The user is supported by the editor `AsmEE` and by `AsmetaVis`, the ASMs visualizer which transforms the textual model into a graphical representation.
- **validation**: the process is supported by the model simulator `AsmetaS`, the scenarios executor `AsmetaV`, and the model reviewer `AsmetaMA`. The simulator `AsmetaS` allows to perform two types of simulation: interactive simulation (the user inserts the value of monitored functions) and random simulation (the

---

[1] http://asmeta.sourceforge.net/.

tool randomly chooses the value of monitored functions among those available). `AsmetaS` executes scenarios written using the `Avalla` language. Each scenario contains the expected system behavior and the tool checks whether the machine runs correctly. The model reviewer `AsmetaMA` performs static analysis. It determines whether a model has sufficient quality attributes (e.g., minimality - the specification does not contain elements defined or declared in the model but never used, completeness - requires that every behavior of the system is explicitly modeled, and consistency - guarantees that locations are never simultaneously updated to different values).

- **verification**: the properties derived from the requirements document are verified to check whether the behavior of the model complies with the intended behavior. The `AsmetaSMV` tool supports this process.
- **testing**: the tool `ATGT` generates abstract unit tests starting from the ASM specification by exploiting the counterexample generation of a model checker (NuSMV).
- **code generation**: given the final ASM specification, the `Asm2C++` automatically translates it into C++ code [12,32]. Moreover, the abstract tests, generated by the `ATGT` tool, are translated to C++ unit tests [13].

2.2 ASM Refinement

The modeling process of an ASM is based on *model refinement*. The designer starts with a high-level description of the system and he/she proceeds through a sequence of more detailed models each introducing, step-by-step, design decisions and implementation details. In ASM, stuttering refinement is introduced in [8]. It consists in adding state functions and rules in a way that one step in the ASM at higher level can be performed by several steps in the refined model. The refinement is correct if any behavior (i.e., run or sequence of states) in the refined model can be mapped to a run in the abstract model. In this way, the refined ASM *preserves* the behaviors of the abstract machine. At the end, the designer builds a chain of refined models $ASM_0, \ldots, ASM_n$ and the `AsmRefProver` tool checks whether ASM_i is a correct refinement of ASM_{i-1}. We note that an important question in this process is when to stop the refinement. In other words, how many details would we consider adequate in the final refined model, i.e., ASM_n? This question is one of the motivations behind the work presented in this paper.

2.3 IEEE 11073 PHD Communication Model

IEEE 11073-20601 defines a communication model that allows personal healthcare devices to exchange data with devices with more computing resources like mobile phones, set-top boxes, and personal computers. The measured health data exchanged between these devices can be transmitted to healthcare professionals for remote health monitoring or health advising.

IEEE 11073 PHD defines an efficient data exchange protocol as well as the necessary data models for communication between two types of devices, i.e., the agent and the manager. Agents are personal healthcare devices that are used to obtain measured health data from the user. They are normally portable, energy-efficient and have limited computing capacity. Examples of agent devices include blood pressure monitors, weighing scales and blood glucose monitors. Managers are computing devices that are used to manage and process the data collected by agents. Managers typically have more computing resources than agents. Examples of managers include mobile phones, set-top boxes, and personal computers.

The messages, called APDUs, at low level are encoded in ASN.1 format, and should support at least the MDER (Medical Device Encoding Rules) standard. The communication must have one primary, reliable virtual channel, plus some secondary virtual channels.

The message types are divided into the following categories:

- messages related to the association procedure: aare (Association Request), aarq (Association Response), rlre (Association Release Response), rlrq (Association Release Request), abrt (Association Abort);
- messages related to the confirmed service mechanism: roiv-* (Remote Operation Invoke messages): roiv-cmip-confirmed-action, roiv-cmip-confirmed-event-report, roiv-cmip-confirmed-set; and rors-* (Reception of Response messages): rors-cmip-confirmed-action, rors-cmip-confirmed-event-report, rors-cmip-get;
- messages related to fault or abnormal conditions: roer (Reception of Error Result), rorj (Reception of Reject Result);
- messages related to the unconfirmed service mechanism: roiv-cmip-action, roiv-cmip-event-report, roiv-cmip-set.

IEEE 11073 State Machine Diagram. There are seven states in the manager state machine defined by the IEEE 11073 specification, as shown in the specification diagram in Fig. 3. We use an example scenario to illustrate how the agent and manager exchange data. In Fig. 4, a weighting scale (our agent device) sends an association request to the manager, containing device configuration information. If the manager recognizes such information, it sends a response of association acceptance, and both devices enter the *Operating* state. Then the agent sends a measured data to the manager with a *Confirmed Event Report* APDU, and the manager responds with the acknowledgment. Finally, the agent requests to release the association; the manager responds to this request, and both devices now enter the *Unassociated* state.

3 Conformance Testing with Model Refinements

The proposal of this paper is to combine model refinement with testing in order to perform more efficient conformance testing of a real system. The process we propose is depicted in Fig. 5 and explained in the following.

We assume that at the beginning the user specifies the core functionalities of the system by means of an initial ASM, ASM_0 in the picture. ASM_0 captures

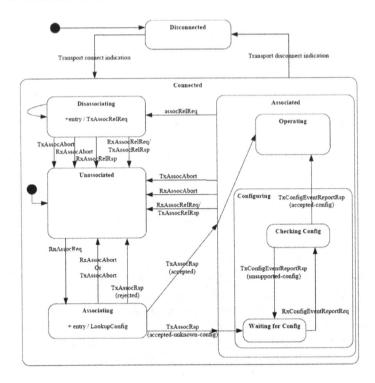

Fig. 3. State machine of the IEEE 11073 PHD Manager

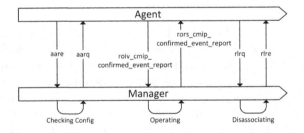

Fig. 4. An example sequence of data exchange

the most critical behaviors but it leaves some details and behaviors out of the specification. ASM_0 is validated by means of the techniques like those introduced in Sect. 2.1. Even if it is simple, ASM_0 must be suitable for test generation and test execution, i.e. it is possible to derive some tests and execute them on the real system. During the testing activity, conformance of the system is checked and information about the coverage of the code is collected. Such coverage information is then used to guide the refinement of ASM_0 in order to obtain a more detailed version ASM_1. For instance, if some code statements and branches are not covered the first time, the user has to insert such functionalities in the new

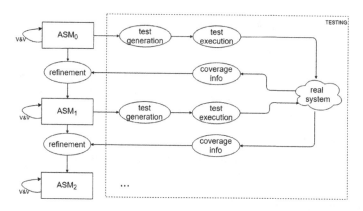

Fig. 5. An overview of the applied framework

version of the abstract state machine. Some V&V activities are then performed over the new specification. Then the process of testing starts over again: tests are derived, executed and then the coverage information collected and used to drive the next refinement step. Such methodology addresses the issues presented in the introduction in several directions:

1. Conformance testing activity can start immediately after a simple first ASM is developed. It is not required to have a complete specification and the most critical behaviors can be tested from the beginning. V&V results on the previous step are not lost during refinement since it preserves the original behaviors (according to the definition given in Sect. 2.2)
2. By analyzing the code coverage, the tester can identify if the specification misses some important areas of functionality that are correctly implemented in the code.
3. Even when no fault has been found, code coverage can give a measure of how much the implementation has been tested and which functionalities and details should be added to the specification.
4. This methodology enables an interleaving approach to perform model verification and testing. Thus, it allows closer interaction between the two activities. In particular, the alternating views of model and implementation could help discover problems that would otherwise not be discovered.

In the following we better explain each step of the process.

Test Generation from ASMs. Starting from an ASM, test sequences can be generated via different approaches present in the literature. We consider test generation based on the following coverage criteria, defined in [20]:

– *Basic Rule Coverage.* A test suite satisfies the basic rule coverage if for every rule r_i there exists at least one test sequence for which r_i fires at least once, and there exists at least one test sequence for which r_i does not fire at least once.

– *All-Rule Coverage.* A test suite satisfies the all-rule coverage if it satisfies the basic rule coverage plus the *Rule Guard coverage* and the *MCDC coverage* described in [20].

According to these criteria, we generate the tests using the tool ATGT, which builds abstract tests starting from the ASM specification by exploiting the counterexample generation of the NuSMV model checker.

Test Execution and Coverage Information. Once abstract tests are generated, they must be executed over the real implementation and coverage information can be collected. To obtain concrete tests cases from abstract ones, there are several methodologies [27]. In our case we use the external tool ProTest [34] which will be presented later.

Model Refinement Guided by the Coverage Information. During the testing activity, coverage information is collected. This requires access to the implementation which must be instrumented somehow to produce some event logs or behavior traces. Our approach is thus not a classical black box testing approach, but rather a gray-box approach. The scope of this activity is to discover which parts or features of the system are not exercised by the tests derived from the abstract model. This information gives a hint to what is missing in the model (i.e., the ASM) and suggests the user what to add. New behaviors are added to the ASM regardless how they are implemented in the code. This must be done by preserving the behavior tested so far, and it is performed by applying the refinement approach explained in Sect. 2.2.

4   Application to the PHD Communication Module

In this section we present how the proposed methodology can be applied to test the conformance of an implementation of the IEEE 11073 PHD communication protocol, to its specification. We present how the tests were executed, which steps of refinements were applied, and which coverage was achieved.

4.1   Test Execution and Coverage Information

The abstract tests generated from ASMs are sequences of abstract states that must be translated into concrete tests that can be executed with the system under test. For this goal, we use ProTest [34] that includes a *test agent*, that interacts with the manager implementation. Each abstract state contains all the necessary information about the transition to be triggered in that state; ProTest builds the APDU message, sends it to the manager implementation, and checks the conformance of the response from the manager.

At each refinement step we added new messages and ProTest took care of the details of the concretization. In addition, the tool can be customized, as it has a configuration file that allows to specify, for each message type, some subtypes by defining the values for the fields in the messages to send. For further customization out of the scope of the PHD protocol, however, it may be necessary to implement the code to automate the concretization function, in our case by extending ProTest code. Using the refinement methodology proposed in this paper, however, it is possible to start testing with just a few implemented concretization functions, and implement the additional ones only as needed, by the model refinement.

We use Antidote 2.0.0[2] as implementation of the manager of the PHD protocol. Antidote source code is written in C, and composed by the following source folders: *api, asn1, communication, dim, resources, specializations, trans,* and *util.* We measure the coverage on the *communication* source folder only, as it is the one containing the code to handle the different messages described by the protocol, and it is the most critical part of the library. The other folders contain mainly utility functions for handling the data types, and for the encoding and decoding of the messages. To compute the code coverage we have instrumented Antidote with GCOV[3] and LCOV[4], open source tools for coverage measurement: the former is a tool that computes the code coverage, while the latter is only a graphical front-end for the visualization of GCOV results. This way we can obtain coverage reports in an automated way. The code for test generation and the ASM models[5] we produced are available open source as part of the ASMETA tool set.

Results are reported in Table 1. For each refinement of the ASM model, and for each applied test generation technique, the table reports the number of sequences composing the generated sequence set, the minimum, the maximum, and the average number of steps per sequence, and the total number of steps composing the generated set of sequences. An execution step corresponds to an execution of the main rule of the ASM model of the system. The test execution time is proportional to the total length (i.e. steps) of the exercised test sequences. Given the same coverage, a test set with fewer total steps is to be preferred in terms of execution time. We ran the process generating the tests with only the basic rule coverage criteria, and with the criteria presented in Sect. 3 altogether. For reference, we also report the coverage achieved with the Finite State Machine integrated in the ProTest tool [34], using the FSM-based test generation criteria edge coverage, and 2-way coverage.

4.2 First ASM: Ground Model

We specify in ASMETA the first model of the manager, *Ground model* $\mathsf{ASM_0}$. This model has only three states: *Disassociating, Unassociated,* and *Operating.* Figure 6 reports a fragment of $\mathsf{ASM_0}$. The signature of $\mathsf{ASM_0}$ contains three functions: status, transition, and message. The transition represents the type of

---

[2] Antidoté: http://oss.signove.com/index.php/Antidote_IEEE_11073_stack_library.

[3] GCOV: https://gcc.gnu.org/onlinedocs/gcc/Gcov.html.

[4] LCOV: http://ltp.sourceforge.net/coverage/lcov.php.

[5] The models are available under: https://sourceforge.net/p/asmeta/code/HEAD/tree/asm_examples/PHD.

Table 1. Results of the application of the test generation strategies to different model refinement versions

# Refinement	Description	Test generation strategy	Test sequences # sequences	steps min	max	total	avg	Code coverage statement	function	branch
ASM$_0$	Ground model	basic	25	2	4	79	3.16	50.1%	61.0%	37.0%
		all-rule	30	2	4	93	3.10	50.3%	61.0%	37.2%
ASM$_1$	Configuration management	basic	52	2	5	173	3.33	77.1%	72.6%	56.4%
		all-rule	64	2	6	216	3.38	77.2%	72.6%	56.6%
ASM$_2$	Error management	basic	62	2	5	208	3.35	78.8%	75.3%	58.8%
		all-rule	77	2	6	266	3.45	78.8%	75.3%	59.0%
ASM$_3$	Protocol error	basic	63	2	5	208	3.30	79.4%	75.3%	59.4%
		all-rule	80	2	6	272	3.40	79.4%	75.3%	59.6%
FSM$_{ProTest}$	Original from [35]	edge	30	2	9	106	3.53	77.2%	72.6%	56.6%
		2-way	51	3	14	336	6.59	77.2%	72.6%	56.6%

request to be sent to the manager, and it is defined as a monitored function, as its value can be driven externally, e.g., by the agent. The status represents the current state of the manager, and the message represents the response from the manager. These two functions are modeled as controlled functions (defined in Sect. 2.1). In terms of Finite State Machines, the status, transition, and message of the ASM represent respectively the status, input, and output of the FSM.

Then, in the *definitions* section, we define the rules; the main rule executes all the rules in parallel at each step. Each rule, based on the current state and the transition, sets the expected next state and the response message. Finally, we need to specify an initial status, defined in the *default init s0* section; the machine starts in *Unassociated* state.

Verification and Validation. The ASM representation allows us to formally verify some properties. Despite the machine was simple in this version, we have specified and verified the following temporal properties:

- the system can reach the *operating* state starting from UNASSOCIATED: AG((status=UNASSOCIATED) implies EF(status=OPERATING))
- if state is UNASSOCIATED and receive a known configuration, then the status in the next state is OPERATING: AG((status=UNASSOCIATED and transition=RX_AARQ_ACCEPTABLE_AND_KNOWN_CONFIGURATION) implies AX(status=OPERATING))
- if state is OPERATING than the system can remain in OPERATING status or not: AG((status=OPERATING) implies EF(status=OPERATING or status!=OPERATING))

The proposerites above were extracted from the official PHD documentation. We verified these properties to gain confidence of the correctness of the specification.

Testing. With the application of all the test generation rules presented in Sect. 3, we have generated 30 test sequences, with a total of 93 steps. This achieved a

```
asm phd_master_v0
import StandardLibrary
signature:
   // DOMAINS
   enum domain Status = {UNASSOCIATED | OPERATING | DISASSOCIATING}
   enum domain Transition = {REQ_ASSOC_REL | REQ_ASSOC_ABORT |
      RX_AARQ_ACCEPTABLE_AND_KNOWN_CONFIGURATION | RX_AARE | RX_RLRQ | RX_RLRE |
      RX_ABRT | RX_AARQ | RX_ROIV | RX_ROER | RX_RORJ | RX_RORS |
      RX_RORS_CONFIRMED_ACTION | RX_RORS_CONFIRMED_SET | RX_RORS_GET}
   enum domain Message = {MSG_NO_RESPONSE | MSG_RX_AARE |
      MSG_RX_ABRT | MSG_RX_RLRQ | MSG_RX_RLRE | MSG_RX_PRST}

   // FUNCTIONS
   controlled status: Status
   monitored transition: Transition //row chosen by the user
   controlled message: Message

definitions:
   rule r_1 = if status = UNASSOCIATED and transition = REQ_ASSOC_REL
      then par status := UNASSOCIATED message := MSG_NO_RESPONSE endpar endif
   rule r_2 = if status = UNASSOCIATED and transition = REQ_ASSOC_ABORT
      then par status := UNASSOCIATED message := MSG_NO_RESPONSE endpar endif
   rule r_3 = if status = UNASSOCIATED and transition =
   RX_AARQ_ACCEPTABLE_AND_KNOWN_CONFIGURATION
      then par status := OPERATING message := MSG_RX_AARE endpar endif
      ...
   main rule r_Main = par r_1[] r_2[] r_3[] ... r_26[] endpar
   // INITIAL STATE
   default init s0:
      function status = UNASSOCIATED
```

Fig. 6. ASMETA specification of the ASM model V0, specifying transitions in the state diagram

statement coverage of the communication folder of just 50.3%. Function coverage and branch coverage are also really low.

4.3   First Refinement: PHD Configuration Management

The coverage of the model ASM_0 was not satisfactory, and in particular the code that manages configurations was not covered since the configuration management was completely missing in the model. In this refinement (ASM_1) we therefore added the states for exchanging the configuration: *Checking Config*, and *Waiting for Config*, with their related transitions, messages, and rules. Figure 7 shows a compact graphical representation of ASM_1.

Testing. Test generation produced 64 sequences, with a total of 216 steps. The code coverage of the communication package increased to 77.2%, mainly due to more functions and statements covered in the configuration management part.

4.4   Second Refinement: Error Management

From coverage analysis, we noticed that all the *rors* APDU messages, related to error management, were missing, and some functions, such as communication_process_rors(ctx, apdu) in communication/operating.c, were never exercised.

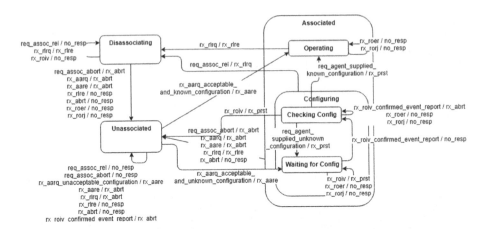

Fig. 7. A graphical view of ASM$_1$ of the IEEE PHD manager

Therefore we designed a new refined model (ASM$_2$) in which we included the *rors* message with its subtypes (rors-*). These messages trigger a relevant part of the protocol between the states *Disassociating* and *Unassociated*, and within the states *Operating*, *Checking Config*, and *Waiting for Config*. Furthermore, we marked the following two *particular* sequences of transitions in the model, since from the coverage report we noticed that these behaviors were not captured by the model:

1. the behavior of rx_roiv_confirmed_event_report that brings from the state *Waiting for Config* to *Checking Config* has to be handled differently depending on whether the state *Waiting for Config* was entered with a transition from the state *Unassociated* or from the state *Checking Config*. In the former case, no configuration similar to the one transmitted by the agent is present in the manager pool of configurations and the function *ext_configurations_get__configuration_attributes* is called; in the latter case, a configuration was transmitted previously, and thus the configuration is already in memory of the Antidote manager.
2. the behavior of rx_roiv_confirmed_event_report, that causes a loop in the *Checking Config* state, is different if executed right after another same message that brought the manager from the state *Waiting for Config* into the *Checking Config* state. The function *configuring_new_measurement_response_tx*, that adds a new measurement from the agent, is executed when this particular sequence occurs.

Testing. Test generation using all the rule-based criteria stated in Sect. 3, has produced 77 sequences, with a total of 266 steps. The statement coverage of the communication package was 78.8%, and function coverage 75.2%, both with an increase of about 3% with respect to the previous refinement of the model.

4.5   Third Refinement: Protocol and Configuration Management

The coverage reached by the previous refinement was quite good, but from coverage analysis we noticed that two important aspects of the connection procedure were not considered. In the first phase, an agent can try to establish a connection with a wrong protocol-id or with an unknown configuration, marked as a specific protocol-id value (0xFFFF) and recognized by Antidote as an external specification. Thus, we added two new variants of the rx_aarq transition in the ASM_3, respectively with an invalid protocol-id and an external protocol-id.

Testing. Test generation using the all-rule criteria stated in Sect. 3, produced 80 sequences, with a total of 272 steps. The statement coverage of the communication package was 79.4%, and the function coverage 75.3%, with an increase of 0.6 % both in statement coverage and in branch coverage, with respect to the previous model in the refinement chain, ASM_2.

5   Process Evaluation

In this section, we evaluate the proposed approach and we compare it with other approaches. In particular, we are interested in answering the following three research questions:

RQ1 Is refinement a viable option in MBT and does it really improve the efficiency of conformance testing in terms of code coverage?

RQ2 Do ASM-based coverage criteria for test generation achieve different results in terms of code coverage?

RQ3 Is our method suitable for discovering faults in the implementation?

5.1   RQ1: How Does Refinement Influence Coverage?

We have observed that refinements always increase code coverage, regardless of the criteria used. For ASM_0, each criteria achieves around 50% in statement coverage. For ASM_1, the coverage is increased to 72%. The highest coverage is obtained by ASM_3, with more than 79% of the statements covered by the test sequences. As expected, the number of generated sequences and total steps increase with the refinements: the sequences vary from a minimum of 16 to a maximum of 80, and the total number of steps from 79 in ASM_0 with the basic-rule coverage to 272 in ASM_3 with the all-rule coverage. A full code coverage is never reached. However, we were able to increase the statement coverage from 50% to around 80%.

By refinements, the average and the maximum length of test sequences increase. In this case, from Table 1 we can see that the maximum sequence length is 6. It is a relatively high length as these ASM models are not so large, and for larger models the length of the generated test sequences could be higher.

Analyzing the statements that are not covered, we have noticed that they are mainly related to procedures of the agent (that was not object of testing), dead code, or negative use cases (exceptions), often regarding internal configurations of the manager. We believe that a further increase in code coverage could not be achieved by adding new messages, but by including in the model different configurations of the manager at startup (in particular to enable some *remote* messages that come from the manager and *actively* ask the associated agent(s) for new data). Full coverage is unachievable due to the presence of some dead code (such as functions declared with an empty body, and never used), but we believe that it is possible to achieve almost full coverage in the *communication* package by exercising Antidote also to act as an agent, thus completing the transition tables of the specification. Nonetheless, testing the agent was beyond the scope of this work.

5.2   RQ2: Comparing Between Coverage Criteria

We have noticed that, regardless of the refinement, the all rule coverage criteria always achieves a higher statement and branch coverage than the basic rule coverage criteria. The difference between the coverage of the two criteria, however, is minimal (just 0.2% gap), in some cases the statement and function coverage are the same. The all-rule coverage criteria, however, leads to a 20% more steps in the generated test sequences, with respect to the basic rule coverage, meaning that it requires more time for test execution. All in all, we can notice that model refinement affects the code coverage more than the choice of coverage criteria: even if one applies a *stronger* test generation criteria, the increase in code coverage (around 0.2% increase) is lower than by applying a refinement (around 1–10% increase). Table 1 reports also the code coverage of combinatorial testing obtained by ProTest [34]. Note that the coverage achieved by our method from the second refinement on, is higher than the coverage obtained by the tests generated with the edge and 2-way coverage of the FSM model in ProTest.

5.3   RQ3: Faults Found

We have found a few mismatches in some of the test executions, namely the actual response from the manager was different from the expected one, according to the model. We analyzed these inconsistencies, and three of them turned out to be real bugs in the implementation, with respect to the protocol specification:

1. The specification of the standard IEEE 11073-20601 requires rx_abrt as response for the sequence "unasocciated + req_assoc_abort". The Antidote implementation uses no response instead. The fault was revealed from the first model ($\mathsf{ASM_0}$).
2. The length of the message rx_roer was computed incorrectly, which results in a rejection by the encoding module. The fault was revealed after the first refinement ($\mathsf{ASM_1}$).
3. The sequence "checking_config + rx_aarq → no response" causes a transition mismatch. A transition labeled by event rx_aarq was defined for state checking_config. However, in the actual code, three transitions were implemented

for three sub-types of event rx_aarq_*, which can never be fired. This bug means that the Antidote Manager only responds to three sub-types of event rx_aarq_*, but does not respond to rx_aarq itself. The fault was revealed after the first refinement (ASM$_1$).

Figure 8 shows an example of test case execution in ProTest, ending with a conformance error between the model and the implementation, denoted by a red cross in the tool. Furthermore, we have found that the state *Associating* is not part of the Antidote FSM table, since it was joined together with *Unassociated* state. In order to make our process work, we had to ignore this state also in the ASMs, but we believe that this is an implementation fault due to oversimplification done by the Antidote team. We have reported the faults to the developers and issued in the tracking system of the Antidote repository in GitHub.

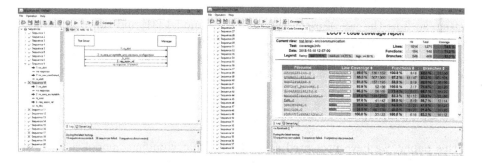

Fig. 8. A test sequence execution, and coverage report, with ProTest [34]

6 Related Work

The works on conformance and interoperability testing for medical/healthcare devices can be classified into two categories: testing health information systems and testing medical or healthcare devices. Snelick et al. [22], and Namli [29] have studied conformance testing strategies for HL-7, a widely used standard for healthcare clinical data exchange. They have compared such testing strategies and proposed a test execution framework for HL7-based systems built on top of an extensible test execution model. This model is represented by an interpretable test description language, which allows dynamic test setup. These works have mainly focused on developing a general test execution framework. This is in contrast with our work, which focuses on test generation and model refinement for the communication model of IEEE 11073 PHD protocol. Garguilo et al. [21] have developed conformance testing tools based on an XML schema derived directly from IEEE 11073 standard, that provides syntactic and semantic validation of individual medical device messages, according to IEEE 11073. This is complementary to our work, as we focus on testing event sequences, and their tool can be used to check the correctness of the individual APDUs. Lim et al. [26] have proposed a toolkit that can generate standard PHD messages using user-defined device information, facilitating users who are not familiar with the standards details. This is another format of representing a model of the protocol messages, as we do in the modeling part of the proposed approach. Yu et al. [34] have proposed a general conformance testing framework for the IEEE 11073 PHD protocol, that streamlines the entire testing process, i.e., from test generation to test execution and evaluation. Our work is built on top of that framework, adding model refinement to improve test coverage, and rule-based test generation to make test sequences more efficient. Similarly to ProTest, there are also methods to generate test cases and to test protocol conformance directly from Finite State Machines, such as in [2,6,18], and many of them are included in a survey by Dorofeeva et al. [17]. Refinement is often used in combination with formal verification of properties [16,24,35]. In this work, instead, we try to combine refinement and testing. There are also other methodologies for protocol testing, such as the use of extended finite state model [31] and timed automata (TA). In timed automata, for instance, different testing techniques have been proposed, based on different coverage criteria as, e.g., transition coverage [7,33] and fault-based coverage [3,4], and they can be used for protocol validation.

7   Conclusion

In this paper, we have presented an approach that combines model refinement with model-based testing capable of improving testing effectiveness. Tests are derived from ASM specifications, obtained using refinement iteratively applied after testing the system under tests. In test execution, coverage info is used to identify system features or behaviors that are not captured in the model. These missing features or behaviors are then added into the model, in a manner that is independent from the implementation. This process has been applied to the case study of the IEEE 11073 PHD's communication model. This work extends the testing framework presented by Yu et al. [34], aiming at streamlining the entire testing process, including test generation, test execution and test evaluation. We have shown that refinement can improve testing results (coverage and faults found) and that rule-based test generation strategies are a good alternative to the t-way test generation. Model refinement is a crucial process to achieve good results. As future work, we will apply this framework also to the Antidote agent, and to some real medical devices to check their compliance with the IEEE 11073 PHD standards. Moreover, we plan to optimize the generated tests among the model refinements, by not executing again in $ASM(n+1)$ the same test sequences in the previous model versions, up to $ASM(n)$. The tests themselves could be also refined between different model versions, for example by using the technique in [10].

The goal of our project is to promote methods that help in testing the conformance of medical devices designed to be compliant with IEEE 11073 PHD protocol, and in general to any other protocol specification.

References

1. ISO/IEC/IEEE international standard - health informatics - personal health device communication - part 20601: Application profile - optimized exchange protocol, June 2016

2. Abu-Ein, A.A.-K.H., Said, M., Hatamleh, A.M., Sharadqeh, A.A.M.: Using finite state machine at the testing of network protocols. Aust. J. Basic Appl. Sci., 956–960 (2011)

3. Aichernig, B.K., Jöbstl, E., Tiran, S.: Model-based mutation testing via symbolic refinement checking. Sci. Comput. Program. **97**(P4), 383–404 (2015)

4. Aichernig, B.K., Lorber, F., Ničković, D.: Time for mutants—model-based mutation testing with timed automata. In: Veanes, M., Viganò, L. (eds.) TAP 2013. LNCS, vol. 7942, pp. 20–38. Springer, Heidelberg (2013). https://doi.org/10.1007/978-3-642-38916-0_2

5. Aichernig, B.K., Peischl, B., Weiglhofer, M., Wotawa, F.: Protocol conformance testing a SIP registrar: an industrial application of formal methods. In: Fifth IEEE International Conference on Software Engineering and Formal Methods (SEFM 2007). IEEE, September 2007

6. Ambrosio, A.M., Pinheiro, A.C., Simão, A.: FSM-based test case generation methods applied to test the communication software on board the ITASAT university satellite: a case study. J. Aerospace Technol. Manag. **6**(4), 447–461 (2014)

7. André, É., Arcaini, P., Gargantini, A., Radavelli, M.: Repairing timed automata clock guards through abstraction and testing. In: Beyer, D., Keller, C. (eds.) TAP 2019. LNCS, vol. 11823, pp. 1–18. Springer, Heidelberg (2019)

8. Arcaini, P., Gargantini, A., Riccobene, E.: SMT-based automatic proof of ASM model refinement. In: De Nicola, R., Kühn, E. (eds.) SEFM 2016. LNCS, vol. 9763, pp. 253–269. Springer, Cham (2016). https://doi.org/10.1007/978-3-319-41591-8_17

9. Arcaini, P., Gargantini, A., Riccobene, E., Scandurra, P.: A model-driven process for engineering a toolset for a formal method. Softw.: Practice Exp. **41**, 155–166 (2011)

10. Arcaini, P., Riccobene, E.: Automatic refinement of ASM abstract test cases. In: 2019 IEEE International Conference on Software Testing, Verification and Validation Workshops (ICSTW), pp. 1–10 (2019)

11. Bannour, B., Escobedo, J.P., Gaston, C., Le Gall, P.: Off-line test case generation for timed symbolic model-based conformance testing. In: Nielsen, B., Weise, C. (eds.) ICTSS 2012. LNCS, vol. 7641, pp. 119–135. Springer, Heidelberg (2012). https://doi.org/10.1007/978-3-642-34691-0_10

12. Bonfanti, S., Carissoni, M., Gargantini, A., Mashkoor, A.: Asm2C++: a tool for code generation from abstract state machines to arduino. In: Barrett, C., Davies, M., Kahsai, T. (eds.) NFM 2017. LNCS, vol. 10227, pp. 295–301. Springer, Cham (2017). https://doi.org/10.1007/978-3-319-57288-8_21

13. Bonfanti, S., Gargantini, A., Mashkoor, A.: Generation of C++ unit tests from abstract state machines specifications. In: 2018 IEEE International Conference on Software Testing, Verification and Validation Workshops (ICSTW), pp. 185–193. IEEE (2018)

14. Börger, E., Stark, R.F.: Abstract State Machines: A Method for High-Level System Design and Analysis. Springer, New York (2003). https://doi.org/10.1007/978-3-642-18216-7

15. Brucker, A.D., Brügger, L., Wolff, B.: Model-based firewall conformance testing. In: Suzuki, K., Higashino, T., Ulrich, A., Hasegawa, T. (eds.) FATES/TestCom - 2008. LNCS, vol. 5047, pp. 103–118. Springer, Heidelberg (2008). https://doi.org/10.1007/978-3-540-68524-1_9

16. Cimatti, A., Demasi, R., Tonetta, S.: Tightening the contract refinements of a system architecture. Formal Methods Syst. Des. **52**(1), 88–116 (2018)

17. Dorofeeva, R., El-Fakih, K., Maag, S., Cavalli, A.R., Yevtushenko, N.: FSM-based conformance testing methods: a survey annotated with experimental evaluation. Inf. Softw. Technol. **52**(12), 1286–1297 (2010)

18. Fujiwara, S., Bochmann, G.V., Khendek, F., Amalou, M., Ghedamsi, A.: Test selection based on finite state models. IEEE Trans. Softw. Eng. **17**(6), 591–603 (1991)

19. Fukada, A., Nakata, A., Kitamichi, J., Higashino, T., Cavalli, A.: A conformance testing method for communication protocols modeled as concurrent DFSMs. Treatment of non-observable non-determinism. In: Proceedings 15th International Conference on Information Networking. IEEE Computer Society (2001)

20. Gargantini, A., Riccobene, E.: ASM-based testing: coverage criteria and automatic test sequence. J. Univ. Comput. Sci. **7**(11), 1050–1067 (2001)

21. Garguilo, J.J., Martinez, S., Cherkaoui, M.: Medical device communication: a standards-based conformance testing approach. In: 9th International HL7 Interoperability Conference (2008)

22. Gebase, L., Snelick, R., Skall, M.: Conformance testing and interoperability: a case study in healthcare data exchange. In: Software Engineering Research and Practice, pp. 143–151 (2008)

23. Hemmati, H.: How effective are code coverage criteria? In: 2015 IEEE International Conference on Software Quality, Reliability and Security. IEEE, August 2015

24. Jeffords, R.D., Heitmeyer, C.L., Archer, M.M., Leonard, E.I.: Model-based construction and verification of critical systems using composition and partial refinement. Formal Methods Syst. Des. **37**(2), 265–294 (2010)

25. Krichen, M., Maâlej, A.J., Lahami, M.: A model-based approach to combine conformance and load tests: an eHealth case study. Int. J. Critical Comput.-Based Syst. **8**(3/4), 282 (2018)

26. Lim, J.H., Park, C., Park, S.J., Lee, K.C.: ISO/IEEE 11073 PHD message generation toolkit to standardize healthcare device. In: 2011 Annual International Conference of the IEEE Engineering in Medicine and Biology Society, EMBC, pp. 1161–1164. IEEE (2011)

27. Utting, B.L.M.: Practical Model-Based Testing. Elsevier LTD, Oxford (2007)

28. Marsso, L., Mateescu, R., Serwe, W.: TESTOR: a modular tool for on-the-fly conformance test case generation. In: Beyer, D., Huisman, M. (eds.) TACAS 2018. LNCS, vol. 10806, pp. 211–228. Springer, Cham (2018). https://doi.org/10.1007/978-3-319-89963-3_13

29. Namli, T., Aluc, G., Dogac, A.: An interoperability test framework for HL7-based systems. IEEE Trans. Inf. Technol. Biomed. **13**(3), 389–399 (2009)

30. Salva, S., Cao, T.-D.: A model-based testing approach combining passive conformance testing and runtime verification: application to web service compositions deployed in clouds. In: Lee, R. (ed.) Software Engineering Research, Management and Applications. SCI, pp. 99–116. Springer, Heidelberg (2014)

31. Sarikaya, B., Bochmann, G.V., Cerny, E.: A test design methodology for protocol testing. IEEE Trans. Softw. Eng. **SE-13**(5), 518–531 (1987)

32. Bonfanti, S., Gargantini, A., Mashkoor, A.: Validation of transformation from abstract state machine models to C++ code. In: Medina-Bulo, I., Merayo, M.G., Hierons, R. (eds.) ICTSS 2018. LNCS, vol. 11146, pp. 17–32. Springer, Cham (2018). https://doi.org/10.1007/978-3-319-99927-2_2
33. Springintveld, J., Vaandrager, F., D'Argenio, P.R.: Testing timed automata. Theoret. Comput. Sci. **254**(1–2), 225–257 (2001)
34. Yu, L., Lei, Y., Kacker, R.N., Kuhn, D.R., Sriram, R.D., Brady, K.: A general conformance testing framework for IEEE 11073 PHD's communication model. In: Proceedings of the 6th International Conference on PErvasive Technologies Related to Assistive Environments, PETRA 2013, pp. 12:1–12:8. ACM, New York (2013)
35. Zhao, Y., Rozier, K.Y.: Formal specification and verification of a coordination protocol for an automated air traffic control system. Sci. Comput. Program. **96**, 337–353 (2014). Special Issue on Automated Verification of Critical Systems (AVoCS 2012)

Evaluating the Complexity of Deriving Adaptive Homing, Synchronizing and Distinguishing Sequences for Nondeterministic FSMs

Nina Yevtushenko[1], Victor Kuliamin[1], and Natalia Kushik[2(✉)]

[1] Ivannikov Institute for System Programming of the Russian Academy of Sciences,
25 Alexander Solzhenitsyn street, 109004 Moscow, Russia
{evtushenko,kuliamin}@ispras.ru

[2] SAMOVAR, CNRS, Télécom SudParis, Université Paris-Saclay,
9 rue Charles Fourier, 91000 Évry, France
natalia.kushik@telecom-sudparis.eu

Abstract. Homing, synchronizing and distinguishing sequences (HSs, SSs, and DSs) are used in FSM (Finite State Machine) based testing for state identification and can significantly reduce the size of a returned test suite with guaranteed fault coverage. However, such preset sequences not always exist for nondeterministic FSMs and are rather long when existing. Adaptive HSs, SSs and DSs are known to exist more often and be much shorter that makes them attractive for deriving test suites and adaptive checking sequences. As nowadays, a number of specifications are represented by nondeterministic FSMs, the deeper study of such sequences, their derivation strategies, and related complexity estimations/reductions is in great demand. In this paper, we evaluate the complexity of deriving adaptive HSs and SSs for noninitialized FSMs, the complexity of deriving DSs for noninitialized merging-free FSMs.

Keywords: Nondeterministic Finite State Machine (FSM) ·
Adaptive homing sequence · Adaptive synchronizing sequence ·
Adaptive distinguishing sequence

1 Introduction

Many problems in automata theory, for example, such as automata/Finite State Machine (FSM) based test derivation methods (see, for example, [1,2,4,5,12, 13]), rely on the state identification sequences in the specification FSM, namely, on distinguishing, homing, and synchronizing sequences (DSs, HSs, and SSs) that can be preset or adaptive [3]. Distinguishing sequences are derived to identify the initial state of the machine of interest, while homing and synchronizing sequences

This work is partially supported by RFBR project N 19-0700327/19.

© IFIP International Federation for Information Processing 2019
Published by Springer Nature Switzerland AG 2019
C. Gaston et al. (Eds.): ICTSS 2019, LNCS 11812, pp. 86–103, 2019.
https://doi.org/10.1007/978-3-030-31280-0_6

allow identifying its final state. Preset input sequences are derived before being applied to the system of interest (FSM, implementation under test, etc.), while for adaptive sequences the next input depends on the outputs produced for the previous inputs. Adaptive sequences can be represented by a tree or an acyclic FSM [14] called a *test case*. Adaptive distinguishing and homing sequences exist more often than the preset ones and are usually shorter.

When deriving adaptive DSs/HSs/SSs for deterministic FSMs one can consider a successor or a spanning tree [12,18]. However, based on the above trees for nondeterministic FSMs, for all types of sequences there are no necessary and sufficient conditions when an adaptive sequence exists. Another approach [8] constructs an adaptive HS for the case when each pair of states has such an adaptive HS and these conditions are necessary and sufficient for a noninitialized complete observable FSM to have an HS. However, for a weakly initialized FSM with a proper subset of initial states the conditions become only sufficient. The same situation holds for adaptive DSs if an FSM under study is merging-free, i.e., an FSM where for each input, the FSM cannot move from two different states to the same state with equal outputs. The pairwise 'homeability' for the set of states can be also effectively used for deriving an adaptive SS for a given nondeterministic FSM. Indeed, it was shown in [11] that such adaptive SS exists for a noninitialized FSM if and only if each state pair is adaptively homing and the FSM has a state that is definitely reachable from any other state. The obtained results allowed to evaluate the upper bound on the length of a shortest adaptive HS/SS for complete noninitialized possibly nondeterministic FSMs; however, the question of the complexity for deriving such corresponding test cases remained open.

The main contribution of this paper is therefore the complexity evaluation of derivation of an adaptive HS/SS for noninitialized complete FSMs and an adaptive DS for noninitialized complete merging-free FSMs. We show that given the FSM under study having n states and q outputs, a corresponding test case has at most $(n-1)^2 n/2 + n + 1$ states and the complexity of deriving such a test case is $O(qn^5)$.

The rest of the paper has the following structure. Section 2 contains the preliminaries. The procedure for deriving adaptive HSs and DSs based on those for each pair of states is presented in Sect. 3 along with its complexity estimation while Sect. 4 describes the construction of SSs. Section 5 briefly describes the related work and Sect. 6 concludes the paper.

2   Preliminaries

A *finite state machine* (FSM), or simply a machine, is a 5-tuple $\mathbf{S} = <S, I, O, h_S, S_{in}>$ where S is a finite nonempty set of states with the set $S_{in} \subseteq S$ of initial states, I and O are finite input and output alphabets, and $h_S \subseteq S \times I \times O \times S$ is a *transition relation*. FSM $\mathbf{S}$ is *noninitialized* if $S_{in} = S$ and in this case, we omit the set S_{in} of initial states and a noninitialized FSM is denoted as a 4-tuple $<S, I, O, h_S>$. FSM $\mathbf{S}$ is an *initialized* FSM if $|S_{in}| = 1$

and FSM **S** with the initial state s_j is denoted $\mathbf{S}/s_j$. If $1 < |S_{in}| < |S|$ then FSM **S** often is called *weakly initialized*. FSM **S** is *nondeterministic* if for some pair $(s, i) \in S \times I$, there exist several pairs $(o, s') \in O \times S$ such that $(s, i, o, s') \in h_S$; otherwise, the FSM is *deterministic*. FSM **S** is *observable* if for every two transitions $(s, i, o, s_1), (s, i, o, s_2) \in h_S$ it holds that $s_1 = s_2$. FSM **S** is *complete* if for every pair $(s, i) \in S \times I$, there exists a transition $(s, i, o, s') \in h_S$. In the following, we consider complete observable possibly nondeterministic FSMs unless something different is explicitly stated. An example of a complete nondeterministic FSM is shown in Fig. 1. A complete observable FSM is *merging-free* [20] if for every two different states s_1 and s_2 and any input i it holds that if (s_1, i, o, s_1'), $(s_2, i, o, s_2') \in h_S$, then $s_1' \neq s_2'$.

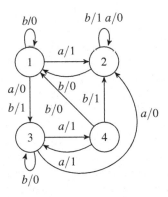

Fig. 1. A complete observable nondeterministic FSM **S**

The behavior relation h_S is extended to input and output sequences in usual way and given an input sequence $i_1 \ldots i_l$, we say that an output sequence $o_1 \ldots o_l \in out(s, i_1 \ldots i_l)$ if and only if there exists a state s' such that $(s, i_1 \ldots i_l, o_1 \ldots o_l, s') \in h_S$. Given an input/output pair io and a state s of a complete observable FSM **S**, state s' is the *io-successor* of state s of FSM **S** if $(s, i, o, s') \in h_S$. The io-successor of state s not necessarily exists and in this case, we say that the io-successor of state s is the empty set. A trace of FSM **S** at state s is a sequence of input/output pairs which label consecutive transitions starting from state s, $tr = i_1 o_1 \ldots i_l o_l$ (or $i_1/o_1 \ldots i_l/o_l$). A sequence $i_1 \ldots i_l$ is an *input* sequence of the trace while $o_1 \ldots o_l$ is an *output* sequence. Since FSM **S** is observable, given state s and a trace γ of the FSM, the γ-successor of state s is state s' which is reached from s via the trace γ. If γ is not a trace at state s then the γ-successor of state s is empty or sometimes we say that in this case the γ-successor of state s does not exist. Given non-empty subset S' of states and a trace γ of the FSM, the γ-successor of S' is the union of γ-successors over all states of the set S'.

Test Case Definition. An input sequence α is called *adaptive* if the next input depends on the output to the previous one. An adaptive input sequence can be represented by a tree or a special FSM that is called a *test case* [14]. Given an input alphabet I and an output alphabet O, a test case $\mathbf{TC}(I,O)$ over an input alphabet I and an output alphabet O is an initialized initially connected observable single-input output-complete FSM that has an acyclic transition graph. In other words, at each state either only one input with all possible outputs is defined or there are no outgoing transitions, and in the latter case, the state is a *deadlock* state. A test case is a partial FSM once $|I| > 1$. By definition, a test case $\mathbf{TC}(I,O)$ represents an adaptive experiment with a complete FSM $\mathbf{S}$ over alphabets I and O in the following way. If input i_1 is a defined input at the initial state t_0 of $\mathbf{TC}(I,O)$ then first, the input i_1 is applied to the FSM $\mathbf{S}$ under investigation and $\mathbf{TC}(I,O)$ moves to the $i_1 o$-successor t_1 of state t_0 if $\mathbf{S}$ produces the output o as the response to the input i_1. The next input to apply is the input defined at state t_1, etc. The procedure terminates when a deadlock state is reached. The *height* of the test case $\mathbf{TC}(I,O)$ is the length of a longest trace from the initial state to a deadlock state of $\mathbf{TC}(I,O)$ and it specifies the length of the longest input sequence that can be applied to an FSM $\mathbf{S}$ during the adaptive experiment.

Given FSM $\mathbf{S} = <S,I,O,h_S>$, a test case $\mathbf{TC}(I,O)$ is a *homing* test case (HTC) for $\mathbf{S}$ if for every trace γ from the initial state to a deadlock state, the γ-successor of the set S_{in} in $\mathbf{S}$ is a singleton or the empty set. FSM $\mathbf{S}$ is *homing* if $\mathbf{S}$ has a homing test case. A homing test case is a *synchronizing* test case (STC) for the FSM $\mathbf{S}$, if there exists a state s such that for every trace γ of $\mathbf{TC}(I,O)$ from the initial to a deadlock state, γ-successor of S_{in} is either $\{s\}$ or the empty set. A homing test case represents an *adaptive homing sequence* and a homing test case for machine $\mathbf{S}$ in Fig. 1 is shown in Fig. 3. By direct inspection, one can assure that an HTC in Fig. 3 is not an STC for $\mathbf{S}$.

A test case $\mathbf{TC}(I,O)$ is a *distinguishing* test case (DTC) if every trace γ from the initial state to a deadlock state can be a trace at most at a single state of the set S_{in}. A distinguishing test case represents an *adaptive distinguishing sequence*.

In [8], it is shown that a noninitialized observable FSM has a homing test case if and only if each pair of states is homing while in [20] it is it is shown that a noninitialized observable merging-free FSM has a distinguishing test case if and only if each pair of states has such test case. For a STC corresponding necessary and sufficient conditions are established in [11]. Given a complete observable noninitialized FSM, there exists a synchronizing test case if and only if the FSM has a homing test case and there exists a state definitely reachable from any other state. State $s' \in S$ is *definitely-reachable* (*d-reachable*) from state $s \in S$ if there exists a test case $\mathbf{P}(s,s')$ over alphabets I and O such that for every trace γ of $\mathbf{P}(s,s')$ from the initial state to a deadlock state, the γ-successor of state s in FSM $\mathbf{S}$ is either the empty set or is the set $\{s'\}$. We hereafter refer to such a test case as a *d-transfer* test case. In [15], necessary and sufficient conditions are established that allow to check if state $s \in S$ is definitely reachable from the initial state s_0 of the initialized FSM $\mathbf{S}$. In particular, it is proven that state s of an initialized FSM $\mathbf{S}$ is definitely reachable from state s_0 if and only if $\mathbf{S}$ has a single-input acyclic submachine $\mathbf{S}'$ with the initial state s_0 and the only deadlock state s such that for each input defined in some state of $\mathbf{S}'$, the state has all the transitions of $\mathbf{S}$ labeled with this input. Moreover, in the same paper, an efficient method is proposed for checking whether a state s is definitely reachable from the initial state of an initialized complete FSM, and in [11], this procedure is adjusted for arbitrary states s and s'.

Note that since any d-transfer test case $\mathbf{P}(s, s')$ is an acyclic submachine of the machine $\mathbf{S}$, then the length of any trace in $\mathbf{P}(s, s')$ does not exceed the number n of states of $\mathbf{S}$; in other words, one needs at most $n - 1$ inputs to adaptively transfer the possibly nondeterministic machine from state s to state s'. Therefore, the length of a longest trace in a shortest test case $\mathbf{P}(s, s')$ is polynomial and is at most $n - 1$.

Given a uninitialized complete observable FSM $\mathbf{S}$, if there is no state s that is definitely reachable from any other state then FSM $\mathbf{S}$ has no synchronizing test case. On the other hand, if there exists state s that is definitely reachable for any other state then this condition does not guarantee that the FSM has a synchronizing test case; the FSM must also be homing.

As an example, consider an FSM $\mathbf{P}$ in Fig. 2. By direct inspection, one can assure that state 3 is d-reachable from state 1 via input b while being d-reachable from state 2 via input a. Note that, for FSM $\mathbf{S}$ in Fig. 1, there is no state that is d-reachable from any other state.

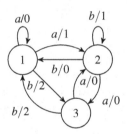

Fig. 2. A complete observable nondeterministic FSM $\mathbf{P}$ where state 3 is d-reachable from states 1 and 2

Despite the fact that there are many research papers on evaluating the complexity of the existence check of adaptive HS/SS/DS and their length (see Sect. 5), the complexity of their derivation even for noninitialized complete nondeterministic FSM is unknown. We furthermore utilize the above cited criteria to estimate the complexity of deriving HTCs, STCs and DTCs for noninitialized nondeterministic FSMs. For the sake of simplicity, we hash states, inputs and outputs by integers; however, for simplifying the reading we still use characters s, i, o.

3   Deriving Homing and Distinguishing Test Cases

We first come back to the definition of k-homing pairs of different states [7]. Given a noninitialized complete observable possibly nondeterministic FSM $\mathbf{S} =$

$<S, I, O, h_S>$ and two different states s_a and s_b, the pair $\{s_a, s_b\}$ is *1-homing* if there exists an input $i_{\{s_a, s_b\}}$ such that for every $o \in O$, the $i_{\{s_a, s_b\}}o$-successor of the pair $\{s_a, s_b\}$ has at most one state. Let all the pairs of k-homing states be determined for some $k > 0$. Then the pair $\{s_a, s_b\}$ is $(k+1)$-*homing* if it is not k-homing and there exists an input $i_{\{s_a, s_b\}}$ such that for every $o \in O$, the pair of $i_{\{s_a, s_b\}}o$-successors of states s_a and s_b either is at most k-homing or the $i_{\{s_a, s_b\}}o$-successor of the pair $\{s_a, s_b\}$ has at most one state. The pair $\{s_a, s_b\}$ is *homing* if $\{s_a, s_b\}$ is k-homing for some $k > 0$.

In fact, the above definition for checking if a pair of different states is homing is constructive and can be used for deriving a homing test case for a homing pair of states. Moreover, when each pair of different states is homing a partial order relation can be established over pairs of different states when $\{s_a, s_b\} > \{s_p, s_m\}$ if and only if $\{s_a, s_b\}$ is a j-homing pair while $\{s_p, s_m\}$ being k-homing for $k < j$. Let the pair $\{s_a, s_b\}$ be j-homing, $j > 0$. If $j = 1$ then there exists an input $i_{\{s_a, s_b\}}$ such that for every $o \in O$, the $i_{\{s_a, s_b\}}o$-successor of $\{s_a, s_b\}$ has at most one state. If $j > 1$ then there exists an input $i_{\{s_a, s_b\}}$ such that for every $o \in O$, the pair of $i_{\{s_a, s_b\}}o$-successors of states s_a and s_b either is at most $(j-1)$-homing or the $i_{\{s_a, s_b\}}o$-successor of the pair $\{s_a, s_b\}$ has at most one state. Correspondingly, we propose to derive an array *Input* where for each pair $\{s_a, s_b\}$ the corresponding input $i_{\{s_a, s_b\}}$ is saved.

Consider FSM **S** in Fig. 1. There are 1-homing pairs $\{2, 3\}$ and $\{2, 4\}$ with $i_{\{2,3\}} = a$ and $i_{\{2,4\}} = b$. Pairs $\{1, 2\}$, $\{1, 3\}$ and $\{1, 4\}$ are 2-homing with the inputs $i_{\{1,2\}}$, $i_{\{1,3\}}$, $i_{\{1,4\}}$ such that for every $o \in O$, $i_{\{1,2\}}o$-successor $(i_{\{1,3\}}o$-successor or $i_{\{1,4\}}o$-successor) of the corresponding pair is either 1-homing or those successors are singletons. Correspondingly, $i_{\{1,2\}} = b$, $i_{\{1,3\}} = i_{\{1,4\}} = a$. Pair $\{3, 4\}$ is 3-homing with the input $i_{\{3,4\}}$ such that for every $o \in O$, the $i_{\{3,4\}}o$-successor of this pair is at most 2-homing or is a singleton and thus, $i_{\{3,4\}} = b$. The array *Input* is shown in Table 1.

Table 1. Array input for FSM **S** in Fig. 1

State pairs	$\{1, 2\}$	$\{1, 3\}$	$\{1, 4\}$	$\{2, 3\}$	$\{2, 4\}$	$\{3, 4\}$
Inputs	b	a	a	a	b	b

The main operation when constructing homing test cases is determining an *io*-successor for a given state (pair of different states). For this reason, we first assume that an FSM is given as a two-dimensional array *IOsuc*. Columns of *IOsuc* correspond to states of the given FSM while the rows correspond to possible *io*-pairs, i.e., given a state and an *io*-pair, the related cell has either the corresponding *io*-successor or it is empty (the transition is not defined). With the help of such structure, the calculation of an *io*-successor of a given state can be considered as an elementary operation. Table 2 has the array *IOsuc* for FSM **S** in Fig. 1. If FSM **S** is homing then we also prepare in advance the array *Input* where for each pair of different states $\{s_a, s_b\}$ the corresponding input $i_{\{s_a, s_b\}}$ is saved as described above. In fact, given these structures, the calculation of an *io*-successor will be reduced to a proper indexing in a certain array.

Table 2. The array $IOsuc$ for FSM **S** in Fig. 1

io-pairs/States	1	2	3	4
$a0$	3	2	2	–
$a1$	2	–	4	3
$b0$	1	1	3	1
$b1$	3	2	–	2

Given a pair $\{s_1, s_2\}$ of different states of a homing complete observable FSM, the following algorithm returns a *special* homing test case $\mathbf{HTC}_{\{s_1,s_2\}}$ for the pair $\{s_1, s_2\}$. Indeed, in test case $\mathbf{HTC}_{\{s_1,s_2\}}$ returned by Algorithm 1 each state pair is listed only once. The reason is that the algorithm constructs a HTC for a state pair in such a way that each state pair representing its current state has a bigger degree of the 'homeability' than its successors (see Proposition 1).

Algorithm 1. Deriving a homing test case $\mathbf{HTC}_{\{s_1,s_2\}}$ for a homing pair $\{s_1, s_2\}$

Input : A homing complete observable, possibly nondeterministic FSM **S** represented by two-dimensional array $IOsuc$ and the array $Input$ that for each pair $\{s_a, s_b\}$ contains the corresponding input $i_{\{s_a,s_b\}}$
Output: A homing test case $\mathbf{HTC}_{\{s_1,s_2\}}$ for the pair $\{s_1, s_2\} \subseteq S$
Construct a test case $\mathbf{HTC}_{\{s_1,s_2\}} = <Q, I, O, h, q_0>$ where
$Q = \{q_0 = \{s_1, s_2\}, D\}$, $h = \emptyset$, the pair $\{s_1, s_2\}$ is unmarked;
while *there exists an unmarked pair* $\{s_a, s_b\} \in Q$ **do**
  Select an unmarked pair $\{s_a, s_b\} \in Q$;
  Extract the input $i_{\{s_a,s_b\}}$ of the array $Input$;
  foreach $i_{\{s_a,s_b\}}o$-*successor* $\{s'_a, s'_b\}$ *of* $\{s_a, s_b\}$ *extracted from the array* $IOsuc$ **do**
    if $s'_a \neq s'_b$ **then**
      Add to h the transition $(\{s_a, s_b\}, i_{\{s_a,s_b\}}, o, \{s'_a, s'_b\})$
      if $\{s'_a, s'_b\} \notin Q$ **then**
        $Q = Q \cup \{\{s'_a, s'_b\}\}$; $\{s'_a, s'_b\}$ is unmarked
    else
      Add to h the transition $(\{s_a, s_b\}, i_{\{s_a,s_b\}}, o, s'_a)$; $Q = Q \cup \{s'_a\}$;
  foreach $o \in O$ *such that* $i_{\{s_a,s_b\}}o$-*successor of the state* $\{s_a, s_b\}$ *does not exist* **do**
    Add to h a transition $(\{s_a, s_b\}, i, o, D)$
  Label state $\{s_a, s_b\}$ as a marked state;
return $\mathbf{HTC}_{\{s_1,s_2\}}$

Given FSM **S** in Fig. 1, the test case is derived by the use of the array *Input* and following partial order over the FSM state pairs: $\{1,3\} > \{2,3\}$, $\{1,3\} > \{2,4\}$.

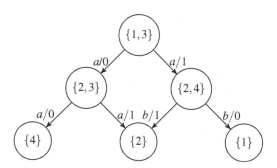

Fig. 3. A homing test case $\mathbf{HTC}_{\{1,3\}}$

By construction of a test case $\mathbf{HTC}_{\{s_1,s_2\}}$, the following statement holds.

Proposition 1. *Given an FSM* **S** *with n states and a homing pair* $\{s_1,s_2\}$ *of* **S***, there exists a homing test case* $\mathbf{HTC}_{\{s_1,s_2\}}$ *such that states of* $\mathbf{HTC}_{\{s_1,s_2\}}$ *are pairs of different states of FSM* **S** *in the union with singletons of S and the deadlock state D. Moreover, given a j-homing state* q_1 *and an m-homing state* q_2, *if* $j \leq m$, *then state* q_2 *is unreachable from state* q_1 *in* $\mathbf{HTC}_{\{s_1,s_2\}}$.

Corollary 1. *The number of states of* $\mathbf{HTC}_{\{s_1,s_2\}}$ *does not exceed* $n(n-1)/2 + n+1$ *while the number of transitions of the test case* $\mathbf{HTC}_{\{s_1,s_2\}}$ *does not exceed* $|O|n(n-1)/2$.

We now discuss the complexity of deriving the array *Input* and test case $\mathbf{HTC}_{\{s_1,s_2\}}$.

For deriving the set of all 1-homing pairs, for each pair of different states all input/output pairs *io* have to be studied, i.e., the complexity of this step is $\mathrm{O}(|I||O||S|^2)$ and each test case for a 1-homing pair has at most $(n+2)$ states and is constructed according to Algorithm 1. If k is the maximum integer such that there exists a pair of states that is k-homing then k is at most $\mathrm{O}(|S|^2)$. For deriving the set of all j-homing pairs, $j \leq k$, the same check should be performed, and thus, the complexity of the check whether each pair of states is homing is $\mathrm{O}(|I||O||S|^2k)$ or at most $\mathrm{O}(|I||O||S|^4)$. The array *Input* is constructed during this check and thus, the derivation of the array *Input* has the same complexity. Therefore, the following proposition holds.

Proposition 2. *Given an FSM* **S** $= <S, I, O, h_S>$ *with n states, the (time) complexity of checking whether this FSM is homing is* $\mathrm{O}(|I||O||S|^4)$. *The problem of deriving the array Input has the same complexity.*

If each pair of states is homing then the noninitialized FSM **S** is homing and at the next step, an HTC for the FSM has to be constructed. Here we notice that in [8], [7], a procedure for deriving HTC was proposed but the complexity of the HTC derivation was not evaluated. In this paper, we propose a modification of that algorithm that allows us evaluating the size of a returned HTC as well as the (time) complexity of the HTC derivation.

Algorithm 2. Deriving a HTC when all pairs of different states are homing

---

Input : A complete observable, possibly nondeterministic homing FSM **S** represented by two-dimensional array $IOsuc$ and the array $Input$ that for each pair $\{s_a, s_b\}$ contains the corresponding input $i_{\{s_a,s_b\}}$

Output: A homing test case HTC for **S**, $|S| = n > 2$

Construct a test case **HTC** $= < Q, I, O, h, q_0 >$ where $Q = \{q_0 = \{s_1, s_2\}^2, D\}$, $h = \emptyset$, the pair $\{s_1, s_2\}^2$ is unmarked;

$j = 2$;

while $j \leq n$ **do**

    while *there exists an unmarked pair* $\{s_a, s_b\}^j \in Q$ **do**

        Select an unmarked pair $\{s_a, s_b\}^j \in Q$;

        Extract the input $i_{\{s_a,s_b\}}$ of the array $Input$;

        foreach $i_{\{s_a,s_b\}}o$-*successor* $\{s'_a, s'_b\}$ *of* $\{s_a, s_b\}$ *extracted from the array* $IOsuc$ **do**

            if $s'_a \neq s'_b$ **then**

                Add to h the transition $(\{s_a, s_b\}^j, i_{\{s_a,s_b\}}, o, \{s'_a, s'_b\}^j)$

                if $\{s'_a, s'_b\} \notin Q$ **then**

                    $Q = Q \cup \{\{s'_a, s'_b\}^j\}$; $\{s'_a, s'_b\}^j$ is unmarked

            else

                Add to h the transition $(\{s_a, s_b\}^j, i_{\{s_a,s_b\}}, o, s'_a)$;

                $Q = Q \cup \{s'_a\}$;

        Label state $\{s_a, s_b\}^j$ as a marked state;

    $j + +$;

    Construct the intersection $\mathbf{HTC} \cap \mathbf{S}/s_j$ of FSMs **HTC** and $\mathbf{S}/s_j$;

    foreach *state* $(\{s_a, s_b\}^r, s)$, $r < j$, *of* $\mathbf{HTC} \cap \mathbf{S}/s_j$ *and io such that the transition function h of* **HTC** *has a transition* $(\{s_a, s_b\}^r, i, o, s_k)$ **do**

        if *the io-successor* s_p *of state* s_j *is different from* s_k **then**

            replace the transition $(\{s_a, s_b\}^r, i, o, s_k)$ in h to

            $(\{s_a, s_b\}^r, i, o, \{s_k, s_p\}^j)$

    foreach *state* $(\{s_a, s_b\}^r, s)$ *of* $\mathbf{HTC} \cap \mathbf{S}/s_j$ *and each input/output pair io, such that state s has no io-successor in* **HTC do**

        Add to h a transition $(\{s_a, s_b\}^r, i, o, D)$;

return HTC

We now investigate some properties of the FSM **HTC** returned by Algorithm 2.

Proposition 3. *An FSM* **HTC** *returned by Algorithm 2 is a homing test case for the FSM* **S**.

Proof. We first show that the FSM **HTC** returned by Algorithm 2 has an acyclic transition graph. By construction, given a state $\{s_a, s_b\}^r$, only states $\{s_k, s_p\}^j$, $j \geq r$, can be reached from state $\{s_a, s_b\}^r$. Moreover, if $r = j$, then due to Proposition 1, if state $\{s_a, s_b\}^r$ is reachable from state $\{s_k, s_p\}^r$ and the pair $\{s_a, s_b\}$ is j-homing, then the pair $\{s_k, s_p\}$ is at most l-homing for $l < r$ and thus, state $\{s_k, s_p\}^r$ is unreachable from state $\{s_a, s_b\}^r$ in **HTC** as only $\mathbf{HTC}_{\{s_p, s_m\}}$, $\{s_p, s_m\} \subseteq S$, are used when deriving **HTC** at the r-th iteration of Algorithm 2. The FSM under construction is indeed single-input as at each iteration of Algorithm 2 the transitions added to h refer to a single input $i_{\{s_a, s_b\}}$. Output completeness is handled by the last instruction at each iteration.

We now should show that when a singleton s_k is reached then for this trace only s_k can be reached from any state of **S**. The statement holds for states s_1 and s_2 by construction of the test case $\mathbf{HTC}_{\{s_1, s_2\}}$. When states $s_3, \ldots, s_n$ are added at the next iterations, if some trace at some of these states does not take the FSM **S** to state s_k then the singleton $\{s_k\}$ would not be a deadlock state in the HTC. $\qquad\qquad\square$

Proposition 4. *Given the FSM* **S** *with n states and the maximum integer k such that FSM* **S** *has a pair of different states that is k-homing but is not $(k-1)$-homing, the FSM* **HTC** *returned by Algorithm 2 has at most $(n-1)^2 n/2 + n + 1$ states and the height at most $(n-1)k$.*

Indeed, Algorithm 2 has at most $(n-1)$ iterations and at each iteration at most $(n-1)n/2$ pairs of states are added. Moreover, there can be at most n singletons and a deadlock state D reached by traces which are not traces at some state of FSM **S**. The height of **HTC** under construction does not exceed the maximal height k of $\mathbf{HTC}_{\{s_p, s_m\}}$, $\{s_p, s_m\} \subseteq S$, attached at most $(n-1)$ times.

Since there is only one defined input with all possible outputs at each intermediate state of **HTC** returned by Algorithm 2, the following statement holds.

Corollary 2. *Given a homing FSM* **S** *with n states, the FSM* **HTC** *returned by Algorithm 2 has at most $|O|(n-1)^2 n/2$ transitions.*

Proposition 5. *The (time) complexity of Algorithm 2 is* $O(|O|n^5)$.

Proof. The proof is performed by evaluating the complexity at an iteration step of Algorithm 2. At the iteration j we have at most $(j-2)n(n-1)/2$ states which are pairs of different states in **HTC** under construction. Correspondingly, the analysis of transitions at this step requires $O(|O|(j-2)n(n-1)/2)$ operations.

At the same time, at the iteration j we perform the intersection of **HTC** under construction and $\mathbf{S}/s_j$, the former having $jn(n-1)/2$ states which are pairs of different states and $|O|$ transitions to process at each state while the latter having n states. Correspondingly, the complexity of checking all the transitions of the intersection needs $O(|O|njn(n-1)/2)$ operations and this number is higher than that for analyzing states of **HTC** under construction. Adding up the number of operations for $j = 2, \ldots, n-1$ we obtain the complexity $O(|O|n^5)$ for Algorithm 2.

As a corollary to the above propositions and keeping in mind Proposition 2, the following statement can be established.

Theorem 1. *Given a homing FSM* $\mathbf{S} = <S, I, O, h_S>$, $|S| = n$, *and the maximum integer* k *such that FSM* $\mathbf{S}$ *has a pair of different states that is* k-*homing but is not* $(k-1)$-*homing, there exists a homing test case of the height at most* $(n-1)k$ *with at most* $(n-1)^2 n/2 + n + 1$ *states, at most* $|O|(n-1)^2 n/2$ *transitions; the (time) complexity of deriving this test case is* $O(|O|n^5)$ *when* $\mathbf{S}$ *is represented by arrays* $IOsuc$ *and* $Input$.

Note that the complexity of **HTC** derivation depends only on the number of states of the FSM under experiment as well as its number of outputs. However, differently from other approaches for deriving homing/synchronizing/distinguishing sequences, it does not directly depend on the number of inputs when the array $Input$ is already derived.

Corollary 3. *Given an FSM where all pairs of different states are at most 1-homing, there exists a homing test case* **HTC** *for the FSM* $\mathbf{S}$ *that has the height at most* $(n-1)$.

Consider an example of FSM $\mathbf{S}$ in Fig. 1 for illustrating Algorithm 2. We start with a pair $\{1, 2\}^2$; the $b0$-successor is $\{1\}$ while the $b1$-successor is $\{2, 3\}^2$. According to the array $Input$ we consider input a for the pair $\{2, 3\}$ and obtain the $a0$-successor $\{2\}$ and the $a1$-successor $\{4\}$. After adding state 3 as an initial state the $b0$-successor $\{1\}$ of $\{1, 2\}^2$ becomes a new state $\{1, 3\}^3$. Since input a corresponds to the pair $\{1, 3\}$ in the array $Input$, we add corresponding transitions to states $\{2, 3\}^3$ and $\{2, 4\}^3$ and to singletons $\{1\}$, $\{2\}$, $\{4\}$. Adding state 4 as an initial state does not add more transitions to the test case.

We also notice that **HTC** returned by Algorithm 2 can be minimized. For example, in **HTC** in Fig. 4 states $\{2, 3\}^2$ and $\{2, 3\}^3$ can be merged into a single state since $\{2, 3\}^3$ is not reachable from any state reachable from $\{2, 3\}^2$ but generally it is not the case and such optimization is out of the scope of this paper.

It also should be mentioned that the observability and completeness of an FSM under investigation are the necessary conditions when using Algorithms 1 and 2 for deriving a homing test case. If the FSM is nonobservable then it can well happen that when adding a new state at the j-th iteration of Algorithm 2 not pairs of states but bigger subsets can be obtained when deriving the intersection $\mathbf{HTC} \cap \mathbf{S}/s_j$. If the FSM is partially specified then as it is shown in [19], even the problem of checking the existence of an adaptive homing sequence is PSPACE-complete.

Another interesting fact is that both above algorithms can be applied for deriving a distinguishing test case for a merging-free FSM. This relies on the following proposition.

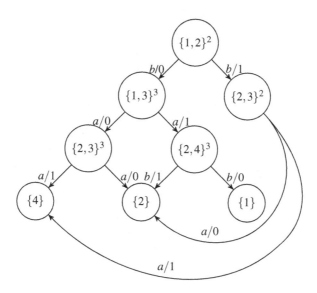

Fig. 4. HTC for FSM **S** in Fig. 1

Proposition 6. *Given a complete merging-free noninitialized observable possibly nondeterministic FSM* **S**, *a test case* **TC** *is a homing test case for* **S** *if and only if the* **TC** *is a distinguishing test case for* **S**.

Indeed, due to properties of merging free FSMs, given a merging-free FSM **S**, a pair of different states of a complete FSM **S** is j-homing, $j > 0$, if and only if this pair is j-distinguishing for **S**.

Note that the FSM in Fig. 2 is merging-free and thus, a homing test case, i.e., the test case in Fig. 5 without transitions from singletons is also a distinguishing test case [1].

In the next section, the complexity of the derivation of an adaptive synchronizing sequence is evaluated based on the complexity for deriving an HTC for a homing FSM.

4   Deriving Synchronizing Test Cases

As mentioned above, there exists a synchronizing test case for a complete noninitialized observable FSM **S** if and only if the FSM **S** has a homing test case and there exists a state $s \in S$ that is definitely-reachable state from any other state. Moreover, in [11], the authors propose just appending the singletons of the HTC with d-transfer test cases. In this paper, we discuss this procedure more detailed in order to evaluate whether the complexity will be increased when a HTC is appended for deriving a STC.

---

[1] Note that for the sake of simplicity, in the Figure we omit the deadlock state D and corresponding incoming transitions.

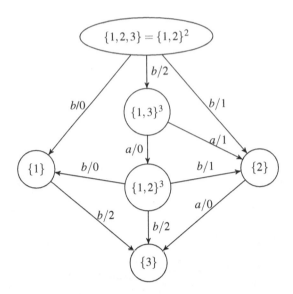

Fig. 5. STC for FSM **S** in Fig. 2

The complexity of the procedure for checking if there exists a state that is d-reachable from any other state requires again considering all pairs of states. Similar to the check of homing pairs, we check each pair $\{i, 1\}$, $i = 2, 3, \ldots, n$, of different states to conclude whether state 1 is d-reachable from any other state. If state 1 does not possess this property we check state pairs $\{i, 2\}$, $i = 1, 3, \ldots, n$, etc. If there is no state that is d-reachable from any other state then the FSM has no synchronizing test case. The complexity of this check is $O(|I||O||S|^2|S|)$ or at most $O(|I||O||S|^3)$. If there exists state s that is d-reachable from any other state then in order to append a HTC with the corresponding transfer test cases, we define the relation of j-d-reachability that also is a partial order over the FSM states.

Given state s' that is d-reachable from any other state, we say that s' is 1-d-reachable from state s if there exists an input i_s such that for each $o \in O$, the $i_s o$-successor of s is empty or is a singleton $\{s'\}$. Given a subset of states from which state s' is j-d-reachable, $j > 0$, we say that state s' is $(j + 1)$-d-reachable from state s if there exists an input i_s that for each $o \in O$, the $i_s o$-successor of state s' is l-d-reachable from state s for $l < j$. In other words, similar to j-homing pairs we establish a partial order relation over states due to the d-reachability of state s'. Similar to the array *Input*, we derive an array *Input-d* where for each state s of the FSM **S** the corresponding input i_s is stored.

Correspondingly, we propose Algorithm 3 for deriving a STC for a complete observable FSM **S**.

As an example, consider an FSM in Fig. 2. The corresponding array *Input-d* is shown in Table 3.

Algorithm 3. Deriving a STC when all pairs of different states are homing and state s' is d-reachable from any other state

---

Input : A complete homing observable, possibly nondeterministic FSM **S** represented by two-dimensional array $IOsuc$,
    HTC, and the array $Input$-d that has for each state s the corresponding input i_s

Output: A synchronizing test case **STC** for **S**, $|S| = n > 2$

STC := **HTC** $=< Q, I, O, h >$;

foreach *singleton* $\{s\}$ *of* **STC do**
> Add to the transition relation h the transition $(\{s\}, i_s, o, \{s'_a\})$ if the $i_s o$-successor s'_a of state s exists

foreach *state* $\{s_a\}$ *of* **STC do**
> **foreach** *and input/output pair io, such that state s_a has no io-successor in* **STC do**
> > Add to h a transition $(\{s_a\}, i, o, D)$

return STC

Table 3. Array $Input$-d for FSM in Fig. 2; state 3 is d-reachable from states 1 and 2

States	1	2	3
Inputs	b	a	$-$

The corresponding synchronizing test case for the FSM in Fig. 2 is presented in Fig. 5. Note that, in Fig. 5 we omitted the transitions to the deadlock state D; some of these transitions are added at the third step of Algorithm 3 for preserving the output completeness of the returned test case. Indexes for state pairs indicate the number of j-th iteration of Algorithm 2 for deriving the corresponding HTC.

Since the d-reachability is a partial order relation and the array $Input$-d inherits the corresponding property, the following statement holds.

Proposition 7. *An FSM* **STC** *returned by Algorithm 3 is a synchronizing test case for the FSM* **S***.*

Similar to HTC derivation, the following statements estimate the complexity of the STC derivation taking advantage of the $Input$-d utilization.

Proposition 8. *Given a FSM* **S** *with n states, the FSM* **STC** *returned by Algorithm 3 has the same set of states as the initial HTC while the number of transitions can be increased at most by $|O|n$.*

Proposition 9. *Given a homing FSM* **S** *with n states and its HTC, the complexity of Algorithm 3 is* $O(|O|n^4)$*.*

As a corollary to Propositions 4 and 9, the following statements hold.

Proposition 10. *Given a homing FSM* **S** *with n states and the FSM* **HTC** *returned by Algorithm 2 of height l, the FSM* **STC** *returned by Algorithm 3 has* at most $(n-1)^2 n/2 + n + 1$ states, at most $|O|(n-1)^2 n/2 + |O|n$ transitions and its height is at most $(l+n)$.

Theorem 2. *Given a homing FSM* **S** *with* n *states where there exists a state that is d-reachable from any other state and the maximal integer* k *such that FSM* **S** *has a pair of different states that is k-homing but is not* $(k-1)$*-homing, there exists a synchronizing test case with at most* $(n-1)^2 n/2 + n + 1$ *states, at most* $|O|((n-1)^2 n/2 + n)$ *transitions, of the height at most* $(n-1)k + n$, *and the complexity of deriving this test case is* $O(|O|n^5)$ *when* **S** *is represented by arrays* IOsuc, Input *and* Input-d.

Note again, that similar to homing test case derivation, the complexity of deriving a STC for a noninitialized observable FSM does not directly depend on the cardinality of its input alphabet when **HTC** and the array *Input-d* are given.

5 Related Work

The problems of checking the existence and derivation of homing, synchronizing and distinguishing sequences have been widely investigated in the past seventy years. Major results obtained in this area mainly concern the deterministic FSM case: for noninitialized complete deterministic minimal machines the existence decision and derivation of an appropriate sequence for the final state identification (HS and SS) can be performed in polynomial time [16]. However, whenever the machine is weakly initialized or partial [19] the corresponding decision problems become PSPACE-complete. There is the same complexity for the existence check of a distinguishing sequence for a uninitialized deterministic machine [12]. However, even for the 'good' case of HS and SS for deterministic FSMs the problem becomes much harder when constructing a shortest HS or SS. Indeed, the problem of deriving a shortest HS/SS is NP-hard even for complete noninitialized deterministic minimal FSMs [16].

In some cases, the complexity of the existence check or derivation of a corresponding state identification sequence can be reduced via adaptive strategy. A remarkable example of such complexity reduction has been considered in [12] where the existence check of an adaptive DS has been proven to be solved in polynomial time with respect to the number of FSM states.

For nondeterministic machines, the problems listed above become harder. Indeed, as homing, synchronizing and distinguishing sequences have exponential length in this case [6,9,17], their existence check and derivation cannot be performed in polynomial time. The adaptive test case length however can be reduced: for homing and synchronizing sequences when considering complete noninitialized FSMs, while for distinguishing sequences for merging-free FSMs. Related decision problems have been considered in [8,10,11,20] and have been proven to have polynomial complexity, as well as polynomial length of the corresponding sequences (with respect to the number of FSM states). In [8], an algorithm for deriving an adaptive homing sequence has been proposed, while

[11] presents a similar contribution for synchronizing sequences. Nevertheless, to the best of our knowledge, the complexity of the derivation of such adaptive sequences for nondeterministic FSMs has not been investigated yet. Therefore, the contributions of the current paper are inline with the current state of the art and moreover, are rather promising as they establish the polynomial complexity of the derivation of adaptive SS and HS for nondeterministic noninitialized FSMs, as well as for adaptive DS for merging-free FSMs.

6 Conclusion

In this paper, we have investigated the complexity of deriving adaptive homing and synchronizing sequences for a complete observable noninitialized possibly non-deterministic FSM as well as the complexity of deriving an adaptive distinguishing sequence for merging-free FSMs. In fact, this complexity can be polynomial with respect to the product of the number of FSM states and the cardinality of its output alphabet. The main trick consists of the proposed data structures for representing the FSM under experiment, that allow considering an io-successor calculation as an elementary operation. Another important contribution lies in the proposal of a partial order over the FSM state pairs identifying the degree of *homeability*.

We note however, that the reachability of the upper bound $O(|O|n^5)$ for an FSM with n states and $|O|$ outputs, for deriving a homing/synchronizing test case might not be tight similar to distinguishing test cases for merging-free nondeterministic FSMs. For the future work, we thus would like to specify the FSM classes where worst theoretical upper bounds are reached while for other classes, we would like to investigate some potential optimizations of the proposed algorithms. We also note that in this work we only consider noninitialized FSMs, and there is still an open problem of evaluating the complexity of adaptive HS/SS/DS derivation for weakly initialized nondeterministic FSMs. The corresponding research is also left for the future work, together with the identification of the class of FSMs where the worst theoretical upper bounds are reached.

Acknowledgement. The authors would like to thank Dr. Hüsnü Yenigün for fruitful discussions on the complexity of FSM state identification sequences; those discussions together with the joint results on the existence check of the related sequences were very helpful for moving forward to the complexity of the HS/SS/DS derivation, i.e., the results presented in this paper.

References

1. von Bochmann, G., Petrenko, A.: Protocol testing: review of methods and relevance for software testing. In: Proceedings of the 1994 International Symposium on Software Testing and Analysis, ISSTA 1994, 17–19 August, Seattle, WA, USA, pp. 109–124 (1994). https://doi.org/10.1145/186258.187153

2. Chow, T.S.: Testing software design modeled by finite-state machines. IEEE Trans. Softw. Eng. **4**(3), 178–187 (1978). https://doi.org/10.1109/TSE.1978.231496
3. Gill, A.: Introduction to the Theory of Finite-State Machines. McGraw-Hill, New York (1962)
4. Hennie, F.C.: Fault detecting experiments for sequential circuits. In: 5th Annual Symposium on Switching Circuit Theory and Logical Design, 11–13 November 1964, Princeton, New Jersey, USA, pp. 95–110 (1964). https://doi.org/10.1109/SWCT.1964.8
5. Hierons, R.M., Ural, H.: Reduced length checking sequences. IEEE Trans. Comput. **51**(9), 1111–1117 (2002). https://doi.org/10.1109/TC.2002.1032630
6. Ito, M., Shikishima-Tsuji, K.: Some results on directable automata. In: Karhumäki, J., Maurer, H., Păun, G., Rozenberg, G. (eds.) Theory Is Forever. LNCS, vol. 3113, pp. 125–133. Springer, Heidelberg (2004). https://doi.org/10.1007/978-3-540-27812-2_12
7. Kushik, N., El-Fakih, K., Yevtushenko, N.: Adaptive homing and distinguishing experiments for nondeterministic finite state machines. In: Yenigün, H., Yilmaz, C., Ulrich, A. (eds.) ICTSS 2013. LNCS, vol. 8254, pp. 33–48. Springer, Heidelberg (2013). https://doi.org/10.1007/978-3-642-41707-8_3
8. Kushik, N., El-Fakih, K., Yevtushenko, N., Cavalli, A.R.: On adaptive experiments for nondeterministic finite state machines. STTT **18**(3), 251–264 (2016). https://doi.org/10.1007/s10009-014-0357-7
9. Kushik, N., Yevtushenko, N.: On the length of homing sequences for nondeterministic finite state machines. In: Konstantinidis, S. (ed.) CIAA 2013. LNCS, vol. 7982, pp. 220–231. Springer, Heidelberg (2013). https://doi.org/10.1007/978-3-642-39274-0_20
10. Kushik, N., Yevtushenko, N.: Adaptive homing is in P. In: Proceedings Tenth Workshop on Model Based Testing, MBT 2015, 18th April 2015, London, UK, pp. 73–78 (2015). https://doi.org/10.4204/EPTCS.180.5
11. Kushik, N., Yevtushenko, N., Yenigün, H.: Reducing the complexity of checking the existence and derivation of adaptive synchronizing experiments for nondeterministic FSMs. In: Proceedings of the International Workshop on domAin specific Model-based AppRoaches to vErificaTion and validaTiOn, AMARETTO@MODELSWARD 2016, 19–21 February 2016, Rome, Italy, pp. 83–90 (2016). https://doi.org/10.5220/0005854500830090
12. Lee, D., Yannakakis, M.: Testing finite-state machines: state identification and verification. IEEE Trans. Comput. **43**(3), 306–320 (1994). https://doi.org/10.1109/12.272431
13. Lee, D., Yannakakis, M.: Principles and methods of testing finite state machines-a survey. Proc. IEEE **84**, 1090–1123 (1996). https://doi.org/10.1109/5.533956
14. Petrenko, A., Yevtushenko, N.: Conformance tests as checking experiments for partial nondeterministic FSM. In: Grieskamp, W., Weise, C. (eds.) FATES 2005. LNCS, vol. 3997, pp. 118–133. Springer, Heidelberg (2006). https://doi.org/10.1007/11759744_9
15. Petrenko, A., Yevtushenko, N.: Adaptive testing of deterministic implementations specified by nondeterministic FSMs. In: Wolff, B., Zaïdi, F. (eds.) ICTSS 2011. LNCS, vol. 7019, pp. 162–178. Springer, Heidelberg (2011). https://doi.org/10.1007/978-3-642-24580-0_12
16. Sandberg, S.: 1 homing and synchronizing sequences. In: Broy, M., Jonsson, B., Katoen, J.-P., Leucker, M., Pretschner, A. (eds.) Model-Based Testing of Reactive Systems. LNCS, vol. 3472, pp. 5–33. Springer, Heidelberg (2005). https://doi.org/10.1007/11498490_2

17. Spitsyna, N., El-Fakih, K., Yevtushenko, N.: Studying the separability relation between finite state machines. Softw. Test. Verif. Reliab. **17**(4), 227–241 (2007)
18. Türker, U.C., Yenigün, H.: Hardness and inapproximability of minimizing adaptive distinguishing sequences. Formal Methods Syst. Des. **44**(3), 264–294 (2014). https://doi.org/10.1007/s10703-014-0205-0
19. Yenigün, H., Yevtushenko, N., Kushik, N.: The complexity of checking the existence and derivation of adaptive synchronizing experiments for deterministic FSMs. Inf. Process. Lett. **127**, 49–53 (2017). https://doi.org/10.1016/j.ipl.2017.07.001
20. Yevtushenko, N., Kushik, N.: Decreasing the length of adaptive distinguishing experiments for nondeterministic merging-free finite state machines. In: 2015 IEEE East-West Design & Test Symposium, EWDTS 2015, 26–29 September 2015, Batumi, Georgia, pp. 1–4 (2015). https://doi.org/10.1109/EWDTS.2015.7493120

Multiple Mutation Testing for Timed Finite State Machine with Timed Guards and Timeouts

Omer Nguena Timo[1][✉], Dimitri Prestat[2], and Antoine Rollet[3]

[1] CRIM - Computer Research Institute of Montréal, Montréal, Canada
omer.nguena-timo@crim.ca
[2] UQAM - University of Québec in Montréal, Montréal, Canada
prestat.dimitri@courrier.uqam.ca
[3] LaBRI, Bordeaux INP, University of Bordeaux, Bordeaux, France
antoine.rollet@labri.fr

Abstract. The problem of generating tests detecting all logical and timing faults which can occur in real-time systems is challenging; this is because the number of (timing) faults is potentially too big or infinite. As a result, it might be time consuming to generate an important number of adequate tests. The traditional model based testing approach considers a fault domain as the universe of all machines with a given number of states and input-output alphabet while mutation based approaches define a list of mutants to kill with a test suite. In this paper, we combine the two approaches by developing a mutation testing technique for real-time systems represented with deterministic timed finite state machines with timed guards and timeouts (TFSM-TG). In this approach, fault domains consisting of fault-seeded versions of the specification (mutants) are represented with non-deterministic TFSM-TG. The test generation avoids the one-by-one enumeration of the mutants and is based on constraint solving. We present the results of an empirical proof-of-concept implementation of the proposed approach.

1 Introduction

This paper deals with mutation testing of timed systems. Traditional model-based testing approaches consist of using the model of the specification as a base for the generation of a test suite, then applying it on the implementation of the system under test. This is a black-box testing, meaning that the implementation is considered as unknown, but with the assumption that it may be described by a formal model. It is the so-called test hypothesis. Since it is generally impossible to generate an exhaustive test suite, several approaches have been proposed to limit the size of test cases while providing enough confidence.

This work was partially supported by MEI (Ministère de l'Économie et Innovation) of Gouvernement du Québec.

Concerning FSM model-based testing, one may consider coverage criteria of the specification: the test may be satisfying if for instance all the transitions or all the states are covered by the test suite. Another approach consists of obtaining a sufficient fault coverage: the test suite is guaranteed to detect all faults of a specific nature, e.g. output faults (the output provided by a transition is not correct) or transfer faults (the arrival state of a transition is not correct). As an example, the so called W-method [6] is known to detect both transfer and output faults whereas TT-method [16][1] focuses only on output faults. Generally, fault coverage based methods consider the traditional fault domain as the universe of all machines with a specific alphabet and a given number of states. On the other side, mutation testing is a technique originally developed to verify if a given test suite has a satisfying detecting power. In model-based testing, the principle consists of applying a certain number of small variations, called mutations, on the specification, then to check if these mutations are detected by the test suite. It is generally called "killing the mutants". Note that mutation testing techniques are also used in code based testing, but in this case, the mutations are applied directly in the source code. Dealing with real-time systems increases the difficulty of testing. For instance, faults related to timing errors should also be detected by a test method. For timed model based testing, many different models and conformance relations have already been proposed in the past. Some of them use a discrete representation of the time in the specification model, such as synchronous models [4,13,23], some other methods extend the so-called *ioco* theory [25] by defining a new conformance relation adapted to timed automata [1] with inputs and outputs [2,3,10,12,15,19]. Another category extends the FSM based testing theory using timed extensions of the FSM model and an adapted fault model [7,11,14,28].

The work in [9] proposes a method to generate a test suite with guarantee fault coverage for partial deterministic TFSM extended with timed guards only. TFSM with timed guards and timeouts (TFSM-TG) can express timed behaviors which cannot be expressed with TFSM with timeouts only [5]. More recently [26] proposes a method to generate tests detecting all the nonconforming implementations of an initialized TFSM with timeouts and TFSM-TG. The implementations belong to the traditional fault domain and they can have more states than the specification, up to a given number. The tests are generated by applying the W-method on an (possible huge) abstraction of TFSM-TG with classical FSM and transforming the resulting abstract tests into timed tests.

In this paper, we combine fault coverage based approaches and mutation testing applied to real-time systems. We propose a mutation testing technique for real-time systems represented with complete and deterministic TFSM-TG. We derive complete test suites from mutation machines. A mutation machine can be designed to represent the traditional fault model; but it can also represent customized fault models as well. Customized fault models could be parts of the traditional fault model and they can be covered with a reduced number of tests. The tests generated for the traditional fault model remain valid to test

---

[1] Without special *status* input.

customized fault models. However they could suffer from redundancy and could include useless tests. Running implementations with tests is time consuming. Then, reducing the number of tests to apply is really useful. This is the main motivation of our work. Our test generation approach is based on constraint resolution. It uses the distinguishing automaton of the specification and the mutation machine to determine revealing combs. They characterized the undetected mutants and serve to encode them with Boolean formula. We use a solver to check the satisfiability of the formula and conclude about the completeness of test and generate new tests if needed. We propose an abstraction of timed states of TFSM-TG and we use it to build the distinguishing automaton. This paper extends the approach proposed in [17,21] in a timed context. This is the main contribution of our paper. It is adapted to be applied on the TFSM-TG model. This contribution includes the abstraction of timed states, the definition of the distinguishing automaton for TFSM-TG, and the representation of the transitions passed during executions of TFSM-TG with the so-called combs.

The paper is organized as follows. The next section introduces the general theoretical background, a fault model for TFSMs-TG and the coverage of fault models with complete test suites. Section 3 characterizes detected mutants with revealing combs. In Sect. 4 we introduce an abstraction for executions of TFSM-TG and we define the distinguishing automaton. Section 5 presents an encoding of undetected mutants with Boolean formulas. We present a method for the test analysis and a method for the complete test suite generation in Sect. 6; we also present the results of an empirical proof-of-concept tool. We conclude the paper in Sect. 7.

2 Preliminaries

A timed guard π is an interval $\pi = \langle l_\pi, u_\pi \rangle$ where l_π is a non-negative integer, while u_π is either a non-negative integer or ∞, $l_\pi \leq u_\pi$, and the symbols $\langle$ and $\rangle$ represent $]$ or $[$. For example, the interval $[0,5[$ contains all the non-negative real numbers smaller than 5. We let Π denote the set of timed guards. Given a timed guard $\pi = \langle l_\pi, u_\pi \rangle$ and a real number x, we define $\pi^{-x} = \langle max(0, l_\pi - x), max(0, u_\pi - x) \rangle$.

2.1 Timed FSM with Timed Guards and Timeouts

Definition 1. *A timed finite state machine with timeouts and timed guards* [5] *(TFSM-TG) is a 6-tuple* $\mathcal{S} = (S, s_0, I, O, \lambda_S, \Delta_S)$ *where* S, I *and* O *are finite non-empty set of* states, inputs *and* outputs, *respectively,* s_0 *is the initial state,* $\lambda_S \subseteq S \times I \times \Pi \times O \times S$ *is an input/output transition relation and* $\Delta_S \subseteq S \times \mathbb{N}_{\geq 1} \cup \{\infty\} \times S$ *is a timeout transition relation.*

Remark that we allow defining multiple timeout transitions in states of TFSM-TG, in the opposite of [5]. Later this will be used to compactly represent sets of implementations of a TFSM-TG specification. $\mathcal{S}$ in state s fires an input/output transition (s, i, π, o, s') to reach the transition's *target state* s' and produces output o if input i is applied in transition's *starting state* s when timed guard π is respected; π expresses the minimal and the maximal delays in s to fire the transition. It fires a timeout transition $(s, \delta, s') \in \Delta_S$ defining timeout δ in s and reaches s' if no input is applied in s before δ expires. Let $\delta_{max}(s)$ denote the maximal (possibly infinite) timeout defined in state s. We require that the maximal finite constant in guards of the transitions defined in every state s should be smaller than $\delta_{max}(s)$. Because multiple timeouts can be defined in the same state, S necessarily fires a timeout transition defining $\delta_{max}(s)$ if no input is applied at s before $\delta_{max}(s)$ expires. A clock measuring the amount of the time elapsed in every state is implicitly reset when transitions are fired.

A *timed state* of TFSM-TG S is a pair $(s, x) \in S \times \mathbb{R}_{\geq 0}$ where $s \in S$ is a state of S and $x \in \mathbb{R}_{\geq 0}$ is the current value of the clock and $x < \delta$ for some $\delta \in \mathbb{N}_{\geq 1} \cup \{\infty\}$ such that $(s, \delta, s') \in \Delta_S$. The initial timed state of S is $(s_0, 0)$.

An *execution step* of S in timed state (s, x) corresponds either to the time elapsing or the firing of an input/output or timeout transition; it is *permitted* by a transition t of S. Formally, a tuple $((s, x), a, t, (s', x')) \in (S \times \mathbb{R}_{\geq 0}) \times (((I \times O) \cup \mathbb{R}_{\geq 0}) \times (\lambda_S \cup \Delta_S)) \times (S \times \mathbb{R}_{\geq 0})$ is an execution step if it satisfies one of the following conditions:

- (timeout) $t = (s, \delta, s') \in \Delta_S$, $a \in \mathbb{R}_{\geq 0}$, $x + a = \delta$ and $x' = 0$
- (time-elapsing) $t = (s, \delta, s'') \in \Delta_S$, $a \in \mathbb{R}_{\geq 0}$, $x + a < \delta$, $x' = x + a$ and $s' = s$
- (input/output) $t = (s, i, \langle l, u \rangle, o, s') \in \lambda_S$, $x \in \langle l, u \rangle$, $a = (i, o)$ with $(i, o) \in I \times O$ and $x' = 0$

In the time-elapsing step, the target state s'' of t and s' can be different. This is because the timeout δ is not expired and t is not fired; $\delta_{max}(s)$ is never exceeded.

An *execution* of S in timed state (s_0, x_0) is a finite sequence of steps $e = stp_1 stp_2 \ldots stp_n$ with $stp_k = ((s_{k-1}, x_{k-1}), a_k, t_k, (s_k, x_k))$, $k \in [1, n]$ such that stp_1 is not an input/output step and stp_k is an input/output step implies that stp_{k-1} is a time-elapsing step for every $k \in [1..n]$. If needed, the elapsing of zero time unit can be inserted before input/output steps which are not immediately preceded with a time-elapsing step. The *timed input/output sequence* of execution e is the sequence $(i_1, o_1)d_1(i_2, o_2)d_2 \ldots (i_l, o_l)d_l$ in $((I \times O) \times \mathbb{R}_{\geq 0})^*$ such that $(i_1, o_1)(i_2, o_2) \ldots (i_l, o_l)$ is the sequence of input/output pairs occurring in the execution and $d_1 d_2 \ldots d_l \in \mathbb{R}_{\geq 0}^l$ is a sequence of non-negative real numbers and t_k is the amount of the time elapsed since the occurrence of i_{k-1} or the beginning of the execution if no input has occurred. l is smaller than the number of steps in the execution. The *timed input sequence* and the *timed output sequence* of the execution e are $inp(e) = i_1 d_1 i_2 d_2 \ldots i_l d_l$ and $out(e) = o_1 d_1 o_2 d_2 \ldots o_l d_l$, respectively; they are said to be applicable and produced in (s, x), respectively. We denote by $inp(s, x)$ the set of timed input sequences applicable in (s, x). Given a timed input sequence α, let $out_S((s, x), \alpha)$ denote the set of all timed output sequences which can be produced by S when α is applied in s, i.e., $out((s, x), \alpha) = \{out(e) \mid e$ is an execution of S in (s, x) and $inp(e) = \alpha\}$.

We let $Execs$ and $Execs(\alpha)$ denote the set of executions of S and the set of executions with the timed input sequence α.

Transitions starting in the same state are called *compatible* if they are timeout transitions or have the same input and the intersection of their timed guards is non-empty. A TFSM-TG S is *deterministic* (DTFSM-TG) if it has no compatible transition; otherwise, it is *non-deterministic*. S is *initially connected* if every state of S is part of a reachable timed state. Let $\lambda_S(s, i)$ denote the set of input/output transitions defined in state s with input i. S is *complete* if the union of the timed guards of the transitions in $\lambda_{S(s,i)}$ equals $[0, \infty[$ for every $(s, i) \in S \times I$; it implies that every $i \in I$ is the input of at least one input/output step from every reachable timed state of S. Note that $inp(s, x) = (I \times \mathbb{R}_{\geq 0})^*$ for every timed state (s, x) of a complete machine S.

We define distinguishability and equivalence relations between timed states of complete TFSMs-TG. Then, we extend these relations to TFSM-TG. Similar notions were introduced in [28]. Intuitively, timed states producing different timed output sequences in response to the same timed input sequence are distinguishable. Formally, let (s, x_s) and (m, x_m) be the timed states of two complete TFSMs-TG defined on the same input and output sets. Given a timed input sequence α, (s, x_s) and (m, x_m) are *distinguishable* with α denoted $(s, x_s) \not\simeq_\alpha (m, x_m)$, if the sets of timed output sequences in $out((s, x_s), \alpha)$ and $out((m, x_m), \alpha)$ differ; otherwise they are *equivalent* and we write $(s, x_s) \simeq (m, x_m)$, i.e., if the sets of timed output sequences coincide for every timed input sequence α. Two TFSM-TG are equivalent if their initial timed states are indistinguishable; otherwise they are distinguishable with a timed input sequence.

Henceforth the TFSMs-TG are complete and initially connected.

2.2   Mutants and Fault Model

Let $S = (S, s_0, I, O, \lambda_S, \Delta_S)$ be a complete DTFSM-TG, called the *specification* machine. A mutant is a variant of the specification and represents a possibly faulty implementation that should be detected by tests; it is also a deterministic and complete TFSM-TG. A mutant can have fewer or more states than the specification, up to a specified bound. The faults can be introduced by performing combinations of the following atomic mutation operations: changing the target state of a transition (transfer fault), changing the output of a transition (output fault), changing a timeout, merging the timed guards of transitions, splitting the timed guard of a transition, adding an extra-state. Similar operations were defined in [20,27] for testing other types of timed machines. Our operations are adapted to TFSM-TG. We compactly represent mutants with a mutation machine. Intuitively, mutants and the specification are all sub-machines of a global mutation machine describing the fault model.

TFSM-TG $S = (S, s_0, I, O, \lambda_S, \Delta_S)$ is a *sub-machine* of TFSM-TG $M = (M, m_0, I, O, \lambda_M, \Delta_M)$ if $S \subseteq M$, $s_0 = m_0$, $\lambda_S \subseteq \lambda_M$ and $\Delta_S \subseteq \Delta_M$.

Definition 2. *A non-deterministic TFSM-TG $M = (M, m_0, I, O, \lambda_M, \Delta_M)$ is a mutation machine of S if S is a sub-machine of M. Transitions in λ_M but not in λ_S or in Δ_M but not in Δ_S are called* mutated.

A *mutant* is a deterministic and complete sub-machine of a mutation machine $\mathcal{M}$ different from the specification. We let $Mut(\mathcal{M})$ denote the set of mutants in $\mathcal{M}$. Let $\Delta_{\mathcal{M}}(m)$ denote the set of timeout transitions defined in m. For a state m, every mutant defines exactly one timeout transition of $\Delta_{\mathcal{M}}$ and a subset z_{mi} of transitions of $\lambda_{\mathcal{M}}(m,i)$, for every $(m,i) \in M \times I$. The subset z_{mi} satisfies the following three *cluster conditions*: (1) it is non-empty, (2) the transitions in z_{mi} are not compatible with each other and (3) the union of their timed guards equals $[0, \infty[$. We let $Z_{mi} = \{z_{mi}^1, z_{mi}^2, \ldots, z_{mi}^l\}$ be the maximal set of subsets of $\lambda_{\mathcal{M}}(m,i)$ such that z_{mi}^k satisfies the three cluster conditions, for each $k = 1 \ldots l$. The number of mutants is $|Mut(\mathcal{M})| = \prod_{(m,i) \in M \times I} |Z_{mi}| \times \prod_{m \in M} |\Delta_{\mathcal{M}}(m)| - 1$.

Faults in mutants are represented with mutated transitions which can be viewed as alternatives for transitions of the specification. Note that changes of delays to fire input/output transitions cannot be expressed if the specification is a TFSM with timeouts only; this is because the timed guard for every input in a TFSM with timeouts is always $[0, \infty[$. Some executions of non-deterministic sub-machines of $\mathcal{M}$ are not executions of any mutants or the specification. We can show that $\bigcup_{P \in Mut(\mathcal{M}) \cup \{S\}} Exec_P(\alpha) \subseteq Exec_{\mathcal{M}}(\alpha)$.

A transition t is *suspicious* in $\mathcal{M}$ if $\mathcal{M}$ defines another transition t' compatible with t. In other words, t and t' specify possible behaviors of different mutants. A transition of the specification is called *untrusted* if it is suspicious in the mutation machine; otherwise, it is *trusted*. Every trusted transition is defined in each mutant. The set of suspicious transitions of $\mathcal{M}$ is partitioned into a set of untrusted transitions all defined in the specification and the set of mutated transitions undefined in the specification. We let $Susp_O$ denote the set of suspicious transitions in an artifact O containing transitions.

Figure 1b presents a mutation machine $\mathcal{M}_1$. Transitions represented with dashed lines are mutated. Transition identifiers appear in brackets. $\mathcal{M}_1$ is non-deterministic because, e.g., t_4 and t_6 are compatible or the two timeout transitions t_8 and t_{11} start from s_2. The suspicious transitions in $Susp_{\mathcal{M}_1}$ are $t_4, t_5, t_6, t_8, t_{11}, t_{12}, t_{13}, t_{16}, t_{17}$; the other transitions are trusted. The specification $\mathcal{S}_1$ in Fig. 1a is deterministic; it defines all the trusted transitions and the untrusted transitions t_4, t_8, t_{12}. $\Delta_{\mathcal{M}_1}(s_1) = \{t_2\}$, $Z_{s_1 a} = \{\{t_1\}\}$, $Z_{s_1 b} = \{\{t_3\}\}$, $\Delta_{\mathcal{M}_1}(s_2) = \{t_8, t_{11}\}$, $Z_{s_2 a} = \{\{t_7, t_9, t_{10}\}\}$, $Z_{s_2 b} = \{\{t_4\}, \{t_5, t_6\}\}$, $\Delta_{\mathcal{M}_3}(s_1) = \{t_{15}\}$, $Z_{s_3 a} = \{\{t_{12}\}, \{t_{13}, t_{16}, t_{17}\}\}$ and $Z_{s_3 b} = \{\{t_{14}\}\}$. $Mut(\mathcal{M}_1)$ contains seven mutants; two of them appear in Fig. 2a and b. The mutants are obtained from the specification by changing the behavior of suspicious transitions, which is done by replacing the untrusted transitions in the specification by other suspicious transitions they are compatible with. The mutant in Fig. 2b has a different behavior in state s_3 for input a. The mutants and the specification have the same behavior in s_1 for input a; this is because t_1 is trusted.

Let $\mathcal{P}$ be a mutant with an initial state p_0 of the mutation machine $\mathcal{M}$ of $\mathcal{S}$. We use the equivalence relation $\simeq$ to define conforming mutants.

Definition 3. *Mutant $\mathcal{P}$ conforms to $\mathcal{S}$, if $(p_0, 0) \simeq (s_0, 0)$; otherwise, it is nonconforming and a timed input sequence α such that $(p_0, 0) \not\simeq_\alpha (s_0, 0)$ is said to detect $\mathcal{P}$. $\mathcal{P}$ survives α if α does not detect $\mathcal{P}$.*

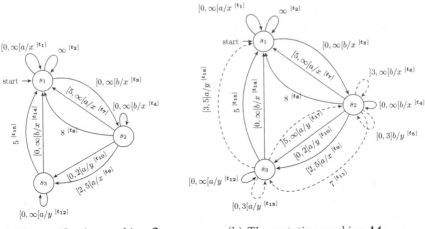

(a) The specification machine $\mathcal{S}_1$ (b) The mutation machine $\mathcal{M}_1$

Fig. 1. A mutation machine for a specification machine; s_1 is the initial state

The set $Mut(\mathcal{M})$ of all mutants in mutation machine $\mathcal{M}$ is called a *fault domain* for $\mathcal{S}$. If $\mathcal{M}$ is deterministic and complete then $\mathcal{M}$ includes only the specification and $Mut(\mathcal{M})$ is empty. A general *fault model* is the tuple $\langle \mathcal{S}, \simeq, Mut(\mathcal{M}) \rangle$ following [18,22]. The conformance relation partitions the set $Mut(\mathcal{M})$ into conforming mutants and nonconforming ones which we need to detect.

Definition 4. *A test for $\langle \mathcal{S}, \simeq, Mut(\mathcal{M}) \rangle$ is a timed input sequence. A complete test suite for $\langle \mathcal{S}, \simeq, Mut(\mathcal{M}) \rangle$ is a set of tests detecting all nonconforming mutants in $Mut(\mathcal{M})$.*

We address the problem of checking the completeness of a test suite and the problem of generating a complete test suite for a fault model $\langle \mathcal{S}, \simeq, Mut(\mathcal{M}) \rangle$, where the specification machine $\mathcal{S}$ is deterministic and complete and the mutation machine can have more states than $\mathcal{S}$. Our approach consists in eliminating, from the fault model, the mutants detected by tests meanwhile avoiding their one-by-one enumeration. Undetected mutants will serve to generate new tests.

3   Revealing Combs for Characterizing Detected Mutants

We introduce combs to characterize mutants having common executions of the mutation machine since mutation machine includes all the mutants. The mutants defining all the transitions in a comb have common executions and can be detected with the same test. The comb for an execution e is the sequence of transitions permitting the steps in e; it is denoted by π_e. The transitions in combs do not necessarily form paths in the state-transition diagram of $\mathcal{M}$. This is because they contain non-fired time-out transitions permitting time-elapsing

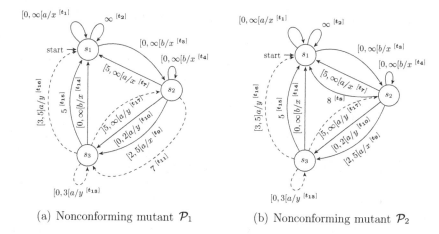

(a) Nonconforming mutant $\mathcal{P}_1$ (b) Nonconforming mutant $\mathcal{P}_2$

Fig. 2. Two mutants included in the mutation machine $\mathcal{M}_1$ in Fig. 1b

steps when timeouts are not expired. Without the time-elapsing steps, input-output steps would not be possible because a certain delay is needed for reaching a timed guard; delays are possible up to the expiration of maximal timeouts. Fired timeout transitions also occur in combs. Let $\Pi_{\mathcal{Q}}(\alpha) = \{\pi_e | e \in Exec_{\mathcal{Q}}(\alpha)\}$ denote the set of combs for the executions of $\mathcal{Q}$ with timed input sequence α and $\Pi_{\mathcal{Q}}$ denote the set of combs for the executions of a TFSM-TG $\mathcal{Q}$. It holds that $\bigcup_{\mathcal{P} \in Mut(\mathcal{M}) \cup \{\mathcal{S}\}} \Pi_{\mathcal{P}}(\alpha) \subseteq \Pi_{\mathcal{M}}(\alpha)$ and $\bigcup_{\mathcal{P} \in Mut(\mathcal{M}) \cup \{\mathcal{S}\}} \Pi_{\mathcal{P}} \subseteq \Pi_{\mathcal{M}}$. An execution $e \in Exec_{\mathcal{M}}(\alpha)$ is called *unexpected* if there is $e' \in Exec_{\mathcal{S}}(\alpha)$ such that $out(e') \neq out(e)$; otherwise it is expected and $out(e)$ is called expected.

Definition 5. *A comb is* deterministic *if its transitions are pairwise non-compatible. A deterministic comb is* revealing *if it corresponds to an unexpected execution of the mutation machine.*

The executions of the mutants correspond to deterministic combs. Only executions of a non-deterministic sub-machine of $\mathcal{M}$ can correspond to a non-deterministic comb. Mutants included in $\mathcal{M}$ can have common executions. Because we want to avoid the enumeration of the mutants one-by-one, we would like to identify the mutants which have an execution in common, i.e., they are *involved* in the execution. A mutant $\mathcal{P}$ is involved in an execution e of $\mathcal{M}$ if $\mathcal{P}$ defines all the suspicious transitions in the comb π_e of e, i.e., $Susp_{\pi_e} \subseteq \lambda_{\mathcal{P}} \cup \Delta_{\mathcal{P}}$. This is because every mutant defines all the trusted transitions in $\mathcal{M}$ and only suspicious transitions vary between the mutants. We let $Rev_{\mathcal{M}}(\alpha)$ denote the set of revealing combs for executions with timed input sequence α. It holds that $Rev_{\mathcal{M}}(\alpha) = \bigcup_{\mathcal{P} \in Mut(\mathcal{M})} Rev_{\mathcal{P}}(\alpha)$. The following lemma indicates that detected mutants are involved in revealing combs of the mutation machine.

Lemma 1. *$Mut(\mathcal{M})$ contains nonconforming mutants if and only if $Rev_{\mathcal{M}}(\alpha) \neq \emptyset$, for some timed input sequence α.*

Lemma 2. *Test α detects mutant $\mathcal{P}$ if and only if there exists $e \in Exec_{\mathcal{M}}(\alpha)$ such that $\pi_e \in Rev_{\mathcal{M}}(\alpha)$ and $Susp_{\pi_e} \subseteq \lambda_{\mathcal{P}} \cup \Delta_{\mathcal{P}}$.*

Corollary 1. *Mutant $\mathcal{P}$ survives α if and only if for every $\pi \in Rev_{\mathcal{M}}(\alpha)$, some transitions in $Susp_{\pi}$ do not belong to $\lambda_{\mathcal{P}} \cup \Delta_{\mathcal{P}}$.*

$e_1 = (s_1, 0)0.5^{[t_2]}(s_1, 0.5)b/x^{[t_3]}(s_2, 0)7^{[t_8]}(s_2, 7)0.5^{[t_8]}(s_2, 7.5)a/x^{[t_7]}(s_1, 0)$ is an execution of $\mathcal{M}_1$ in Fig. 1b; it is also an execution of $\mathcal{S}_1$. The transitions permitting the steps appear in brackets and also serve to identify the comb. The first, third and fourth steps in e_1 are time-elapsing. t_8 permits the fourth step. A distinct execution, let us call it e_2, could involve t_{11} at the fourth step. Another distinct execution is possible by making a timeout step at the third step, i.e., by firing t_{11}. The comb $\pi_{e_1} = t_2 \curvearrowright t_3 t_8 t_8 \curvearrowright t_7$ is for e_1 does not form a path in $\mathcal{M}_1$; the symbol "$\curvearrowright$" is inserted between timeout transitions permitting time-elapsing steps which just precede input/output steps. π_{e_1} is deterministic and a mutant can define all the suspicious transitions in it. π_{e_1} is not revealing because the timed output sequence of e_1, $x0.5x7.5$ is expected. The mutants defining only the suspicious transitions occurring in π_{e_1} and all the trusted transitions cannot be detected by $b0.5a7.5$. $\pi_{e_2} = t_2 \curvearrowright t_3 t_8 t_{11} \curvearrowright t_7$ is not deterministic because t_8 and t_{11} are compatible and suspicious; a mutant cannot define these two transitions. π_{e_2} is not revealing since it is not deterministic.

4   Distinguishing Automaton and Revealing Combs

The distinguishing automaton for a specification $\mathcal{S}$ and a mutation machine $\mathcal{M}$ is aimed to represent synchronous executions of $\mathcal{S}$ and the mutants in $\mathcal{M}$. It will be used to identify unexpected executions of the mutants and the corresponding combs without enumerating the mutants one-by-one. Each of its states is composed of a timed state of $\mathcal{S}$ and a timed state of $\mathcal{M}$. Each transition between two states of the automaton represents a synchronization between a transition of $\mathcal{S}$ and a transition of $\mathcal{M}$. Because $\mathcal{S}$ and $\mathcal{M}$ could have an infinite number of reachable timed states, a naive definition of the distinguishing automaton could include an infinite number of the automaton's states. For this reason our definition is based on a new notion of abstract timed states for TFSM-TG.

4.1   Abstract Timed State for TFSM-TG

We introduce a new notion of abstract execution which we show to be equivalent to the notion of execution described in Sect. 2. In abstract executions the range for clock values is finite while it is infinite in executions. In particular, by increasing a clock value by one in a state which defines the infinite timeout, the value of the clock will continuously increase up to a value which depends on the number of time-elapsing steps. It happens that after a certain threshold value, the exact value of the clock is not necessary to determine transitions which can be fired. In state m, the threshold value is the maximal finite integer used in input-output and timeout transitions starting at state m, denoted by max_m.

We let max_m^+ be a special number representing any real number greater than max_m, the maximal finite value in transitions starting from m; it has the following arithmetic properties: $max_m^+ \in]max_m, \infty[$, $max_m^+ + k = max_m^+$ for every finite real number $k \geq 0$ and $max_m^+ + \infty = \infty$.

The abstract time domain for the clock when the TFSM-TG is in state m is $Atd_m = [0, max_m] \cup \{max_m^+\}$ where $[0, max_m]$ is an integer interval. For machine with states in M, the abstract time domain is $Atd_S = \bigcup_{m \in S} Atd_m$. An abstract execution of a TFSM-TG is defined with abstract execution steps which only consider abstract time domains for clocks and arithmetic properties introduced for the domain. Every execution corresponds to an abstract execution. The latter can be obtained from the former by replacing every timed state (s, x) with (s, max_m^+) wherever x is greater than max_m. We can show that there is an abstract execution of a TFSM-TG with timed input/output sequence α/β if and only if there is an execution of the TFSM-TG with α/β. This indicates that abstract executions can be used instead of executions.

4.2   Distinguishing Automaton

Definition 6. *Given a specification machine* $\mathcal{S} = (S, s_0, I, O, \lambda_\mathcal{S}, \Delta_\mathcal{S})$ *and a mutation machine* $\mathcal{M} = (M, m_0, I, O, \lambda_\mathcal{M}, \Delta_\mathcal{M})$, *a finite automaton* $\mathcal{D} = (C \cup \{\nabla\}, c_0, I, \lambda_\mathcal{D}, \Delta_\mathcal{D}, \nabla)$, *where* $C \subseteq S \times S \times Atd_S \times Atd_M$, $\lambda_\mathcal{D} \subseteq C \times I \times \Pi \times C$ *is the input transition relation,* $\Delta_\mathcal{D} \subseteq C \times (\mathbb{N}_{\geq 1} \cup \{\infty\}) \times C$ *is the timeout transition relation and* ∇ *is the accepting (sink) state, is the* distinguishing automaton with timeouts and timed guards *for* $\mathcal{S}$ *and* $\mathcal{M}$*, if it holds that:*

- $c_0 = (s_0, m_0, 0, 0)$
- *For each* $(s, m, x_s, x_m) \in C$ *and* $i \in I$
  $(\mathcal{R}_1) : ((s, m, x_s, x_m), i, \pi_s^{-x_s} \cap \pi_m^{-x_m}, (s', m', 0, 0)) \in \lambda_\mathcal{D}$ *if there exists*
  $(s, i, \pi_s, o_s, s') \in \lambda_\mathcal{S}, (m, i, \pi_m, o_m, m') \in \lambda_\mathcal{M}$ *s.t.* $\pi_s^{-x_s} \cap \pi_m^{-x_m} \neq \emptyset$ *and*
  $o_s = o_m$
  $(\mathcal{R}_2) : ((s, m, x_s, x_m), i, \pi_s^{-x_s} \cap \pi_m^{-x_m}, \nabla) \in \lambda_\mathcal{D}$ *if there exists* (s, i, π_s, o_s, s')
  $\in \lambda_\mathcal{S}, (m, i, \pi_m, o_m, m') \in \lambda_\mathcal{M}$ *s.t.* $\pi_s^{-x_s} \cap \pi_m^{-x_m} \neq \emptyset$ *and* $o_s \neq o_m$
- *For each* $(s, m, x_s, x_m) \in C$ *and the only timeout transition* $(s, \delta_s, s') \in \Delta_\mathcal{S}$
  defined in the state of the deterministic specification
  $(\mathcal{R}_3) : ((s, m, x_s, x_m), \delta_m - x_m, (s', m', 0, 0)) \in \Delta_\mathcal{D}$ *if there exists* (m, δ_m, m')
  $\in \Delta_\mathcal{M}$ *s.t.* $\delta_s - x_s = \delta_m - x_m$ *and* $\delta_m - x_m > 0$
  $(\mathcal{R}_4) : ((s, m, x_s, x_m), \delta_m - x_m, (s, m', max_s^+, 0)) \in \Delta_\mathcal{D}$ *if there exists*
  $(m, \delta_m, m') \in \Delta_\mathcal{M}$ *such that* $\delta_m - x_m > 0$, $\delta_s - x_s > \delta_m - x_m$, *and*
  $x_s + \delta_m - x_m > max_s$
  $(\mathcal{R}_5) : ((s, m, x_s, x_m), \delta_m - x_m, (s, m', x_s + \delta_m - x_m, 0)) \in \Delta_\mathcal{D}$ *if there exists*
  $(m, \delta_m, m') \in \Delta_\mathcal{M}$ *such that* $\delta_m - x_m > 0$, $\delta_s - x_s > \delta_m - x_m$, *and*
  $x_s + \delta_m - x_m \leq max_s$
  $(\mathcal{R}_6) : ((s, m, x_s, x_m), \delta_s - x_s, (s', m, 0, max_m^+)) \in \Delta_\mathcal{D}$ *if there exists*
  $(m, \delta_m, m') \in \Delta_\mathcal{M}$ *such that* $\delta_s - x_s > 0$, $\delta_s - x_s < \delta_m - x_m$, *and*
  $x_m + \delta_s - x_s > max_m$

$(\mathcal{R}_7) : ((s, m, x_s, x_m), \delta_s - x_s, (s', m, 0, x_m + \delta_s - x_s)) \in \Delta_{\mathcal{D}}$ *if there exists*
$(m, \delta_m, m') \in \Delta_{\mathcal{M}}$ *such that* $\delta_s - x_s > 0$, $\delta_s - x_s < \delta_m - x_m$, *and*
$x_m + \delta_s - x_s \leq max_m$

- $(\nabla, i, [0, \infty[, \nabla) \in \lambda_{\mathcal{D}}$ *for all* $i \in I$ *and* $(\nabla, \infty, \nabla) \in \Delta_{\mathcal{D}}$

In a state (s, m, x_s, s_m) of $\mathcal{D}$, (s, x_s) and (m, s_m) represents timed state of the specification and mutation machines. The two machines synchronize on input actions (see $\mathcal{R}_1$, $\mathcal{R}_2$) and time delays. They do not synchronize on timeout, i.e., the expiration of a timeout in a machine is not necessarily synchronized with the expiration of a timeout in the other machine (case of $\mathcal{R}_4$ to $\mathcal{R}_7$); A synchronization of timeout transitions may occur depending on the respective clocks (see $\mathcal{R}_4$). The automaton also uses a sink state ∇ to identify synchronizations on an input but with different outputs. An execution of $\mathcal{D}$ from a timed state (c, x) is a sequence of steps between timed states of $\mathcal{D}$; it can be defined similarly to that for a TFSM-TG. An execution starting from $(c_0, 0)$ and ending at ∇ is called *accepted*. $\mathcal{D}$ is complete because $\mathcal{S}$ and $\mathcal{M}$ are complete. Every execution of $\mathcal{D}$ corresponds to an execution of the specification $\mathcal{S}$ and an execution of the mutation machine $\mathcal{M}$. Indeed, transitions in $\mathcal{D}$ are directly defined by execution steps of $\mathcal{S}$ and $\mathcal{M}$ and indirectly by transitions of $\mathcal{S}$ and $\mathcal{M}$ permitting the steps. We let $e = (e_1, e_2)$ represent an execution of $\mathcal{D}$, where e_1 and e_2 are the corresponding executions of $\mathcal{S}$ and $\mathcal{M}$. Clearly $inp(e) = inp(e_1) = inp(e_2)$. For every execution e_1 of $\mathcal{S}$ there is an execution e_2 of $\mathcal{M}$ such that $e = (e_1, e_2)$ is an execution of $\mathcal{D}$. For every execution e_2 of $\mathcal{M}$ there is an execution e_1 of $\mathcal{S}$ such that $e = (e_1, e_2)$ is an execution of $\mathcal{D}$. Moreover e_1 and e_1' have the same timed input/output sequence whenever (e_1, e_2) and (e_1', e_2) represent executions of $\mathcal{D}$. It means that $\mathcal{D}$ represents the comparisons of timed input/output sequences of $\mathcal{M}$ with an expected timed input/output sequence of $\mathcal{S}$.

Lemma 3. *An execution e_2 of $\mathcal{M}$ is unexpected if and only if there is an execution e_1 of $\mathcal{S}$ such that $e = (e_1, e_2)$ is an accepted execution of $\mathcal{D}$.*

Only unexpected executions of $\mathcal{M}$ having deterministic combs can be executions of mutants; the combs for such executions are revealing; they could be identified in checking whether $Mut(\mathcal{M})$ contains nonconforming mutants.

Lemma 4. $Rev_{\mathcal{M}}(\alpha) \neq \emptyset$ *if and only if there exists an accepted execution $e = (e_1, e_2)$ of $\mathcal{D}$ such that π_{e_2} is a deterministic comb and $\alpha = inp(e_2)$.*

The deterministic revealing combs for a test α can be computed from the distinguishing automaton for the specification and mutation machines. Their computation works as follows. First we compute the accepted executions of the distinguishing automaton $\mathcal{D}$ with α; this can be done by defining a product an automaton for α and $\mathcal{D}$, which we do not formalize for the sake of simplicity. Each accepted execution corresponds to an execution of the specification and an unexpected execution of the mutation machine; the deterministic combs for the unexpected execution of the mutation machine belong to $Rev_{\mathcal{M}}(\alpha)$.

The following corollary is a consequence of Lemmas 4 and 1.

Corollary 2. *Mut($\mathcal{M}$) contains nonconforming mutants detectable with α if and only if there exists an accepted execution $e = (e_1, e_2)$ of $\mathcal{D}$ such that π_{e_2} is a deterministic comb and $\alpha = inp(e_2)$.*

5   Boolean Formulas Encoding (Un)Detected Mutants

We encode the test-surviving mutants with Boolean formulas over Boolean variables; each variable corresponds to a transition in $\mathcal{M}$. Henceforth we let variable t represent both a transition in $\mathcal{M}$ and the corresponding variable. A solution of a Boolean formula assigns *True* or *False* to the variables, which we can use to choose a (mutant) sub-machine in $\mathcal{M}$. Intuitively, we can replace in a mutant a suspicious transition by another (compatible) suspicious transition to obtain a different mutant. However, every mutant defines all the trusted transitions. We say that a sub-machine (possibly a mutant) of $\mathcal{M}$ is *determined* by a Boolean formula φ defined over the transition variables of $\mathcal{M}$ if: (1) the sub-machine includes all the trusted transitions in $\mathcal{M}$ and, (2) there exists a solution of φ which assigns *True* to a transition variable if and only if the corresponding transition is in the sub-machine. The encoding Boolean formula is the conjunction of two sub-formulas. The first sub-formula encodes the complementary of the detected mutants, which can contain mutants and non-deterministic sub-machines of the mutation machine as well. The second sub-formula encodes all the mutants only.

The encoding of the detected mutants uses the suspicious transitions in revealing combs corresponding to the tests in a test suites. This encoding is inspired by Lemma 2. Given a set of revealing combs $Rev_{\mathcal{M}}(\alpha)$ for test α, we let $\varphi_\alpha = \bigvee_{\pi \in Rev_{\mathcal{M}}(\alpha)} \left(\bigwedge_{t \in Susp_\pi} t \right)$ be a Boolean formula over the variables for the suspicious transitions in revealing combs of $Rev_{\mathcal{M}}(\alpha)$. φ_α encodes all the mutants and also non-deterministic sub-machines involved in revealing combs; this means that every solution of φ_α determines a sub-machine of $\mathcal{M}$ that defines all the transitions in a comb $\pi \in Rev_{\mathcal{M}}(\alpha)$. So, φ_α determines all the sub-machines with unexpected outputs for input α. Let $\neg\varphi$ denote the negation of φ. Every solution of $\neg\varphi_\alpha$ sets variables for some suspicious transitions in every revealing comb to *False*; this indicates that every mutant determined by $\neg\varphi_\alpha$ does not define some suspicious transitions from each comb in $Rev_{\mathcal{M}}(\alpha)$.

Lemma 5. *For every $\mathcal{P}$ determined by $\neg\varphi_\alpha$ and every $\pi \in Rev_{\mathcal{M}}(\alpha)$, there exists $t \in Susp_\pi$ which does not belong to $\lambda_\mathcal{P} \cup \Delta_\mathcal{P}$.*

The following lemma is a consequence of Lemma 5 and Corollary 1.

Lemma 6. *Every mutant determined by $\neg\varphi_\alpha$ survives α.*

Let $TS = \{\alpha_1, \alpha_2, \ldots, \alpha_n\}$ be a test suite. We define $\varphi_{TS} = \bigvee_{\alpha_i \in TS} \varphi_{\alpha_i}$. The formula φ_{TS} determines all the sub-machines which produce unexpected outputs for an input $\alpha_i \in TS$, i.e., the sub-machines detected by at least one test in TS. A determined sub-machine is not necessarily a mutant; so we need to encode all the mutants in $\mathcal{M}$. We can proof the following lemma by using Lemma 6.

Lemma 7. *Every mutant determined by $\neg\varphi_{TS}$ survives the test suite TS.*

Note that $\neg\varphi_{TS}$ determines not only mutants but also non-deterministic sub-machines of the mutation machine $\mathcal{M} = (M, m_0, I, O, \lambda_{\mathcal{M}}, \Delta_{\mathcal{M}})$. In other to exclude these non-deterministic sub-machines of $\mathcal{M}$, we encode the set of mutants with a Boolean formula $\varphi_{\mathcal{M}}$. Each of its solutions determines exactly one timeout transition in every state (which is expressed by (Eq. 2)) and a subset $z_{mi} \in Z_{mi}$, where Z_{mi} is the maximal set of subsets of $\lambda_{\mathcal{M}}(m, i)$ satisfying the cluster conditions introduced in Sect. 2.2. Let us define:

$$\varphi_{\mathcal{M}} = \bigwedge_{m\in M}\left(\varphi_{\Delta m} \wedge \bigwedge_{i\in I}\varphi_{mi}\right) \wedge \bigvee_{t\in\lambda_S\cup\Delta_S} \neg t \tag{1}$$

where

$$\varphi_{\Delta m} = \bigvee_{t\in\Delta_{\mathcal{M}}(m)}\left(t \wedge \bigwedge_{t'\in\Delta_{\mathcal{M}}(m),t'\neq t} \neg t'\right) \tag{2}$$

$$\varphi_{mi} = \bigvee_{z\in Z_{mi}}\left(\varphi_z \wedge \bigwedge_{w\in Z_{mi},w\neq z} \neg\varphi_w\right) \text{ and } \varphi_z = \bigwedge_{t\in z} t \tag{3}$$

Each solution of $\varphi_{\Delta m}$ sets to *True* the variable of exactly one timeout transition defined in m. All the variables in exactly one set Z_{mi} has all its variables assigned to *True* by each solution of φ_{mi}. The variable for each trusted transition is set to *True* in every solution of $\varphi_{m\delta}$; this is because they are not compatible with any other transitions and thus defined by every mutant. We can conclude that each solution of $\varphi_{\mathcal{M}}$ determines a mutant in $Mut(\mathcal{M})$ and every mutant is determined by a solution of $\varphi_{\mathcal{M}}$, i.e., $\varphi_{\mathcal{M}}$ determines all the mutants in $Mut(\mathcal{M})$. According to its definition, every solution of $\varphi_{\mathcal{M}}$ never assigns *True* to the variables for compatible transitions and determines a mutant.

Lemma 8. *$\varphi_{\mathcal{M}}$ determines the mutants in $Mut(\mathcal{M})$.*

We can prove the following theorem by using Lemmas 8 and 7.

Theorem 1. *Formula $\varphi_{\mathcal{M}} \wedge \neg\varphi_{TS}$ determines exactly the mutants undetected by the test suite TS.*

For $\mathcal{M}_1$ in Fig. 1b, $\varphi_{\Delta s_2} = (t_8 \wedge \neg t_{11}) \vee (t_{11} \wedge \neg t_8)$, $\varphi_{s_2 a} = t_7 \wedge t_9 \wedge t_{10}$ and $\varphi_{s_2 b} = (t_4 \wedge \neg t_5 \wedge \neg t_6) \vee (t_5 \wedge t_6 \wedge \neg t_4)$. $\varphi_{\Delta s_2} \wedge \varphi_{s_2 a} \wedge \varphi_{s_2 b}$ determines the transitions starting at s_2 in a mutant. We can make similar formulas for s_1 and s_3, according to the sets $Z_{s_1 a}, Z_{s_1 b}, Z_{s_2 a}, Z_{s_2 b}, Z_{s_3 a}$ and $Z_{s_3 b}$ presented before Definition 3. Finally, $\varphi_{\mathcal{M}_1} = \varphi_{\Delta s_1} \wedge \varphi_{s_1 a} \wedge \varphi_{s_1 b} \wedge \varphi_{\Delta s_2} \wedge \varphi_{s_2 a} \wedge \varphi_{s_2 b} \wedge \varphi_{\Delta s_3} \wedge \varphi_{s_3 a} \wedge \varphi_{s_3 b}$.

The test $\alpha_1 = b0.5a7.5$ triggers executions in the distinguishing automaton for $\mathcal{M}_1$. These executions correspond to the expected execution e_1, e_2 and :
$e_3 = (s_1, 0)0.5^{[t_2]}(s_1, 0.5)b/x^{[t_3]}(s_2, 0)7^{[t_{11}]}(s_3, 0)0.5^{[t_{15}]}(s_3, 0.5)a/y^{[t_{12}]}(s_1, 0)$ and
$e_4 = (s_1, 0)0.5^{[t_2]}(s_1, 0.5)b/x^{[t_3]}(s_2, 0)7^{[t_{11}]}(s_3, 0)0.5^{[t_{15}]}(s_3, 0.5)a/y^{[t_{13}]}(s_1, 0)$.

The comb for e_3 and e_4 are $\pi_{e_3} = t_2 \curvearrowright t_3 t_{11} t_{15} \curvearrowright t_{12}$ and $\pi_{e_4} = t_2 \curvearrowright t_3 t_{11} t_{15} \curvearrowright t_{13}$; they are revealing because the produced timed output sequence $x0.5y7.5$ is unexpected; so they characterize the mutants detected by test α_1. We recall that π_{e_1} and π_{e_2} are not revealing. The formula $\neg\varphi_{\alpha_1} = \neg((t_{11} \wedge t_{12}) \vee (t_{11} \wedge t_{13}))$ encodes the mutants surviving α_1, e.g., the mutant $\mathcal{P}_2$ in Fig. 2b.

6   Test Analysis and Test Generation

Consider a test suite TS and a fault model $\langle \mathcal{M}, \simeq, Mut(\mathcal{M}) \rangle$. The test analysis problem consists in verifying whether the test suite is complete for the fault model. The test generation problem aims at generating a complete test suite, by adding new tests to the given one. Solving the test analysis problem, we encode the mutants undetected by the tests with the Boolean formula $\varphi_{\mathcal{M}} \wedge \neg\varphi_{TS}$; then we use a solver to determine a mutant undetected by TS, according to Theorem 1 TS is complete if no mutant can be determined or only conforming mutants can be determined. We exclude encountered conforming mutants from the fault domain; this is done by making the conjunction of $\varphi_{\mathcal{M}} \wedge \neg\varphi_{TS}$ with the formula $\bigvee_{t \in \lambda_{\mathcal{P}} \cup \Delta_{\mathcal{P}}} \neg t$ encoding the mutants different from $\mathcal{P}$.

Theorem 2. *TS is complete for $\langle \mathcal{M}, \simeq, Mut(\mathcal{M}) \rangle$ if and only if $\varphi_{\mathcal{M}} \wedge \neg\varphi_{TS}$ is not satisfiable or all the mutants it determines are conforming.*

In order to generate a complete test suite, our procedure analyzes the current test suite TS. If it is complete the procedure stops and return TS; otherwise we generate a test α detecting nonconforming mutants from a mutant surviving TS. α can be the timed input sequence of an execution of the distinguishing automaton for the specification and a surviving mutant (which is a part of the mutation machine), according to Corollary 4. Then we compute φ_α and we analyze the new test suite $TS' = TS \cup \{\alpha\}$ by solving the formula $\varphi_{\mathcal{M}} \wedge \neg\varphi_{TS} \wedge \neg\varphi_\alpha$; this may trigger the generation of a new test. We generate iteratively new tests until all the procedure stops and a complete test suite is returned.

For example, the test suite $TS = \{b0.5a7.5\}$ is not complete for $\mathcal{M}_1$ in Fig. 1b because $\varphi_{\mathcal{M}_1} \wedge \neg\varphi_{TS}$ determines the nonconforming mutant $\mathcal{P}_2$ in Fig. 2b, where $\varphi_{TS} = \varphi_{\alpha_1}$ and $\alpha_1 = b0.5a7.5$. An implementation of our approach generates the complete test suite $\{\alpha_1 = b0.5a7.5, \alpha_2 = b0.5a0.5a3.5a0.5, \alpha_3 = b0.5b0.5\}$ detecting all the seven nonconforming mutants. α_2 detects $\mathcal{P}_2$; it is the timed input sequence of an accepted execution of the distinguishing automaton of $\mathcal{S}_1$ and $\mathcal{P}_2$. A nonconforming mutant undetected by α_1 and α_2 was used to generate α_3; it defines transition t_5.

Let us compare our complete test suite generation approach with the one proposed in [26]. We focus on detecting specific faults represented in the mutation machine which can have more states than the specification, so do the mutants. The specification machine is not necessarily "minimal". We believe that for the traditional fault model, the method in [26] could be faster than ours (especially if the time required to minimize the specification is not considered), but the method in [26] could generate redundant tests. The reason is that the method

in [26] is an application of the W-method over a classical TFSM which represents
an abstraction of TFSM-TG and the W-method was developed for minimal classical FSM. The size of the abstract TFSM-TG [26] could contribute to decrease
the efficiency of the test generation [8,26]. The W-method generates tests by
combining input sequences (namely, state cover sets, all input sequences of a
certain length and state identification input sequences or characterization sets);
it does not check whether each generated test actually detects faults and several
generated tests can detects only one mutant. Thus the number of generated tests
can be bigger and less adequate to focus on faults specified in customized fault
models represented with mutation machines. Where [26] will generate a huge
test suite to detect all possible faults, our method will generate test suites of
reduced sizes for customized fault models.

We performed an empirical evaluation of our approach with a proof-of-
concept tool developed in C++ and randomly generated TFSM-TG with two
inputs and outputs, with a maximal timeout of 5 (resp. 10) for the specification (resp. the mutations machines). The tool uses cryptoSAT [24]. Preliminary
results appear in Table 1 which presents sizes and generating times for test suites
from mutation machines defining multiple of mutants with few states. For each
number of states and number of mutants, we generated tests for several mutation machines. The tool can take a long time in encoding the fault domain; this
may happen when there are too many compatible (not necessarily equal) timed
guards and timeouts defined in the same state. Since this operation is done for
every state, it could be distributed. In most of the situations, the tool can rapidly
encode the fault domain and the test generation becomes faster.

Table 1. Size of the generated complete test suites and generating time; for an entry
(x, y), x is the size of the test suite and y is the generating time in seconds

	#mutants in the fault domain		
#states	$\simeq 10^4$	$\simeq 10^8$	$\simeq 10^{12}$
8 states	(6, 0.22)	(7, 0.32)	(12, 45.57)
10 states	(3, 0.16)	(8, 2.34)	(21, 46.94)
12 states	(5, 0.72)	(5, 2.77)	(15, 4.45)

7 Conclusion

We have proposed a multiple mutation testing theory to testing real-time systems
represented with finite state machine extended with timed guards and timeouts
(TFSM-TG). We developed an approach to generate complete test suites for
fault models represented with mutation machines. The approach relies on the
definition of distinguishing automaton for mutation machine and the construction of Boolean formulas encoding the (faulty) implementations undetected by
tests. We implemented the approach in a proof-of-concept tool which we used

to evaluate the efficiency of the approach. The experimental results show that the approach can be used to derive tests for non-trivial TFSM-TG fault models representing an important number of faults.

Ongoing work includes developing open access benchmarks and use them to compare the existing test generation methods for TFSM-TG. We also plan to generate symbolic tests, i.e., timed input sequences with delay intervals instead of simple delays, and complete test suites consisting of a single test.

References

1. Alur, R., Dill, D.L.: A theory of timed automata. Theoret. Comput. Sci. **126**(2), 183–235 (1994)
2. Bertrand, N., Jéron, T., Stainer, A., Krichen, M.: Off-line test selection with test purposes for non-deterministic timed automata. In: Abdulla, P.A., Leino, K.R.M. (eds.) TACAS 2011. LNCS, vol. 6605, pp. 96–111. Springer, Heidelberg (2011). https://doi.org/10.1007/978-3-642-19835-9_10
3. Bohnenkamp, H., Belinfante, A.: Timed testing with TorX. In: Fitzgerald, J., Hayes, I.J., Tarlecki, A. (eds.) FM 2005. LNCS, vol. 3582, pp. 173–188. Springer, Heidelberg (2005). https://doi.org/10.1007/11526841_13
4. Bousquet, L.D., Ouabdesselam, F., Richier, J.L., Zuanon, N.: Lutess: a specification-driven testing environment for synchronous software. In: Proceedings of ICSE 1999, pp. 267–276 (1999)
5. Bresolin, D., El-Fakih, K., Villa, T., Yevtushenko, N.: Deterministic timed finite state machines: equivalence checking and expressive power. In: GandALF (2014)
6. Chow, T.S.: Testing software design modeled by finite-state machines. IEEE Trans. Softw. Eng. **SE-4**(3), 178–187 (1978)
7. Derderian, K., Merayo, M.G., Hierons, R.M., Núñez, M.: Aiding test case generation in temporally constrained state based systems using genetic algorithms. In: Cabestany, J., Sandoval, F., Prieto, A., Corchado, J.M. (eds.) IWANN 2009. LNCS, vol. 5517, pp. 327–334. Springer, Heidelberg (2009). https://doi.org/10.1007/978-3-642-02478-8_41
8. Dorofeeva, R., El-Fakih, K., Maag, S., Cavalli, A.R., Yevtushenko, N.: FSM-based conformance testing methods: a survey annotated with experimental evaluation. Inf. Softw. Technol. **52**(12), 1286–1297 (2010)
9. El-Fakih, K., Yevtushenko, N., Fouchal, H.: Testing timed finite state machines with guaranteed fault coverage. In: Núñez, M., Baker, P., Merayo, M.G. (eds.) FATES/TestCom -2009. LNCS, vol. 5826, pp. 66–80. Springer, Heidelberg (2009). https://doi.org/10.1007/978-3-642-05031-2_5
10. Krichen, M., Tripakis, S.: Conformance testing for real-time systems. FMSD **34**, 238–304 (2009)
11. Lallali, M., Zaidi, F., Cavalli, A.: Timed modeling of web services composition for automatic testing. In: 2007 Third International IEEE Conference on Signal-Image Technologies and Internet-Based System, pp. 417–426. IEEE (2007)
12. Larsen, K.G., Mikucionis, M., Nielsen, B., Skou, A.: Testing real-time embedded software using Uppaal-Tron: an industrial case study. In: Proceedings of EMSOFT 2005, pp. 299–306. ACM (2005)
13. Marre, B., Arnould, A.: Test sequences generation from LUSTRE descriptions: GATEL. In: Proceedings ASE 2000, pp. 229–237 (2000)

14. Merayo, M.G., Núñez, M., Rodríguez, I.: Formal testing from timed finite state machines. Comput. Netw. **52**(2), 432–460 (2008)
15. Mikucionis, M., Larsen, K.G., Nielsen, B.: T-Uppaal: online model-based testing of real-time systems. In: Proceedings of ASE 2004, pp. 396–397. IEEE (2004)
16. Naito, S., Tsunoyama, M.: Fault detection for sequential machines by transition-tours. In: Proceedings of Fault Tolerant Computer Systems, pp. 238–243 (1981)
17. Nguena Timo, O., Petrenko, A., Ramesh, S.: Multiple mutation testing from finite state machines with symbolic inputs. In: Yevtushenko, N., Cavalli, A.R., Yenigün, H. (eds.) ICTSS 2017. LNCS, vol. 10533, pp. 108–125. Springer, Cham (2017). https://doi.org/10.1007/978-3-319-67549-7_7
18. Nguena Timo, O., Petrenko, A., Ramesh, S.: Checking sequence generation for symbolic input/output FSMs by constraint solving. In: Fischer, B., Uustalu, T. (eds.) ICTAC 2018. LNCS, vol. 11187, pp. 354–375. Springer, Cham (2018). https://doi.org/10.1007/978-3-030-02508-3_19
19. Nguena Timo, O., Rollet, A.: Conformance testing of variable driven automata. In: WFCS 2010, pp. 241–248. IEEE (2010)
20. Nilsson, R., Offutt, J., Mellin, J.: Test case generation for mutation-based testing of timeliness. Electr. Notes Theor. Comput. Sci. **164**(4), 97–114 (2006)
21. Petrenko, A., Nguena Timo, O., Ramesh, S.: Multiple mutation testing from FSM. In: Albert, E., Lanese, I. (eds.) FORTE 2016. LNCS, vol. 9688, pp. 222–238. Springer, Cham (2016). https://doi.org/10.1007/978-3-319-39570-8_15
22. Petrenko, A., Yevtushenko, N.: Test suite generation from a FSM with a given type of implementation errors. In: Proceedings of the IFIP TC6/WG6.1 Twelfth International Symposium on Protocol Specification, Testing and Verification, pp. 229–243 (1992)
23. Raymond, P., Nicollin, X., Halbwachs, N., Waber, D.: Automatic testing of reactive systems. In: Proceedings of RTSS 1998, pp. 200–209. IEEE (1998)
24. Soos, M., Nohl, K., Castelluccia, C.: Extending SAT solvers to cryptographic problems. In: Kullmann, O. (ed.) SAT 2009. LNCS, vol. 5584, pp. 244–257. Springer, Heidelberg (2009). https://doi.org/10.1007/978-3-642-02777-2_24
25. Tretmans, J.: Test generation with inputs, outputs, and repetitive quiescence. Softw.-Concepts Tools **17**, 103–120 (1996)
26. Tvardovskii, A., El-Fakih, K., Yevtushenko, N.: Deriving tests with guaranteed fault coverage for finite state machines with timeouts. In: Medina-Bulo, I., Merayo, M.G., Hierons, R. (eds.) ICTSS 2018. LNCS, vol. 11146, pp. 149–154. Springer, Cham (2018). https://doi.org/10.1007/978-3-319-99927-2_13
27. Vega, J.J.O., Perrouin, G., Amrani, M., Schobbens, P.: Model-based mutation operators for timed systems: a taxonomy and research agenda. In: Proceedings of QRS 2018, pp. 325–332. IEEE (2018)
28. Zhigulin, M., Yevtushenko, N., Maag, S., Cavalli, A.R.: FSM-based test derivation strategies for systems with time-outs. In: Proceedings of QSIC 2011, pp. 141–149 (2011)

Empirical Approaches

An Empirical Evaluation of Search Algorithms for App Testing

Leon Sell, Michael Auer, Christoph Frädrich, Michael Gruber,
Philemon Werli, and Gordon Fraser[✉]

University of Passau, Passau, Germany
gordon.fraser@uni-passau.de

Abstract. Automated testing techniques can effectively explore mobile applications in order to find faults that manifest as program crashes. A number of different techniques for automatically testing apps have been proposed and empirically compared, but previous studies focused on comparing different *tools*, rather than *techniques*. Although these studies have shown search-based approaches to be effective, it remains unclear whether superior performance of one tool compared to another is due to fundamental advantages of the underlying search technique, or due to certain engineering choices made during the implementation of the tools. In order to provide a better understanding of app testing as a search problem, we empirically study different search algorithms within the same app testing framework. Experiments on a selection of 10 nontrivial apps reveal that the costs of fitness evaluations are inhibitive, and prevent the choice of algorithm from having a major effect.

Keywords: Software testing · Android · Genetic algorithm

1 Introduction

Mobile applications (apps) have become an important branch of software engineering. To support the development and analysis of mobile applications, automated testing techniques have been tailored towards the specifics of mobile applications. In particular, automated testing techniques which interact with apps through the user interface are frequently applied to automatically find faults leading to program crashes.

Different techniques for automatically testing apps have been proposed and empirically compared. In particular, techniques based on random exploration and on meta-heuristic search algorithms have emerged as the most effective [15,19]. However, previous empirical studies focused on comparing different *tools*, rather than *techniques*. Consequently, it remains unclear whether superior performance of one tool compared to another is due to fundamental advantages of the underlying technique, or due to certain engineering choices made during the implementation of the tools.

© IFIP International Federation for Information Processing 2019
Published by Springer Nature Switzerland AG 2019
C. Gaston et al. (Eds.): ICTSS 2019, LNCS 11812, pp. 123–139, 2019.
https://doi.org/10.1007/978-3-030-31280-0_8

In order to better understand the factors influencing the effectiveness of app test generators, we empirically study the best-working search algorithms and technical choices, according to previous research (e.g., [4,19]), re-implemented within the same app testing framework. This increases internal validity, as it reduces the influence of engineering aspects on the outcome of the comparison.

Since previous empirical comparisons suggest that multi-objective search achieves the best performance [19], we aim to scrutinise this insight in particular. We implemented the multi-objective search algorithm NSGA-II as used in the Sapienz [12] tool, a simple mono-objective genetic algorithm (GA), the many-objective optimisation algorithms MOSA [13] and MIO [3], and random testing as well as heuristic improvements based on the Stoat [17] tool into the MATE [8] framework for app testing. Given this setup, we aim to answer the following research questions:

RQ1: What is the influence of using multi-objective optimisation, rather than the generally common approach of optimising simply for code coverage?

RQ2: Do recent many-objective search techniques that have been specifically designed for test generation outperform multi-objective optimisation?

RQ3: Does meta-heuristic search perform better than basic random testing?

Experiments on 10 non-trivial apps suggest that there is little difference between the individual search algorithms. The main problem is that test executions, and thus fitness evaluations, take so much time on Android that the search algorithms hardly get a chance to perform meaningful evolution.

2   Background

In order to understand testing of Android apps, we first explain how an Android app is composed. Android apps can be divided into the following components [6]: Activities (user interface), Services (background processes), Broadcast Receivers (inter-process communication), and Content Providers (sharing data between apps). Components are configured in the Android manifest, an XML file that maintains permissions of each Android app, e.g., internet access. Activities, services and broadcast receivers can be invoked by internal messages called *Intents*. While progress on testing services has been made (e.g., intent fuzzing [16]), most effort is put into testing the UI. Activities implement handling of user interaction with the app (e.g., logic behind a button click) and can assign callback functionality to its life-cycle methods. Activities navigate to other activities and potentially trigger services, broadcast receivers and content providers. Exploring activities most often leads to code being executed. Therefore, testing the UI in a more sophisticated way often results in higher code coverage.

A UI test case consists of a sequence of UI events (e.g., clicks). Different methods to automatically generate such test cases have been proposed and empirically compared. Choudhary et al. [15] compared different tools in terms of the effectiveness of the search strategy (e.g., random or systematic), the fault detection ability (how many crashes were found), the ease of use (how difficult is it to

---

Algorithm 1. Random exploration using only available events

    Input   : Termination Condition C, length of the test cases n
    Output: test suite TS with test cases of length n
1 $TS \longleftarrow \{\}$
2 **while** $\neg C$ **do**
3      $test \longleftarrow []$
4   **for** 0 **to** n **do**
5         $A \longleftarrow$ getListOfAvailableEvents()
6         $a \longleftarrow$ selectNextEvent(A)
7   execute(a)
8         $test$.push(a)
9      $TS \longleftarrow TS \cup \{test\}$
10 **return** TS

---

install and run the testing tool) and the Android framework compatibility (is the testing tool compatible with several Android API levels). The study looked at 68 different open-source apps and reported that the tools Monkey [7] and Dynodroid [10] (both using random exporation) outperformed the remaining tools on average. More recently, Wang et al. [19] examined 68 industrial apps with state-of-the-art test generation tools, motivated by the assumption that industrial apps have higher complexity. However, Monkey still obtained the highest coverage on most apps, closely followed by the tool Sapienz [12], which in contrast builds on an evolutionary algorithm for the test generation. Based on this insight, Zeng et al. [20] added some heuristics to random exploration, resulting in overall highest coverage. In the following, we take a closer look at these test generation techniques.

2.1 Random Exploration

To create a test case for an Android application, the application needs to be explored. The simplest way to do this is to randomly click anywhere on the screen and record these events. Random exploration is one of the most frequently applied strategies as it is implemented in the state-of-current-practice tool Monkey, which comes with Android [11]. However, test cases that were created by random clicks on the screen can contain events that do not trigger any code in the source code [2], for example when clicking on an area of the screen that does not contain any widgets. To improve the exploration, the set of events to choose from can be minimized to the set of available events on the current activity. Algorithm 1 describes random selection based on available events (Line 6).

    Since random selection of available events may likely choose events that do not lead to exploration of previously unvisited activities, a heuristic can be used to improve the selection process. In particular, a heuristic reported as effective in the literature is the Stoat approach [17]. Each available event is assigned an execution weight, which is used to rank the events based on the potential increase of test coverage. The execution weight consists of three parts:

Type of the Event T_e. A navigation event (scroll and back) is assigned a value of 0.5, whereas menu events are assigned the value 2. All other events have the value 1.

Number of Unvisited Child Widgets C_e. An event that has more previously unvisited child widgets will be executed more likely than ones with fewer unvisited child widgets.

Number of Executions E_e. If an event has been executed previously during exploration, it should have a lower priority of being selected again compared to other events that have not been executed before, in order to increase the probability of discovering new activities.

Each of these parts is multiplied with a factor α, β, γ, resulting in an overall execution weight computed as follows:

$$execution\_weight_e = \frac{\alpha \cdot T_e + \beta \cdot C_e}{\gamma \cdot E_e} \tag{1}$$

The event with the highest execution weight is then selected and added to the test case (cf. Algorithm 1, Line 6). If two or more events have the same execution weight, one of those events is randomly selected and added to the test case.

2.2   Searching for Test Suites with Multi-objective Search

Search-based testing describes the use of meta-heuristic search algorithms, such as GAs, to evolve tests. A common approach is to encode test suites as chromosomes of the GA, and then guide evolution with a fitness function based on code coverage [9]. In the context of Android testing, this approach has been popularised by the Sapienz tool [12]. In contrast to previous work on whole test suite generation, Sapienz optimises not only for code coverage, but also the number of crashes and event sequence length: Maximising the code coverage assures that most parts of the app are tested. Finding as many as possible crashes is the main goal of automated Android testing in general. Minimising the total number of events in a test suite helps with reducing the number of steps that need to be taken to reproduce a crash and keeps the amount of time needed to execute one chromosome at reasonable level.

To address multiple objectives at once, Sapienz uses the Non-dominated Sorting Genetic Algorithm II (NSGA-II), a popular multi-objective algorithm, shown in Algorithm 2. In each iteration, NSGA-II successively applies ranks to non-dominated individuals to build Pareto-optimal sets, starting at optimum 1 (Line 7). An individual x dominates another individual y if x is at least as good in all objectives and better than y in at least one objective. Using non-domination, individuals with a good score for only one objective have a higher chance of surviving. To sort individuals with the same rank, crowding distance is applied to all individuals (Line 10). At the end of each iteration, individuals are sorted by crowding distance (Line 13) and the population is reduced to its size limit (Line 14). Once terminated, the current population is returned.

Algorithm 2. NSGA-II algorithm

Input : Termination Condition C, population size limit n
Output: P_t, population of individuals

1 $t \longleftarrow 0$ // generation count
2 $P_t \longleftarrow$ GenerateRandomPopulation(n)
3 $P_t \longleftarrow$ Non-Dominated-Sort(P_t)
4 **while** $\neg C$ **do**
5 $\quad$ $R_t \longleftarrow P_t \cup$ GenerateOffspring(P_t)
6 $\quad$ $r \longleftarrow 1$
7 $\quad$ $\{F_1, F_2, \ldots\} \longleftarrow$ Non-Dominated-Sort(R_t)
8 $\quad$ $P_{t+1} \longleftarrow \{\}$
9 $\quad$ **while** $|P_{t+1}| \leq n$ **do**
10 $\quad\quad$ AssignCrowdingDistance(F_r)
11 $\quad\quad$ $P_{t+1} \longleftarrow P_{t+1} \cup F_r$
12 $\quad\quad$ $r \longleftarrow r + 1$
13 $\quad$ CrowdingDistanceSort($P_t + 1$)
14 $\quad$ $P_{t+1} \longleftarrow P_{t+1}\big[1 : n\big]$
15 $\quad$ $t \longleftarrow t + 1$
16 **return** P_t

2.3 Searching for Test Cases with Many-Objective Optimisation

Traditionally, search-based test generation used individual test cases as representation, and there are several approaches for Android testing that also use such a representation [1,11,14]. While the whole test suite generation approach has superseded the optimisation of individual goals in many scenarios, recently new specifically tailored many-objective optimisation algorithms have popularised test case representation again, in particular the Many-Objective Sorting Algorithm (MOSA) [13] and the Many Independent Objective Algorithm (MIO) [3]. Similar to the Sapienz approach, MOSA and MIO are population based GAs. Each coverage goal (e.g., individual branch) is viewed as an independent objective by both MOSA and MIO. An objective is represented by a corresponding fitness function, which allows us to evaluate whether an individual reaches an objective, i.e., whether a test case covers a certain branch or statement.

MOSA: MOSA [13] is an extension of NSGA-II [5] and optimises test cases as individuals for not one, but multiple independent objectives (e.g., individual branches). It extends the ranking system of NSGA-II and adds a second population, called *archive*. Algorithm 3 illustrates how MOSA works. Extensions to NSGA-II are marked with a bold background.

The archive contains the best individual for each fulfilled objective. Individuals which fulfill an objective first are added to the archive; these objectives are ignored for future optimisation. If, however, an individual fulfills an already

---

Algorithm 3. MOSA algorithm

Input : Termination Condition C, population size limit n
Output: *archive*, a set of optimised test cases

1 $t \longleftarrow 0$ // generation count
2 $P_t \longleftarrow$ GenerateRandomPopulation(n)

3 *archive* $\longleftarrow$ UpdateArchive(P_t)

4 **while** $\neg C$ **do**
5      $R_t \longleftarrow P_t \cup$ GenerateOffspring(P_t)
6      $r \longleftarrow 0$
7      $\{F_0, F_1, \ldots\} \longleftarrow$ PreferenceSorting(R_t)
8      $P_{t+1} \longleftarrow \{\}$
9   **while** $|P_{t+1}| + |F_r| \leq n$ **do**
10   AssignCrowdingDistance(F_r)
11         $P_{t+1} \longleftarrow P_{t+1} \sqcup F_r$
12         $r \longleftarrow r + 1$
13   CrowdingDistanceSort(F_r)
14     $P_{t+1} \longleftarrow P_{t+1} \cup F_r\left[1 : \left(n - |P_{t+1}|\right)\right]$
15   *archive* $\longleftarrow$ UpdateArchive(P_{t+1})
16     $t \longleftarrow t + 1$

17 **return** *archive*

---

satisfied objective, but with a shorter sequence length than the individual in the archive, it replaces the existing in the archive (Line 15).

NSGA-II selects individuals based on ranks, which start from an optimum of 1. MOSA extends the ranking system with a *preference sorting criterion* to avoid losing the best individual for each non-fulfilled objective, i.e., closest to fulfilling (Line 7). The best individuals for non-fulfilled objectives are given the new optimal rank 0, independent of their relation to other individuals. For all other individuals, NSGA-II ranking is applied.

At the end, MOSA returns the archive, which contains the individuals for all satisfied objectives (Line 17).

MIO: The Many Independent Objective Algorithm [3] is based on the $(1+1)$ EA and uses archives with a dynamic population. For each testing target one archive exists. The best n tests are kept in the archive, where n is the maximum size of the archives. If a target is reached, then the maximum size of the corresponding archive is set to 1 and all but the covering test are removed from the archive.

To better control the trade-off between exploitation and exploration of the search landscape MIO uses a parameter P_r, according to which new tests are sampled or old ones mutated (Line 7). A second parameter F defines, when the focused search phase should start: Similar to Simulated Annealing the amount

---

Algorithm 4. Many Independent Objective Algorithm

Input : Termination Condition C, Random sampling probability P_r, List of fitness functions L, Population size limit n, Start of focused search F

Output: Archive of optimised individuals

1 T ⟵ createInitialPopulation ()
2 A ⟵ {}
3 **while** $\neg C$ **do**
4   **if** *rand()* $< P_r$ **then**
5 | p ⟵ createRandomIndividual ()
6   **else**
7 | p ⟵ sampleIndividual (T)
8   ⌊ p ⟵ mutate (p)
9   **for** k ⟵ L **do**
10   fitness = k.getFitness (p)
11   **if** *target is covered* **then**
12   addToArchive(A, p)
13   T_k ⟵ {p}
14   T ⟵ $T \setminus \{T_k\}$
15   **else if** *target is partially covered* **then**
16   T ⟵ $T_k \cup \{p\}$
17   resetCounter(k)
18   **if** $|T_k| > n$ **then**
19   ⌊ removeWorstTest(T_k, k)
20   updateParameters(F, P_r, n)

21 **return** A

---

of exploration is reduced over time when the focused search starts (Line 20). An additional feature of MIO is Feedback-Directed Sampling. Simply put, it is an approach to prefer targets for which we continuously see improvements. To achieve this, each target has a counter c_k. It is increased every time we sample a test from the targets (Line 7) archive and is reset to 0 when the new test performs better than the ones already in the archive (Line 17). The algorithm always samples tests from the archive of the target with the lowest counter.

3 Experimental Setup

3.1 Study Subjects

For experiments we used ten different Android apps which we obtained from the F-Droid platform[1]. A main criterion for the apps was to allow a comparison of search algorithms without being inhibited by the technical limitations of the underlying Android testing framework. Therefore, the ten open-source apps (the

---

[1] https://f-droid.org/en/.

code was necessary for the instrumentation) were primarily selected in a random fashion with the following restrictions:

▷ The latest available version of each app has been used to avoid finding bugs that have already been fixed.
▷ Apps that require certain permissions, e.g., camera or GPS, for their core functionality were discarded as the MATE framework [8] cannot provide meaningful real world data for those sensors which could prevent a comprehensive exploration of the app.
▷ Apps that require authentication as a basic prerequisite were discarded as this too will prevent a comprehensive exploration of the app.
▷ Apps with less than four activities were discarded as those apps are often too small in scope to generate meaningful data during testing.
▷ Apps that do not primarily use native Android UI elements such as menus, text fields, buttons and sliders were discarded since we use native Android UI elements to deduce actions that can be performed on the current screen.

If any of those criteria do not apply for the selected app, a new random app was selected. This process was repeated until we found ten apps that fulfil all the criteria. The resulting apps are listed in Table 1.

Table 1. Randomly selected apps.

App name (abbreviation)	Version	#Activities	#LoC
com.oriondev.moneywallet (**moneywallet**)	4.0.4.1	35	23081
com.woefe.shoppinglist (**shoppinglist**)	0.11.0	4	1242
de.arnowelzel.android.periodical (**periodical**)	1.22	7	1558
de.rampro.activitydiary (**activitydiary**)	1.4.0	11	3652
de.drhoffmannsoftware (**drhoffmansoftware**)	1.16-9	9	896
de.retujo.bierverkostung (**bierverkostung**)	1.2.1	13	7297
de.tap.easy_xkcd (**easy_xkcd**)	6.1.2	9	4972
net.gsantner.markor (**markor**)	1.6.0	7	5691
org.quantumbadger.redreader (**redreader**)	1.9.9	19	16019
protect.rentalcalc (**rentalcalc**)	0.5.1	12	1770

3.2 Experimental Infrastructure

We implemented the different approaches described in Sect. 2 on top of the MATE framework [8]. MATE was previously used to identify accessibility flaws in apps by exploring the app using various heuristics. The framework was extended to support different search algorithms and to measure code coverage.

For the search algorithms random exploration is used as a basis for creating the initial population in order to be able to compare it to solely using the heuristic exploration introduced in Sect. 2.1. Unlike Android Monkey, random exploration chooses only from events that are available on the current activity. To ensure that there is no influence between individual test cases, for each test execution the app is re-installed and re-initialized to provide a consistent and clean starting state. This is also done by other test generation tools like Sapienz [12].

As proposed in the Sapienz paper [12], random selection was used for NSGA-II and also MOSA, to choose the chromosomes which are crossed over and mutated. MIO selects chromosomes according to Feedback-Directed Sampling. Simple GA uses a fitness proportionate selection. For the Sapienz reimplementation the crossover and mutation function were matched as closely as possible. For the other GAs (which all operate on test cases instead of test suites) a crossover function was implemented that tries to match the screen state after an event of the first parent with the screen state before an event of the second parent. The offspring is an event sequence that starts with the events leading up to the matching point of the first parent after which it is continued with the events succeeding the match in the second parent. The search is started from a random element of the event sequence of the first parent with a bias towards the middle and is continued in an alternating fashion until a matching screen state is found. While executing the resulting new test case if an event cannot be execute because a new screen state was reached, random events will be selected from that point onward until the original event sequence length has been reached. For the mutation function a random element of the event sequence is chosen after which new events will be generated that will be executed instead of the old events. Parameters of the GAs were chosen based on the values in the respective papers that introduced the search algorithms:

Population size	50	[12]
pMutate	0.3	[12]
pCrossover	0.7	[12]
Start of focused Search	0.5	[3]
pSampleRandom	0.5	[3]
Maximal number of events (per test case)	50	[12]
Number of test cases per test suite	5	[12]

All experiments were carried out on the Android Emulator version 28.0.22.0, using an x86 image of Android 7.1.1. For each run, the emulator had full access to 4 physical cores (8 hyper-threads) and 16 GB of RAM. Physically, we used Intel(R) Xeon(R) E5-2650 v2 @ 2.60 GHz CPUs. Each approach was executed ten times on each of the ten different study subjects for 8 hours per execution. We instrumented the apps using JaCoCo[2]. Measurement of line coverage and logging of occurred crashes were performed during the entire run. After a run has finished we calculate the unique number of crashes of the run by comparing the entire stacktrace of each crash. Two crashes are considered the same unique crash if the strings of both of the crashes' stacktraces are identical.

---

[2] https://www.eclemma.org/jacoco/.

3.3 Experiment Procedure

For each research question we use the Vargha-Delaney $\hat{A}_{1,2}$ effect size and the Wilcoxon-Mann-Whitney U test, with a 95% confidence level, to statistically compare the performance of the algorithms. If the effect size is calculated for a comparision of two algorithms X and Y, $\hat{A}_{X,Y} = 0.5$ indicates that both approaches achieve the same coverage or crashes, and $\hat{A}_{X,Y} = 0.0$ means that algorithm X has a 100% probability of achieving lower coverage or crashes.

RQ1: In order to answer RQ1, we compare the NSGA-II algorithm to a simple GA that solely optimises test suites for coverage. The simple GA uses the same representation, mutation, and crossover as NSGA-II, but only optimises for line coverage, whereas the NSGA-II algorithm additionally uses (1) a fitness function minimizing the number of events executed in the test suite and (2) a fitness function maximising the number of crashes produced by the test suite, both also used in the Sapienz approach. Based on the NSGA-II variant used in Sapienz, NSGA-II selects individuals for reproduction randomly; in contrast, the simple GA uses standard fitness proportionate selection. We compare the number of unique crashes found and the coverage achieved to determine if the multi-objective approach yields a benefit over a simple mono objective approach.

RQ2: In order to answer RQ2, we compare NSGA-II to the many-objective optimisation algorithms MOSA and MIO in terms of line coverage and unique crashes. For many-objective optimisation, each line of the app under test becomes an independent testing target to optimise. MOSA and MIO use the same fitness function for each line, which yields results between 0.0 and 1.0 (covered). An executed line in the same package as the target line adds 0.25 and same class as the target line adds 0.25. The remaining possible 0.5 are calculated from the distance inside the class to the target line. Since our line coverage fitness function maximises towards 1.0 and MOSA usually minimises its fitness functions, we adjust our implementation of MOSA to maximise towards 1.0 as well.

RQ3: In order to answer RQ3, we implemented a random exploration that only takes available events into account, and creates test cases of a fixed length. For our studies we set the length of a single test case to 50 events, which matches the length of individuals in the search algorithms. This strategy is then compared in terms of code coverage achieved and unique crashes found to the heuristic strategy based on Stoat (Sect. 2.1), and NSGA-II. The values for the weights we choose for the heuristic approach are the same ones that the researchers of Stoat [17] have used. These values are 1 for the value of α, the weight for the type of event, 1.4 for the value of β, the weight for the number of unvisited children widgets, and 1.5 for γ, the weight of the number of executions of the event. Since we do not know the number of unvisited children widgets for events that have not been executed before during exploration, we set this value twice as high as the highest number of unvisited children widgets from all known events.

3.4   Threats to Validity

To reduce threats to *internal validity* caused by the randomised algorithms, we ran each experiment 10 times and applied statistical analysis. To avoid possible confounding factors when comparing algorithms, they were all implemented in the same tool. We used the same default values for all relevant parameters, and used recommended values for algorithm-specific ones. Threats to *external validity* result from our limited choice of algorithms and study subjects. However, we used the best algorithms based on previous empirical studies. The 10 open source apps were chosen as representatives for a wide range of functionality, but results may not generalise to other apps.

4   Results

In this section, we investigate each proposed research question with results from our experiments. Tables 2 and 3 summarise the results of our experiments in terms of the line coverage achieved and number of unique crashes found for each of the algorithms. Statistical comparisons are summarised in Tables 4 and 5.

Table 2. Mean line coverage of the different algorithms

App	NSGA-II	Random	Heuristic	Simple GA	MOSA	MIO
moneywallet	0.20	0.21	0.35	0.22	0.22	0.19
shoppinglist	0.77	0.80	0.73	0.77	0.77	0.77
periodical	0.85	0.87	0.87	0.84	0.83	0.85
drhoffmannsoftware	0.44	0.48	0.43	0.44	0.46	0.48
activitydiary	0.74	0.75	0.78	0.73	0.74	0.75
bierverkostung	0.43	0.47	0.58	0.44	0.45	0.49
easy_xkcd	0.62	0.62	0.61	0.57	0.59	0.60
markor	0.62	0.63	0.58	0.61	0.60	0.60
redreader	0.55	0.55	0.45	0.52	0.54	0.52
rentalcalc	0.67	0.69	0.70	0.68	0.68	0.71
Mean	0.59	0.61	0.61	0.58	0.59	0.60

4.1   RQ1: Mono-Objective vs. Multi-objective Optimisation

In order to determine if multi-objective optimisation is an improvement over mono-objective GAs optimising for code coverage, we compare the coverage achieved by both approaches. As shown in Tables 2 and 4, NSGA-II and the simple GA perform similar in terms of overall coverage with NSGA-II having a slight edge over the simple GA. NSGA-II achieves better coverage for the apps

Table 3. Mean unique crashes of NSGA-II, random, heuristic, simple GA, MOSA & MIO

App	NSGA-II	Random	Heuristic	Simple GA	MOSA	MIO
moneywallet	0.37	0.17	0.36	0.20	0.30	0.20
shoppinglist	0.00	0.00	0.00	0.00	0.00	0.00
periodical	0.00	0.00	0.00	0.00	0.00	0.00
drhoffmannsoftware	11.50	12.36	11.45	8.90	10.40	11.00
activitydiary	0.00	0.08	0.00	0.00	0.00	0.00
bierverkostung	3.30	4.09	8.00	4.00	3.60	3.80
easy_xkcd	3.30	3.38	0.64	2.80	3.40	2.80
markor	0.40	0.38	0.00	0.20	0.10	0.30
redreader	0.10	0.00	0.00	0.00	0.00	0.10
rentalcalc	1.40	2.17	4.18	1.90	1.80	2.90
Mean	2.04	2.26	2.46	1.80	1.96	2.11

Table 4. Comparison of mean coverage of NSGA-II vs. Random, heuristic, simple GA, MOSA & MIO

NSGA-II	vs. Random		vs. Heuristic		vs. Simple GA		vs. MOSA		vs. MIO	
App	P-Value	$\hat{A}_{1,2}$	P-Value	$\hat{A}_{1,2}$	P-Value	$\hat{A}_{1,2}$	P-Value	$\hat{A}_{1,2}$	P-Value	$\hat{A}_{1,2}$
moneywallet	0.13	0.26	<0.01	0.00	0.23	0.31	0.27	0.32	0.71	0.56
shoppinglist	0.16	0.30	**0.02**	0.81	0.79	0.46	0.79	0.46	0.38	0.38
periodical	<0.01	0.10	0.14	0.30	0.41	0.61	0.16	0.69	0.91	0.48
drhoffmannsoftware	**0.03**	0.20	0.15	0.69	1.00	0.49	0.34	0.36	**0.01**	0.15
activitydiary	0.36	0.37	<0.01	0.09	0.88	0.52	0.31	0.64	0.60	0.42
bierverkostung	**0.01**	0.15	<0.01	0.00	0.57	0.58	0.43	0.39	<0.01	0.12
easy_xkcd	0.96	0.51	0.41	0.61	<0.01	0.94	0.16	0.69	0.12	0.71
markor	0.92	0.52	<0.01	1.00	0.08	0.74	**0.01**	0.84	<0.01	0.89
redreader	0.31	0.64	<0.01	1.00	<0.01	0.90	0.52	0.59	<0.01	0.90
rentalcalc	0.43	0.39	0.21	0.33	1.00	0.50	0.82	0.46	0.05	0.23
Mean	0.33	0.34	0.09	0.48	0.50	0.61	0.38	0.54	0.28	0.48

easy_xkcd and redreader, where the results are well within the margin of significance, with a mean difference in overall coverage of 5% for easy_xkcd and 3% for redreader. For all other apps neither algorithm significantly outperforms the other. Overall, NSGA-II achieves about 1% more line coverage on average.

In terms of mean unique crashes per app, which are shown in Tables 3 and 5, NSGA-II is also doing slightly better. There is only one statistically significant difference in mean crashes, i.e., for the markor app where NSGA-II discovers about 0.2 crashes more than the simple GA on average. Overall NSGA-II discovers about 0.24 crashes more than the simple GA.

Our conjecture is that NSGA-II triggers a few more unique crashes than the simple GA because it keeps test suites containing crashes in its population. Intuitively, because of defect clustering crashes may often occur in proximity to

Table 5. Comparison of mean unique crashes of NSGA-II vs. Random, heuristic, simple GA, MOSA & MIO

NSGA-II App	vs. Random		vs. Heuristic		vs. Simple GA		vs. MOSA		vs. MIO	
	P-Value	$\hat{A}_{1,2}$	P-Value	$\hat{A}_{1,2}$	P-Value	$\hat{A}_{1,2}$	P-Value	$\hat{A}_{1,2}$	P-Value	$\hat{A}_{1,2}$
moneywallet	0.64	0.55	0.94	0.50	0.64	0.55	0.94	0.50	0.94	0.51
shoppinglist	-	-	-	-	-	-	-	-	-	-
periodical	-	-	-	-	-	-	-	-	-	-
drhoffmannsoftware	0.25	0.35	0.57	0.57	**<0.01**	0.91	**0.04**	0.77	0.17	0.68
activitydiary	0.37	0.45	-	-	-	-	-	-	-	-
bierverkostung	0.29	0.36	**<0.01**	0.00	0.41	0.39	0.94	0.48	0.53	0.41
easy_xkcd	0.29	0.35	**<0.01**	1.00	0.45	0.60	0.88	0.47	0.45	0.60
markor	0.67	0.56	**0.03**	0.70	0.37	0.60	0.14	0.65	0.68	0.55
redreader	0.37	0.55	0.37	0.55	0.37	0.55	0.37	0.55	0.94	0.50
rentalcalc	0.50	0.41	**<0.01**	0.04	0.31	0.36	0.67	0.44	0.10	0.28
Mean	0.42	0.44	0.27	0.48	0.36	0.57	0.57	0.55	0.54	0.50

other crashes. This could explain why NSGA-II discovers more unique crashes by mutating and crossing test suites that already contain crashes.

This could also explain the slight edge in coverage NSGA-II has over the simple GA: More unique crashes found might mean covering more catch-blocks, whereas the "easy" parts of the code will be covered similarly by both approaches.

4.2 RQ2: Multi-objective vs. Many-Objective Optimisation

To test how multi-objective optimisation compares to many-objective optimisation we compare NSGA-II with MOSA and also with MIO.

In terms of coverage, Table 2 indicates an insignificant advantage of NSGA-II compared to MOSA. The comparison in Table 4 shows one significant difference for the `markor` app. In this case, NSGA-II outperforms MOSA with an effect size of 0.84 as NSGA-II achieves 62% coverage vs. the 60% achieved by MOSA. In terms of unique crashes, we observe a similar behaviour. As shown in Table 3, NSGA-II has a minor advantage over MOSA. For the only significant result, the `drhoffmannsoftware` app, NSGA-II covers 11.5 unique crashes while MOSA only covers 10.4 as depicted in Table 5.

Tables 2 and 3 show that NSGA-II and MIO have the same mean code coverage and number of unique crashes. When comparing code coverage, NSGA-II and MIO perform significantly better than the other for two apps as shown in Table 4. In comparison, NSGA-II achieves significant results for `markor` and `redreader`, while MIO does so for `drhoffmannsoftware` and `bierverkostung`. For unique crashes, no results are close to statistical significance (Table 5).

Our results indicate that neither multi-objective nor many-objective optimisation have a clear advantage over the other. We conjecture that the search space contains many states that are equally easy to reach for both types of optimisations, while very specific sequences of actions or inputs are needed to reach the

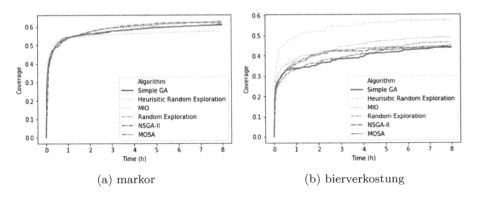

(a) markor   (b) bierverkostung

Fig. 1. Cumulative coverage over time for the tested apps. Values averaged every full minute using linear interpolation of the nearest respective previous and subsequent data point.

remaining states. Figure 1a illustrates how coverage evolves over time: Even after eight hours the search has not converged. Consequently, the search algorithms are likely to require much more time to cover more difficult states.

4.3   RQ3: Random vs. Search-Based Testing

To answer RQ3, we compare the random and the heuristic approach to NSGA-II. Tables 2 and 3 suggest that, on average, NSGA-II achieves slightly less coverage and crashes. Table 4 shows that NSGA-II achieved significantly lower coverage than random exploration in three cases, and for heuristic exploration it is significantly worse in three cases but significantly better in three other cases. Table 5 shows that in terms of crashes, there are no significant differences between NSGA-II and random, and compared to heuristic exploration NSGA-II is significantly better in two and significantly worse in two other cases. Overall, differences are small and mostly insignificant, although averages are slightly in favour of random and heuristic exploration.

This is also reflected by Fig. 1a and b which illustrate that, depending on whether it is better in terms of coverage to interact with unexplored widgets or to interact with the same widgets multiple times, the heuristic exploration performs a little better or a little worse. Random exploration, on the other hand, very closely matches the search-based approaches.

Overall, our results suggest that mono-objective and multi-objective optimisations do not achieve better results than random or heuristic exploration, and on average even appear to be slightly worse.

4.4   Discussion

Our experiments suggest that the actual search algorithm used only has a minor impact on the results. A closer look at the number of generations executed suggests that the search-based approaches simply do not receive sufficient time for meaningful evolution to take place. For example, NSGA-II on average over all apps achieved only 12.3 generations per run. This means that a substantial part of the search budget is used simply for evaluating the initial population, which means that the search behaves identical to random exploration for that time. For successive generations, the search mainly makes small changes through mutations and crossover, and the low number of generations leads to only small coverage increases over the initial population. Random exploration, in contrast, in the same time executes independently generated random tests, which likely explore more diverse aspects of the app under test, thus leading to the slight improvement in terms of coverage and crashes. To better understand what causes the high test execution costs, we took a closer look at the main cost factors:

▷ MATE uses a delay of 0.5 s in between actions to conservatively allow the UI to react to user events. However, the UIAutomator, which is used by Android testing tools to send user events, has an additional overhead, such that on average, each action takes 1.5 s.
▷ Code coverage information is stored in a local file on the emulated device, and this file needs to be retrieved after each test execution. This action takes another 0.7–2.5 s.
▷ In between test executions, the app is reset to a clean state. This is necessary to avoid dependencies between tests, and thus flaky tests. On average, it takes 8 s to reset an app.

When optimising test suites using NSGA-II, we used a population size of 50 test suites, each with 5 test cases and a maximum of 50 events per test case (i.e., a maximum of 12.500 events per generation of the search). Thus, only considering the values listed above, evaluating a single generation can take up to $50 \times 5 \times 1.5\,\text{s} + 50 \times 5 \times 8\,\text{s} + 50 \times 50 \times 5 \times 1.5\,\text{s} = 21125\,\text{s} = 5.87\,\text{h}$. However, test execution results are cached, and thus tests are only executed if they are mutated, which only happens with a certain probability. In practice, we observed that evaluating the initial generation takes around 3.6 h, and successive generations take about 38 min. The search algorithms using test cases rather than test suites potentially require fewer test executions, since each individual in the search is a test case rather than a whole test suite. However, the different representation means that chances of the tests being mutated are higher (when optimising test suites, on average only one test in the test suite is mutated if an individual is mutated). In our experiments, evaluating the initial population of test case based algorithms took only 46 min, but then evaluating successive generations took around 76 min, leading to an overall comparable number of generations to NSGA-II. Note that these execution costs are not specific to MATE but apply to other tools as well; for example, Vogel et al. [18] report execution times of up to 5 h to run Sapienz for 10 generations.

5   Conclusions

Search-based testing is one of the most popular approaches for testing mobile apps, and has been popularised by the Sapienz tool. In this paper we aimed to better understand how search algorithms influence the effectiveness of search-based testing for Android apps. In contrast to prior studies, we implemented different search algorithms within the same framework, such that our comparisons are not skewed by the engineering of the underlying tool. Our experiments suggest that the high costs of executing tests on Android devices or emulators makes fitness evaluations so expensive that the search algorithms can run only for few iterations, and hardly get a chance to perform meaningful evolution. As a result, random exploration performs slightly better than the search algorithms. This finding is also in line with previous, tool-based comparisons, in which random exploration tools like Android Monkey performed well. As future work, we therefore plan to investigate ways of reducing the execution costs, to allow search algorithms to perform better, and we plan to investigate other technical choices such as the influence of choosing widgets rather than random positions.

Acknowledgements. This work is supported by EPSRC project EP/N023978/2, Erasmus+ project IMPRESS 2017-1-NL01-KA203-035259 and DFG grant FR 2955/ 2-1.

References

1. Amalfitano, D., Amatucci, N., Fasolino, A.R., Tramontana, P.: Agrippin: a novel search based testing technique for Android applications. In: Proceedings of the 3rd International Workshop on Software Development Lifecycle for Mobile, pp. 5–12. ACM (2015)
2. Amalfitano, D., Fasolino, A.R., Tramontana, P., De Carmine, S., Memon, A.M.: Using GUI ripping for automated testing of Android applications. In: Proceedings of the 27th IEEE/ACM International Conference on Automated Software Engineering, pp. 258–261 (2012)
3. Arcuri, A.: Test suite generation with the many independent objective (MIO) algorithm. Inf. Softw. Technol. **104**, 195–206 (2018)
4. Campos, J., Ge, Y., Fraser, G., Eler, M., Arcuri, A.: An empirical evaluation of evolutionary algorithms for test suite generation. In: Menzies, T., Petke, J. (eds.) SSBSE 2017. LNCS, vol. 10452, pp. 33–48. Springer, Cham (2017). https://doi. org/10.1007/978-3-319-66299-2_3
5. Deb, K., Agrawal, S., Pratap, A., Meyarivan, T.: A fast elitist non-dominated sorting genetic algorithm for multi-objective optimization: NSGA-II. In: Schoenauer, M., et al. (eds.) PPSN 2000. LNCS, vol. 1917, pp. 849–858. Springer, Heidelberg (2000). https://doi.org/10.1007/3-540-45356-3_83
6. Android Developers: Application fundamentals, October 2018. https://developer. android.com/guide/components/fundamentals
7. Android Developers: Ui/application exerciser monkey, September 2018. https:// developer.android.com/studio/test/monkey

8. Eler, M.M., Rojas, J.M., Ge, Y., Fraser, G.: Automated accessibility testing of mobile apps. In: 2018 IEEE 11th International Conference on Software Testing, Verification and Validation (ICST), pp. 116–126 (2018)

9. Fraser, G., Arcuri, A.: Whole test suite generation. IEEE Trans. Softw. Eng. **39**(2), 276–291 (2013)

10. Machiry, A., Tahiliani, R., Naik, M.: Dynodroid: an input generation system for android apps. In: Proceedings of the 9th Joint Meeting on Foundations of Software Engineering, ESEC/FSE, pp. 224–234. ACM (2013)

11. Mahmood, R., Mirzaei, N., Malek, S.: Evodroid: segmented evolutionary testing of Android apps. In: Proceedings of the 22nd ACM SIGSOFT International Symposium on Foundations of Software Engineering, pp. 599–609 (2014)

12. Mao, K., Harman, M., Jia, Y.: Sapienz: multi-objective automated testing for android applications. In: Proceedings of the 25th International Symposium on Software Testing and Analysis, ISSTA, pp. 94–105. ACM (2016)

13. Panichella, A., Kifetew, F.M., Tonella, P.: Reformulating branch coverage as a many-objective optimization problem. In: 2015 IEEE 8th International Conference on Software Testing, Verification and Validation (ICST), pp. 1–10 (2015)

14. Rohella, A., Takada, S.: Testing Android applications using multi-objective evolutionary algorithms with a stopping criteria. In: 30th International Conference on Software Engineering and Knowledge Engineering, SEKE 2018, pp. 308–313. Knowledge Systems Institute Graduate School (2018)

15. Roy Choudhary, S., Gorla, A., Orso, A.: Automated test input generation for Android: Are we there yet? (e). In: Proceedings of the IEEE/ACM International Conference on Automated Software Engineering (ASE), pp. 429–440 (2015)

16. Sasnauskas, R., Regehr, J.: Intent fuzzer: crafting intents of death. In: Proceedings of Joint International Workshop on Dynamic Analysis (WODA) and Software and System Performance Testing, Debugging, and Analytics (PERTEA), pp. 1–5 (2014)

17. Su, T., et al.: Guided, stochastic model-based GUI testing of android apps. In: Proceedings of the 11th Joint Meeting on Foundations of Software Engineering, pp. 245–256 (2017)

18. Vogel, T., Tran, C., Grunske, L.: Does diversity improve the test suite generation for mobile applications? In: Proceedings of the 11th Symposium on Search-Based Software Engineering (SSBSE 2019). Springer, Heidelberg (2019, to appear)

19. Wang, W., et al.: An empirical study of Android test generation tools in industrial cases. In: Proceedings of the 33rd ACM/IEEE International Conference on Automated Software Engineering, pp. 738–748 (2018)

20. Zeng, X., et al.: Automated test input generation for Android: are we really there yet in an industrial case? In: SIGSOFT FSE (2016)

Performance Comparison of Two Search-Based Testing Strategies for ADAS System Validation

Florian Klück[1(✉)], Martin Zimmermann[1(✉)], Franz Wotawa[1(✉)], and Mihai Nica[2(✉)]

[1] Christian Doppler Laboratory for Quality Assurance Methodologies for Autonomous Cyber-Physical Systems, Institute for Software Technology, Graz University of Technology, Graz, Austria
{fklueck,mzimmerm,wotawa}@ist.tugraz.at
[2] AVL List GmbH, Graz, Austria
mihai.nica@avl.com

Abstract. In this paper, we compare the performance of a genetic algorithm for test parameter optimization with simulated annealing and random testing. Simulated annealing and genetic algorithm both represent search-based testing strategies. In the context of autonomous and automated driving, we apply these methods to iteratively optimize test parameters, to aim at obtaining critical scenarios that form the basis for virtual verification and validation of Advanced Driver Assistant System (ADAS). We consider a test scenario to be critical if the underlying parameter set causes a malfunction of the system equipped with the ADAS function (i.e., near-crash or crash of the vehicle). To assess the criticality of each test scenario we rely on time-to-collision (TTC), which is a well-known and often used time-based safety indicator for recognizing rear-end conflicts. For evaluating the performance of each testing strategy, we set up a simulation framework, where we automatically run simulations for each approach until a predefined minimal TTC threshold is reached or a maximal number of iterations has passed. The genetic algorithm-based approach showed the best performance by generating critical scenarios with the lowest number of required test executions, compared to random testing and simulated annealing.

Keywords: Autonomous vehicles · Genetic algorithm · Simulated annealing · System verification · Automatic testing

1 Introduction

In order to improve functionality, increase user experience, or improve safety there is a trend of adding more and more automated and autonomous functions into our currently used devices and systems including cars. In case of the

© IFIP International Federation for Information Processing 2019
Published by Springer Nature Switzerland AG 2019
C. Gaston et al. (Eds.): ICTSS 2019, LNCS 11812, pp. 140–156, 2019.
https://doi.org/10.1007/978-3-030-31280-0_9

latter, Advanced Driver Assistant Systems (ADASs) have become more and more important in order to automate certain functions like keeping a lane on a highway or braking in case of an emergency, maybe finally leading to real autonomous driving not requiring human drivers anymore. Obviously, it is of uttermost importance to keep systems safe especially in case of increased autonomy. Failing to provide an appropriate testing method results in severe accidents causing harm to people. One way of providing measures for keeping systems safe is to come up with a rigorous testing methodology that potentially identifies critical situations a system has to deal with. In this paper, we follow this research direction and provide an automated method for obtaining critical test scenarios.

In the context of our paper, a test scenario is a test case for an autonomous system comprising values for certain test parameters. These parameters are, for example, for setting the speed of the ego vehicle, i.e., the system under test, determining the number of pedestrians crossing a street or the behavior of any other entity that might interact with the system under test. Test scenarios can, therefore, be seen as instances of a general test scenario blueprint where we assign values for the parameters. The objective now is to find critical test scenarios, i.e., test scenarios that lead the system under test to crash (or at least to be close to such a situation). In order to find critical scenarios, we have to search for appropriate parameter values in an n-dimensional space where n is the number of parameters. Considering, in addition, that the parameters are often continuous numbers like the vehicle speed, there is a need for an efficient search procedure.

In this paper, we make use of two of such search algorithms, i.e., the genetic algorithm and simulated annealing, and compare them regarding their appropriateness for being used in the autonomous driving domain. We suggest an algorithm to be more appropriate if the algorithm requires fewer trials for finding a critical test scenario. A trial comprises setting the parameters and calling a simulation engine for executing the test scenario. Since simulation, requiring 3D simulation and physical simulation as well, is computationally demanding and time-consuming, limiting the number of necessary trials is, therefore, significant to make the approach practical. For making the comparison, we make use of the autonomous emergency braking system case study.

In contrast to our previous work [13], where we already introduced the general concept and the use of a genetic algorithm compared to random testing, we report on the following contributions in this paper:

- Introducing simulated annealing for finding parameters leading to a critical scenario in case of testing automated and autonomous systems.
- Comparing the performance of simulated annealing with random testing and our genetic algorithm approach using the autonomous emergency braking system case study.
- Introducing a novel heuristics function for evaluating the quality of tests during searching.

We organized the paper as follows: We first discuss the preliminaries comprising the tool-chain and the algorithmic foundations behind genetic algorithms and simulated annealing. Afterward, we compare the two search algorithms relying on previous research and introduce the underlying case study. The description of the case study comprises details of the setup, the obtained results, and a discussion. Finally, we discuss related research and conclude the paper.

2   Preliminaries

In this paper, we carry forward our previous work [13], where we contributed to automatic test case generation in an automotive context, by identifying critical scenarios that form the basis for virtual verification and validation of ADAS based driving functions. Again, we assume to have a set of parameters that comprise specific values in one particular driving scenario. We are interested in identifying specific values for parameter assignments that result in a driving scenario that can be classified as critical by means of our oracle function. In our case, the driving scenario can be seen as the input for testing and the classification regarding criticality as the output. The oracle function is explained in detail later in this paper.

Given a finite set of parameters P and a function *dom* that returns the domain, i.e., a set of values, for each parameter $p \in P$ as well as an oracle function Γ that returns *critical* $\perp$, in case the execution of the system under test (SUT) together with a given parameter value assignment leads to a critical situation, and *not critical* $\top$, otherwise. From a general perspective the main testing problem is based on the question, if there is an assignment of values PA from $dom(p)$ for all parameters $p \in P$ such that $\Gamma(\text{SUT}, PA)$ returns $\perp$, when executing the SUT. Notably, this testing problem may not be decidable for continuous parameter domains, since we are not able to exhaustively try all different parameter value combinations. For discrete parameter domains, the problem is decidable but it may still be infeasible to solve, due to the huge corresponding search space. In our previous work [13], we concluded that generally, at least for a simple testing problem, both genetic algorithm and random testing are able to find these value to parameter assignments that result in critical driving scenarios. However, evaluating every single execution is costly and time-consuming. Therefore, in this paper we want to investigate which testing strategy requires the least number of executions to find one suitable assignment of continuous values PA from $dom(p)$ for all parameters $p \in P$ such that $\Gamma(\text{SUT}, PA)$ returns $\perp$ at least once. We set up a case study to compare the performance of different search-based testing strategies in finding a suitable value to parameter assignment. As a reference, we compared the genetic algorithm and simulated annealing to random testing. All investigated testing strategies are explained in more detail in the upcoming chapters. The underlying tool-chain for automatic test scenario generation, execution and evaluation is based on previous work in this field [14, 23].

2.1   General Tool-Chain Setup

To facilitate our rather comprehensive testing procedure, we designed the underlying tool-chain to automatically generate, execute and evaluate test scenarios, as pictured in Fig. 1.

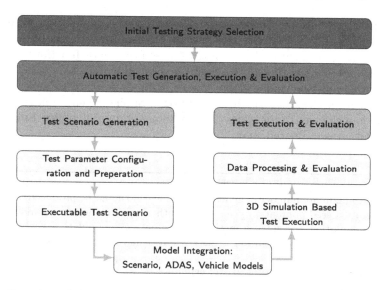

Fig. 1. Overview of the underlying tool chain for automatic test scenario generation, execution and evaluation.

As an initial step, we select and prepare the testing strategy we want to apply and then use a script to configure and initiate the automatic testing procedure. A set of parameter values can be seen as a single test case that forms an executable test scenario when assigned to the appropriate parameters. Test cases are handed over one by one to a model integration and co-simulation platform called AVL Model.Connect [3]. This platform connects different models used for testing (e.g., vehicle models), driving functions as well as an interface to the 3D simulation platform Vires VTD [21]. Model.Connect generates a particular executable driving scenario, based on the obtained test case, and hands it over to Vires VTD for test execution. VTD exploits the input signals and gathers all required information about the virtual environment, for instance, sensor data. Next, all the data collected during test execution is sent back to Model.Connect, where we can access the gathered information via a script, to evaluate the driving scenario regarding criticality. Utilizing this framework allows us to not only carry out multiple experimental runs in sequence but also to execute and evaluate a theoretically unlimited number of test scenarios. Regarding time for testing, we enabled the simulation to run faster than real time and therefore reduced the total test duration by about one third.

2.2   Genetic Algorithm

Generally, genetic algorithms are based on the natural process of reproduction of an organism. The algorithm starts with an initial population and through reproduction and mutation, the algorithm evolves the initial population to a better, i.e., more optimal population. To solve an optimization problem, we can follow Algorithm 1. First, it generates a random start population, where the genes of each individual encode one variant of a solution to the optimization problem. Each individual is then evaluated based on a cost function. Until the number of desired generations is reached, the best individuals are selected from the current population and will be crossed with each other to generate new individuals. In addition to crossing, a mutation of single genes might happen, where random changes to the genes occur with a certain probability. Finally, the new population is evaluated again [9].

Algorithm 1. Basic genetic algorithm

Require: A maximum number of generations G, which should be produced, a method to generate a seed population *generate*, a method to select a new population from an old population *select(P)*, a method to evaluate the population *evaluate(P)*, a method to cross the population *cross(P)* and a method to mutate a population *mutate(P)*.

1: **procedure** GENETICALGORITHM(G, *generate, select, evaluate, cross, mutate*)
2:    $P \leftarrow generate()$
3:    $evaluate(P)$
4:    **for** $g = 0$ to G **do**
5:        $P \leftarrow select(P)$
6:        $P \leftarrow cross(P)$
7:        $P \leftarrow mutate(P)$
8:        $evaluate(P)$
9:    **end for**
10: **end procedure**

The biggest challenge when using a genetic algorithm is to find a suitable encoding for the genes and to design appropriate functions that accurately guide the key processes of generation, selection, crossing and mutation. For our case study, we are using a modified version of the DEAP Python library [7]. The main modification applied for this paper solely stops the GA right after our target value is reached, i.e., this means stopping the GA in the middle of evaluating a generation. As mentioned above, selecting the right encoding for the genes and defining appropriate functions is not trivial and often can only be done by trial and error. We decided to encode the parameters for our case study directly as values from $\mathbb{R}$ in the genes. Our initial population consists of 100 randomly generated individuals. To select individuals for the next generation we use tournament selection with a tournament size of 3. As a crossing function, we are using uniform crossing. After the crossing, each parameter of an individual has a 50% chance to be mutated in the following way. First, we choose a random value between $-\Delta p_i$ and Δp_i, where Δp_i is a value defined per parameter, which indicates how much the mutation is allowed to deviate from the current value. This random value is then added to the current parameter value. The evaluation function will be described in detail in Sect. 4.

2.3 Simulated Annealing

Simulated annealing and genetic algorithm are two distinct optimization techniques that share one particular commonality: they are both inspired by natural processes. While a genetic algorithm models the process of natural selection, simulated annealing is based on the metallurgic challenge to heat and cool a metal properly during processing so that an optimal crystal structure forms. Metals with high temperature and therefore high thermodynamic energy show a loose and very flexible crystal structure that becomes more and more rigid with decreasing temperature. However, if the metal is rapidly quenched, the formed crystal structure is uneven and the metal becomes brittle. During the cooling process, however, to change from an initial sub-optimal crystal structure to an optimal structure, sometimes an intermediate state is required that is even worse, compared to the initial crystal structure. Therefore, simulated annealing also considers bad solutions on a transitional basis, when approximating the global optimum for a given function. The general process behind simulated annealing can be described by the help of two main parameters: temperature and energy. Objects in nature commonly pursue a state with the lowest level of energy possible. Transferred to simulated annealing, a low level of energy represents a good solution. Therefore, the initial solution is modified until a new better solution is found that results in a lower level of energy, compared to the initial solution. Based on the temperature, a probability for intermediately accepting a worse solution is defined. As long as the temperature is high, worse solutions are more likely to be accepted as intermediate states in order to maintain the possibility to leave a local optimum on the way to the global optimum. However, the temperature parameter decreases over time, therefore the chance to leave local optima decreases over time as well. The general working principle for simulated annealing is illustrated in Algorithm 2.

In our case study, we first used a standard version of the simulated annealing algorithm (SA), where the move function behaves the same as the mutation function of the genetic algorithm. Second, we implemented an improvement suggested by Locatelli [16] (Loc. SA) where a sphere around the point, from which new solutions are drawn, shrinks with decreasing temperature. In our case, the sphere covers the whole parameter range at maximum temperature and shrinks proportional until it collapses to a point at the minimum temperature. For both algorithms, we used the Python library Simanneal [18] as a base and modified it accordingly, to include Locatelli's algorithm. We decrease the temperature linearly and the acceptance function is the standard simulated annealing acceptance function depicted in Eq. 1, where e' is the evaluation of the new solution, e is the evaluation of the old solution, and t is the current temperature. Hence, the acceptance function always accepts if the new solution is better or equal to the old solution. If not, a value between 0 and 1 is returned depending on the temperature and the difference between the evaluations of the two solutions. When the system still has a high temperature, the probability for accepting a worse solution will be higher. Similar if the evaluations of the two solutions are close together, the probability for accepting a worse solution will be higher, and

---

Algorithm 2. Basic simulated annealing algorithm

Require: A maximum number of generated solutions S, a method to generate a starting solution *generate*, a method to evaluate a solution *evaluate(s)*, a method that
lowers the temperature $T(t)$, a method to pick a new solution from an existing one
move(s) and an acceptance function $P(e', e, t)$.

1: **procedure** SIMULATEDANNEALING(S, *generate, move, evaluate, P*)
2:     $s \leftarrow generate()$
3:     $e \leftarrow evaluate(s)$
4:     **for** $i = 0$ to S **do**
5:         $t \leftarrow T(t)$
6:         $s' \leftarrow move(s)$ ▷ Is changed to $s' \leftarrow move(s, t)$ in Locatelli's algorithm
7:         $e' \leftarrow evaluate(s')$
8:         **if** $P(e', e, t) \geq random(0, 1)$ **then**
9:             $s \leftarrow s'$
10:             $e \leftarrow e'$
11:         **end if**
12:     **end for**
13: **end procedure**

---

if the evaluations of the solutions are far apart, the probability will be smaller.
As for the genetic algorithm, we will describe the evaluation function in Sect. 4.

$$
P(e', e, t) \begin{cases} 1, & \text{if } e \leq e' \\ \exp(\dfrac{-(e' - e)}{t}), & \text{otherwise} \end{cases} \tag{1}
$$

3   Comparison of Genetic Algorithm and Simulated Annealing

As introduced in the previous sections genetic algorithm and simulated annealing represent two search techniques that utilize heuristic meta information to
find an optimal solution to a problem. In most applications, these algorithms
are used to solve combinatorial optimization problems, e.g., the traveling sales-
man problem. However, they have also successfully been applied to continuous
optimization problems as described in [6]. In our case study, we want to follow
this path of research and apply simulated annealing to a continuous optimization
problem in the context of automated and autonomous systems. Furthermore, we
want to investigate the performance of simulated annealing by comparing it to
the genetic algorithm as done by [17]. Here, Manikas and Cain compared the
performance of simulated annealing and genetic algorithm on a combinatorial
optimization problem, namely the circuit partitioning problem. As a conclusion
they stated that the genetic algorithm is probably more suitable than simulated
annealing when approximating the optimal solution to a function comprising
discrete values. However, they did not provide much information on how many
individual solutions they considered to get to these results, or in other words,

how long it took the two algorithms to come up with the optimal solutions. Regarding execution time, a better indication is provided by [1], where Akinwale et al. compared simulated annealing and the genetic algorithm by applying both search techniques on the timetabling problem, representing another combinatorial problem. They stated that both algorithms produce feasible solutions, however, the execution time for simulated annealing to find such a solution was found to be 2.5 times higher than for the genetic algorithm. Hereafter, Fredrikson and Dahl further investigated the timetabling problem and concluded that the genetic algorithm is faster in the beginning while simulated annealing performs better in the later stages [8]. While most related work in this direction concludes that a genetic algorithm is probably better suited for approximating the optimal solution to a problem, we could not find any work that compares the performance of both algorithms regarding execution time in detail. Therefore, our case study will follow this path of research and analyze the required execution time of both algorithms to find a certain threshold value, representing a good solution to a continuous optimization problem in the context of automated driving based on Advanced Driver Assistant Systems.

4   Case Study

In the following, we report on the results obtained from the case study. First, we describe the underlying experimental setup, followed by presenting and discussing the obtained empirical results.

4.1   Setup

The case study described in this paper is a continuation based on previous research [13], where we investigated the effectiveness of our genetic algorithm approach in finding critical scenarios by comparing it to results obtained when using random testing. Here, we demonstrated that the genetic algorithm reliably finds parameter value combinations that lead to critical driving scenarios. Furthermore, we showed that invalid test scenarios are iteratively eliminated, when the genetic algorithm modifies the generation of new scenarios accordingly. However, random testing did also produce suitable results, which led to the assumption that the genetic algorithm might perform better on driving scenarios with higher complexity, containing more traffic participants, various driving maneuvers and in general more underlying parameters to control.

For the current case study, we made several extensions to the driving scenario in order to increase the complexity. The new driving scenario covers 16 different parameter domains and describes the ego vehicle (EGO) driving behind another vehicle, the global vehicle target (GVT), on a straight road with a cluster of two parking vehicles on the right side as shown in Fig. 2. In addition, two pedestrians are moving either aside or across the road. The first pedestrian can cross the street in various angles from the left, the second pedestrian can walk across the street either behind the second car, between the two cars, or in front of the first

Fig. 2. This exemplary simulation run shows the Ego vehicle (following vehicle), the GVT vehicle (leading vehicle) as well as a cluster of parked vehicles aside the road with one pedestrian ready to cross the street. Within the sensor range (yellow cone) green bounding boxes are drawn around detected objects. (Color figure online)

car. In total we have 16 different parameter domains that act as placeholders in the predefined scenario template, forming an executable driving scenario as soon as continuous parameter values are assigned accordingly. This executable driving scenario is then simulated for 90 s in our tool-chain as described in Sect. 2.1. Hereby, the genetic algorithm approach iteratively optimizes test parameter values from a given seed population. Simulated annealing modifies parameter values by selecting new values within a variable range embracing the current parameter values. For random testing an arbitrary set of parameter values is selected to form an executable scenario. The resulting driving scenarios form the basis for virtually testing the ego vehicle equipped with an AEB system. The AEB system is a vehicle active safety function, designed to automatically trigger a braking maneuver in response to the detection of a potential collision. The system comprises two main modules, first the vision system and second the brake control system. The vision system (I) is based on a perfect radar sensor model, enabling the system to detect even covered objects, as well as an object detection algorithm. As soon as an object enters the radar's cone-shaped field of view (i.e., within 250 m), the system detects the object and identifies its position and speed. Based on that, the brake control system (II) calculates the minimum required braking distance towards the object and adds a velocity dependent safety margin. As soon as the calculated distance is equal to or goes below the actual headway distance, an appropriate braking maneuver is triggered in accordance with the situation.

The main objective of the case study, presented in this paper, is to investigate how long it takes, for each of the three different approaches, to find a satisfiable solution (i.e., a critical driving scenario). In other words, for each approach, we want to investigate how many test executions are required to generate a solution that meets the predefined evaluation target. Regarding evaluation, we rely on time-to-collision (TTC), a well-known and commonly used indicator to identify potential rear-end conflicts [12]. According to previously conducted experiments, based on the virtual driving scenario we consider in this case study, we found that a TTC below 0.3 s represents the transition area from a near-crash scenario to an actual crash scenario. Therefore, we set the target value for our evaluation criteria to 0.3 s, i.e., the oracle function Γ returns *critical* $\perp$ in this case. Furthermore, based on previous work as described in [13], we made several improvements to the evaluation function itself, to guide the generation of a critical scenario more efficiently. Therefore, we introduced five different criticality zones that we monitor throughout the simulation and use the obtained information as additional input for our evaluation function. The zones are listed from least critical to most critical.

1. No object is within a 250 m radius of the EGO
2. An object is anywhere within a 250 m radius of the EGO
3. An object is in the lane of the EGO and less than 250 m away
4. An object is in front of the EGO produces a TTC of less than 20 s
5. An object is in front of the EGO produces a TTC of less than 0.3 s

The genetic algorithm and simulated annealing are designed to modify parameter assignments such that the resulting driving scenario traverses from low criticality zones to higher criticality zones over time. We automatically executed each method seven times to compare how many test executions are required in average and median to find a driving scenario for which the oracle function Γ returns *critical* $\perp$ (i.e., TTC below 0.3 s), before a maximum number of 500 iterations has passed.

4.2   Results

As described in the previous section, we carried out further experiments based on the AEB case study, described in [13], to investigate how many test executions are required in order to find a suitable solution (i.e., a driving scenario for which the oracle function Γ returns *critical* $\perp$), when applying genetic algorithm, simulated annealing and random parameter selection. Therefore, we executed each method seven times until either a resulting TTC of 0.3 s was detected or a maximum number of 500 iterations has passed. Clearly, we are hereby searching for a solution that meets a certain threshold value, rather than searching for the global optimum. In the following, we want to report on the empirical results obtained from our experiments, as summarized in Table 1.

Table 1. Overview on the test results obtained from seven experimental runs for every investigated test methods.

	Average	Minimum	1. Quartile	Median	3. Quartile	Maximum
GA	41.71	18	19	35	65	70
RA	83.85	4	20	53	127	235
SA	268.57	40	131	213	500	500
Loc. SA	228.42	6	20	49	500	500

As the first column of Table 1 shows, overall it took the genetic algorithm
(GA) the lowest number of test executions, in average 42 executions, to generate
a test scenario that results in a TTC value below 0.3 s. In addition, the genetic
algorithm showed very consistent performance and reliably found a suitable solution in each of the seven experimental runs. In comparison, the second row of
Table 1 summarizes the results obtained when applying random parameter value
selection (RA). For random testing in average 84 executions are required to generate a test scenario that results in a TTC value below 0.3 s. Also for random
testing a suitable solution (i.e., a driving scenario for which the oracle function Γ
returns *critical* $\perp$) was found in each of the seven test runs. The highest number
of executions is on average required for both simulated annealing approaches,
where it took the basic algorithm (SA) on average 269 executions and the algorithm proposed by Locatelli (Loc. SA) on average 229 executions, to generate a
suitable solution. The high number of test executions for Loc. SA in the 3. Quar-
tile in contrast to low median shows that it either finds a suitable solution really
fast or not at all (i.e., termination after 500 iterations), which can be explained
by the general working principle of the Loc. SA. Not finding a solution at all
might happen when the initial solution, which the Loc. SA randomly generates,
is very far away from the global optimum and it also does not find a good solution within the first few iterations. Both simulated annealing algorithms have in
common that when searching for the global optimum, the algorithms are very
likely to get stuck in one of the several local optima, which are better than
the initial solution. With decreasing temperature over time, also the possibility
of leaving such a better suited but still insufficient local optimum is decreasing.
The advantage of the simulated annealing algorithm proposed by Locatelli, compared to the basic SA, is that the algorithm is able to take significantly greater
steps through the search space, depending on the temperature. This advantage
becomes clearly visible if we compare the average and the median number of
required executions, as visualized for all investigated test methods in Fig. 3.

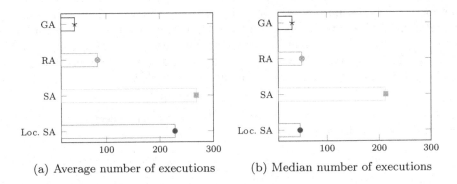

(a) Average number of executions   (b) Median number of executions

Fig. 3. Comparison of (a) average and (b) median number of required execution per
test method.

Here it can be seen that for genetic algorithm (GA), random testing (RA) as well as for the basic simulated annealing algorithm (SA), the difference between average and median number of required executions is comparatively small. However, for the simulated annealing algorithm as proposed by Locatelli (Loc. SA), we observe a major gap with an average number of 229 and a median number of 49 required executions. Considering every individual result obtained from the seven Loc. SA runs, we observe that if the Loc. SA has not found a suitable solution after 49 executions, it will not find a solution at all but run into the stop criterion instead, which is triggered after 500 test executions. This observation is reasonable due to the fact that for the Loc. SA algorithm the temperature parameter is proportionally decreasing with every execution towards a minimal temperature value, which is reached after 500 executions. In other words, with an increasing number of test executions, the sphere that defines the search space around the current solution is steadily tightening until no new solutions are produced at all. In contrast, the basic SA works with a fixed search space and could technically still accept better solutions after 500 iterations, eventually finding a suitable solution if an arbitrary number of test executions would be permissible. It would be interesting to see if the performance of the Loc. SA can be further increased if we define an individual stop criterion that restarts the algorithm, if no suitable solution is found after a certain number of test executions, indicating an unsuitable initial solution. We will follow this approach as part of our future research. The summarized results in Table 1 are visualized in Fig. 4 to be further investigated and to be compared in more detail.

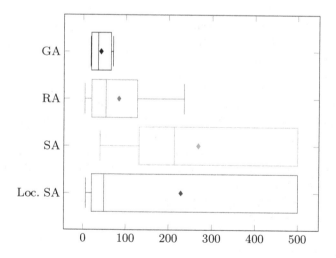

Fig. 4. Comparison of Box-Plots comprising the results obtained from seven test run for each investigated method

Here again, we see that the genetic algorithm finds suitable solutions in the fastest and most effective manner. The corresponding box plot summarizes the distribution of results obtained from all seven experimental runs. It can be observed that the minimum number (vertical line on the left) of 18 required executions and the maximum number (vertical line on the right) of 70 required executions closely embrace the interquartile range (box), showing that 50% of all test runs required between 19 and 65 executions until a suitable solution was found. Notably, the median number (vertical line in box) of 35 required executions does not deviate much from the average number (diamond in box) of 42 required executions. This leads to the interpretation that the genetic algorithm performs very consistently and produces results that are not much affected by any outliers.

For random testing, it can be observed that 50% of all test runs required between 20 and 127 executions until a solution was found, for which the oracle function Γ returns *critical* $\perp$. However, random testing is slightly stronger affected by outlier results in both directions compared to the genetic algorithm, as indicated by a minimum number of 4 required executions and a maximum number of 235 required executions. This observation is also supported by a bigger deviation between the average and the median number of required executions. Based on our results, the basic simulated annealing algorithm performed worse, compared to the other investigated methods. Here, on average 269 executions were required to find a solution. 50% of all test runs required more than 213 executions to find a suitable solution, as indicated by the median, or terminated before finding any good solution at all. The deviation between average and median required number of executions is greater than for the genetic algorithm and for random testing, indicating that the basic simulated annealing algorithm is strongly affected by outlier results.

Finally, for the simulated annealing algorithm as proposed by Locatelli we can observe that the box plot more or less covers the whole area of possible results. Notably, 50% of all test runs required between 6 and 49 executions to find a suitable solution, which is comparable to the performance we observed for the genetic algorithm and random testing. However, in this case, the deviation between average and median required number of executions is significantly greater than for all the other investigated methods. This underlines our previously described assumption, that also the Loc. SA either finds a suitable solution very fast or not at all, depending on the quality of the initial solution. As previously mentioned, we find this observation quite interesting and will make further adjustments to the Loc. SA as part of our future work. Hereby, we plan to introduce a new internal stopping criterion that triggers the generation of a new initial solution, if necessary.

4.3   Discussion

In the subsection Results, we discussed the experimental results obtained from the case study, where we investigated which testing strategy requires the lowest number of executions to generate a critical scenario (i.e., resulting in TTC values below 0.3 s). In the course of the case study, we compared the performance of a genetic algorithm to simulated annealing and random testing. Hereby, the genetic algorithm showed the best performance in finding the desired value to parameter assignments that lead to a critical driving scenario, with regards to the required number of test executions. Furthermore, for the basic simulated annealing algorithm as well as for the simulated annealing algorithm proposed by Locatelli, both strength and weaknesses were detected. On the one hand, depending on the quality of the initial solution, both simulated annealing algorithms are generally able to find a suitable solution within a low number of test executions. However, on the other hand, if the initial solution is of bad quality, both simulated annealing algorithms are very likely to get stuck in local optima rather than generating a critical driving scenario. Although the observed data is very interesting, we acknowledged that the results of only 7 test runs per method do not represent a sufficiently large data set to conduct meaningful statistical analysis. However, we consider the presented evaluation as an initial basis for conducting larger experiments in our further work. Also based on the observation that Loc. SA performance either good or bad, we plan to make further improvements to the simulated annealing algorithm proposed by Locatelli as part of our future research.

5   Related Work

One of the biggest challenges for testing ADAS systems is caused by the near infinite input domain. Due to that, Rafaelli proposed that stochastic approaches should be preferably used for ADAS systems verification and validation, rather than deterministic approaches and test protocols [19]. Therefore, the idea to use stochastic and search-based testing methods for system testing is not novel. In their paper Gross et al. compared search-based testing on module or unit level to search-based testing on system level. They concluded that search-based testing is only meaningful when it is performed on a system level. Otherwise, a large number of false positive test cases is generated that only reveal the execution of an invalid input sequence. However, when search-based testing methods are used on system level all revealed faults have been shown to be actual faults of the system [10].

In the automotive direction, there are also a few papers available that describe frameworks for testing ADAS functions [15, 20, 25, 26]. However, none of these frameworks provide an automated method for ADAS system testing. In literature we can also find some papers on parameter optimization utilizing a genetic algorithm [22, 24], as well as utilizing a simulated annealing algorithm [11]. In these papers, both methods are usually described to perform better or comparably good compared to a random selection of parameter values. Furthermore, genetic algorithms have also been used in software testing, for example, to find tests that cause extreme processing times as described in [2].

Moreover, a few studies have also been conducted on testing ADAS functions by utilizing a genetic algorithm or similar search-based algorithms. Ben Abdessalem et al. have created their own algorithm based on a genetic algorithm and applied it for testing a pedestrian detection system [4]. Similar to our paper, [5] compared random testing with evolutionary test case generation. However, they left a few research questions unanswered, which we took into account in our last paper [13], where we also focused on testing an AEB function and compared random test case generation to test case generation guided by a genetic algorithm.

6   Conclusion

In this paper, we have compared the use of a genetic algorithm and simulated annealing for test parameter optimization in the context of autonomous and automated driving. Especially in case of advanced driver assistant systems, it is of uttermost importance to find instances of usage scenarios that might lead to crash situations in order to verify the implemented functionality. Because of the limited amount of resources it is, therefore, important to introduce an automated method. For this purpose we suggest a combination of search-based testing and system simulation. The goal of this paper is to evaluate two algorithms for implementing search-based testing using the autonomous emergency braking system. In addition to previous research, we also modified and improved the heuristics function for evaluating solutions.

The results of the empirical evaluation showed that the genetic algorithm is superior compared to simulated annealing and also random testing. Using a genetic algorithm for test parameter optimization for the autonomous emergency braking system requires fewer test executions on average and on median compared to the other methods. In future research, besides improving the Loc. SA, we will further investigate on this comparison using more and larger case studies from the autonomous driving domain.

Acknowledgment. The financial support by the Austrian Federal Ministry for Digital and Economic Affairs and the National Foundation for Research, Technology and Development is gratefully acknowledged. We also want to thank our colleague Jianbo Tao for supporting the tool-chain set-up and AVL List GmbH for providing the underlying simulation models and software tools required for the empirical evaluation. The investigated prototypical AEB function was developed in the course of internal research activities and is solely used for demonstration purpose.

References

1. Akinwale, C., Olatunde, S., Olusayo, E., Babalola, J., et al.: Performance evaluation of simulated annealing and genetic algorithm in solving examination timetabling problem. Sci. Res. Essays **7**(17), 1727–1733 (2012)
2. Alander, J.T., Mantere, T., Turunen, P.: Genetic algorithm based software testing. In: Smith, G.D., Steele, N.C., Albrecht, R.F. (eds.) Artificial Neural Nets and Genetic Algorithms, pp. 325–328. Springer, Vienna (1998). https://doi.org/10.1007/978-3-7091-6492-1_71
3. AVL List GmbH: Model.connect. https://www.avl.com/-/model-connect-

4. Ben Abdessalem, R., Nejati, S., Briand, L.C., Stifter, T.: Testing advanced driver assistance systems using multi-objective search and neural networks. In: Proceedings of the 31st IEEE/ACM International Conference on Automated Software Engineering, ASE 2016, pp. 63–74. ACM, New York (2016). https://doi.org/10.1145/2970276.2970311

5. Buehler, O., Wegener, J.: Evolutionary functional testing of a vehicle brake assistant system. In: 6th Metaheuristics International Conference, Vienna, Austria. Citeseer (2005)

6. Erdogmus, P., Ozturk, A., Tosun, S.: Continuous optimization problem solution with simulated annealing and genetic algorithms. J. Eng. Res. Appl. Sci. **2**(1), 116–121 (2013)

7. Fortin, F.A., De Rainville, F.M., Gardner, M.A., Parizeau, M., Gagné, C.: DEAP: evolutionary algorithms made easy. J. Mach. Learn. Res. **13**, 2171–2175 (2012)

8. Fredrikson, R., Dahl, J.: A comparative study between a simulated annealing and a genetic algorithm for solving a university timetabling problem (2016)

9. Goldberg, D.E.: Genetic Algorithms in Search, Optimization and Machine Learning, 1st edn. Addison-Wesley Longman Publishing Co., Inc., Boston (1989)

10. Gross, F., Fraser, G., Zeller, A.: Search-based system testing: high coverage, no false alarms. In: Proceedings of the 2012 International Symposium on Software Testing and Analysis, ISSTA 2012, pp. 67–77. ACM, New York (2012). https://doi.org/10.1145/2338965.2336762

11. Haddock, J., Mittenthal, J.: Simulation optimization using simulated annealing. Comput. Ind. Eng. **22**(4), 387–395 (1992). https://doi.org/10.1016/0360-8352(92)90014-B. http://www.sciencedirect.com/science/article/pii/036083529290014B

12. Kircher, K.: A comparison of headway and time to collision as safety indicators. Accid. Anal. Prev. **35**, 427–433 (2003). https://doi.org/10.1016/S0001-4575(02)00022-2

13. Klück, F., Zimmermann, M., Wotawa, F., Nica, M.: Genetic algorithm-based test parameter optimization for ADAS system testing. In: Proceedings of the 19th International Conference on Software Quality, Reliability and Security (2019)

14. Klueck, F., Li, Y., Nica, M., Tao, J., Wotawa, F.: Using ontologies for test suites generation for automated and autonomous driving functions. In: 2018 IEEE International Symposium on Software Reliability Engineering Workshops (ISSREW), pp. 118–123, October 2018. https://doi.org/10.1109/ISSREW.2018.00-20

15. Lattarulo, R., Pérez, J., Dendaluce, M.: A complete framework for developing and testing automated driving controllers. IFAC-PapersOnLine **50**(1), 258–263 (2017). https://doi.org/10.1016/j.ifacol.2017.08.043. http://www.sciencedirect.com/science/article/pii/S2405896317300587. 20th IFAC World Congress

16. Locatelli, M.: Simulated annealing algorithms for continuous global optimization: convergence conditions. J. Optim. Theory Appl. **104**(1), 121–133 (2000). https://doi.org/10.1023/A:1004680806815

17. Manikas, T.W., Cain, J.T.: Genetic algorithms vs. simulated annealing: a comparison of approaches for solving the circuit partitioning problem. Comput. Sci. Eng. Res. 1 (1996)

18. Perry, M.: simanneal: Python module for simulated annealing. https://github.com/perrygeo/simanneal (2013–2019)

19. Raffaelli, L.: Facing ADAS validation complexity with usage oriented testing. In: ERTS 2016, Toulouse, France, p. 13, January 2016. https://hal.inria.fr/hal-01277494

20. Semrau, M., Erdmann, J.: Simulation framework for testing ADAS in Chinese traffic situations. SUMO 2016 Traffic Mobil. Logist. **30**, 103–115 (2016)
21. VIRES Simulationstechnologie GmbH: Vtd – virtual test drive. https://vires.com/vtd-vires-virtual-test-drive/
22. Wang, Q.: Using genetic algorithms to optimise model parameters. Environ. Model. Softw. **12**(1), 27–34 (1997). https://doi.org/10.1016/S1364-8152(96)00030-8. http://www.sciencedirect.com/science/article/pii/S1364815296000308
23. Wotawa, F., Peischl, B., Klück, F., Nica, M.: Quality assurance methodologies for automated driving. e & i Elektrotechnik und Informationstechnik **135**(4), 322–327 (2018). https://doi.org/10.1007/s00502-018-0630-7
24. Wright, A.H.: Genetic algorithms for real parameter optimization. Found. Genet. Algorithms **1**, 205–218 (1991). https://doi.org/10.1016/B978-0-08-050684-5.50016-1. http://www.sciencedirect.com/science/article/pii/B9780080506845500161
25. Zhou, J., Schmied, R., Sandalek, A., Kokal, H., del Re, L.: A framework for virtual testing of ADAS (2016). https://doi.org/10.4271/2016-01-0049
26. Zofka, M.R., Klemm, S., Kuhnt, F., Schamm, T., Zöllner, J.M.: Testing and validating high level components for automated driving: simulation framework for traffic scenarios. In: 2016 IEEE Intelligent Vehicles Symposium (IV), pp. 144–150, June 2016. https://doi.org/10.1109/IVS.2016.7535378

Testing and Verification Techniques

Bounded Exhaustive Testing with Certified and Optimized Data Enumeration Programs

Clotilde Erard and Alain Giorgetti[⊠]

FEMTO-ST Institute, Univ. of Bourgogne Franche-Comté, CNRS, Besançon, France
`alain.giorgetti@femto-st.fr`

Abstract. Bounded exhaustive testing (BET) is an elementary technique in automated unit testing. It consists in testing a function with all input data up to a given size bound. We implement BET to check logical and program properties, before attempting to prove them formally with the deductive verification tool Why3. We also present a library of enumeration programs for BET, certified by formal proofs of their properties with Why3. In order to make BET more efficient, we study and compare several strategies to optimize these programs.

Keywords: Bounded exhaustive testing · Formal verification · Algorithmic efficiency

1 Introduction

Bounded Exhaustive Testing (BET, for short) automates unit testing of a function by checking one of its properties for all admissible inputs up to some size. Although this method is limited to small input data, its relevance is recognized [15,21] since it facilitates debugging by providing the smallest counterexamples, and provides confidence by guaranteeing the absence of errors below some size bound. This makes BET complementary to methods adapted to data of larger size, such as random testing. Whatever, the subject of this paper is not to compare BET with other test methods, but to improve the quality and availability of BET tools.

BET has first been used to check properties of functional languages, as exemplified by SmallCheck in Haskell [20]. Then, BET has been adapted to several proof assistants, e.g., to Isabelle in Quickcheck [4] and more recently to Coq, in an extension of QuickChick [14] named CUT (Coq Unit Testing) [7].

BET is also relevant to check properties produced by deductive verification, aka. *verification conditions* that a given program satisfies a given specification. We present a prototypical implementation of BET in the deductive verification tool Why3 [3]. Programs for Why3 are written in WhyML, a verification-oriented dialect of ML with some functional features, such as polymorphic algebraic types, but also imperative features, such as loops or records with mutable

© IFIP International Federation for Information Processing 2019
Published by Springer Nature Switzerland AG 2019
C. Gaston et al. (Eds.): ICTSS 2019, LNCS 11812, pp. 159–175, 2019.
https://doi.org/10.1007/978-3-030-31280-0_10

fields. The functional behavior of WhyML programs can be specified with formal annotations: preconditions, postconditions, invariants and loop variants, assertions, etc., in a first-order logic with polymorphic types. Why3 standard library defines theories or data structures for common types such as integers, lists or arrays. Why3 reduces programs and specifications to logical verification conditions whose satisfiability entails that the programs meet their specifications. Then, automated provers (e.g., SMT solvers) or proof assistants (e.g., Coq) can be used to prove these logical statements. Why3 also provides extraction to get correct-by-construction OCaml programs.

Some BET tools implement techniques such as constraint solving or local choice with backtracking, either to enumerate data or to derive enumeration programs from data definitions (see [6, Section 7] for references). However, these techniques may fail or enumerate data too slowly. For effectiveness, we consider BET using a distinct handwritten enumeration program for each family of data of interest. Dubois and Giorgetti proposed BET for Coq with such *custom* enumeration programs, defined either in Coq or in Why3 language [6].

Confidence in BET is increased if its enumeration programs are certified, ideally with formal proofs of their properties. Genestier et al. [10] developed a first version of the ENUM library, gathering enumeration programs in C language, formally specified with ACSL clauses and proved with Frama-C plugin WP for deductive verification. An adaptation to Why3 of a small fragment of this library has been presented to the French community [11,12]. Here we present a larger version of this library and its certification with Why3.

Another challenge for BET is to design and implement efficient enumeration algorithms. We examine here several ways to reduce their algorithmic cost: by implementing algorithms in a more efficient language (C versus WhyML), or by using optimized compilation. We also study the negative impact that these optimizations might have on certification.

The first contribution of this work is an implementation of BET to check Why3 properties (Sect. 2). The second contribution is a library of enumeration programs certified with Why3 (Sect. 3). The third contribution is an experimental study to optimize enumeration programs without sacrificing too much their certification (Sects. 4 and 5).

2   Bounded Exhaustive Testing for Why3

This section presents our implementation of bounded exhaustive testing for Why3 properties. It consists of a generic BET function (described in Sect. 2.2) and a library of enumeration programs (detailed in Sect. 3). All enumeration programs implement the same interface, described in Sect. 2.1. Two examples of BET are given in Sects. 2.3 and 2.4, respectively with success and exhibiting a counterexample.

2.1   Common Interface of Enumeration Programs

Since enumeration is a particular form of iteration, we specify and implement enumeration programs (sometimes hereafter called *generators*) by adapting the modular iterators defined by Filliâtre and Pereira [8,9]. Our generators modify a state, called a *cursor*, whose type is

```
type cursor = { current: array int; mutable new: bool; }
```

in WhyML. The field `current` stores the last data generated so far. For simplicity, it is here a mutable array of integers, but other types can be used similarly. The Boolean flag `new` is set to `false` if and only if the data stored in the `current` field has already been exploited, for instance to test a property.

The generators presented in this paper are composed of two functions (declared on Lines 3 and 4 in Listing 1.1): a constructor `create_cursor` initiates the cursor with the first element of the iteration, and a function `next` replaces the data in the cursor with the next one, if it exists. Otherwise, it sets the field `c.new` to false.

2.2   BET Function

BET is implemented by the generic function `small_check` in Listing 1.1, whose execution tests the property defined by the `oracle` function (first parameter) for all data of size n (second parameter). The first parameter of the module `SmallCheck` (on Line 2) is a characteristic predicate of the enumerated data.

Note that the input type for the `oracle` function is a list rather than an array, because Why3 has limited support for function parameters that are functions working with mutable data. For the same reason, the generator functions cannot be input parameters for `small_check` function. Therefore we define them as module parameters (on Lines 3–4). They can be instantiated thanks to Why3's module cloning mechanism, as detailed in Sect. 2.3.

The return type `verdict` is composed of the field `witness` storing either a counterexample, if it exists, or the empty list (`Nil`) otherwise, and the field `rank` storing either the number of data tested when the witness is found, or the total number of tested data if there is no counterexample. The function `small_check` first creates the cursor (line 12), then converts the cursor array into a list (line 18), by using the `to_list` function from Why3 standard library. Finally, `small_check` tests each generated data with the `oracle` (line 19). If a counterexample is found, it is stored in the local variable `ce` (line 22), the enumeration is stopped and the function returns the counterexample and the number of data tested so far. Otherwise, the function stops when all data have been tested.

The `diverges` clause (on Line 10) declares that the function is not guaranteed to terminate. To prove its termination it is necessary to annotate its `while` loop with a *variant*, an integer expression whose value is non-negative before the loop and strictly decreases between two successive loop iterations. Defining a unique variant for all kinds of enumerated data is a challenging task out of the scope of the present study.

```
 1 module SmallCheck
 2   predicate is_XXX (a: array int)
 3   val create_cursor (n: int) : cursor
 4   val next (c: cursor) : unit
 5
 6   type verdict = { witness: list int; rank: int; }
 7
 8   let small_check (oracle: list int → bool) (n: int) : verdict
 9     requires { n ≥ 0 }
10     diverges
11   =
12     let c = create_cursor n in
13     let ref r = 0 in
14     let ref ce = Nil in
15     while c.new do
16       r := r+1;
17       let a = c.current in
18       let l = to_list a 0 a.length in
19       if oracle l then
20         next c
21       else begin
22         ce := l;
23         c.new ← false
24       end
25     done;
26     { witness = ce; rank = r }
27 end
```

Listing 1.1. BET function in WhyML.

2.3   Example of BET

We illustrate our BET for Why3 with functions and properties on permutations
of a given size. Permutations on a finite set is an important topic in combinatorics
and group theory. They have recently been formalized as injective endofunctions
in Coq [6, Section 3]. The present example is the first step of an adaptation of
that case study to Why3.

The permutation p on the set $[0..n-1]$ of first n natural numbers is encoded
by the Why3 integer array a of its images, i.e., $a[i] = p(i)$ for $0 \leq i < n$. We
characterize these permutation arrays with the predicate

```
predicate is_permut (a: array int) = range a ∧ injective a
```

where (range a) specifies that the values of array a are in $[0...a.\texttt{length} - 1]$
and (injective a) specifies injectivity of the function represented by a, i.e.,
uniqueness of values in a.

Let us consider the **reverse** function in Listing 1.2. The function reverses the
order of the elements of its input array. For instance, it turns the array 4 1 0 7
into the array 7 0 1 4. It proceeds by exchanging symmetrical elements with

respect to the middle of the array. We want to prove that the function `reverse` preserves permutations. This property is specified by the precondition and the postcondition on Lines 2–3.

```
1 let reverse (a: array int) : unit
2   requires { is_permut a }
3   ensures { is_permut a }
4 =
5   let n = a.length in
6   let ref x = 0 in
7   let ref y = n-1 in
8   while x < y do
9     let v = a[x] in
10    a[x] ← a[y];
11    a[y] ← v;
12    y := y - 1;
13    x := x + 1
14  done
```

Listing 1.2. Reverse function under test.

Since WhyML predicates are not necessarily decidable, all specifications are ignored when a program is run. In particular, the postcondition (`is_permut a`) is not executable. In order to test it, a Boolean function implementing the logical predicate `is_permut` has to be provided. A Boolean function implementing a logical predicate, when it exists, is a *decision procedure* for this predicate. The Boolean function and a proof that it corresponds to the predicate are together called a *Boolean reflection*. This mechanism has several applications, e.g., proof automation [13].

The Boolean function

```
let function b_permut (a: array int) : bool = b_range a && b_injective a
```

decides the predicate `is_permut` if `b_range` and `b_injective` respectively are decision procedures for the predicates `range` and `injective`. We only detail the Boolean reflection `b_range` of the predicate

```
predicate range (a: array int) =
  ∀ i: int. 0 ≤ i < a.length → in_interval a[j] 0 n
```

a naive (i.e., non-optimized) implementation of the predicate `injective` being similar. The predicate

```
predicate in_interval (x l u: int) = l ≤ x < u
```

is a specificity of WhyML. It is indeed both a logical predicate and a Boolean function, because it is also the case for comparison operators on integers. Thus, we have its Boolean reflection for free.

The Boolean function `b_range` in Listing 1.3 is a decision procedure for the predicate `range`. The universal quantification is implemented by a `for` loop that stops at the first array value not in the interval $[0..n-1]$. The postcondition (on Line 2) ensures that the Boolean function decides the logical predicate `range`: the function returns `true` if and only if the predicate holds for the input array `a`.

```
1 let function b_range (a: array int) : bool
2   ensures { result ↔ range a }
3 =
4   let n = a.length in
5   for j = 0 to n - 1 do
6     invariant { range_sub a 0 j n }
7     if not (in_interval a[j] 0 n) then return false
8   done;
9   true
```

Listing 1.3. Boolean function b_range.

A loop invariant (on Line 6) helps to prove the postcondition. It uses the generalization

```
predicate range_sub (a: array int) (l u b: int) =
  ∀ i: int. l ≤ i < u → in_interval a[i] 0 b
```

of range which controls that each element of the subarray $a[l..u-1]$ is in the interval $[0...b-1]$.

Whereas implementing a decision procedure is in general a difficult problem, it becomes simple for the family of first-order properties on integer arrays where all quantifications on array indices and values are bounded. All such universal quantifications (∀) can be implemented by a for loop as in the former example, and implementing an existential quantification (∃) is similar. Genestier et al. [10] showed that these array properties are common in combinatorics. They proposed a general pattern of Boolean reflection, when the properties are specified by ACSL predicates and implemented by Boolean functions in C language. The decidability property is proved generically, once for all, for all kinds of predicates. So, it holds for free (without requiring specific annotations) for each pattern instantiation. The adaptation of this feature to WhyML is left as future work.

```
1 use permutation.Permutation
2 use permutation.Enum
3
4 clone SmallCheck with
5   predicate is_XXX = is_permut,
6   val create_cursor = create_cursor,
7   val next = next
8
9 let test () : verdict
10   diverges
11 =
12   let n = 6 in
13   small_check (fun l → let a = to_array l in reverse a; b_permut a) n
```

Listing 1.4. Test program.

A simple program to test that the reverse function preserves permutations is presented in Listing 1.4. The declarations on Lines 1 and 2 import other modules. The module Permutation provides the predicate is_permut and its Boolean reflection b_permut. The module Enum provides a cursor and its functions to enumerate permutations. The declaration on Lines 4–7 imports a clone of the generic module `SmallCheck`, instantiated with the characteristic predicate `is_permut` and the enumeration functions for permutations. This cloning provides the type `verdict` and the right instance of the generic function `small_check` to test properties for all permutations with a given size. For the size $n = 6$ the test program (on Lines 9–13) uses this instance and an anonymous oracle function working as follows: as required by `small_check`, its input `l` is a list of integers. The function `to_array` from Why3 standard library transforms it into an array `a`, then reversed in-place by application of the `reverse` function. Finally the Boolean function `b_permut` is applied to the resulting array.

For efficiency and to get an explicit test result, the test code is executed in OCaml, after extraction of the test program and related modules. Thanks to some additional lines of OCaml code, the test result is displayed as follows:

```
Test passed. 720 data tested.
```

meaning that the test was successful for the $6! = 720$ permutations of size 6. This BET is executed in less than one second, in the environment used for the experimentation described in Sect. 4, where more efficiency results are provided.

The current prototype does not allow to set a time limit for BET, but it can be completed with this feature. The approach is suitable for arrays containing integers in a small interval, as it is the case for permutations here. For larger integer ranges, random generation is preferable.

2.4 Counterexample

What happens if there is an error in a tested function? To illustrate the behavior of `small_check` in that case we inject an error on Line 9 of the `reverse` function (in Listing 1.2) that becomes the following one:

```
let v = a[y] in
```

When running the same test (in Listing 1.4) for this erroneous version, the following output

```
Test failed after 1 test(s). Counterexample:
[0 1 2 3 4 5 ]
```

provides as counterexample a permutation that the false version of the `reverse` function transforms into the array

```
[4 4 3 3 4 4 ]
```

which is not a permutation. This BET discovers this error only after generating one test case. In general, more test cases may be required.

3 Certified Library of Enumeration Programs

ENUM is a library of certified enumeration programs for BET, freely distributed at https://github.com/alaingiorgetti/enum.[1] Its first releases were composed of

---

[1] The work presented in this paper is in release 1.2 of ENUM.

C programs specified in ACSL language and verified with Frama-C plugin WP for deductive verification [10]. This section presents a new part of ENUM, composed of enumeration programs specified and implemented in WhyML. It is an almost complete adaptation in WhyML of the C/ACSL enumeration programs, completed by new generators. Its programs implement algorithms that enumerate combinatorial structures [2] and have various applications in combinatorics.

Section 3.1 introduces some expected properties of these generators and their formalization in WhyML. Section 3.2 presents a simple way to define a generator, by filtering the output of another generator. Section 3.3 describes the techniques we use to assist formal proofs that the generators satisfy their expected properties. Finally, the content of the library is detailed in Sect. 3.4.

3.1 Properties

Each data enumeration program is expected to satisfy the following three behavioral properties. *Soundness* is the property that each generated data satisfies the characteristics (or *data invariant*) of its family, such as being a duplicate-free or a sorted array. *Completeness* is the property that the program produces all existing data with a given size, without omitting any of them. Generally, proving completeness is more challenging than proving soundness. Therefore, we limit ourselves to algorithms enumerating data in a predefined strict total order, hereafter denoted by $\prec$, and we adopt two strategies. The first strategy is to specify completeness as the conjunction of the following three properties: the property *min* that the first generated data is the smallest one, the property *max* that the last generated data is the largest one, and the property *inc* (for "incrementality") that each data a_2 generated from data a_1 is the smallest data strictly greater than a_1. In other words, no sound data a_3 is such that $a_1 \prec a_3 \prec a_2$. When proving completeness seems too difficult, the second strategy is to address the less challenging property – named *progress* – that each generated data is strictly greater than the former generated data. Since we assume that there are finitely many data with each size, progress entails termination of bounded-exhaustive enumeration.

```
1 val create_cursor (n: int) : cursor
2   requires { n ≥ 0 }
3   ensures { c.new → sound result }
4   ensures { c.new → min result.current }
5
6 val next (c: cursor) : unit
7   requires { sound c }
8   ensures { c.new → sound c }
9   ensures { c.new → lt (old c.current) c.current }
10  ensures { c.new → inc (old c.current) c.current }
11  ensures { not c.new → max (old c.current) }
```

Listing 1.5. Contracts of enumeration functions.

Listing 1.5 shows a declaration of the enumeration functions with their contracts (pre- and postconditions) formalizing these properties in WhyML. The precondition on Line 2 specifies that the size n of data should be a natural number. The function `create_cursor` (resp. `next`) should set the cursor field `c.new` to false if and only if there is no data for a given size n (resp. the input cursor contains the last data). Therefore, most of the properties are formalized by postconditions guarded by the condition that the Boolean flag `c.new` is true.

We assume that a predicate

```
predicate sound (c: cursor)
```

encapsulates the data invariant. Then, the generator is sound if the first generated data satisfies this predicate (postcondition on Line 3) and if the output of the `next` function satisfies this predicate (postcondition on Line 8) whenever its input does (precondition on Line 7). The progress property is formalized on Line 9, with a predicate `lt` formalizing the strict total order $\prec$. (The expressions (`old e`) and `e` in a function postcondition respectively denote the values of the expression `e` before and after the function call.) The properties *min, inc* and *max* (entailing completeness) are respectively formalized on Lines 4, 10 and 11, with predicates `min`, `inc` and `max` respectively formalizing minimality, incrementality and maximality of the restriction of the order $\prec$ to data satisfying the data invariant `sound`.

3.2   Enumeration by Filtering

Assume you already have implemented, specified and certified an enumeration program for some family of data. Then an enumeration program for those data that satisfy an additional constraint can easily be implemented by running your program and selecting among its outputs those satisfying that constraint. Of course, the more data are rejected, the less effective is the resulting program. However, we show in this section that this *filtering* technique provides a specification, an implementation and a certification of the resulting enumeration program almost for free.

The generic module in Listing 1.6 formalizes filtering in WhyML. It provides an enumeration program for a family `Z` of integer arrays by filtering those arrays in a family `X` (characterized by the predicate `is_X`) that satisfy the additional constraint `is_Y`, implemented by the Boolean function `b_Y`. The module is parameterized by the predicates `is_X` and `is_Y`, the Boolean function `b_Y` and the enumeration functions `create_cursor_X` and `next_X` of `X` data. The module provides enumeration functions `create_cursor` and `next` of data in family `Z`.

The function `create_cursor` searches the first `Z` data by enumeration of `X` data started from the first one (given by `create_cursor_X`) and selection of the first enumerated data satisfying `is_Y`, if it exists. (Otherwise, the field `c.new` is set to `false` by the function `next_X`.)

The function `next` proceeds similarly, but from the current cursor `c`. If the current data in the cursor is the last one satisfying `is_Z` but subsequent `X` data exist, then they are enumerated (by `next_X`) in the cursor. If furthermore none of them are in the `Z` family, then the cursor no longer contains a sound data. This is acceptable because, in that case, the new field is set to false. As specified on Line 11 of Listing 1.5, the cursor is expected to contain the maximal data only as input of the next function when it sets the c.new field to false, not necessarily as its output. It is possible to restore the maximal Z data in the output cursor, but this makes the generator less effective.

When the Boolean function b_Y decides the predicate is_Y and the enumeration functions create_cursor_X and next_X satisfy their contract given in Listing 1.5, the resulting enumeration functions create_cursor and next satisfy the same contract. This is automatically proved by Why3. So, it also holds for all instantiations of the module Filter, for free.

```
 1 module Filter
 2   predicate is_X (a: array int)
 3   predicate is_Y (a: array int)
 4   predicate is_Z (a: array int) = is_X a ∧ is_Y a
 5
 6   val b_Y (a: array int) : bool
 7     ensures { result ↔ is_Y a }
 8
 9   val create_cursor_X (n: int) : cursor
10     requires { n ≥ 0 }
11   val next_X (c: cursor) : unit
12
13   let create_cursor (n: int) : cursor
14     requires { n ≥ 0 }
15     diverges
16   =
17     let c = create_cursor_X n in
18     while c.new && not (b_Y c.current) do
19       next_X c
20     done;
21     c
22
23   let next (c: cursor) : unit
24     diverges
25   =
26     if c.new then next_X c;
27     while c.new && not (b_Y c.current) do
28       next_X c
29     done;
30 end
```

Listing 1.6. Filtering in WhyML.

3.3   Auto-active and Interactive Verification

We combine the following two techniques to assist deductive verification of the enumeration programs. *Auto-active verification* [16] consists in providing additional specifications, such as variants (for termination), invariants, assertions and lemmas (for partial correctness), before running an automated prover. *Interactive verification* consists in reducing the proof goal step by step, by applying rules – named *tactics* in Coq and *transformations* in Why3.

3.4   Contents of ENUM Library

Metrics on the library and its contents are collected in Table 1. The first column assigns a name to each generator. The number of lines of code (resp. WhyML annotations) is recorded in the second (resp. third) column. The fourth (resp. fifth) column gives the number of transformations (resp. lemmas) needed for the proof of the soundness, progress and completeness properties. All of them have been proved automatically with Why3 1.2.0 and the SMT solvers Alt-Ergo 2.2.0, CVC4 1.6 and Z3 4.7.1, except the completeness property for the generator of permutations, which required an interactive proof of two lemmas with Coq 8.9.0.

The first block of lines in Table 1 concerns effective enumeration programs. The first four are adaptations of C++ programs proposed in [2]. The program RGF (for "Restricted Growth Function") enumerates the arrays a of length n such that $a[0] = 0$ and $a[i] \leq a[i-1]+1$ for $1 \leq i \leq n-1$. SORTED generates all arrays from $\{0, ..., n-1\}$ to $\{0, ..., k-1\}$ sorted in increasing order. PERM enumerates the permutations on $\{0, ..., n-1\}$. BARRAY (for "bounded array") (resp. ENDO) (for "endo-array") enumerates the arrays of length n whose values are in $\{0, ..., k-1\}$ (resp. $\{0, ..., n-1\}$). FACT enumerates the $n!$ *factorial* arrays [12] f of length n such that $0 \leq f[i] \leq i$ for $1 \leq i \leq n-1$.

Table 1. Verification results.

Array family	Code	Spec.	Trans.	Lemma	Time (s)
RGF	26	22	1	0	1.98
SORTED	22	26	4	0	3.21
PERM	42	86	5	16	16.35
BARRAY	22	23	3	0	3.14
FACT	22	20	1	0	1.53
ENDO	22	22	0	0	1.13
SORTED ⊂ BARRAY	24	15	0	0	1.05
INJ ⊂ BARRAY	24	16	0	0	0.92
SURJ ⊂ BARRAY	34	25	0	0	1.1
COMB ⊂ BARRAY	17	10	0	0	0.84

The second block concerns enumeration programs obtained by filtering (Sect. 3.2). We denote by $Z \subset X$ an enumeration program of data Z by filtering among more general data X. For instance, SORTED ⊂ BARRAY enumerates increasing arrays filtered among bounded arrays. By filtering from BARRAY we get generators for the following data families: arrays sorted in increasing order, injections from $\{0, ..., n-1\}$ to $\{0, ..., k-1\}$, for $n \leq k$ (INJ $\subset$ BARRAY), surjections from $\{0, ..., n-1\}$ to $\{0, ..., k-1\}$, for $n \geq k$ (SURJ $\subset$ BARRAY), and combinations of n elements selected from k, (COMB $\subset$ BARRAY), which are encoded by arrays c of length n such that $0 \leq c[0] < ... < c[n-1] \leq k-1$.

4   Experimentation Protocol

This section presents the experimental protocol we have designed in order to compare various ways of implementing, certifying and optimizing data enumeration programs. We consider two programming and specification languages, C/ACSL and WhyML, the properties detailed in Sect. 3.1, and the execution techniques (interpretation, extraction and compilation) detailed in Sect. 4.1. The goal of the experimentation is to answer the research questions detailed in Sect. 4.2.

All proofs and time measures were performed on a Ubuntu 18.04 virtual machine, with a Core i5-8259U processor.

4.1   Execution

There are several ways to run an enumeration program: With Why3 as interpreter (command `why3 execute`), by executing code compiled from OCaml source code extracted from WhyML code, or by compiling and executing C code, either extracted from WhyML code or written by hand. Indeed, Rieu-Helft [19] has developed a method to extract in C language a subset of programs written in WhyML. The C code can be compiled with `gcc` or with the certified C compiler CompCert [17]. Indeed, when you compile a program with an ordinary compiler like `gcc`, you have no assurance that the executed code has the same semantics as the source code. In contrast, the CompCert compiler is formally verified, using machine-assisted mathematical proofs, to be exempt from miscompilation issues.

4.2   Research Questions

We gather experimental data in order to answer the following research questions. In a nutshell, RQ1 is about certification only, RQ2 about efficiency only and RQ3 about how to find a good compromise between both quality criteria.

RQ1: What is the most convenient approach to certify the enumeration programs? Since we have two versions, one in C/ACSL and another one in WhyML, we want to compare the effort required to prove their properties with Frama-C/WP and Why3. We quantify this proof effort with the number of lines of specification. These numbers for WhyML version are in Table 1.

RQ2: What is the most efficient way to run our programs? The efficiency of our generators is estimated by computing their speed, i.e., the number of data generated per second, for all the ways to run our programs presented in Sect. 4.1. Indeed, we implement algorithms already optimal in memory, producing each data on the fly, starting from the data previously produced. Thus, only one data is stored in memory at a time.

RQ3: Since certification and optimization are two desirable but potentially antagonistic quality criteria, which language and tool combination provides the best compromise between both? From the answers to the former two questions we try to derive a good compromise between data generation speed and proof effort.

5   Experimentation Results

This section exploits experimental results to answer our research questions.

To answer RQ1 we first analyze some metrics collected in Table 1 for the version in WhyML and the metrics in Table 2 for the version in C/ACSL, for the most effective programs (the first 5 in Table 1, without filtering). These metrics are the numbers of lines of code and specification and the time required for proofs. The number of transformations is not comparable, as Frama-C/WP does not offer a transformation mechanism. We also do not compare the number of lemmas, because all lemmas in WhyML are used to prove completeness, but completeness is neither specified nor proved in the C/ACSL version. Nevertheless, the average proof time with C/ACSL is 1.69 times longer than with WhyML. The total numbers of lines of code and specifications are 76 and 154 in C/ACSL and 134 and 174 in WhyML program, i.e. not much more for one more specified property.

Table 2. Verification results with the C/ACSL version.

Array family	Code	Spec.	Trans.	Lemma	Time (s)
RGF	13	29	0	0	5.71
SORTED	13	32	0	0	5.50
PERM	24	35	0	0	22.98
BARRAY	13	29	0	0	5.19
FACT	13	29	0	0	5.14

Since the completeness property was not proved formerly with Frama-C/WP, we have tried to adapt to that environment its specification and successful proof with Why3. Although the adaptation of the specification to ACSL language did not require much effort, we have not yet managed to demonstrate any fragment of the completeness property with Frama-C/WP. We assume that this is due to the different memory models used by Why3 and WP. A memory model defines links between the program variables and the mathematical terms used in the proof obligations. It represents a mapping of the memory, management processes (reading, writing, allocating, releasing) and their properties. While Why3 has a simple memory model for arrays, producing concise proof obligations, the WP memory model produces more complex proof obligations. This convinces us that Why3 is more convenient than Frama-C/WP for the certification of ENUM.

To answer RQ2 we compare the speed of data generation of various interpretations or compilations of implementations and extractions in WhyML, OCaml and C of the same enumeration algorithm. We consider an algorithm to enumerate permutations [2, p. 243], and assume that speeds would be classified in the same order for other generators.

The first column of Table 3 gives the size of the generated permutations. The other columns display the number of millions of data generated per second, for four implementations and execution scenarios. A dash (-) indicates that generation exceeds the 6 h time limit.

Table 3. Speed of data generation (number of millions of data per second).

Size	WhyML	OCaml (extraction)	C (extraction)	C/ACSL (handwritten)
7	0.011	0.3	0.8	1
8	0.019	1.75	5.7	6.7
9	0.02	4.59	21.34	27.91
10	0.021	5.41	43.72	60.48
11	0.021	5.57	50.52	71.28
12	0.021	5.58	51.33	73.57
13	-	5.6	51.53	74.4
14	-	-	51.76	75.62

The interpretation of WhyML code is the least efficient enumeration method. It is not surprising since the other methods include a compilation, usually more efficient than an interpretation. Next comes the execution of its extraction in OCaml. For instance, the OCaml program enumerates 5.58×10^6 permutations of size 12 in 1 s. This may be appropriate in some applications, but is well below the speeds of the C programs. Indeed, C is a low-level imperative programming language. It has been designed to provide low-level memory access, which allows it to reduce the memory allocation required and optimize performance, particularly through the use of pointers.

Although the extracted C code is behind the handwritten one, its speed is much higher than that of the OCaml code. Its performance allows us to continue our efficiency study only for the C code extracted from the WhyML code. Figure 1 shows data generation speeds for this C code compiled with gcc (without and with -O3 optimization option) and CompCert compilers. This experiment confirms the claim that code compiled with CompCert is about twice as fast as that compiled by `gcc` without optimization, and quantifies the claim that it is a bit slower than that compiled by `gcc` with higher levels of optimization[2]: the code compiled by `gcc` with its third level of optimization is about 40% faster than the one compiled by CompCert.

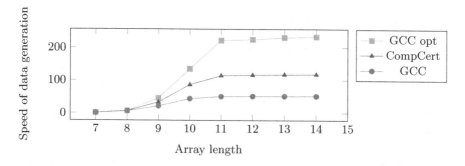

Fig. 1. Speed of data generation for different compilations.

To answer RQ3 we first draw some conclusions from the former answers to RQ1 and RQ2. Firstly, thanks to its elementary theory of arrays, Why3 makes it possible to prove more challenging properties – such as completeness – than Frama-C and its WP plugin. Moreover, C code automatically extracted from WhyML code is almost as fast as handwritten C code, for a much lower implementation effort. If a higher speed (resp. more confidence) is expected, the C code can be compiled with `gcc -O3` (resp. CompCert).

It remains to evaluate the additional effort required to specify and implement in WhyML enumeration programs suitable for C extraction. For the pointer-adapted permutation generator, we had to write 49 lines of code (only 7 lines more than for the original program), and 107 lines of specifications, so 21 lines more than the original code. The number of specification lines is mainly related to the fact that we control the memory manually. To download the proofs, we need 56.31 s, 3.44 times more than the original code. In addition, in the case of this program, completeness is not proved. Other generators (BARRAY and FACT) were also adapted for extraction. All properties were proven for these programs, but the specification effort was also greater than for their original codes. However, we noted that many specifications were common to all programs.

6   Conclusion

We have presented a prototypical implementation of a bounded exhaustive testing tool to check properties in the deductive verification tool Why3. It relies on

---

[2] http://compcert.inria.fr/compcert-C.html.

enumeration programs which are specified, implemented and certified by formal proofs with Why3. The impact of several execution scenarios on their efficiency has been evaluated experimentally.

Obviously, we do not claim that BET and our prototype are competing with advanced property testing tools, such as QuickCheck and its commercial version QuviQ [1]. Such a comparison would be of little interest, because we pursue different goals. Our first goal is to certify the test tool, which as far as we know has already been done only for and with the Coq proof assistant, in the Quickchick tool [18]. Our second goal is to offer a free test tool to Why3 users, complementing prover-based counterexample generation [5].

This is ongoing work and directions for future work are numerous. First, the presented certification of enumeration programs should be extended to the entire testing tool. Data enumeration should be generalized to address functions with several parameters, complex datatypes (e.g. tree-like) and constraints between parameters. The specification and certification of more efficient enumeration programs may also be explored.

An important possible improvement concerns Boolean reflection, i.e., implementation and certification of a decision procedure for the characteristic predicate of test data. We have shown two applications of this procedure: as a test oracle, and as a filter to select the test data among a wider family. In the presented prototype the user has to write each procedure manually. A small-term objective is to provide her with an automated mechanism of derivation of these procedures, covering at least a first-order theory including integers and integer arrays.

Acknowledgements. The authors warmly thank Raphaël Rieu-Helft for his help in using extraction of WhyML programs in C, and Jean-Christophe Filliâtre for many suggestions.

References

1. QuviQ testing tools (2019). http://www.quviq.com
2. Arndt, J.: Matters Computational - Ideas, Algorithms, Source Code [The fxtbook] (2010). https://www.jjj.de/fxt/fxtpage.html
3. Bobot, F., Filliâtre, J.-C., Marché, C., Melquiond, G., Paskevich, A.: The Why3 Platform (2018). http://why3.lri.fr/manual.pdf
4. Bulwahn, L.: The new Quickcheck for Isabelle - random, exhaustive and symbolic testing under one roof. In: Hawblitzel, C., Miller, D. (eds.) CPP 2012. LNCS, vol. 7679, pp. 92–108. Springer, Heidelberg (2012). https://doi.org/10.1007/978-3-642-35308-6_10
5. Dailler, S., Hauzar, D., Marché, C., Moy, Y.: Instrumenting a weakest precondition calculus for counterexample generation. J. Logic Algebraic Methods Program. **99**, 97–113 (2018). https://doi.org/10.1016/j.jlamp.2018.05.003
6. Dubois, C., Giorgetti, A.: Tests and proofs for custom data generators. Formal Aspects Comput. **30**, 659–684 (2018)
7. Dubois, C., Giorgetti, A., Genestier, R.: Tests and proofs for enumerative combinatorics. In: Aichernig, B.K.K., Furia, C.A.A. (eds.) TAP 2016. LNCS, vol. 9762, pp. 57–75. Springer, Cham (2016). https://doi.org/10.1007/978-3-319-41135-4_4

8. Filliâtre, J.-C., Pereira, M.: Itérer avec confiance. In: Journées Francophones des Langages Applicatifs (JFLA 2016) (2016). https://hal.inria.fr/hal-01240891
9. Filliâtre, J.-C., Pereira, M.: A modular way to reason about iteration. In: Rayadurgam, S., Tkachuk, O. (eds.) NFM 2016. LNCS, vol. 9690, pp. 322–336. Springer, Cham (2016). https://doi.org/10.1007/978-3-319-40648-0_24
10. Genestier, R., Giorgetti, A., Petiot, G.: Sequential generation of structured arrays and its deductive verification. In: Blanchette, J.C., Kosmatov, N. (eds.) TAP 2015. LNCS, vol. 9154, pp. 109–128. Springer, Cham (2015). https://doi.org/10.1007/978-3-319-21215-9_7
11. Giorgetti, A., Lazarini, R.: Preuve de programmes d'énumération avec Why3. In: AFADL 2018, pp. 14–19 (2018). http://afadl2018.ls2n.fr/wp-content/uploads/sites/38/2018/06/AFADL_Procs_2018.pdf
12. Giorgetti, A., Dubois, C., Lazarini, R.: Combinatoire formelle avec Why3 et Coq. In: Journées Francophones des Langages Applicatifs (JFLA 2019), Les Rousses, France, pp. 139–154, January 2019. https://hal.inria.fr/hal-01985195
13. Gonthier, G., Mahboubi, A.: An introduction to small scale reflection in Coq. J. Formaliz. Reason. **3**, 95–152 (2010)
14. Hriţcu, C., Lampropoulos, L., Dénès, M., Paraskevopoulou, Z.: QuickChick: randomized property-based testing plugin for Coq (2018). https://github.com/QuickChick/QuickChick
15. Jackson, D., Damon, C.: Elements of style: analyzing a software design feature with a counterexample detector. IEEE Trans. Softw. Eng. **22**(7), 484–495 (1996)
16. Leino, K.R.M., Moskal, M.: Usable auto-active verification. In: Usable Verification Workshop (2010). http://fm.csl.sri.com/UV10/
17. Leroy, X.: Formal verification of a realistic compiler. Commun. ACM **52**(7), 107–115 (2009)
18. Paraskevopoulou, Z., Hriţcu, C., Dénès, M., Lampropoulos, L., Pierce, B.C.: Foundational property-based testing. In: Urban, C., Zhang, X. (eds.) ITP 2015. LNCS, vol. 9236, pp. 325–343. Springer, Cham (2015). https://doi.org/10.1007/978-3-319-22102-1_22
19. Rieu-Helft, R., Marché, C., Melquiond, G.: How to get an efficient yet verified arbitrary-precision integer library. In: Paskevich, A., Wies, T. (eds.) VSTTE 2017. LNCS, vol. 10712, pp. 84–101. Springer, Cham (2017). https://doi.org/10.1007/978-3-319-72308-2_6
20. Runciman, C., Naylor, M., Lindblad, F.: Smallcheck and lazy smallcheck: automatic exhaustive testing for small values. In: Proceedings of the 1st ACM SIGPLAN Symposium on Haskell, pp. 37–48. ACM (2008). https://doi.org/10.1145/1411286.1411292
21. Sullivan, K.J., Yang, J., Coppit, D., Khurshid, S., Jackson, D.: Software assurance by bounded exhaustive testing. In: Proceedings of the ACM/SIGSOFT International Symposium on Software Testing and Analysis, ISSTA 2004, pp. 133–142. ACM (2004)

A Mechanised Proof of an Adaptive State Counting Algorithm

Robert Sachtleben[1], Robert M. Hierons[2], Wen-ling Huang[1],
and Jan Peleska[1(✉)]

[1] Department of Mathematics and Computer Science, University of Bremen,
Bremen, Germany
{rob_sac,huang,peleska}@uni-bremen.de
[2] Department of Computer Science, The University of Sheffield, Sheffield, UK
r.hierons@sheffield.ac.uk

Abstract. In this paper it is demonstrated that the capabilities of state-of-the-art proof assistant tools are sufficient to present mechanised and, at the same time, human-readable proofs establishing completeness properties of test methods and the correctness of associated test generation algorithms. To this end, the well-known Isabelle/HOL proof assistant is used to mechanically verify a complete test theory elaborated by the second author for checking the reduction conformance relation between a possibly nondeterministic finite state machine (FSM) serving as reference model and an implementation whose behaviour can also be represented by an FSM. The formalisation also helps to clarify an ambiguity in the original test generation algorithm which was specified in natural language and could be misinterpreted in a way leading to insufficient fault coverage.

Keywords: Complete test methods · Finite state machines · Reduction · Proof assistants · Isabelle/HOL · Mechanised proofs

1 Introduction

Objectives. In this paper, we present a comprehensive mechanised proof for a complete test strategy originally published in [7] by the second author. The strategy allows for verifying the reduction conformance relation between two finite state machines (FSMs); the first serving as reference model, and the second representing the true behaviour of the system under test (SUT). Both FSMs may be nondeterministic. The test strategy uses an adaptive state counting approach to generate finite test suites guaranteeing complete fault coverage under the assumption of an upper bound for the number of states contained in the (unknown) observable, minimised FSM representing the SUT behaviour. In many situations, this results in significantly fewer test cases than the well-

© IFIP International Federation for Information Processing 2019
Published by Springer Nature Switzerland AG 2019
C. Gaston et al. (Eds.): ICTSS 2019, LNCS 11812, pp. 176–193, 2019.
https://doi.org/10.1007/978-3-030-31280-0_11

known "brute force" strategy based on product FSMs[1], which requires $O(a^{mn})$ test cases[2] to guarantee full fault coverage.

Motivation. We advocate an approach to systematic testing where fault coverage capabilities of test suites are formally proven, so that no doubt with respect to their test strength and their underlying hypotheses, such as the specification of fault domains, remains. Preferably, the proofs should be mechanically checked by proof assistants, as it cannot be expected that every new strategy and its variants and specialisations will be manually checked for correctness by many members of the testing community. Since complete test strategies are of considerable importance for the verification of safety-critical systems, the correctness of fault coverage claims for a given strategy is crucial from the system certification perspective. In absence of a "social process", where the scientific community can be expected to re-verify every detail of a completeness argument, the mechanised re-verification and publication of the tool-based proofs is the best alternative from our perspective. Ideally, these proofs could be presented to the certification authorities responsible for authorisation of safety-critical systems becoming operative, to show that the complete testing strategy applied really has the test strength (i.e. the fault detection capabilities) that was claimed for the strategy.

Main Contributions. To our best knowledge, this is the first time that a mechanised proof for the complete reduction testing strategy from [7] is presented. Moreover, a formalised version of the associated test case generation algorithm is presented and proven to be correct as well, while in [7], only a textual description of the algorithm has been given. The formalisation has the advantage of removing an ambiguity in the algorithm's textual presentation, that could lead to a misinterpretation and, in turn, to the generation of incomplete test suites.

Related Work. The first complete state counting approach to reduction testing has been published in [14]. It specialised on the case of deterministic implementations to be tested for language inclusion against nondeterministic reference models. This work has been optimised later in [13] by using adaptive state counting. The general problem admitting both nondeterministic reference models and implementations has been studied in [7] – this is the article the present paper is based on – and [15], where it is stated that the complete, adaptive strategy elaborated there results in fewer test cases than for the strategy published in [7].

Applying proof assistants to testing has first been advocated in [3]. In [4], the same authors present an integrated testing framework with Isabelle/HOL at its core, which allows for test strategy elaboration (a strategy is called a *test theorem* in [4]), fault coverage proof, test case and test data generation in the same tool. The authors present several cases of mechanised proofs establishing

---

[1] This strategy has been described, for example, in the lecture notes [11, Section 4.5].
[2] a is the size of the input alphabet, n the number of states in the observable, minimised reference model, and m an upper bound for the number of states in the SUT model.

the completeness of testing theories. They do not, however, prove the theory analysed in the present paper.

Our general approach to model-based testing (MBT) contrasts to the one advocated in [4], since we favour specialised tools for strategy elaboration (Isabelle/HOL), modelling (FSM and SysML modelling tools), and test case and test data generation (RT-Tester [10] with SMT solver [12]). We agree with [2] that the use of SMT solvers in testing requires less specialised expertise than the interactive handling of proof assistants, since SMT solving can often be performed internally, without requiring explicit interactions with the users.

Reference to Comprehensive Online Resources. The Isabelle/HOL files containing the theories and proofs elaborated with the tool are publicly available for download on https://bitbucket.org/RobertSachtleben/formalisation-of-an-adaptive-state-counting-algorithm. The adaptive test algorithm has been implemented and made available in the *fsmlib-cpp* library, an open source project programmed in C++. The library contains fundamental algorithms for processing Mealy Machine FSMs and a variety of model-based test generation algorithms. Download, contents, and installation of the library is explained in the lecture notes [11, Appendix B] which are also publicly available.

Overview. In Sect. 2, the adaptive state counting test strategy from [7] is explained, in order to make this paper sufficiently self-contained. In Sect. 3, our mechanised proof is presented. First, an informal overview of the proof strategy is given. Then the main features of the theory and proof mechanisation in Isabelle/HOL are explained. Finally, the ambiguity in the informal description of the test generation algorithm in [7] is illustrated by an example, and it is shown that the algorithm's new formalised version produces a complete test suite for this example. In Sect. 4, we present the conclusions.

2   Adaptive State Counting

The adaptive state counting algorithm re-verified in this paper serves to check the reduction conformance relation between a reference model M_1, given as a finite state machine, and an SUT whose behaviour is assumed to correspond to some unknown finite state machine M_2.

Finite State Machines. A *Finite State Machine* (also called a *Mealy Machine*) is usually defined as a tuple $M = (Q, q_0, \Sigma_I, \Sigma_O, h)$, consisting of a finite set of states Q containing an initial state q_0, a finite input alphabet Σ_I, a finite output alphabet Σ_O and a transition relation $h \subseteq Q \times \Sigma_I \times \Sigma_O \times Q$ where $(q_1, x, y, q_2) \in h$ if and only if there exists a transition from q_1 to q_2 for input x that produces output y. We write $initial(M)$ to denote the initial state of M and $|M|$ to denote the number of states of M. The *language* of state $q \in Q$ of an FSM $M = (Q, q_0, \Sigma_I, \Sigma_O, h)$, denoted $L(M, q)$, is the set of all input-output

(IO) sequences $\bar{x}/\bar{y} \in (\Sigma_I \times \Sigma_O)^*$ such that q can react to $\bar{x}$ with outputs $\bar{y}$. The language of M, denoted $L(M)$, is the language of its initial state.

FSM M is said to be *observable* if for each q in Q, input x and output y there is at most one state q' that is reached from q through a transition with input/output x/y, i.e. there is at most one state q' in Q such that $(q, x, y, q') \in h$. If from any state of M there exists a transition for any input in the input alphabet, then M is said to be *completely specified*. Finally, M is said to be *minimised*, if $L(M, q) \neq L(M, q')$ holds for every pair $q \neq q'$ of states of M. If M is observable, then the state reached by an IO-sequence $\bar{x}/\bar{y} \in L(M, q)$ applied to state q, denoted $io\_target(M, q, \bar{x}/\bar{y})$ is uniquely determined. In the remainder of this paper, we assume every FSM to be completely specified over the same alphabet, observable and minimised. Recall that this is no restriction, since every FSM can be completed using one of the three methods described in [7] and transformed into a language-equivalent observable minimised machine [8].

A state q of FSM M is *deterministically reached* (d-reached) by an input sequence $\bar{v}$ if there exists some sequence $\bar{v}/\bar{v}' \in L(M)$ that reaches q and every sequence $\bar{v}/\bar{v}'' \in L(M)$ also reaches q. Such a state is called *d-reachable*. A *deterministic state cover* of M is a minimal set of input sequences V containing the empty sequence ϵ such that every d-reachable state of M is d-reached by some $\bar{v} \in V$. Finally, the *product machine* of two FSMs $M_1 = (S, s_1, \Sigma_I, \Sigma_O, h_1)$ and $M_2 = (T, t_1, \Sigma_I, \Sigma_O, h_2)$ is an FSM PM $= (S \times T, (s_1, t_1), \Sigma_I, \Sigma_O, h)$, where h is constructed as follows, ensuring that $L(\text{PM}) = L(M_2) \cap L(M_1)$ holds: $((s, t), x, y, (s', t')) \in h \iff (s, x, y, s') \in h_1 \wedge (t, x, y, t') \in h_2$.

Adaptive Testing for Reduction. M_2 is a *reduction* of M_1, denoted $M_2 \preceq M_1$, if and only if $L(M_2) \subseteq L(M_1)$. Intuitively speaking, $M_2 \preceq M_1$ states that M_2 can only behave in ways that are also admissible in M_1. Analogously, M_2 is a reduction of M_1 on a set U *of input sequences*, denoted $M_2 \preceq_U M_1$, if every reaction of M_2 to an input sequence $\bar{x} \in U$ is also a reaction of M_1 to $\bar{x}$.

The latter definition is required, as it is generally infeasible to test for reduction by enumerating the languages of both machines. Thus, the algorithm tests for reduction by only applying a finite number of input sequences to both machines and checking whether the reactions of M_2 to each input sequence can also be observed in M_1. In doing so, some input sequence $\bar{x}$ may produce an output $\bar{y}$ in M_1 which is never produced by the implementation M_2. In such a situation, it is unnecessary to check whether M_2 conforms to the behaviour of M_1 after having run through $\bar{x}/\bar{y}$.

An *adaptive test case (ATC)* serves to apply inputs to M_2 depending on previously observed outputs, thus possibly reducing the number of applied inputs by omitting certain inputs if specific outputs are not observed. ATCs are tree-like structures whose nodes are either leaves, denoted *null*, or pairs (x, f), where x is an input and f maps outputs to ATCs. Applying an ATC $\sigma = (x, f)$ to an FSM M is performed by applying x to M and next applying ATC $f(y)$ where y is the reaction of M to x. Applying *null* produces just ϵ. The *response set* of all responses observed when applying an ATC to M in state q is calculated by function IO, defined as follows.

$$IO(M, q, null) := \{\epsilon\}$$

$$IO(M, q, (x, f)) := \bigcup_{x/y \in L(M,q)} \{x/y\}.IO(M, io\_target(M, q, x/y), f(y))$$

From this, we define additional functions ($\bar{x}/\bar{y} \in L(M)$, Ω a set of ATCs).

$$B(M, \bar{x}/\bar{y}, \Omega) := \bigcup_{\sigma \in \Omega} IO(M, io\_target(M, initial(M), \bar{x}/\bar{y}), \sigma)$$

$$D(M, U, \Omega) := \{B(M, \bar{x}/\bar{y}, \Omega) \mid \bar{x} \in U \wedge \bar{x}/\bar{y} \in L(M)\}$$

Function B maps $(M, \bar{x}/\bar{y}, \Omega)$, to the set of all IO sequences $\bar{x}.\bar{x}_1/\bar{y}.\bar{y}_1$, where $\bar{x}/\bar{y}$ reaches some q in M, $\bar{x}_1/\bar{y}_1 \in IO(M, q, (x, f))$, and ATC (x, f) is in Ω. Function D comprises all sets $B(M, \bar{x}/\bar{y}, \Omega)$, such that $\bar{x}$ is an input sequence from U and $\bar{y}$ is a possible response of M, when applying $\bar{x}$ to its initial state.

In testing, sets U of input sequences are *followed* by ATC sets Ω in the sense that Ω is applied to every state reached by some sequence in U. We say that M_2 is a reduction of M_1 on U followed *with* Ω, denoted $M_2 \preceq_{U.\Omega} M_1$, if the following property holds:

$$M_2 \preceq_U M_1 \wedge \forall \bar{x} \in U. \; \forall \bar{y}. \; \bar{x}/\bar{y} \in L(M_2) \Longrightarrow B(M_2, \bar{x}/\bar{y}, \Omega) \subseteq B(M_1, \bar{x}/\bar{y}, \Omega)$$

This requires M_2 to be a reduction of M_1 on U, while for any $\bar{x}/\bar{y} \in L(M_2)$ with $\bar{x} \in U$ the responses observed by applying Ω to the states reached in M_2 by $\bar{x}/\bar{y}$ are also observed by applying Ω to all states reached by $\bar{x}/\bar{y}$ in M_1.

The idea behind this application of ATCs is to *distinguish* states: If the same Ω applied after two distinct IO sequences produces different response sets, then these sequences must reach distinct states. We say that two states s and s' in M_1 are *r-distinguishable* if there exists an ATC $\sigma \neq null$ such that $IO(M_1, s, \sigma) \cap IO(M_1, s', \sigma) = \emptyset$. Then, for some states t, t' of M_2, if both $IO(M_2, t, \sigma) \subseteq IO(M_1, s, \sigma)$ and $IO(M_2, t', \sigma) \subseteq IO(M_1, s', \sigma)$ hold, σ is also sufficient to distinguish t from t'. To increase the potential to distinguish states of the implementation, the set Ω used in the algorithm is thus preferably an *adaptive characterising set* of M_1, which is a set containing for each pair of r-distinguishable states of M_1 an ATC that r-distinguishes them.

2.1 Overview of the Adaptive State Counting Algorithm

The adaptive state counting algorithm introduced in [7] describes a procedure to generate a finite set of input sequences TS for completely specified, observable, minimised FSMs M_1 and M_2 over the same alphabet and for an adaptive characterising Ω of M_1 such that $M_2 \preceq M_1 \Longleftrightarrow M_2 \preceq_{TS.\Omega} M_1$ holds. FSM M_2 is assumed to have at most m states. Then the application of TS followed with Ω is sufficient to test for reduction. Starting from some deterministic state cover V of M_1 and iteratively extending this set of input sequences until a termination criterion is met, the *test suite* $TS.\Omega$ is generated by a breadth-first search for a minimal length input sequence $\bar{x}$ such that, for some $\bar{v} \in V$, M_2 reacts to $\bar{v}\bar{x}$ in a way not observed in M_1. This criterion is based on *state counting* in the sense that a *lower bound function LB* is used to calculate for some IO-sequence $\bar{v}\bar{x}/\bar{v}'\bar{y} \in L(M_2)$ with $\bar{v} \in V$ a lower bound on the number of states that M_2 must contain for any extension of $\bar{x}/\bar{y}$ to be a minimal sequence to a failure if applied after $\bar{v}/\bar{v}'$. If this lower bound exceeds m, then no extension of $\bar{x}/\bar{y}$ applied after $\bar{v}/\bar{v}'$ can be minimal. Hence, $\bar{v}\bar{x}/\bar{v}'\bar{y}$ needs not be considered further. Moreover, if *no* response of M_2 to some input sequence $\bar{x}$ needs to be considered further, then $\bar{x}$ does not need to be extended. The search terminates as soon as no sequence needs to be extended further or an examined sequence has uncovered a failure.

Lower Bound Function LB. The calculation of the lower bound by function LB is based on two parts: First, the number of sequences reaching certain states in M_1 and second, the number of distinct response sets observed by applying the same set of ATCs after different input sequences to M_2, not counting response sets observed by applying the ATCs after the sequences of the first part. The first part is calculated using functions R and RP as defined below. For state s of M_1, function R collects all prefixes of $\bar{v}\bar{x}/\bar{v}'\bar{y}$ longer than $\bar{v}/\bar{v}'$ reaching s. Function RP adds to this certain $\bar{w}/\bar{w}' \in V'' \subseteq L(M_2)$ observed while testing M_2 that also reach s in M_1.

$$R(M, s, \bar{v}/\bar{v}', \bar{x}/\bar{y}) \qquad := \{\bar{v}\bar{x}'/\bar{v}'\bar{y}' \mid \bar{x}'/\bar{y}' \in \mathit{pref}(\bar{x}/\bar{y}) \setminus \{\epsilon\}$$
$$\wedge\, s = \mathit{io\_target}(M, \mathit{initial}(M), \bar{v}\bar{x}'/\bar{v}'\bar{y}')\}$$
$$RP(M, s, \bar{v}/\bar{v}', \bar{x}/\bar{y}, V'') := R(M, s, \bar{v}/\bar{v}', \bar{x}/\bar{y}) \cup \{\bar{w}/\bar{w}' \in V'' \mid$$
$$s = \mathit{io\_target}(M, \mathit{initial}(M), \bar{w}/\bar{w}')\}$$

The lower bound function is then defined for arguments M_1, M_2, IO sequences $\bar{v}/\bar{v}'$ and $\bar{x}/\bar{y}$, a set U of input sequences, a subset S_1 of states of M_1, a set Ω of ATCs, and some $V'' \subseteq L(M_2)$ as follows.

$$LB(M_1, M_2, \bar{v}/\bar{v}', \bar{x}/\bar{y}, U, S_1, \Omega, V'') :=$$

$$\sum_{s \in S_1} \left| RP(M_1, s, \bar{v}/\bar{v}', \bar{x}/\bar{y}, V'') \right| + \tag{LB1}$$

$$\left| D(M_2, U, \Omega) \setminus \right. \tag{LB2}$$

$$\left. \{B(M_2, \bar{x}_1/\bar{y}_1, \Omega) \mid s' \in S_1 \wedge \bar{x}_1/\bar{y}_1 \in RP(M_1, s', \bar{v}/\bar{v}', \bar{x}/\bar{y}, V'')\} \right|$$

Splitting Sequences. In the algorithm, the V'' argument passed to the lower bound function is always contained in the set of all permutations of reactions of M_2 to V, denoted $\mathit{Perm}(M_2, V)$ and defined for $V = \{\bar{v}_1, \ldots, \bar{v}_k\}$ as follows:

$$\mathit{Perm}(M_2, V) := \{\{\bar{v}_1/\bar{v}_1', \ldots, \bar{v}_k/\bar{v}_k'\} \mid \forall\, 1 \le i \le k.\ \bar{v}_i/\bar{v}_i' \in L(M_2)\}$$

Furthermore, when calculating a lower bound for some IO-sequence $\bar{x}'/\bar{y}'$ and some V'', $\bar{x}'/\bar{y}'$ is split into a prefix $\bar{v}/\bar{v}'$ and a suffix $\bar{x}/\bar{y}$ such that $\bar{x}'/\bar{y}' = \bar{v}\bar{x}/\bar{v}'\bar{y}$

and $\bar{v}/\bar{v}'$ is the maximum length prefix of $\bar{x}'/\bar{y}'$ in V''. Depending on the V'' considered, sequence $\bar{x}'/\bar{y}'$ might thus be split in many different ways. We avoid this ambiguity by introducing function N to further restrict possible choices of V'' in such a way that for all remaining V'', sequence $\bar{x}'/\bar{y}'$ is split in the same way. This function N is defined as follows, using helper function mcp:

$$mcp(\bar{z}, W) = \bar{z}' \Leftrightarrow \bar{z}' \in \mathit{pref}(\bar{z}) \cap W \wedge \forall \bar{z}'' \in \mathit{pref}(\bar{z}) \cap W. \ |\bar{z}''| \leq |\bar{z}'|$$
$$N(\bar{x}/\bar{y}, M_2, V) := \{V'' \in \mathit{Perm}(M_2, V) \mid \exists \bar{v}/\bar{v}' \in \mathit{pref}(\bar{x}/\bar{y}).$$
$$\bar{v}/\bar{v}' = mcp(\bar{x}/\bar{y}, V'') \wedge \bar{v} = mcp(\bar{x}, V)\}$$

Function N thus for a sequence $\bar{x}/\bar{y}$ *narrows* the result of *Perm* to only those sets of responses V'' where the maximal prefix of $\bar{x}$ in V is also the input portion of the maximal prefix of $\bar{x}/\bar{y}$ in V''. In Subsect. 3.2 we use this narrowing to avoid an ambiguity in the description of the algorithm given in [7].

Test Suite Generation. Using the LB function as the main termination criterion, we define the test suite generated by the adaptive state counting algorithm using families of sets TS, C, and RM indexed by an iteration counter. $TS_i.\Omega$ then describes the test suite generated up to iteration i. Similarly, C_i contains all sequences considered for further extension and $RM_i \subseteq C_i$ contains those sequences not extended. We say that a sequence $\bar{x} \in RM_i$ is *removed* in iteration i. The families are defined as follows:

$$C_1 \quad := V \qquad C_{i+1} := ((C_i \setminus RM_i).(inputs(M_1))) \setminus TS_i$$
$$TS_0 \quad := \emptyset \qquad TS_{i+1} := TS_i \cup C_{i+1}$$
$$RM_0 \quad := \emptyset$$

$$RM_{i+1} := \Big\{ \bar{x}' \in C_{i+1} \ \Big|$$
$$(\exists \bar{x}'/\bar{y}' \in L(M_2). \tag{F}$$
$$\bar{x}'/\bar{y}' \notin L(M_1) \vee B(M_2, \bar{x}'/\bar{y}', \Omega) \not\subseteq B(M_1, \bar{x}'/\bar{y}', \Omega))$$
$$\vee \forall \bar{x}'/\bar{y}' \in L(M_2). \ \exists S_1 \subseteq S, \bar{x}/\bar{y}. \tag{L}$$
$$\exists V'' \in N(\bar{x}'/\bar{y}', M_2, V), \bar{v}/\bar{v}' \in V''.$$
$$\bar{v}\bar{x}/\bar{v}'\bar{y} = \bar{x}'/\bar{y}'$$
$$\wedge \ \bar{v}/\bar{v}' = mcp(\bar{x}'/\bar{y}', V'')$$
$$\wedge \ \forall s_1, s_2 \in S_1, s_1 \neq s_2.$$
$$\forall \bar{x}_1/\bar{y}_1 \in RP(M_1, s_1, \bar{v}/\bar{v}', \bar{x}/\bar{y}, V'').$$
$$\forall \bar{x}_2/\bar{y}_2 \in RP(M_1, s_2, \bar{v}/\bar{v}', \bar{x}/\bar{y}, V'').$$
$$B(M_2, \bar{x}_1/\bar{y}_1, \Omega) \neq B(M_2, \bar{x}_2/\bar{y}_2, \Omega)$$
$$\wedge \ LB(M_1, M_2, \bar{v}/\bar{v}', \bar{x}/\bar{y}, TS_i \cup V, S_1, \Omega, V'') > m \Big\}$$

Starting from a deterministic state cover V of M_1, the test suite is thus generated by iteratively extending all sequences currently considered and not removed with every element of the input alphabet (see C_{i+1} and TS_{i+1}).

Some sequence $\bar{x}'$ is removed only if it uncovers a failure (F) or if for every reaction $\bar{x}'/\bar{y}'$ of M_2 to it, $\bar{x}'/\bar{y}'$ can be split into $\bar{v}/\bar{v}'$ and $\bar{x}/\bar{y}$ where $\bar{v}/\bar{v}'$ is the maximum length prefix of $\bar{x}'/\bar{y}'$ also contained in $V'' \in N(\bar{x}'/\bar{y}', M_2, V)$, Ω pairwise distinguishes the states reached in M_2 via sequences in the RP-sets for distinct states in some subset S_1 of the states of M_1, and the lower bound calculated by LB for these parameters exceeds m (L). Note here that if Ω is an adaptive characterising set of M_1, no failure is observed when applying Ω after $TS_i \cup V$, and S_1 contains a pair of r-distinguishable states s and s' of M_1, then, by construction, Ω must distinguish the states of M_2 reached by sequences in the RP-set for s from those reached by sequences in the RP-set for s'.

The presented method of iterative test suite generation can be implemented in a WHILE-language in a straightforward way, for example by Algorithm 1.

3   The Mechanised Proof

Isabelle/HOL. Isabelle is a generic proof assistant featuring an extensive implementation of higher-order logic (Isabelle/HOL). We have based our formalisation of the adaptive state counting algorithm in this logic, as it is highly expressive and already contains many useful definitions and theorems. For an introduction see Nipkow et al. [9]. The Isabelle core libraries are further extended by the *Archive of Formal Proofs* (see www.isa-afp.org). The Isar (*Intelligible Semi-Automated Reasoning*) proof language offered in Isabelle distributions allows for proofs to be written in a human-readable style [16]. An example is given in Sect. 3.1. Finally, we make use of Isabelle's *locales* [1] facilitating the management of parametric theories, type hierarchies and structured contexts, by reusing the definition of transition systems given in [5] to define finite state machines.

Data Structures. In our Isabelle/HOL formalisation, we define FSMs by the following parametrised record-type:

```
record ('in, 'out, 'state) FSM =
  initial ::  "'state"
  inputs  ::  "'in set"
  outputs ::  "'out set"
  succ    ::  "('in × 'out) ⇒ 'state ⇒ 'state set"
```

Our definition thus syntactically deviates from the initial definition by using a successor function *succ* instead of the transition relation. This is no restriction, as $(q_1, x, y, q_2) \in h \equiv q_2 \in succ((x, y), q_1)$. We also omit explicitly enumerating the state set; instead, it is assumed to be the set of all states that can be reached from the initial states by some sequence of transitions. This state set of FSM M is denoted by $nodes(M)$, and its cardinality is denoted by $|M|$.

Algorithm 1. A simple implementation of an adaptive state counting algorithm

1: **function** $performAdaptiveStateCounting(M_1, M_2, V, \Omega, m)$
2:    $ts \leftarrow \emptyset$;
3:    $c \leftarrow V$;
4:    $rm \leftarrow \emptyset$;
5:    $obs_1 \leftarrow \{\bar{x}/\bar{y} \in L(M_1) \mid \bar{x} \in c\}$;   ▷ Observed responses of M_1, M_2 to c
6:    $obs_2 \leftarrow \{\bar{x}/\bar{y} \in L(M_2) \mid \bar{x} \in c\}$;
7:    $obs_1^\Omega \leftarrow \bigcup_{\bar{x}/\bar{y} \in L(M_1) \wedge \bar{x} \in c}(\{\bar{x}/\bar{y}\} \times B(M_1, \bar{x}/\bar{y}, \Omega))$;   ▷ Response to Ω after c
8:    $obs_2^\Omega \leftarrow \bigcup_{\bar{x}/\bar{y} \in L(M_2) \wedge \bar{x} \in c}(\{\bar{x}/\bar{y}\} \times B(M_2, \bar{x}/\bar{y}, \Omega))$;
9:    $iter \leftarrow 1$;   ▷ Iteration counter
10:   **while** $(c \neq \emptyset \wedge obs_1 \subseteq obs_2 \wedge obs_1^\Omega \subseteq obs_2^\Omega)$ **do**
11:      $iter \leftarrow iter + 1$;
12:      $rm \leftarrow \{\bar{x}' \in c \mid$
              $(\exists \bar{x}'/\bar{y}' \in L(M_2).$
                 $\bar{x}'/\bar{y}' \notin L(M_1) \vee B(M_2, \bar{x}'/\bar{y}', \Omega) \not\subseteq B(M_1, \bar{x}'/\bar{y}', \Omega))$
              $\vee \, \forall \bar{x}'/\bar{y}' \in L(M_2). \, \exists S_1 \subseteq S, \bar{x}/\bar{y}.$
                 $\exists V'' \in N(\bar{x}'/\bar{y}', M_2, V), \bar{v}/\bar{v}' \in V''.$
                    $\bar{v}\bar{x}/\bar{v}'\bar{y} = \bar{x}'/\bar{y}'$
                    $\wedge \, \bar{v}/\bar{v}' = mcp(\bar{x}'/\bar{y}', V'')$
                    $\wedge \, \forall s_1, s_2 \in S_1, s_1 \neq s_2 :$
                       $\forall \bar{x}_1/\bar{y}_1 \in RP(M_1, s_1, \bar{v}/\bar{v}', \bar{x}/\bar{y}, V'').$
                       $\forall \bar{x}_2/\bar{y}_2 \in RP(M_1, s_2, \bar{v}/\bar{v}', \bar{x}/\bar{y}, V'').$
                          $B(M_2, \bar{x}_1/\bar{y}_1, \Omega) \neq B(M_2, \bar{x}_2/\bar{y}_2, \Omega)$
                    $\wedge \, LB(M_1, M_2, \bar{v}/\bar{v}', \bar{x}/\bar{y}, ts \cup V, S_1, \Omega, V'') > m\}$
13:      $ts \leftarrow ts \cup c$;
14:      $c \leftarrow ((c \setminus rm).(inputs(M_1))) \setminus ts$;
15:      $obs_1 \leftarrow obs_1 \cup \{\bar{x}/\bar{y} \in L(M_1) \mid \bar{x} \in c\}$;
16:      $obs_2 \leftarrow obs_2 \cup \{\bar{x}/\bar{y} \in L(M_2) \mid \bar{x} \in c\}$;
17:      $obs_1^\Omega \leftarrow obs_1^\Omega \cup \bigcup_{\bar{x}/\bar{y} \in L(M_1) \wedge \bar{x} \in c}(\{\bar{x}/\bar{y}\} \times B(M_1, \bar{x}/\bar{y}, \Omega))$;
18:      $obs_2^\Omega \leftarrow obs_2^\Omega \cup \bigcup_{\bar{x}/\bar{y} \in L(M_2) \wedge \bar{x} \in c}(\{\bar{x}/\bar{y}\} \times B(M_2, \bar{x}/\bar{y}, \Omega))$;
19:   **end while** ;
20:   **return** $(obs_1 \subseteq obs_2 \wedge obs_1^\Omega \subseteq obs_2^\Omega)$ ▷ Check for observed failures
21: **end function**

Furthermore, this definition of FSMs by itself does neither enforce the finiteness and non-emptiness of the alphabets and the set of reachable states, nor restrict the successor function to allow only transitions over the input and output alphabets. We alleviate this problem by encoding these requirements in a predicate `well_formed`, which is then explicitly assumed to hold for relevant FSMs (see the assumptions of the example lemma in Sect. 3.1). Furthermore, we say that a value of type FSM is an *OFSM* if it is well-formed, observable and completely specified.

We interpret values of type FSM as transition systems with initial states as defined by Brunner in [5]. This interpretation allows us to reuse a large number of theorems, in particular concerning paths and reachability.

Finally, we define ATCs as a data type such that a value of this type is either a `Leaf` (*null*) or a `Node` containing an input and a function from outputs to ATCs:

datatype (*'in, 'out) ATC = Leaf | Node 'in "'out ⇒ ('in, 'out) ATC"*

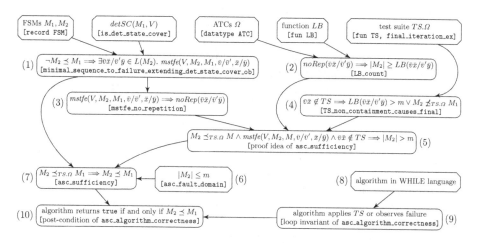

Fig. 1. Overview of the main proof steps and their dependencies.

3.1 Proof Strategy

The strategy employed in mechanising and proving the adaptive state counting algorithm correct is given schematically by Fig. 1. In this figure, definitions are given in rectangles with cut corners, whereas rectangles with rounded corners represent lemmata. The corresponding definitions and lemmata in the Isabelle code are given in brackets in the lower half of the corresponding rectangle. The information flow from definitions and lemmata to other lemmata is indicated by arrows. Note that, due to size constraints, the lemmata and deductions do not list all assumptions. Figure 1 makes use of the following abbreviations: (a) $detSC(M_1, V)$ states that V is a deterministic state cover of M_1, (b) $mstfe(V, M_2, M_1, \bar{v}/\bar{v}', \bar{x}/\bar{y})$ states that $\bar{v} \in V$ and $\bar{x}/\bar{y}$ is a minimal sequence to a failure from the state reached by $\bar{v}/\bar{v}'$, and (c) $noRep(\bar{v}\bar{x}/\bar{v}'\bar{y})$ states that $\bar{x}/\bar{y}$ applied to M_2 after $\bar{v}/\bar{v}'$ contains no repetitions (as defined below).

Following the depicted strategy, we first prove that it is sufficient to search for minimal sequences to failures extending a deterministic state cover of M_1 (1). Next, we show that a value calculated by the LB function in the algorithm is a valid lower bound on $|M_2|$ (2) under certain assumptions, which are proven to be met by minimal sequences to failures (3). Additionally, we show that if an input sequence is not contained in TS, then either $TS.\Omega$ uncovers a failure or the lower bound for any reaction of M_2 to that input sequence exceeds m (4). Using these results, we prove that if $TS.\Omega$ does not uncover an existing failure, then M_2 must contain more than m states (5), providing a contradiction under the assumption that $|M_2| \leq m$ holds (6). Thus, applying TS followed with Ω is sufficient to test for reduction (7). Finally, we provide an implementation of the algorithm in a simple WHILE-language (8) and show that it generates and applies $TS.\Omega$ until it has been fully applied or a failure has been observed (9), therefore being able to decide whether M_2 is a reduction of M_1 (10).

Our Isabelle/HOL code is split into *theory files* accordingly: First, FSM.thy defines FSMs and proves (1). Next, FSM_Product.thy and ATC.thy introduce product machine and data type ATC, respectively. ASC_LB.thy then defines LB, establishing (2), and ASC_Suite.thy defines TS, C and RM as functions, providing (4). Thereafter, ASC_Sufficiency.thy proves (3) and then (7) via (5,6). Finally, an implementation (8) is proven correct (9,10) in ASC_Hoare.thy.

Sequences to Failures. To provide a concrete example of an Isabelle lemma and its proof, we consider a sequence to a failure. This is an IO-sequence $\bar{v}\bar{x}/\bar{v}'\bar{y} \in L(M_2) \setminus L(M_1)$ *extending* a deterministic state cover V of M_1 such that every proper prefix is contained in $L(M_2) \cap L(M_1)$ and $\bar{v} \in V$. Such a sequence $\bar{v}\bar{x}/\bar{v}'\bar{y}$ is called *minimal* if furthermore no sequence $\bar{x}'/\bar{y}'$ shorter than $\bar{x}/\bar{y}$ constitutes a sequence to a failure extending V if appended to some $\bar{w}/\bar{w}'$ with $\bar{w} \in V$. If M_2 is not a reduction of M_1, then some sequences to a failure extending V must exist, since, by definition, a deterministic state cover contains the empty input sequence. Hence, any sequence to a failure extends V. From these, a minimal sequence to a failure extending V can then finally be selected. We express this result and proof in Isabelle as follows, where [ ] denotes the empty list and @ denotes list concatenation:

```
lemma minimal_sequence_to_failure_extending_det_state_cover_ob :
  assumes "well_formed M2"
  and     "well_formed M1"
  and     "is_det_state_cover M1 V"
  and     "¬ M2 ⪯ M1"
obtains vs xs
where "minimal_sequence_to_failure_extending V M2 M1 vs xs"
proof -
  — The set of all IO-sequences that extend some reaction of M2 to V to a failure:
  let ?exts = "{xs. ∃ vs' ∈ L_{in} M2 V.
                     sequence_to_failure M2 M1 (vs'@xs)}"
  — Select an arbitrary sequence to failure.
  — This sequence must be contained in ?exts, as V contains the empty sequence.
  obtain stf where "sequence_to_failure M2 M1 stf"
    using assms sequence_to_failure_ob by blast
  then have "sequence_to_failure M2 M1 ([] @ stf)"
    by simp
  moreover have "[] ∈ L_{in} M2 V"
    by (meson assms(3) det_state_cover_initial
              language_state_for_inputs_empty)
  ultimately have "stf ∈ ?exts"
    by blast
```

— Select an arbitrary minimal-length sequence ?xsMin from ?exts.
— By construction, ?xsMin is a minimal sequence extending V to a failure.
let ?xsMin = "arg_min length (λxs. xs ∈ ?exts)"
have xsMin_def : "?xsMin ∈ ?exts

$$\wedge\ (\forall xs \in\ ?exts.\ length\ ?xsMin \leq length\ xs)"$$

  by (metis (no_types, lifting) ⟨stf ∈ ?exts⟩ arg_min_nat_lemma)
then obtain vs **where** "vs ∈ L_{in} M2 V

$$\wedge\ sequence\_to\_failure\ M2\ M1\ (vs\ @\ ?xsMin)"$$

  by blast
moreover have "¬(∃xs . ∃ws ∈ L_{in} M2 V.

$$sequence\_to\_failure\ M2\ M1\ (ws@xs)$$
$$\wedge\ length\ xs < length\ ?xsMin)"$$

  using leD xsMin_def **by** blast
ultimately have
  "minimal_sequence_to_failure_extending V M2 M1 vs ?xsMin"
  by auto
then show ?thesis **using** that **by** auto
qed

Observe the use of the **by** keyword to apply automatic proof methods (e.g. blast, auto, metis) to mechanically verify each individual proof step. Note that most of these steps are so simple that they would very likely not be proven explicitly in a manual proof "on paper".

Furthermore, note that a sequence $\bar{v}\bar{x}x/\bar{v}'\bar{y}y$ to a failure extending V is not minimal in the above sense if $\bar{x}/\bar{y}$ applied after $\bar{v}/\bar{v}'$ visits any state of the product machine of M_1 and M_2 twice: in this case $\bar{x}x/\bar{y}y$ can be shortened by removing the resulting loop. It is also not minimal if $\bar{x}/\bar{y}$ applied after $\bar{v}/\bar{v}'$ visits some state that is reached by some sequence $\bar{w}/\bar{w}' \in L(M_2)$ with $\bar{w} \in V$ and $\bar{w} \neq \bar{v}$, as in this case a proper suffix of $\bar{x}/\bar{y}$ applied after $\bar{w}/\bar{w}'$ is a shorter sequence to a failure extending V. The absence of repetitions of the first and second kind is denoted by predicates $\neg\mathbf{Rep\_Pre}(M_1, M_2, \bar{v}/\bar{v}', \bar{x}/\bar{y})$ and $\neg\mathbf{Rep\_Cov}(M_1, M_2, V'', \bar{v}/\bar{v}', \bar{x}/\bar{y})$, respectively, where $V'' \subseteq L(M_2)$ usually is a set of reactions of M_2 to V.

Lemma `mstfe_no_repetition` then encodes that for a minimal sequence $\bar{v}\bar{x}/\bar{v}'\bar{y}$ to a failure extending V and some $\bar{x}'/\bar{y}' \in pref(\bar{x}/\bar{y})$, repetition properties $\mathbf{Rep\_Pre}(M_1, M_2, \bar{v}/\bar{v}', \bar{x}'/\bar{y}')$ and $\mathbf{Rep\_Cov}(M_1, M_2, V'', \bar{v}/\bar{v}', \bar{x}'/\bar{y}')$ do not hold if V'' is contained in $N(\bar{v}\bar{x}/\bar{v}'\bar{y}, M_2, V)$.

Validity of the Calculated Lower Bound. Let s be some state of M_1. All sequences contained in $R(M, s, \bar{v}/\bar{v}', \bar{x}/\bar{y})$ by definition reach s in M_1. If it is assumed that $\mathbf{Rep\_Pre}(M_1, M_2, \bar{v}/\bar{v}', \bar{x}/\bar{y})$ does not hold, then each contained sequence must reach a distinct state in M_2, as otherwise some state in the product automaton is visited twice. Similarly, if $\mathbf{Rep\_Cov}(M_1, M_2, V'', \bar{v}/\bar{v}', \bar{x}/\bar{y})$ is assumed not to hold and V'' is an element of $N(\bar{v}\bar{x}/\bar{v}'\bar{y}, M_2, V)$, then the additional sequences of V'' contained in $RP(M, s, \bar{v}/\bar{v}', \bar{x}/\bar{y}, V'')$ must also reach distinct states in M_2. Hence, M_2 contains at least $|RP(M, s, \bar{v}/\bar{v}', \bar{x}/\bar{y}, V'')|$ distinct states.

When this function is applied in the algorithm, it is ensured that Ω is sufficient to distinguish states of M_2 reached by sequences calculated by RP for distinct states $s, s' \in S_1$. Then no sequence in $RP(M, s, \bar{v}/\bar{v}', \bar{x}/\bar{y}, V'')$ reaches a state in M_2 that is also reached by some sequence in $RP(M, s', \bar{v}/\bar{v}', \bar{x}/\bar{y}, V'')$, which guarantees that, under the assumption that no repetitions occur, part (LB1) of LB is a valid lower bound. Adding to this, part (LB2) calculates the number of response sets observed by applying Ω to M_2 after every input sequence in T, not counting those already observed by applying Ω after sequences in the RP-sets. Any such distinct response set indicates the existence of at least one state of M_2 not reached via the RP-sets and hence the value calculated by LB is an actual lower bound on the number of states in M_2. This result is encoded in lemma LB_count.

Properties of the Generated Test Suite. Every removed sequence either uncovers a failure directly or, following from $|M_2| \leq m$, cannot be prefix of a minimal sequence to a failure extending V (see mstfe_no_repetition). Note that by this iterative process of extension, C_{i+1} contains only sequences created by extending V with sequences of length i.

In order to ensure practical applicability of this test suite generation process, we first show that it terminates in the sense that after a finite number of iterations the test suite does not change for any further iteration. We call such an iteration *final*. Some final iteration must exist: Consider some IO-sequence $\bar{x}'/\bar{y}'$ with $\bar{x}' \in C_{|M_1|*m+1}$. Then $\bar{x}'/\bar{y}'$ is of the form $\bar{v}\bar{x}/\bar{v}'\bar{y}$ such that $\bar{v} \in V$, $\bar{x}/\bar{y}$ is of length $|M_1|*m$ and $\bar{v}\bar{x}$ has not been removed in some RM_j with $j < |M_1|*m+1$. Then $\bar{x}/\bar{y}$ applied after $\bar{v}/\bar{v}'$ either uncovers a failure, or visits states of the product machine of M_1 and M_2 a total of $|M_1|*m+1$ times and must hence visit some state s of M_1 at least $m+1$ times, which causes the RP-set for s to contain $m+1$ sequences. By choosing $S_1 = \{s\}$ it is then possible to select parameters such that the lower bound is at least $m+1 > m$. By this argument, every sequence in $C_{|M_1|*m+1}$ is removed and $|M_1| * m + 1$ is a final iteration. In our Isabelle code, this result is given in lemma final_iteration_ex.

Finally, let i be a final iteration, implying $C_i = \emptyset$, and note that $TS_i = \bigcup_{j \leq i} C_j$ holds by construction. Therefore, $TS_i = \bigcup_{j \leq i} RM_j$ follows (i.e., every sequence contained in TS_i has been removed at some point). As the test suite is generated by iteratively extending it with every input in the input alphabet Σ_I of M_1, if some sequence $\bar{x}$ over Σ_I is not contained in TS_i, then there must exist some $j \leq i$ such that a proper prefix $\bar{x}'$ of $\bar{x}$ is contained in RM_j. This constitutes lemma TS_non_containment_causes_final. Note that the removal of $\bar{x}'$ indicates that it either already uncovers a failure or that the lower bounds calculated for the reactions of M_2 to it all exceed m.

Sufficiency for Proving Reduction. We show next that the test suite $TS_i.\Omega$ for some final iteration i is sufficient to test for reduction (i.e., that $M_2 \preceq_{TS_i.\Omega} M_1$ implies $M_2 \preceq M_1$).

Assume that $M_2 \preceq_{TS_i.\Omega} M_1$ and hence also $M_2 \preceq_{TS_i} M_1$ holds. For $M_2 \preceq M_1$ not to hold, there must thus exist some minimal sequence to a failure $\bar{v}\bar{x}/\bar{v}'\bar{y}$ extending V such that $\bar{v}\bar{x} \notin TS$. By lemma TS_non_containment_causes_final, this is only possible if for a proper prefix $\bar{v}\bar{x}'/\bar{v}'\bar{y}'$ of $\bar{v}\bar{x}/\bar{v}'\bar{y}$ its input portion $\bar{v}\bar{x}'$ has been removed, which, in turn, requires the lower bound calculated for $\bar{v}\bar{x}'/\bar{v}'\bar{y}'$ to exceed m. Following from lemma mstfe_no_repetition applied to $\bar{v}\bar{x}/\bar{v}'\bar{y}$, no repetitions occur for $\bar{x}'/\bar{y}'$ applied after $\bar{v}/\bar{v}'$, and hence this lower bound is valid, implying that M_2 has more than m states. Thus, the assumption of $|M_2| \leq m$ is contradicted, proving that no minimal sequence to a failure can exist whose input portion is not contained in TS_i. This is the proof idea for lemma asc_sufficiency.

Note that the reverse implication, $M_2 \preceq M_1 \implies M_2 \preceq_{TS_i.\Omega} M_1$, trivially holds by definition. From the above lemma it thus follows directly that M_2 is a reduction of M_1 if and only if it is a reduction of M_1 on $TS_i.\Omega$.

Also observe that the above proofs do not require Ω to be an adaptive characterising set of M_2. Yet, as described for the calculation of the lower bound, choosing an adaptive characterising set for Ω ensures that for pairs of r-distinguishable states in M_1, the application of Ω either uncovers a failure or successfully distinguishes the states reached by sequences in the corresponding RP-sets, thus possibly enabling earlier removal of sequences.

Correctness of an Implementation. The idea behind Algorithm 1 is to first initialise variables ts, c and rm with TS_0, C_1 and RM_0, respectively, and then to loop, calculating the values for the next iterations of those sets, until a failure has been observed or $c = \emptyset$ holds, indicating a final iteration. During this process, the observed reactions of M_1 and M_2 to the input sequences in c and the response sets to Ω applied after c are stored in corresponding obs-variables. Finally, the algorithm is to return true if and only if no failure has been observed. In our Isabelle/HOL code, this algorithm is defined within lemma asc_algorithm_correctness.

We prove the correctness of Algorithm 1 (i.e., whether it returns true if and only if $M_2 \preceq M_1$ holds) using Hoare-logic by first establishing a *loop-invariant*: If variables ts, c and rm contain TS_{iter-1}, C_{iter} and RM_{iter-1}, respectively, before executing the body of the loop, then they contain the respective sets for the updated value of *iter* after having executed the loop body. As *iter* is incremented by 1 during each execution of the body, this shows that each such execution performs a single iteration in the calculation of the test suite. Since the invariant trivially holds before first execution of the loop body, this proves that the algorithm iteratively generates the desired test suite.

By lemma final_iteration_ex, a final iteration i must exist. Therefore, the loop terminates with the value of *iter* not exceeding $i + 1$. Furthermore, from the loop-invariant and the construction of the obs-sets it follows that $(obs_1 \subseteq obs_2 \wedge obs_1^\Omega \subseteq obs_2^\Omega)$ holds if and only if $M_2 \preceq_{(ts \cup c).\Omega} M_1$. Hence, if the loop terminates because $(obs_1 \subseteq obs_2 \wedge obs_1^\Omega \subseteq obs_2^\Omega)$ does not hold, then a failure has been observed and the algorithm correctly returns false. Finally, if the loop terminates due to c being empty, then a final iteration has been reached and the truth value of $M_2 \preceq_{ts.\Omega} M_1 \equiv M_2 \preceq_{TS_i.\Omega} M_1$ is returned. Thus, by lemma asc_sufficiency, the algorithm returns **true** if and only if $M_2 \preceq M_1$ holds.

3.2   Ambiguity

The following example serves to highlight an ambiguity in the original natural language specification of the algorithm, where the ambiguity allows for the generation of a test suite that is not sufficient to uncover an existing failure.

Consider M_1 and M_2 given in Fig. 2, where M_2 is not a reduction of M_1 on any input sequence of length at least 3. Let $m = 2$ be the assumed upper bound on the number of states of M_2 and let $V = \{\epsilon, a\}$. Then $Perm(V, M_2) = \{V_0'', V_1''\}$ where $V_i'' = \{\epsilon, a/i\}$. Furthermore, let $\Omega = \{(a, f)\}$ with f mapping every output to *null*. Note that applying (a, f) is equivalent to applying input a and thus sufficient to distinguish states in both FSMs.

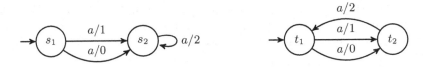

Fig. 2. FSMs M_1 (left) and M_2 (right)

The first iteration of the algorithm thus applies $C_1.\Omega = V.\Omega$, which is equivalent to applying $\{a, aa\}$, and observes no failure. As the extension of ϵ by $\Sigma_I = \{a\}$ is $a \in TS_1$ and hence cannot be contained in C_2, it remains only to check whether a is contained in RM_1. This reduces to checking whether the removal conditions are met for the two responses of M_2 to a: $a/0$ and $a/1$. Consider first the case of $a/0$: The original description of the algorithm can be read in a way that allows for V'' to be chosen arbitrarily from $Perm(V, M_2)$, in particular allowing the choice of $V'' = V_1''$. This is not possible in the definition of RM given here, which requires V'' to be contained in $N(a/0, M_2, V) = \{V_0''\}$. By choosing $V'' = V_1''$, $S_1 = \{s_1, s_2\}$, $\bar{v}/\bar{v}' = \epsilon$ and $\bar{x}/\bar{y} = a/1$, the RP-set for s_1 contains ϵ and that for s_2 contains $a/0$ and $a/1$, together containing three sequences. The calculated lower bound then is $3 > m$ and all requirements for the removal of $a/1$ are satisfied. Analogously, by choosing $V'' = V_0''$ for case $a/1$, the removal condition can again be satisfied and hence $a \in RM_1$ holds, C_2 is empty and the final iteration is already reached by $TS_1 = V$. Thus, only $TS_1.\Omega = \{a, aa\}$ is applied, which is insufficient to uncover a failure.

In contrast, the algorithm formalised in this paper does not remove a, as restricting the choices of V'' to V_0'' for $a/0$ and V_1'' for $a/1$ results in lower bounds not exceeding m. Hence, a is extended to aa, which, followed by Ω, uncovers the failure $aaa/022 \in L(M_2) \setminus L(M_1)$. Therefore, aa is removed from $C_2 = \{aa\}$ and the complete test suite is $TS_2.\Omega = \{a, aa, aaa\}$.

3.3   Effort, Challenges and Benefits

The implementation in Isabelle of the proof strategy presented in Sect. 3.1 has required a combined effort equivalent to about 6 weeks work of a single person to complete, not including the time the authors required to familiarise themselves with Isabelle/HOL, and some subordinate activities concerning cleanup and reformatting of the theory and proof files created. This work resulted in several theory files with a combined size of about 11,000 lines of code, proving a total of 241 lemmata of various complexities. On a computer running Isabelle2018 on Ubuntu 18.04 and equipped with an Intel Core i7-4700MQ processor, all proofs are verified within 149 s. Details for each theory file are presented in Table 1.

Table 1. Sizes and verification times of the Isabelle theory files

Theory file	Lines	Lemmata	Time (s)
FSM.thy	2000	85	16.94
FSM_Product.thy	1600	34	27.60
ATC.thy	800	36	10.43
ASC_LB.thy	2900	42	49.69
ASC_Suite.thy	1900	33	30.20
ASC_Sufficiency.thy	800	7	7.74
ASC_Hoare.thy	1000	4	6.16
Σ	11000	241	148.76

The data structures and functions defined in the Isabelle code closely resemble those used in the manual proof. For finite state machines and adaptive test cases, the Isabelle definitions have already been discussed above. Furthermore, most functions defined in [7] (e.g. function LB) did not require any rephrasing other than finding the corresponding Isabelle functions for the operations performed in their calculation. Functions whose definitions rely on $io\_target(M, q, \bar{x}/\bar{y})$ being uniquely determined (e.g. function B) are slightly rewritten in the Isabelle code so that the resulting definitions do not assume that input FSMs are observable. Instead, the functions operate on all states reached by $\bar{x}/\bar{y}$. Finally, the definitions of functions C, RM, TS and algorithm $performAdaptiveStateCounting$ follow directly from the original textual description of the algorithm and thus constitute only a simple transcription.

Similarly, the overall proof strategy of the mechanised proof follows the strategy used in the manual proof, resulting in closely related intermediate steps. For example, lemma LB_count in the mechanised proof is a specialisation of Lemma 12 of [7]. The proofs performed in Isabelle differ from manual proofs mainly by explicitly stating all assumptions and by the necessity to prove correct all those intermediate properties that are often omitted in manual proofs, because they are considered to be trivial or analogous to previous steps. Proofs of such intermediate properties can usually be found in a fully automated way using the Sledgehammer tool (part of Isabelle). If some intermediate property is used in several proofs, we introduce and prove it as a separate lemma, which can then be reused in different contexts. This method of handling intermediate properties results in a large number of lemmata. This holds in particular for FSMs, as shown in Table 1, where many lemmata describe rather simple properties. For example, lemma `language_state_prefix` in `FSM.thy` states that if $\bar{x}/\bar{y} \in L(M, q)$, then any prefix of $\bar{x}/\bar{y}$ is contained in $L(M, q)$.

Thus, the challenges encountered in mechanising the manual proof consisted mainly in the large number of such intermediate properties to prove, caused by the complexity of the algorithm, and in the requirement to provide a formalisation of the algorithm that does not include the ambiguity discussed in Sect. 3.2.

For reasons described above, the mechanised proof presented here is much longer than the manual proof given in [7], but provides also many theorems concerning finite state machines and adaptive test cases, which might be reused in other mechanised proofs. For example, the existence of minimal sequences to failures extending the state cover, proven in Sect. 3.1, is also used in a proof given in [11] about the completeness of test suites generated using the H-Method, originally presented in [6]. More generally, theory file `FSM.thy` proves various properties about paths and languages of finite state machines (focusing on observable FSMs), which are not specific to the presented adaptive state counting algorithm. This theory file might therefore be used as a starting point to mechanise other algorithms for generating complete test suites based on finite state machines.

4   Conclusions

For the first time, a comprehensive mechanised verification of a complete test strategy and its associated test case generation algorithm previously elaborated by the second author has been presented. The underlying theories and proofs have been developed using the Isabelle/HOL tool. The results presented show that today's proof assistant tools are powerful enough and do possess adequate usability, so that such an undertaking can be achieved with acceptable effort, provided that some expertise in working with proof assistant tools is available. We advocate mechanised proofs for complete testing theories, since these theories are of considerable value for the verification of safety-critical system. Errors in theories or algorithms, however, may lead to fatal discrepancies between their claimed and actual fault coverage. This could be illustrated by an ambiguity in the original informal description of the test case generation algorithm.

References

1. Ballarin, C.: Locales: a module system for mathematical theories. J. Autom. Reasoning **52**(2), 123–153 (2014). https://doi.org/10.1007/s10817-013-9284-7
2. Bjørner, N.: Z3 and SMT in industrial R&D. In: Havelund, K., Peleska, J., Roscoe, B., de Vink, E.P. (eds.) FM 2018. LNCS, vol. 10951, pp. 675–678. Springer, Cham (2018). https://doi.org/10.1007/978-3-319-95582-7_44

3. Brucker, A.D., Wolff, B.: Interactive testing with HOL-TestGen. In: Grieskamp, W., Weise, C. (eds.) FATES 2005. LNCS, vol. 3997, pp. 87–102. Springer, Heidelberg (2006). https://doi.org/10.1007/11759744_7

4. Brucker, A.D., Wolff, B.: On theorem prover-based testing. Formal Aspects Comput. **25**(5), 683–721 (2013). https://doi.org/10.1007/s00165-012-0222-y

5. Brunner, J.: Transition systems and automata. Archive of Formal Proofs, October 2017. http://isa-afp.org/entries/Transition_Systems_and_Automata.html

6. Dorofeeva, R., El-Fakih, K., Yevtushenko, N.: An improved conformance testing method. In: Wang, F. (ed.) FORTE 2005. LNCS, vol. 3731, pp. 204–218. Springer, Heidelberg (2005). https://doi.org/10.1007/11562436_16

7. Hierons, R.M.: Testing from a nondeterministic finite state machine using adaptive state counting. IEEE Trans. Comput. **53**(10), 1330–1342 (2004). https://doi.org/10.1109/TC.2004.85

8. Luo, G., von Bochmann, G., Petrenko, A.: Test selection based on communicating nondeterministic finite-state machines using a generalized Wp-method. IEEE Trans. Softw. Eng. **20**(2), 149–162 (1994). https://doi.org/10.1109/32.265636

9. Nipkow, T., Paulson, L.C., Wenzel, M.: Isabelle/HOL - A Proof Assistant for Higher-Order Logic. LNCS, vol. 2283. Springer, Heidelberg (2002). https://doi.org/10.1007/3-540-45949-9

10. Peleska, J., Brauer, J., Huang, W.: Model-based testing for avionic systems proven benefits and further challenges. In: Margaria, T., Steffen, B. (eds.) ISoLA 2018. LNCS, vol. 11247, pp. 82–103. Springer, Cham (2018). https://doi.org/10.1007/978-3-030-03427-6_11

11. Peleska, J., Huang, W.L.: Test automation - foundations and applications of model-based testing. University of Bremen, January 2017. http://www.informatik.uni-bremen.de/agbs/jp/papers/test-automation-huang-peleska.pdf

12. Peleska, J., Vorobev, E., Lapschies, F.: Automated test case generation with SMT-solving and abstract interpretation. In: Bobaru, M., Havelund, K., Holzmann, G.J., Joshi, R. (eds.) NFM 2011. LNCS, vol. 6617, pp. 298–312. Springer, Heidelberg (2011). https://doi.org/10.1007/978-3-642-20398-5_22

13. Petrenko, A., Yevtushenko, N.: Adaptive testing of deterministic implementations specified by nondeterministic FSMs. In: Wolff, B., Zaïdi, F. (eds.) ICTSS 2011. LNCS, vol. 7019, pp. 162–178. Springer, Heidelberg (2011). https://doi.org/10.1007/978-3-642-24580-0_12

14. Petrenko, A., Yevtushenko, N., von Bochmann, G.: Testing deterministic implementations from nondeterministic FSM specifications. In: Baumgarten, B., Burkhardt, H.-J., Giessler, A. (eds.) Testing of Communicating Systems. ITIFIP, pp. 125–140. Springer, Boston (1996). https://doi.org/10.1007/978-0-387-35062-2_10

15. Petrenko, A., Yevtushenko, N.: Adaptive testing of nondeterministic systems with FSM. In: 15th International IEEE Symposium on High-Assurance Systems Engineering, HASE 2014, Miami Beach, FL, USA, 9–11 January 2014, pp. 224–228. IEEE Computer Society (2014). https://doi.org/10.1109/HASE.2014.39

16. Wenzel, M.: Isabelle/Isar - a versatile environment for human readable formal proof documents. Ph.D. thesis, Technical University Munich, Germany (2002). http://tumb1.biblio.tu-muenchen.de/publ/diss/in/2002/wenzel.pdf

A Model Checking Based Approach
for Detecting SDN Races

Evgenii Vinarskii[1], Jorge López[2(✉)], Natalia Kushik[2], Nina Yevtushenko[3],
and Djamal Zeghlache[2]

[1] Lomonosov Moscow State University,
1 Leninskiye Gory Street, 119991 Moscow, Russia
vinevg2015@gmail.com
[2] SAMOVAR, CNRS, Télécom SudParis, Université Paris-Saclay,
9 rue Charles Fourier, 91000 Évry, France
{jorge.lopez,natalia.kushik,djamal.zeghlache}@telecom-sudparis.eu
[3] Ivannikov Institute for System Programming of the Russian Academy of Sciences,
25 Alexander Solzhenitsyn Street, 109004 Moscow, Russia
evtushenko@ispras.ru

Abstract. The paper is devoted to the verification of Software Defined Networking (SDN) components and their compositions. We focus on the interaction between three basic entities, an application, a controller, and a switch. When the application submits a request to the controller, containing a set of rules to configure, these rules are expected to be 'pushed' and correctly applied by the switch of interest. However, this is not always the case, and one of the reasons is the presence of races or concurrency issues in SDN components and related interfaces. We propose a model checking based approach for deriving test sequences that can identify SDN races. The test generation strategy is based on model checking, and related formal verification is performed with the use of extended automata specifying the behavior of the components of interest; Linear Temporal Logic (LTL) formulas are utilized to express the properties to check. We generalize the races of interest and propose an approach for deriving the corresponding LTL formulas that are later used for verification. The Spin model checker is used for that purpose and thus, Promela specifications for interacting components are also provided; those are: the ONOS REST API, the ONOS controller and an OpenFlow Switch. An experimental evaluation with the aforementioned components showcases the existence of race conditions in their compositions.

Keywords: Software Defined Networking (SDN) · Races · Controller · Switch · Verification · Testing

1 Introduction

Software Defined Networking (SDN) technologies are actively developing nowadays and are utilized in future network standards, such as for example 5G. Therefore, thor-

The results in this work were partially funded by the Celtic-Plus European project SENDATE, ID C2015/3-1, and the Russian Foundation for Basic Research (RFBR), grant No. 18-01-00854.

ough testing, verification and validation of the components of such networks are crucial. A number of works are in fact dedicated to the verification and testing of SDN enabled switches and SDN controllers (see, for example [13, 14, 20]). At the same time, even if two SDN components have been carefully verified up to some extent, it is still possible that their composition can cause network misconfigurations and inconsistencies. That is the reason why in this work, we focus on the *interaction* of three crucial SDN components, namely an SDN application, an SDN controller and an SDN enabled switch. Generally speaking, the communication between the latter two takes place via the Open-Flow protocol [10], and therefore in this work we focus on the OpenFlow specification as the base for further validation [4].

We note that the OpenFlow protocol does not guarantee that requests between the controller and switch are delivered in the same order as they have been sent; thus races between the requests are possible in the OpenFlow channels. In [16], the authors analyze the reasons and impact of such races. In fact, they identify three types of races: (i) packet races on the data plane, (ii) Post/Get/Delete races on the *southbound* interface (between the controller and the switch), and (iii) a combination of data and control races on the southbound interface. To identify races in the components of interest, i.e., to simulate the races and conditions of those using a formal finite state model (or a composition of those) we propose another classification. We identify the following race types: races between inputs and outputs at a given state of the automaton and races in the communication channel when two or more automata are working in a dialog mode.

We note that the problem of SDN races has been previously raised and existing utilities, such as for example SDNracer, are quite effective [3]. The proposed approaches rely on the definition of a specific (partial) order between the possible SDN events and further monitoring if the defined order is violated. For example, in [11] the authors derive a specific *HB graph (happens-before model)* to identify the order of events. Another possibility is to take a *preventive path*, i.e., to derive the SDN components that are carefully synchronized, so that races cannot show up [9].

In this paper, we propose a complementary approach which is based on proactive testing, i.e., on generation of specific application requests that can lead to a race in an SDN framework. Test sequences that are executed against an SDN framework under test are derived using formal verification approaches. In particular, we employ the Spin model checker [5] that produces a counterexample to generate a sequence of actions that can induce a race. For this reason, we derive extended automata simulating the behavior of the interacting SDN components and later on verify potential (race) properties for this composition. Such properties are described in Linear Temporal Logic (LTL) formulas [1], which can be verified by Spin; likewise, the absence/presence of livelocks/deadlocks in the composition of interest can be verified. We highlight the necessity of the execution of a derived counterexample signaling a potential race in a given SDN component or in their composition. The reason is that in some cases an implementation under test can still be race insensible even if its model does not possess this property. Therefore, such proactive testing against SDN frameworks allows detecting races in *real* SDN enabled components.

When deriving the extended automata models for interacting components we have used both, an OpenFlow specification (OpenFlow 1.4.0), as well as the description of one of the widely utilized controllers. In this work, the experiments have been performed with the ONOS controller [2] and thus, we have extracted a state model specifying its behavior. We note however, that without loss of generality, the controller and/or switch specifications can be easily modified/substituted. All the communicating components have been described in the Promela language (required by Spin). The derived composition has been later on verified by the Spin model checker. Once a counterexample is returned by Spin, the proactive race testing is performed, i.e., counterexamples for concurrency violations are applied to the implementations under study. These counterexamples in fact serve as test sequences to be applied to the implementation under test, in order to make sure the property violation over the model indeed corresponds to a race condition in the implementation.

The main contributions of this work are therefore (i) a proactive model checking based testing method for SDN race detection; (ii) extended automata specifications describing the behavior of an SDN controller, an SDN switch and a communication channel (southbound interface), as well as their Promela specifications that can be downloaded from [17] (which can be easily extended for specific needs); (iii) the description of the potential races of two types for the considered composition in LTL, and iv) experimental results identifying an inconsistency in a common SDN composition (ONOS with Open vSwitch) with respect to the time constraints and delays for the rules to be pushed.

The structure of the paper is as follows. Section 2 presents the background. Section 3 is devoted to the description of the obtained automata together with the related Promela descriptions of the components of interest. Section 4 proposes a solution for deriving LTL formulas for detecting SDN races, as well as the algorithms for the race verification in a given application-controller-switch composition and includes an assessment of the probability to detect races for the SDN composition. Section 5 contains the experimental results while Sect. 6 concludes the paper and presents some avenues for future work.

2   Background

2.1   Software Defined Networking

Software defined networking is a technology that dynamically allows to centrally manage the network behavior via open interfaces by abstracting from the lower-level functionality [4]. This is done by decoupling the control plane from the data plane responsible for forwarding the traffic. The communication between the two critical SDN components, namely the controller and the switch, is performed according to a well-defined protocol (referred to as a southbound protocol). As an example, one can consider the widespread OpenFlow [4] protocol, and in fact, the specifications of the switch and communication channel with the controller in this work are extracted from the OpenFlow descriptions. In the OpenFlow protocol, the flow rules of the switch are configured by the application via the controller, through a defined set of protocol messages. Each flow rule is responsible for forwarding (or dropping) a received packet to an appropriate set of output ports; at the same time, each flow rule has a predefined set of values to which the packet header has to match. Additionally, rules can have timeouts so that they are deleted when a certain timeout expires after their installation (hard timeouts), or so that they are deleted after certain time units when they are not used/matched (soft timeouts). Finally, rules are grouped in (flow) tables and each rule has a defined priority. Rules grouped in the tables with higher numbers are processed first, and in fact, the rule with the highest priority matching a given packet is applied. Network packets are processed according to the rules within flow tables. To better outline the working principles of SDN rules, consider the following rules installed at a given switch:

ID	Priority	Hard Timeout	TCP DST PORT	DST IP	Action
1	5000			10.0.1.22	OUT(2)
2	5001		22		OUT(3)
3	6000	20		10.0.1.23	CTRLLR

To simplify our explanation, and without loss of generality we consider that the rules are installed in the first table of the SDN-enabled switch (table 0). TCP DST PORT is the TCP destination port and DST IP is the destination IP (for further information on basic networking concepts the reader can refer to [8]). A network packet with the destination IP address 10.0.1.22 and destination TCP port 22 will be forwarded to the output 2 (due to the higher priority of Rule 1). Likewise, a network packet with destination IP address 10.0.1.21 and destination TCP port 22 will be forwarded to port 3 (the highest priority rule matching the network packet). Finally, if a network packet going to the destination IP address 10.0.1.23 (and the destination TCP port not equal to 22) arrives within the next 20 s, the switch sends this packet to the controller, asking for the action to take with the packet; after 20 s have passed, the rule will 'disappear', and a packet with destination IP 10.0.1.23 follows the default table policy, which is usually to drop the packet.

2.2 Extended Input/Output Automata and Related Races

In this paper, we model the SDN components by a simplified version of an Extended Finite Input/Output Automata, EIOA, for short. An EIOA **A** is a tuple (S, I, O, V, T, s_0), where S is a finite nonempty set of states with the designated initial state s_0; I and O are finite *input and output alphabets*; V is a finite, possibly empty set of *context variables* with the set D_V of vectors of context variables' values if $V \neq \emptyset$; T is a set of transitions. In our case, inputs and outputs are parameterized, i.e., inputs and outputs of the EIOA are pairs (*input, vector of input parameters' values*) or (*output, vector of output parameters' values*) and D_I (D_O) is the set of vectors of input (output) parameters' values if the set of parameters is not empty. A transition is a 6-tuple (s, a, P, v_p, v_o, s') where $s, s' \in S$ are initial and final states of the transition; $a \in I \cup O$; $P : D_V \times D_I \rightarrow \{True, False\}$ is *the transition predicate*; $v_p : D_V \rightarrow D_V$ is *the context update transition function*. The transition (s, a, P, v_p, v_o, s') is executed only when the transition predicate P evaluates to *true* and the vectors of context variables' values and output parameters' values are updated according to the functions v_p and v_o after the transition execution. We note, however, that the EIOA model can be more complicated, for example, the set of states can have a defined subset of the final states or non-observable actions can be considered, etc. Nevertheless, these cases are not taken into account in the derived models for the controller, switch and application and we furthermore demonstrate that such simplification does not limit the targeted model checking with respect to the race related properties.

As usual, we also assume that when dealing with an EIOA, no input is accepted and no output is produced when a transition is executed. However, when both an input and an output are defined at a state, they can 'compete' between themselves, i.e., what the machine does first - accepts the input or produces the output is nondeterministically decided. We hereafter refer to such 'competition' as an *input/output race* (a race between input and output actions).

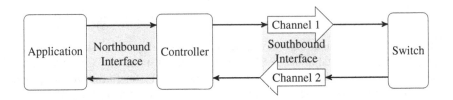

Fig. 1. SDN topology considered in the paper

EIOA Composition and Related Races. When an EIOA works in isolation, the races can occur within certain states, as discussed above. However, when the machine acts as a component of a multi-agent system, other types of races can take place. In particular, the communication channels can serve as 'tunnels' where the actions 'compete' to be faster for reaching the output, we refer to this type of races as *intra-channel* races. In this paper, we are concerned with the interactions of three entities, namely the application, controller, and switch. Therefore, potential races in the channels cover either the northbound or southbound interface. The interacting entities (application, controller and switch) are depicted in Fig. 1. Races of the latter type can occur for example if a message for deleting a rule is delivered to the switch after the rule expires via a timeout, i.e., the deletion is not performed as defined in the OpenFlow specification. We note, that it can also happen that due to races in the communication channel, both components can reach states where they wait for an input. If this happens, then a deadlock in the composition occurs as a consequence of such 'competition'.

2.3 Linear Temporal Logic

For the race detection in EIOAs and their compositions, formal verification can be used and in this paper, we use Linear Temporal Logic (LTL) [6] formulas and the correlation between LTL formulas and EIOA properties.

The notion of an LTL formula is closely related to the Kripke structure [6]. A Kripke structure is a labeled directed graph where each state (node) s is labeled by a set $L(s)$ of *atomic propositions* which are *true* (at s). Correspondingly, a path: $\pi = s_1 \rightarrow s_2 \rightarrow \cdots \rightarrow s_j \rightarrow \ldots s_n \rightarrow \ldots$ is a possibly infinite sequence of consecutive states of the Kripke structure. For each $j \geq 1$, $\pi|^j$ is a suffix $s_j \rightarrow \ldots s_n \rightarrow \ldots$ of path π started with s_j.

An LTL formula is a formula $\varphi ::= a|\varphi_1 \wedge \varphi_2|\neg\varphi|\mathbf{X}\varphi|\varphi_1\mathbf{U}\varphi_2|\mathbf{F}\varphi|\mathbf{G}\varphi$, where: a is *an atomic proposition*, $\mathbf{X}$ denotes the 'next' operator, $\mathbf{U}$ denotes the 'until' operator, $\mathbf{F}$ denotes the 'eventually' operator and $\mathbf{G}$ denotes the 'globally' operator. We briefly remind the conditions when a path $\pi = s_1 \rightarrow s_2 \rightarrow \cdots \rightarrow s_n \rightarrow \ldots$ *satisfies* ($\models$) the LTL formula φ:

- if $\varphi = a$ then $\pi \models \varphi$ iff $a \in L(s_1)$;
- if $\varphi = \mathbf{X}\varphi_1$ then $\pi \models \varphi$ iff $\pi|^2 \models \varphi_1$;
- if $\varphi = \mathbf{F}\varphi_1$ then $\pi \models \varphi$ iff there exists $i \geq 1$ such that $\pi|^i \models \varphi_1$;
- if $\varphi = \mathbf{G}\varphi_1$ then $\pi \models \varphi$ for all $i \geq 1$ $\pi|^i \models \varphi_1$;
- if $\varphi = \varphi_1\mathbf{U}\varphi_2$ then $\pi \models \varphi$ iff there exist $i \geq 1$ $\pi|^i \models \varphi_2$ and for all $1 \leq j < i, \pi|^j \models \varphi_1$.

In this paper, atomic propositions are rather simple; an atomic proposition is *true* if and only if the value of a variable of interest is equal to a given integer.

3   Modeling the Application-Controller-Switch Interaction

In this section, we describe some of the EIOAs derived for checking the application-controller-switch interaction. We have derived the corresponding automaton for each of the interacting components and have elaborated a list of properties to be checked, described as corresponding LTL formulas. We note, that the chosen level of abstraction when modeling the SDN components' behavior plays a crucial role in their further verification.

We hereafter assume that the SDN infrastructure includes only one controller, one switch and one application. The latter means we abstract from any other entity on the data or control plane except the components of interest. To decrease the abstraction level in this case, a composition of switches or a whole data plane can be considered instead of a single switch. We however, note that even such restricted composition allows detecting the races of interest. At the same time, we consider two input channels for the controller, i.e., to accept inputs from the switch and the application of interest. Input and output alphabets of the components of interest can be defined in different ways. For the switch, for example, an OpenFlow specification provides the set of messages which the controller and the switch use for interacting while available specifications for the controllers of interest can also be considered. As a case study, for evaluating our methodology we chose the ONOS controller and thus, to extract the information about the controller-to-application interaction, we use ONOS documentation [2]. For the application of interest, in our experiments we consider a REST service [7] which allows defining the corresponding behavior of the application.

Given the assumptions listed above, we consider the topology shown in Fig. 1. The ONOS documentation, the OpenFlow specification and ONOS REST service documentation allow to extract the following alphabets:

- An application-controller channel alphabet: $\{PostFlow, DeleteFlow, GetFlow\}$;
- A controller-application channel alphabet: $\{FlowRemoveExpire, ReplyFlow\}$;
- A controller-switch channel alphabet: $\{PostFlow, DeleteFlow, GetFlow\}$;
- A switch-controller channel alphabet: $\{FlowRemoveExpire, ReplyFlow\}$.

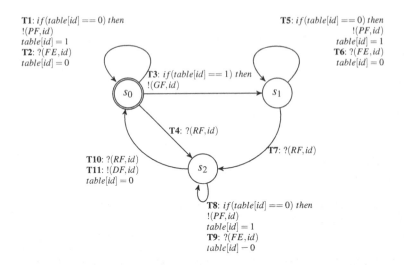

T1: $if(table[id] == 0)$ *then*
$!(PF, id)$
$table[id] = 1$
T2: $?(FE, id)$
$table[id] = 0$

T3: $if(table[id] == 1)$ *then*
$!(GF, id)$

T5: $if(table[id] == 0)$ *then*
$!(PF, id)$
$table[id] = 1$
T6: $?(FE, id)$
$table[id] = 0$

T4: $?(RF, id)$

T7: $?(RF, id)$

T10: $?(RF, id)$
T11: $!(DF, id)$
$table[id] = 0$

T8: $if(table[id] == 0)$ *then*
$!(PF, id)$
$table[id] = 1$
T9: $?(FE, id)$
$table[id] - 0$

Fig. 2. EIOA modeling the controller behavior

3.1 Extended Automaton Modeling the Behavior of a Controller

In this work, the EIOA for modeling the controller behavior has three states s_0, s_1, s_2. These states naturally correspond to the situations when messages from the controller to the switch (or vice-versa) change the behavior of the system. For example, at state s_0 a *GetFlow* (GF) request is not being processed; likewise, the *DelFlow* (DF) request cannot be produced. State s_1 describes the situation when a GF request has been produced from the controller (to the switch); at this state the EIOA can get *ReplyFlow* (RF) and should move to state s_2. At state s_2, the DF signal can be produced. We note that this interaction is a part of the aforementioned specifications (OpenFlow, ONOS, etc.).

The EIOA has a context variable; this variable corresponds to the number of installed flow rules, and thus, its domain is the set of integers $\{0, \dots, n-1\}$. The EIOA has 11 transitions, and seven of them are unconditional, i.e., the transitions have no predicates. As an example, the transition $(s_0, GetFlow, s_1)$ models the situation when the controller has sent the *GetFlow* request moving to state s_1. The transition diagram of the EIOA modeling the controller behavior is shown in Fig. 2.

For further model checking, namely races' detection, we describe the EIOA in Promela which is accepted by Spin as an input. In this case, the Promela code contains the variable IDflow, the rule's ID. Note that for convenience and without loss of generality the value of the IDflow is equal to the rule's priority. Moreover, the Promela description has an array app_table that contains all the current switch flow rules. The description of the controller behavior includes one process. A fragment[1] of the Promela description of the controller is illustrated in Fig. 3. The complete version of the related program, as well as the Promela code for other interacting components, are available at [17].

---

[1] The actual description contains 632 lines.

```
 1  proctype Controller(chan AppCont, ContApp, Ch2Cont,        19        ContApp!FlowExpire(id_flow_cont);
 2                    ContCh1) {                                20        app_table[id_flow_cont] = false;
 3  mtype mess_app_cont;                                        21        mess = FlowExpire;
 4  int id_flow_app, id_flow_cont;                              22        flow_id = id_flow_cont;
 5  S0:                                                         23        goto S0;
 6      if                                                      24     :: Ch2Cont?ReplyFlow(id_flow_cont);
 7      ::  AppCont?(mess_app_cont, id_flow_app);               25        ContApp!ReplyFlow(id_flow_cont);
 8          goto S0;                                            26        mess = ReplyFlow;
 9      ::  (app_table[0] == false) ->                          27        flow_id = id_flow_cont;
10          atomic {                                            28        goto S0;
11              do                                              29     :: Ch2Cont?ReplyFlow(id_flow_cont);
12              ::  ContCh1!PostFlow(0);                        30        ContApp!ReplyFlow(id_flow_cont);
13                  app_table[0] = true;                        31        mess = ReplyFlow;
14                  mess = PostFlow;                            32        flow_id = id_flow_cont;
15                  flow_id = 0;                                33        goto S2;
16                  goto S0;                                    34     od;
17              ::  Ch2Cont?FlowExpire(id_flow_cont);           35   }
```

Fig. 3. Controller description in Promela

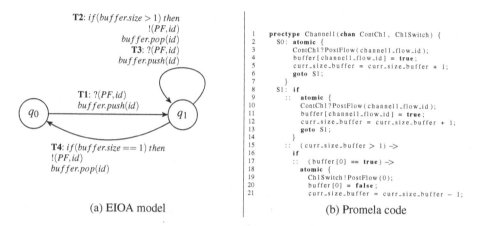

(a) EIOA model

```
 1  proctype Channel1(chan ContCh1, Ch1Switch) {
 2  S0:  atomic {
 3      ContCh1?PostFlow(channel1_flow_id);
 4      buffer[channel1_flow_id] = true;
 5      curr_size_buffer = curr_size_buffer + 1;
 6      goto S1;
 7      }
 8  S1:  if
 9      ::    atomic {
10          ContCh1?PostFlow(channel1_flow_id);
11          buffer[channel1_flow_id] = true;
12          curr_size_buffer = curr_size_buffer + 1;
13          goto S1;
14          }
15      ::  (curr_size_buffer > 1) ->
16          if
17      ::  (buffer[0] == true) ->
18          atomic {
19              Ch1Switch!PostFlow(0);
20              buffer[0] = false;
21              curr_size_buffer = curr_size_buffer - 1;
```

(b) Promela code

Fig. 4. Channel 1 descriptions

3.2   Extended Automaton Modeling the Behavior of Channel 1

The EIOA that models channel 1's behavior has two states, namely q_0 and q_1. These states correspond to the state of the buffer. In particular, state q_0 corresponds to the situation when the buffer is empty while state q_1 reflects the opposite. The context variable buffer.size corresponds to the number of messages in the buffer. The EIOA has four transitions, and two of them are unconditional. As an example, a transition (q_1, PF, q_0) can be considered: it models the situation when channel 1 has sent a *PostFlow* request for a rule with ID *id* moving to state q_0. The transition diagram of the corresponding EIOA is shown in Fig. 4a.

This EIOA is also described in the Promela language. In this case, the Promela code contains the IDflow variable, the identifier for a given rule. Similarly, the Promela description has an array buffer that contains the messages in the buffer. A fragment of the Promela description of channel 1 (channel 2) is illustrated in Fig. 4b.

Given the room constraints, we do not include the detailed EIOA descriptions of other interacting components, such as the switch or application. For detailed description one can access the corresponding Promela code via [17].

4   Race Detection in the Application-Controller-Switch Interaction

This section is devoted to the verification of the Application-Controller-Switch (ACS) interaction. We propose a methodology for detecting races of two types discussed above. Namely, we propose two randomized algorithms for two types of races. These are Monte Carlo algorithms, i.e., if a race is detected by the method then we guarantee that such race can happen in the ACS interaction under proper conditions, namely, for proper timeouts. However, if the algorithm returns '*FALSE*' then this answer can still be wrong, i.e., it cannot be guaranteed that the ACS interaction is free of races described above. The main reasons for that are the following: (i) the approach relies on the Spin model checker that does not guarantee that a counterexample is always found, and (ii) the approach depends on the time each message spends in a channel and this time is nondeterministic.

4.1   Input/Output Races

These races can occur when there exists a state of a corresponding EIOA where an input and an output which have a parameter in common are allowed, i.e., at a given state the decision of accepting an input or producing an output is made nondeterministically. However, if the system is race insensible, then this fact does not influence the system behavior. In order to check this, the Spin model checker can be used. Therefore, the problem is reduced to constructing an appropriate LTL formula that checks whether the system is sensible to races between inputs and outputs at a given state.

We propose (a probabilistic approach in) Algorithm 1, that assures the presence and the detection of an input/output race. The algorithm is based on a choice of a state s of the EIOA, where both input i and output o *related via some parameter* are defined. The Spin model checker is used for verifying the LTL formula *prohibiting* a race between i and o. Let *curr_mess* denote an input or an output action (message) at state s while *next_mess* denote the action at the next time instance. To guarantee that the output o is never produced before the input i is received, an LTL formula of the following kind can be verified: $\mathbf{G}(\neg((curr\_mess == o) \rightarrow (next\_mess == i)))$[2].

If the formula of interest can be violated for the component of interest, then Spin produces a counterexample α. Note that not each counterexample is feasible for the topology of interest; further checking should be performed by applying a sequence of inputs simulating α, with appropriate timeouts to an implementation (component of interest). Determining such timeouts is a separate task which for the moment is performed heuristically for input/output races; while for intra-channel races (see Sect. 4.2), we propose an algorithmic solution (Algorithm 3). As the approach proposed in this paper is proactive, we execute the derived counterexample α potentially leading to a race against the implementation of the SDN framework. For that reason, we rely on an automated script; the script is executed at most N times, simulating α as an input to the component of interest. If during the execution of the script the *competition* between an input and output can be observed, then the script returns *TRUE*. Therefore, when

---

[2] The reader might notice that the formula is quite generic and can be adjusted accordingly for various particular cases, for example, states, input/output parameters can be added.

Execute_script(S) returns *TRUE* a race is indeed detected in the implementation. Note that the execution of the script can be performed against any application, controller, and switch, from different providers, as long as the corresponding versions are compatible.

Algorithm 1. Input/output race detection

Input : A composition Promela model $\mathcal{M}$; a number n of flow rules; a number N of testing iterations

Output: A Boolean value indicating if the race is detected

Choose an SDN component C of interest from the composition $\mathcal{M}$

Choose a state s of C where both input i and output o are defined // The procedure can be repeated iteratively for a subset of states $J \subseteq S$

Derive an *LTL*-formula Φ simulating that the output o was produced before the input i was accepted

Verify Φ over $\mathcal{M}$ (e.g., using Spin)

if *a counterexample* α *is found (by Spin)* **then**

    if *Obtain_timeout_vector*(α) $==$ *FALSE* **then**

        // *Obtain_timeout_vector* heuristically derives a timeout vector if it is feasible

        return *FALSE*

    Given the timeout vector, and the counterexample α, derive script S stimulating the SUT with α

    foreach $i \in \{1,\ldots,N\}$ **do**

        if *Execute_script*(S) $==$ *TRUE* **then**

            return *TRUE*

return *FALSE*

An important step of Algorithm 1 concerns the choice of the component of interest and its state (or a subset of those) for further verification. As an example, consider an SDN controller whose model is presented in Fig. 2. Note that, at state s_2 both input (FE, id) and output (DF, id) are defined. These actions can compete and it must be assured that indeed (DF, id) occurs first. In other words, it should be checked that the controller can send a *DelFlow* message to remove a flow rule with the *flow_id* number only if this rule currently exists. This property can be expressed using the following LTL formula: $\mathbf{G}(((mess == DelFlow)\&\&(flow\_id == id)) \rightarrow (flow\_table[id] == true))$.

Algorithm 1 is a randomized algorithm that can be *trusted* on a race detection. The probability of such reply significantly depends on the structure of the specification EIOA **A**. If the simulation of this EIOA represents a Markov chain then the probability of success and, in some cases, its limit, can be evaluated.

Assume that the transitions of the EIOA **A** of interest are augmented with their probabilities of execution. In the simplest case, we assume that all the transitions are equally probable at a given state. Let Π denote the stochastic matrix for the related Markov process, i.e., $\Pi = \{p_{i,j}\}$, and $p_{i,j}$ is the probability to reach s_j from state s_i. Let also $J \subseteq S$ denote the set of *critical* states of **A** where a given input can compete with certain output. The probability of Algorithm 1 to terminate with a positive reply depends on the probability of reaching one of the states $j \in J$ from the initial state $s_0 \in S$. The latter is determined by the following proposition.

Proposition 1. $Pr(s_1 \xrightarrow{\alpha} j \in J) = \sum_{j \in J} [p_{1,j}]^m$, where $\{[p_{i,j}]^m\} = \Pi^m$, and $|\alpha| = m$.

Proof. Indeed, matrix Π^m consists of items $[p_{i,j}]^m$ for $i, j \in \{1, \ldots, |S|\}$. Moreover, state s_j is reached from state s_i via a sequence α, $|\alpha| = m$, i.e., $i \xrightarrow{\alpha} j$ with the probability $[p_{i,j}]^m$. Therefore, the probability of reaching any state of set J via a sequence of length m equals $\sum_{j \in J} [p_{1,j}]^m$. $\square$

Corollary 1. *If the sum $\sum_{j \in J} [p_{1,j}]^m$ has the limit, then the probability of reaching a state where a race is possible equals* $\lim_{m \to \infty} \sum_{j \in J} [p_{1,j}]^m$.

The matrix Π^m can be computed by direct multiplication of Π matrices, or in some cases, the spectral decomposition of Π can be utilized (for more details one can see [15], for example), to improve the scalability of the Π^m as well as for the checking the criterion when such decomposition is possible.

We note also that the race sensibility in the SDN components of interest can be avoided by setting appropriate timeouts for processing inputs and producing outputs. However, as our experiments show (Sect. 5), for the ONOS controller those timeouts are not appropriately set.

4.2 Intra-channel Races

Having discussed the input/output races at a given state, we now turn to the detection of another type of races. In particular, this subsection is devoted to the intra-channel races, when for example the rules or requests submitted into a channel by a given component can be permutated. In other words, the order of the rules/requests cannot necessarily be preserved once submitted into the channel. In the case of our experimental evaluation those are the rules submitted by the controller and later on pushed to the switch. Such detection is essential as it leads to different 'understanding' of a current network state at the control and data plane, and thus can cause network misconfigurations. In order to detect if there exists a potential permutation in the channel, we try to proactively create this race condition. To do so, the SDN application installs rules with their ID in chronological order; moreover, each rule has a hard timeout equal to its ID. For instance, the SDN application installs a rule with ID i and timeout i before installing the rule $i + 1$ with timeout $i + 1$. Thus, to check the possibility of permutations, we propose Algorithm 4 that either detects an intra-channel race or returns *FALSE* if a race cannot be detected. The Promela model $\mathcal{M}$ of the composition of interest serves as one of the inputs. At the first step, the LTL formulas are derived via the call to Algorithm 2. The strategy to detect this type of races is to stimulate 'competing' messages in a channel. In order to better understand the properties that are investigated, we further explain the motivation behind them.

- Consider the following property: $\mathbf{G}((table[id] == true) \to (table[id'] == true))$. This guarantees that if the rule with the id number is pushed before the rule with id' number and has a timeout value less than that of id', then the id rule should be deleted before the id' one. In other words, the presence of the id rule in the flow table implies the presence of the id' as well.
- Consider the property: $(mess == (PF, id)) \to ((mess \neq (DF, id))\mathbf{U}(table[id] == true))$. This means that if a controller requested to push the rule with the id number, then at some point this rule will be pushed. Moreover, the rule cannot be deleted unless it was pushed.

Algorithm 2. Deriving LTL formulas

Input : The global variables of the Promela model ($\mathcal{V}_{\mathcal{M}}$)
Output: Φ, LTL-formulas to check intra-channel races
return *the following formulas*
foreach $i \in \{1, \ldots, size\_of(table) - 1\}$ **do**
$\quad\lfloor\ \mathbf{G}((table[i+1] == 0) \to (table[i] == 0));$
$\mathbf{G}((app\_send\_mess == (Post\_flow, id)) \to \mathbf{F}(table[id] == 1))$
$\mathbf{G}((app\_send\_mess == (Delete\_flow, id)) \to \mathbf{F}(table[id] == 0))$

At the next step, the derived properties together with the original model are 'fed' to Spin. If Spin does not detect a violation of any of the properties then not a single race of interest can be detected. This does not necessarily guarantee the absence of such races. On the other hand, if a counterexample α is produced then its feasibility is first verified (Algorithm 3)[3]. A non-feasible counterexample again results in the '*not detected*' conclusion. On the contrary, if α is feasible, the result is a vector τ representing the timeouts for each of the n rules. Similar to Algorithm 1, at the last step each feasible counterexample is executed N times as it is possible that the system does not incur into a race condition at all times. In this case, we analyze the probability of success to actually observe the race in the given implementation. In other words, given a counterexample α produced by Spin and a vector $\tau = (\tau_1, \ldots, \tau_n)$ of timeouts, we further define the probability of the randomized Algorithm 4 to terminate returning a *FALSE* verdict.

A message may spend an unknown time in a channel, we assume that this time is bounded by certain interval $[T_{min}, T_{max}]$; t_i defines the time that a message i spends in a channel, and there is no guarantee that the time spent in the channel is closer either to the left or to the right bound. Let us denote the timeout for a given rule i as τ_i, and the differences between the neighbour rule timeouts as d_i, i.e., $d_1 = \tau_2 - \tau_1$, $d_2 = \tau_3 - \tau_2, \ldots, d_{n-1} = \tau_n - \tau_{n-1}$. Note that the rules in a switch are installed without permutations if and only if $\forall i \in \{1, \ldots, n-1\}\ 0 < \tau_i < \tau_{i+1}$, $t_i \in [T_{min}, T_{max}]$ it holds that $t_i + \tau_i < t_{i+1} + \tau_{i+1}$. The latter means that $\forall i \in \{1, \ldots, n-1\}\ \tau_{i+1} - \tau_i > t_i - t_{i+1}$, i.e., $d_i > t_i - t_{i+1}$. We assume that for all i, t_i are absolutely continuous random variables defined over the interval $[T_{min}, T_{max}]$ with the probability density functions $f_i(z)$.

---

[3] Note that the equation in Algorithm 3 can be solved using classical approaches, see for example Gauss-Jordan elimination [15].

Algorithm 3. Permutation feasibility check

Input : T_{min} - the minimum time a message spends in a given channel; T_{max} - the maximum time a message spends in a given channel; n - the number of messages (rules) to submit to the channel

Output: A vector τ of timeouts or *FALSE* if races are not possible

Solve the following inequality // Can be done using classical approaches, see for example Gauss-Jordan elimination [15]

$$t_i + \tau_i \geq t_j + \tau_j$$

where
$$t_i, t_j \in [T_{min}, T_{max}]$$
$$i < j$$
$$\tau_i < \tau_j$$
$$\tau_i > 0$$
$$\tau_j > 0$$

if *the inequality has a feasible solution* $(t'_i, t'_j, \tau'_i, \tau'_j)$ **then**
$\quad$ select any $\tau = (\tau_1, \ldots, \tau'_i, \ldots, \tau'_j, \ldots, \tau_n)$ where
$\quad 0 < \tau_1 < \tau_2 < \cdots < \tau'_i < \ldots < \tau'_j < \cdots < \tau_n$
$\quad$ **return** τ
return *FALSE*

Algorithm 4. Intra-channel race detection

Input : A composition Promela model $\mathcal{M}$; A minimal and a maximal time T_{min}, T_{max} to cross the controller-to-switch Openflow channel by messages; A number n of *flow_rules*; A number N of testing iterations

Output: A Boolean value indicating if the race is detected

Obtain a set of *LTL*-formulas $\Phi = $ Deriving_LTL_formulas $(\mathcal{V}_{\mathcal{M}})$ // $\mathcal{V}_{\mathcal{M}}$ represents the global variables of $\mathcal{M}$

Verify Φ over $\mathcal{M}$

if *a counterexample* α *is found* **then**
$\quad$ **if** $(\tau == $ *Permutation_feasibility_check* $(T_{min}, T_{max}, n))$ **then**
$\quad\quad$ Obtain the script $S = $ *Produce_script* (α, τ)

$\quad$ **else**
$\quad\quad$ **return** *FALSE*

$\quad$ **foreach** $i \in \{1, \ldots, N\}$ **do**
$\quad\quad$ **if** *Execute_script* $(S) == TRUE$ **then**
$\quad\quad\quad$ **return** *TRUE*

return *FALSE*

We denote the length of this interval as $D = T_{max} - T_{min}$. We therefore assume that $t_i, i \in \{1, \ldots, n-1\}$, are independent and uniformly distributed on $[T_{min}, T_{max}]$, i.e.,

$$\forall i \in \{1, \ldots, n\} \ f_i(z) = \begin{cases} \frac{1}{D}, & z \in [T_{min}, T_{max}] \\ 0, & z \notin [T_{min}, T_{max}] \end{cases}$$. In this case, $c_i = t_i - t_{i+1}$ are absolutely

continuous random variables defined on the interval $[-D, D]$ with the probability density function $\varphi_i(z)$, for each $i \in \{1, \ldots, n-1\}$. Taking into account the uniform distribution hypothesis for t_i and t_{i+1}, for all $i \in \{1, \ldots, n-1\}$, c_i are also independent and uniformly distributed on the interval $[-D, D]$ with the probability density functions

$$\varphi_i(z) = \begin{cases} \frac{1}{2*D}, & z \in [-D, D] \\ 0, & z \notin [-D, D] \end{cases}.$$

Proposition 2. *Given the uniform distribution hypothesis, the probability that no rules are permutated, i.e., no races occur in the channel, is equal to* $Pr(no\_permutations) = \frac{1}{(2*D)^{n-1}} * \prod_{i=1}^{n-1} (D + d_i)$.

Proof. According to the independence of random variables [19], it holds that: $Pr(no\_permutations) = Pr(d_1 > c_1, \ldots, d_{n-1} > c_{n-1}) = Pr(c_1 < d_1) * \cdots * Pr(c_{n-1} < d_{n-1}) = \int_{-D}^{d_1} \varphi_1(z)dz * \cdots * \int_{-D}^{d_{n-1}} \varphi_{n-1}(z)dz$.

Under the assumption that $c_1, \ldots, c_{n-1}$ are uniformly distributed, and $d_i \in [0, D]$, it holds that $Pr(no\_permutations) = \frac{1}{(2*D)^{n-1}} * \prod_{i=1}^{n-1} (D + d_i)$. $\square$

Therefore, the probability of having races, caused by the rules' permutation in the channel is $Pr(permutations) = 1 - Pr(no\_permutations) = 1 - \frac{1}{(2*D)^{n-1}} * \prod_{i=1}^{n-1} (D + d_i)$.

We however note that the probability distribution for the time a rule spends in a channel is crucial. If it is known in advance the probability density function should be recalculated accordingly, for example, due to an experimental evaluation of the channel and corresponding communicating components. This affects the success of the randomized Algorithm 4, i.e., the positive reply when the races are detected. In our experiments, we however relied on the uniform distribution assumption and were able to detect the permutation and related races for the controller and switch of interest.

5   Experimental Results

Experiments were performed with the ONOS Controller and the Mininet [12] simulator, executed under a virtual machine running on VirtualBox Version 5.1.34 for Ubuntu 16.04 LTS with 4 GB of RAM, and a quad AMD A6-7310 APU with AMD Radeon R4 Graphics processor. Our experimental setup corresponds to the topology in Fig. 1, i.e., the simulated network contains a single switch running Open vSwitch version v2.11.0 and a single application implemented as a Perl [18] script. The goal of the experiments was to estimate the efficiency of the proposed algorithms for race detection and their impact on available SDN components of wide use, namely, on the communication between the ONOS controller and an Open vSwitch. All the Perl scripts utilized in the experimental setup are accessible at [17].

5.1 Input/Output Races

The first set of experiments was performed to detect the potential input/output races (at a given state). In this case, the component under test is the ONOS controller. With the proposed approach (Algorithm 1) we managed to detect a race at state s_2 for the specification provided in Fig. 2. Consider the property: *an input (DelFlow, flow_id) should not be sent if the rule with the number flow_id is not defined in the flow table.* The corresponding LTL formula in this case is as follows: $\mathbf{G}(((mess == DelFlow) \wedge (flow\_id == id)) \rightarrow (flow\_table[id] == true))$.

A flow rule with a timeout with the number $flow\_id$ may expire in the switch before the controller sends the *DelFlow* request to remove the flow rule with this number. Thus, in such composition, the controller can be sensible to this type of races.

To detect such a race we used three rules ($n = 3$). The probability of success of the race detection can be estimated using the EIOA in Fig. 3. Assume that the transitions at each state are equally probable, then the stochastic matrix $\Pi - \begin{bmatrix} 1/2 & 1/4 & 1/4 \\ 0 & 2/3 & 1/3 \\ 1/2 & 0 & 1/2 \end{bmatrix}$. The spectral decomposition allows computing $Pr(s_1 \xrightarrow{\alpha} s_3) = \lim_{m \to \infty} p_{1,3}^m = \frac{1}{3}$.

Given the probability of success, we executed the model checking and Spin found a counterexample (available at [17]) of length 21. To comply with the order of the requests in the counterexample α, following Algorithm 1 we derived a vector of timeouts τ that were implemented with the *sleep*() procedure. The counterexample α (together with the values τ_i in the comments of the Perl script) can be checked at [17]. The script of interest was executed 10 times, i.e., $N = 10$ and at the 4-th iteration an unexpected behavior was observed. A rule deleted via a timeout, produced a *FlowExpire* message from the switch to the controller, however, the controller at a later time instance produced a *FlowDelete* message for the same rule ID. The latter means that the flow table *of the controller* can be dis-synchronized, i.e., the controller's knowledge of the network state is not always relevant and up-to-date. Moreover, it cannot be predicted which action removed the rule: *FlowExpire* or *DelFlow*. The detailed logs of the script execution and race detection are also available at [17]. In the files logs/test_1.txt, logs/test_2.txt and logs/test_3.txt the *FLOW_REMOVED* signal is sent 5 times, however, in logs/test_4.txt the *FLOW_REMOVED* signal is sent 3 times. This means that to delete a rule with number 5000 in first 3 cases the controller sent *FLOW_REMOVED* signal and in the fourth case the switch sent a *FLOW_EXPIRE* message earlier. Thus, the input/output race is possible.

5.2 Intra-channel Races

When detecting races of this type in an SDN framework, we focused on the channel 1, i.e., the controller-to-switch interface. In particular, in our experiments we tried to detect a race between the *PostFlow* requests in the related channel.

For that reason, Algorithm 4 was executed with the following parameters: $T_{min} = 0$, $T_{max} = 1.5$, $n = 5$, $N = 10$ and for each i, $d_i = 1$. Therefore $D = 1.5$ and, thus, $Pr(no\_permutations) = \frac{2.5^4}{3^4}$. Consequently, $Pr(permutations) = 1 - \frac{2.5^4}{3^4} \approx 0,52$.

The counterexample α produced by Spin contains 10 requests (5 inputs and 5 outputs); the vector τ provided by Algorithm 3 is as follows: $\tau = \langle 5, 6, 7, 8, 9 \rangle$. Thus, for a rule with ID $5000 + i$, its timeout value is set to $i + 5$ seconds. Following Algorithm 4, the counterexample α was executed with the timeouts τ, using the corresponding Perl script. We executed the Perl script $N = 10$ times and at the 8-th execution an unexpected behavior was observed. Figure 5 showcases the flow table in the controller, which exhibits a race condition; Fig. 5a presents the rules as initially installed while Fig. 5b presents the rules at the end. Note that the rules 5003 and 5004 expired, however, the rule 5002 is still present, although the value of the timeout in the rule 5002 is set to 7 s while the timeout of the rules 5003 and 5004 are set to 8 and 9 s, correspondingly. Indeed, the nondeterministic behavior of the controller can lead to a rule permutation in the channel. In the counterexample of interest, two rules with the IDs 2 and 3 accordingly happened to permutate. The iterative execution of a Perl script allows to detect such permutations. Likewise, the permutation of rules with the numbers 5002 and 5003 can be observed (Fig. 5). The latter means, that the sequence of actions executed by the controller can be different from the implemented sequence of actions.

Flows for Device of:0000000000000001 (7 Total)

STATE	PACKETS	DURATION	FLOW PRIORITY	TABLE NAME
Added	0	594	40000	0
Added	0	594	40000	0
Added	0	3	5000	0
Added	0	3	5001	0
Added	0	3	5002	0
Added	0	2	5004	0
Added	0	3	5003	0

Flows for Device of:0000000000000001 (3 Total)

STATE	PACKETS	DURATION	FLOW PRIORITY	TABLE NAME
Added	0	474	40000	0
Added	0	474	40000	0
Added	0	4	5002	0

(a) Initial rules   (b) Final rules

Fig. 5. Rule permutation

6 Conclusions

In this paper, we considered concurrency issues in the SDN framework. In particular, we studied two different types of races for an application-controller-switch composition. For each of these types, we proposed a proactive testing approach for detecting such concurrency. The proposed approach complements the existing ones that are mostly based on effective monitoring and run-time verification, i.e., a model checking based design of test sequences that can push certain race to show, can be integrated into monitoring systems and thus, can later serve for the SDN components' certification.

This work opens a number of directions for future work. First, additional types of races should be considered, taking into account other types of interfaces, such as for example between controllers. Despite the fact that the proposed approach is generic, experiments were only carried for the ONOS controller and one Open vSwitch, more experiments are needed to investigate other SDN components of wide use and their (in-) tolerance to certain types of races. The proposed approach relies on the LTL based model checking solutions for describing and detecting races in SDN; in the future, we plan to investigate other formal verification and model checking techniques and their applicability to the problem of interest. We plan to extend the proposed approach for stating clear recommendations for avoiding races in SDN frameworks, probably, taking advantage of some other model based techniques, such as for example Game Theory. Moreover, adaptive approaches are of a particular interest of the authors, namely we plan to investigate various testing strategies that could be used depending on the implemented race-avoidance mechanisms in an SDN framework. Finally, the application areas of the proposed approach are not limited with SDN, and in the future we plan to consider other distributed systems and related race conditions.

References

1. Baier, C., Katoen, J.P.: Principles of Model Checking. The MIT Press, Cambridge (2008)
2. Berde, P., et al.: ONOS: towards an open, distributed SDN OS. In: Proceedings of the Third Workshop on Hot Topics in Software Defined Networking, pp. 1–6. ACM (2014)
3. El-Hassany, A., Miserez, J., Bielik, P., Vanbever, L., Vechev, M.T.: SDNRacer: concurrency analysis for software-defined networks. In: Proceedings of the 37th ACM SIGPLAN Conference on Programming Language Design and Implementation, PLDI 2016, Santa Barbara, CA, USA, 13–17 June 2016, pp. 402–415 (2016). https://doi.org/10.1145/2908080.2908124
4. Open Networking Foundation: OpenFlow switch specification version 1.4.0 (2013). https://www.opennetworking.org/images/stories/downloads/sdn-resources/onf-specifications/openflow/openflow-spec-v1.4.0.pdf
5. Holzmann, G.: The Spin Model Checker: Primer and Reference Manual. Addison-Wesley Professional, Boston (2003)
6. Huth, M., Ryan, M.: Logic in Computer Science: Modelling and Reasoning About Systems. Cambridge University Press, Cambridge (2004)
7. Koshibe, A., et al.: ONOS - Appendix B: REST API (2014). https://wiki.onosproject.org/display/ONOS/Appendix+B%3A+REST+API. Accessed 02 June 2019
8. Kozierok, C.M.: The TCP/IP Guide: A Comprehensive, Illustrated Internet Protocols Reference. No Starch Press, San Francisco (2005)
9. McClurg, J., Hojjat, H., Černý, P.: Synchronization synthesis for network programs. In: Majumdar, R., Kunčak, V. (eds.) CAV 2017. LNCS, vol. 10427, pp. 301–321. Springer, Cham (2017). https://doi.org/10.1007/978-3-319-63390-9_16
10. McKeown, N., et al.: OpenFlow: enabling innovation in campus networks. ACM SIGCOMM Comput. Commun. Rev. **38**(2), 69–74 (2008)
11. Miserez, J., Bielik, P., El-Hassany, A., Vanbever, L., Vechev, M.T.: SDNRacer: detecting concurrency violations in software-defined networks. In: Proceedings of the 1st ACM SIGCOMM Symposium on Software Defined Networking Research, SOSR 2015, Santa Clara, California, USA, 17–18 June 2015, pp. 22:1–22:7 (2015). https://doi.org/10.1145/2774993.2775004
12. de Oliveira, R.L.S., Schweitzer, C.M., Shinoda, A.A., Prete, L.R.: Using mininet for emulation and prototyping software-defined networks. In: 2014 IEEE Colombian Conference on Communications and Computing (COLCOM), pp. 1–6 (2014). https://doi.org/10.1109/ColComCon.2014.6860404
13. Scott, C., et al.: Troubleshooting blackbox SDN control software with minimal causal sequences. In: Proceeding of the ACM SIGCOMM 2014 Conference, Chicago, Illinois, USA (2014)

14. Shalimov, A., Zuikov, D., Zimarina, D., Pashkov, V., Smeliansky, R.: Advanced study of SDN/OpenFlow controllers. In: 9th Central & Eastern European Software Engineering Conference in Russia. ACM (2013)
15. Strang, G.: Introduction to Linear Algebra, vol. 3. Wellesley-Cambridge Press, Wellesley (1993)
16. Sun, X.S., Agarwal, A., Ng, T.S.E.: Controlling race conditions in OpenFlow to accelerate application verification and packet forwarding. IEEE Trans. Netw. Serv. Manag. **12**(2), 263–277 (2015). https://doi.org/10.1109/TNSM.2015.2419975
17. Vinarskii, E.: Perl scripts, promela descriptions and counterexamples for SDN race detection (2019). http://mks1.cmc.msu.ru/EvgeniiEM/detecting_SDN_races
18. Wall, L., Christiansen, T., Orwant, J.: Programming Perl. O'Reilly Media Inc., Sebastopol (2000)
19. William, F.: A Introduction to Probability Theory and Its Applications. Wiley, New York (1971)
20. Zhang, Z., Yuan, D., Hu, H.: Multi-layer modeling of OpenFlow based on EFSM. In: 4th International Conference on Machinery, Materials and Information Technology Applications, pp. 209–214 (2016)

Security and Performance Testing

Towards an Efficient Performance Testing Through Dynamic Workload Adaptation

Osvaldo Huerta-Guevara$^{(\boxtimes)}$, Vanessa Ayala-Rivera, Liam Murphy,
and A. Omar Portillo-Dominguez

Lero@UCD, School of Computer Science, University College Dublin, Dublin, Ireland
osvaldo.huertaguevara@ucdconnect.ie,
{vanessa.ayalarivera,liam.murphy,andres.portillodominguez}@ucd.ie

Abstract. Performance testing is a critical task to ensure an acceptable user experience with software systems, especially when there are high numbers of concurrent users. Selecting an appropriate test workload is a challenging and time-consuming process that relies heavily on the testers' expertise. Not only are workloads application-dependent, but also it is usually unclear how large a workload must be to expose any performance issues that exist in an application. Previous research has proposed to dynamically adapt the test workloads in real-time based on the application behavior. By reducing the need for the trial-and-error test cycles required when using static workloads, dynamic workload adaptation can reduce the effort and expertise needed to carry out performance testing. However, such approaches usually require testers to properly configure several parameters in order to be effective in identifying workload-dependent performance bugs, which may hinder their usability among practitioners. To address this issue, this paper examines the different criteria needed to conduct performance testing efficiently using dynamic workload adaptation. We present the results of comprehensively evaluating one such approach, providing insights into how to tune it properly in order to obtain better outcomes based on different scenarios. We also study the effects of varying its configuration and how this can affect the results obtained.

Keywords: Software engineering · Performance testing ·
Performance bug · Workload · Web systems and applications

1 Introduction

Performance testing plays a critical role in the software industry in order to successfully engineer reliable systems and guarantee the best experience for the final users. When a system exhibits failures or errors, it can cause severe damages to companies such as economic and reputational losses. Moreover, the risk of suffering performance degradation in systems is exacerbated with the increase

© IFIP International Federation for Information Processing 2019
Published by Springer Nature Switzerland AG 2019
C. Gaston et al. (Eds.): ICTSS 2019, LNCS 11812, pp. 215–233, 2019.
https://doi.org/10.1007/978-3-030-31280-0_13

of services residing in the cloud, which must support millions of users interacting with the system at the same time through web or mobile applications [11].

The goal of performance testing is to evaluate how well an application can perform under a particular workload [21,30]. However, it is difficult to generate effective test cases that can expose performance issues promptly as it requires testers to evaluate multiple combinations of workloads, actions, and data [24]. Additionally, a large number of enterprise systems that were developed as data-centric applications are now deployed as software as a service (SaaS) in the cloud. The problem with services in the cloud is that they are difficult to test because their backend components are distributed, thus, making it difficult to emulate the flow of the application, especially when the services are consumed by multiple users at the same time [16,31].

Conducting performance testing typically requires a lot of effort and expertise from testers. The performance of each application is unique and although the application could be the same, different versions and releases are still distinctive, so the set of performance tests needs to be updated accordingly [34]. This problem emphasizes the need for an expert on the application under test in order to get some insights regarding its weakness [38]. However, this situation could lead to dependencies and bottlenecks in the workflow of the testing team [2]. Moreover, due to the strict demands for shorter time-to-market products, testers are required to automate as much as possible their test plans so they can move at the same rate of emerging methodologies such as Agile, Continuous Integration, and Continuous Deployment. In addition, complete coverage of performance testing is not always achievable, as there are no automated oracles that can assure that a system is completely safe in terms of performance [40]. Load testing, an important part of performance testing, is the standard approach for assessing how an application behaves under different loads to find scenarios where it suffers performance issues (e.g., CPU bottlenecks, deadlocks) leading to high response time or low throughput [24] that affect the user experience.

One important problem in load testing is that most of the tools used to assess the performance of applications depend on static (i.e., pre-configured) workloads [32] such as Apache JMeter[1] and IBM RPT[2]. A major disadvantage of these tools is that, in order to define a correct load to stress the applications, they require human expertise and several runs of trial-and-error, hence, taking a lot of time. Additionally, manually designing, executing, and analyzing the values of a test workload can be very difficult due to the scale of the test, increasing the risk of overlooking problems or potential bugs [10].

An innovative approach in the literature is to adapt the workloads, in real time, based on the behavior of the application under test. These types of approaches aim to reduce the effort and expertise needed to carry out performance testing efficiently. A representative example of this type of approach is DYNAMO [3], which can automatically find an adequate workload for a web application without requiring multiple test runs while increasing the number of

---

[1] http://jmeter.apache.org/.
[2] https://www.ibm.com/us-en/marketplace/ibm-rational-performance-tester.

performance bugs found. This is achieved by dynamically defining the appropriate workloads on the fly based on the analysis of the intermediate testing results. However, despite its potential benefits, one disadvantage of DYNAMO is that users are required to define several parameters in order to configure it properly (otherwise, there is a risk that results may vary and have negative impacts in the testing process), a characteristic which might hinder its usability and effectiveness. Hence, there are improvements that can be done in terms of identifying the proper combination of the different variables involved in the configuration of DYNAMO, and of this type of approach in general.

To address the above issue, the contributions of this paper are the following:

1. A comprehensive evaluation of the DYNAMO approach, assessing a broad range of configuration alternatives to conduct performance testing efficiently using dynamic workload adaptation.
2. A set of rules of thumb, derived from our experiments using DYNAMO, that advise practitioners in the appropriate usage of these types of approaches.
3. An insightful analysis of how the different configuration variables can affect DYNAMO's behavior and its results.

The rest of this paper is structured as follows: Sect. 2 presents the background and related work. Section 3 explains the DYNAMO approach, while Sect. 4 describes the experimental evaluation and results obtained from the use of DYNAMO. Finally, Sect. 5 presents the conclusions and future work.

2   Background and Related Work

Performance testing is a type of testing whose objective is to ensure that an application-under-test (AUT) is capable of running its business operations under certain varieties of loads [21,29]. As shown in Fig. 1, a performance tester typically configures a Load tool (e.g., Apache JMeter) to run a test for a certain amount of time, usually several hours or even days in the case of industrial applications. In this context, a test workload is comprised of many concurrent virtual customers and a series of operations such as logins, searches, and click events to emulate the real use of the AUT. In order to identify performance issues, monitoring tools collect performance-related information, such as throughput and response time, during the execution of the test. Finally, the tester analyzes the outputs from the monitoring tool to identify trends in the collected data and determine possible bottlenecks or failures in the system.

Software testing automation has become crucial for organizations as oftentimes they require faster deployments and reduced time-to-market. Therefore, testing automation is incorporated as a crucial step in the software development life cycle to minimize the appearance of bugs in production code and reduce the testing efforts. Test suits are collections of test cases designed to evaluate the behavior of software applications. Nevertheless, testing is complex and expensive, then the approach presented in [20] explains how to focus the testing using a property-oriented technique to reduce the complexity of the test suits and yet

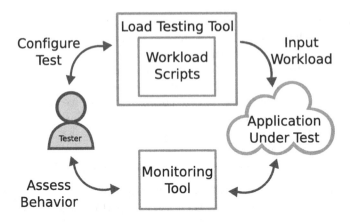

Fig. 1. Performance testing - Contextual view

obtain complete coverage. The authors of [8] propose an architecture to automate the performance testing of microservices by monitoring key indicators like
the throughput, response time, and availability, which are used to detect bottlenecks. A framework is proposed by [23] to combine the use of conformance
testing and load testing in order to save time and efforts during the validation
of web services. Traditionally these types of testing are run by different teams
verifying distinctive inputs and outputs. This work is an extension of [25] implementing timed automata and a test generation algorithm to discover bugs and
system degradations that appear during high loads of users because of the lack
of optimization in the code. Also, in [7], the authors define metrics to test web
applications focusing on the stability, quality, and the difficulties involved to
automate a test case. Other approaches use model-based testing to reduce the
test case derivation efforts [13,14,26]. In [14], the author examines techniques
for model-based testing of web applications and websites that apply statistical
usage models to generate and evaluate appropriate test suites. Similarly, the
works in [13,26] explore the automation of test case derivation to facilitate testing for automotive software.

Conducting performance testing of software systems is particularly challenging as it requires a significant amount of effort to carry out. For instance, identifying the limits of a system is not trivial. Testers require to have previous
experience and knowledge about the system to define the correct workloads [27].
Another problem is that there are no methods to assess the effectiveness of performance testing. So the authors of [35] propose the use of mutation testing
during performance testing to measure the efficiency of the test suits to discover errors. Mutation testing is a type of test that involves the introduction
of faults (mutants) into the code through some predefined rules to unveil errors
in the system. Effective performance testing techniques are required to cover
a system from high-priority bugs. In [37], the authors propose a model-based
approach to test web applications generating synthetic workloads based on the

data dependencies and transactions of the application under test. The authors in [4] explain that it is not feasible to test all the possible inputs in multi-core applications. Therefore, automation is applied to generate appropriate test cases using genetic algorithms. The work presented in [15] defines a declarative approach to incorporate performance testing into continuous software development. With such approach it is possible to model goal-oriented performance tests into the development life cycle.

More recent approaches incorporate new emerging technologies. Machine learning, for instance, uses black box testing, which identifies performance problems based on the feedback and outputs provided by the application. Other methods take into account the use of cloud resources [17] to calculate how many resources are needed to run an application without affecting the performance. In [18], the authors explore the detection of software defective modules using clustering-based under-sampling and artificial neural network. Metamorphic testing [36], on the other hand, aims to reduce the complexity of the testing configuration, the human-based expertise and the use of diagnostic tools to analyze variables like the optimization of Garbage Collection [29].

In general, the process of defining an appropriate test workload to detect performance issues in systems is a difficult problem. Workloads must be representative of the application under test and they must reflect the variability of human behavior [12]. Moreover, workloads are related to specific variables depending on the application under test and it is difficult for a human to identify patterns [5]. Despite there are tools to generate synthetic workloads for testing [9,39] these rely on static techniques for workload generation. This type of technique requires to invest more time and resources to identify an adequate workload for the system. With static workloads, a predetermined number of users are defined per run, whereas in an adaptive approach various diverse workloads will be generated in-test until a high workload (maximum number of users) is found such that the system can handle it without crashing. Other performance testing approaches are based on static code analysis. For instance, the authors of [34] determine the performance tests based on commits and the usage of unit-tests. Meanwhile, the work presented in [33] describes the performance analysis of software systems as a comparison of two versions of software and their performance results to find possible (regression) bugs. In response to these limitations, approaches that dynamically adapt the workload have been proposed [3,22]. This paper conducts an evaluation of DYNAMO because of its advantages of adjusting the workload on the fly using the analysis of key performance metrics to create a customized workload for the AUT with minimal knowledge or experience from the tester. Moreover, in relation to bug accuracy, previous work [3,22] has proved the benefits of using DYNAMO to find bugs in comparison with static approaches.

3   DYNAMO Overview

The goal of DYNAMO [3] is to help testers to define appropriate workloads without a trial-and-error process. To achieve this, DYNAMO relies on the use of adaptive workloads. Applying adaptive workloads can help to reduce the time invested to find a suitable workload, therefore saving money and resources. This is because an inappropriate low test workload can overlook performance issues in the application [21]. In contrast, using a "too" high load can saturate the system and prevent the detection of some issues due to critical failures that may arise on the system (as presented in Fig. 2 for illustrative purposes only, as the actual workload curves are application-specific).

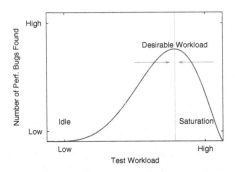

Fig. 2. Bugs vs Test workload example

DYNAMO works by constantly monitoring key performance indicators (during the test run execution) to automatically adjust the workload as required. To adjust the workload, a set of the functional transactions are incremented, based on a threshold evaluation that identifies those transactions to be increased, as well as by how much. The transactions that will be stressed are called workload sensitive (WKS). DYNAMO works in two phases: Phase 1 (Ph1), whose objective is to identify the workload sensitive transactions (WKS) involved in the test, and Phase 2 (Ph2), whose goal is to exercise the WKS as much as possible, while avoiding the saturation of the system (as shown in Fig. 3).

During Ph1, DYNAMO conducts two test runs (TR1, TR2) in order to identify the WKS transaction. In TR1, a known low workload is used, while a higher workload (w.r.t. TR1) is used in TR2. After TR1 and TR2 have finished, DYNAMO calculates the performance differences (deltas) per transaction between both runs in order to identify which transactions are the most workload-sensitive. For example, a basic welcome page could be a non-sensitive transaction because its content is static, while executing a login operation is typically more sensitive due to all the internal process triggered to verify a user (e.g., interfacing with a Single Sign-On service). Finally, the transactions are sorted in descending order of their deltas, and the leading ones are considered WKS.

In Ph2, DYNAMO keeps monitoring the performance of the WKS transactions (identified in Ph1) during the rest of the test run execution. Furthermore, their performance is iteratively evaluated, using an adjustment strategy, to identify those transactions that need a workload increment. DYNAMO currently supports 3 strategies to perform the workload adjustments: *Min*, which

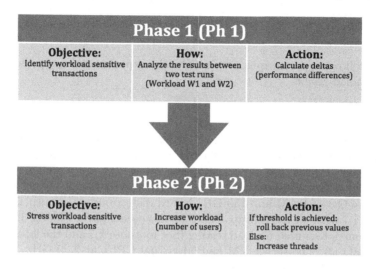

Fig. 3. DYNAMO's phases summary

increases the WKS transactions with the best performance; *Max*, which increases the WKS transactions with the worst performance; and *Random*, which selects a random set of WKS transactions to be adjusted.

In terms of configuration, DYNAMO requires several user inputs: (1) the test duration (e.g., 1 day). (2) the duration ratio between phases (i.e., 50/50%). (3) Two known seed workloads (WK1,WK2), one low (e.g., 1 user) and the other relatively higher than the first (e.g., 10 users). They are used by Ph1 to conduct the two calibration test runs (i.e., TR1, TR2). (4) A percentage of transactions of interest (%WKS), used by Ph1 to define how many (starting from the top) of the sorted transactions will be tagged as WKS. (5) A sample interval (SI), used by Ph2, to define how often the performance of the workloads will be evaluated (e.g., 5 min). (6) An error rate threshold (ERT), used by Ph2, to define what is considered saturation (e.g., 90%). (7) An adjustment strategy (ADS), used by Ph2, to identify the transactions whose workloads need to be increased. (8) A workload increment (WKINC) to define how big the increment will be (e.g., 20 users). (9) A percentage (%WKINC) to define how many WKS transactions will be increased, based on the chosen adjustment strategy (i.e., 30%).

4   Experimental Evaluation

Our experiments aimed to evaluate DYNAMO's accuracy, in terms of both WKS labeling and bug finding, with a special emphasis on any trade-offs existing between the accuracies w.r.t. DYNAMO's configuration. Specifically, the conducted experiments addressed the following research questions:

- **RQ**$_1$. *Which is the best ratio (between DYNAMO Ph1 and Ph2) w.r.t. WKS labeling accuracy?*

- **RQ$_2$**. *Which is the best ratio (between DYNAMO Ph1 and Ph2) w.r.t. bug finding accuracy?*

In the following paragraphs, we describe the experimental setup used as well as the obtained results.

4.1   Experimental Setup

The test environment consisted of two virtual machines (VMs) running in isolated conditions to avoid noise during the experiments. One VM worked as the client running JMeter and DYNAMO. The other VM ran a web server hosting the application-under-test (AUT). The client VM had 2 virtual CPUs at 2.20 GHz, 4 GB of RAM and 150 GB of hard disk, running Ubuntu 14.04 with OpenJDK 1.7 with a 1.6 GB heap. This VM also used Apache JMeter 3.2 (a leading open-source tool used for load testing (See footnote 1)) and the latest version of DYNAMO [3]. The server VM had 20 virtual CPUs at 2.20 GHz, 50 GB of RAM and 150 GB of hard disk, running Ubuntu 14.04 with IBM JVM 1.8 with a 25 GB heap and Apache Tomcat 7.0 as web server container. Additionally, IBM WAIT was used as diagnostic tool due to its robust capabilities to detect performance errors [29,41] such as memory leaks and resource bottlenecks.

Table 1. DaCapo programs

Name	Description
avrora	It simulates a program running on a grid
batik	It processes vector-based images
eclipse	It executes tests in an Eclipse development environment
fop	It generates PDF files
h2	It runs banking transactions in a database system
jython	It runs Python scripts
luindex	It indexes documents
lusearch	It runs keyword searches over a data corpus
pmd	It reviews a set of Java classes
sunflow	It renders images
tomcat	It runs queries in a Tomcat server
tradebeans	It runs stock transactions through Java Beans
tradesoap	It runs stock transactions through SOAP
xalan	It transforms XML files into HTML files

The AUTs used were DaCapo[3] and SPECJVM[4], which are two well-known Java benchmarks that are highly used in the literature. In order to utilize them

---

[3] http://dacapobench.org/.

[4] https://www.spec.org/jvm2008/.

as web applications, we used a servlet-based tool that enables their access and execution via web, so that each program (within the benchmark) can be used as a different functional transaction [28]. The Dacapo test plan consisted of its 14 benchmark programs (shown in Table 1) configured to run using their *small* size, 1 iteration, and 2 threads. Meanwhile, due to the complexity of SPECJVM, some benchmarks were executed by their specific sub-benchmarks (i.e., scimark: fft, lu, sor, sparse and monte_carlo) to create a test plan of 13 operations, as shown in Table 2. The configuration used to run the benchmarks was 0 s warm-up time, 10 s iteration, small data sets, and 2 threads.

Furthermore, to monitor the key performance indicators, we used JMeter for the throughput (tps), error rate (%) and, response time (ms) while nmon[5] collected CPU utilization (%) and memory consumption (MB). Additionally, WAIT was used to monitor the number (and criticalness) of the identified performance issues.

Table 2. SPECJVM programs

Name	Sub-benchmark	Description
compiler	.compiler	It compiles Java source files
compress	all	It runs a data compression alg
crypto	.rsa	It encrypts/decrypts files
MPEGaudio	all	It decodes audio files
scimark	fft, lu, sor, sparse and monte_carlo	It executes floating point ops
serial	all	It serialises/deserialises objects and primitives
startup	.helloworld	It runs a hello word program
sunflow	all	It runs visualization operations
XML	.transform	It transforms XML documents

The response time during Ph1 determines which transactions are WKS. In Ph2, the error rate evaluates if the overall workload has reached the threshold and decides whether to increase the load applying one of the three available strategies or to rollback to a previous value and try a different combination to increase the workload. CPU utilization and Memory consumption were monitored to validate the minimal overhead introduced by the use of DYNAMO in the client machine.

DYNAMO has several configuration options to generate adaptive workloads. Therefore, choosing a different combination of parameters can lead to distinct results. The values used in the experiments were defined to cover as many scenarios as possible. The configurations we used for DYNAMO are shown in Table 3.

---

[5] http://nmon.sourceforge.net/.

It is worth mentioning that the test durations and the workload values were defined, per AUT, based on the maximum capacity supported by our test environment.

4.2 Results

To answer RQ_1, our analysis initially focused on assessing how well Ph1 could identify WKS transactions. To accomplish this, we firstly executed DYNAMO using all the in-scope Ph1/Ph2 ratios. Then, the obtained results were compared against a baseline, which was used to calculate the accuracy of Ph1 for labeling WKS transactions. The baseline was created following the traditional performance testing approach, typically utilized in the industry, of using static (i.e., pre-configured) test workloads [19]. Thus, the baseline was calculated with the average results of 10 test runs carried out (per AUT) using a range of static workloads (their consolidated response time information is shown in Table 4).

Table 3. Experimental configuration parameters for DYNAMO

Phase	Parameter	Value
Initial Settings	(1) Test duration	100 min for SPECJVM and 200 min for DaCapo
	(2) Ph1 and Ph2 ratios	10/90, 20/80, 40/60, 60/40, and 80/20
Phase 1 Settings	(3) Calibration workloads [WK1, WK2]	[1,10] for SPECJVM and [2,20] for DaCapo
	(4) Number of transactions considered as WKS (%WKS)	30% and 50%
Phase 2 Settings	(5) Sample interval (SI)	5 min
	(6) Error rate threshold (ERT)	90%
	(7) Adjustment strategy (ADS)	*Min*
	(8) Workload increment (WKINC)	5 users
	(9) WKS transactions to be increased (%WKINC)	50%

To maximize the representativeness of the baseline (i.e., covering the full spectrum of potential test workloads, starting with a close-to-idle scenario and ending with a saturated environment), both AUTs were initially tested with a very low workload (i.e., 1 and 2 concurrent users for SPECJVM and DaCapo, respectively). Then, the workload was gradually increased, per test run, by 100% (w.r.t. the initial workloads used), until reaching a high enough workload that provoked saturation in the system (i.e., 10 and 20 concurrent users for SPECJVM and DaCapo, respectively).

Table 4. Baselines sorted by response time

Trans. ID	**DaCapo** Average response time (ms)	Trans. ID	**SPECJVM** Average response time (ms)
10	34,076.66	01	15,514.34
09	37,903.85	07	26,085.40
08	42,888.26	06	26,319.86
14	43,272.39	08	27,039.00
04	51,381.02	04	29,763.84
07	62,803.12	02	31,332.79
01	63,576.74	03	32,090.00
13	69,162.31	10	33,366.21
02	70,003.78	09	34,099.33
12	73,513.73	05	45,603.02
11	82,565.42	12	48,367.00
05	107,204.49	11	71,762.47
06	118,468.68	13	354,635.71
03	208,623.71	-	-

Furthermore, we calculate of the accuracy of Ph1 to correctly label WKS transactions. It was based on a set B of baseline transactions and a set S of labeled transactions (which is the main output of Ph1) in order to determine how many of the S transactions belong to the B set. Let B be a finite set of (baseline) transactions $B = \{b_1, b_2, \ldots, b_n\}$ and $n(B)$ its cardinality. Let S be the set of sample transactions $S = \{s_1, s_2, \cdots, s_n\}$ sorted in descending order according to their response time. Now, a function $f(s_i)$ is defined to indicate whether a given sample transaction s_i will be taken into account when calculating the percentage of accuracy (as depicted in Eq. 1).

$$f(s_i) = \begin{cases} 0, & \text{if } s_i \notin B \\ 1, & \text{if } s_i \in B \end{cases} \tag{1}$$

Then, the percentage of accuracy can be computed as the sum of the values for all $s_i \in S$ from the previously defined function, all divided by the cardinality of B. This is depicted in Eq. 2.

$$\text{percentage of accuracy} = \frac{\sum\limits_{s_i \in S} f(s_i)}{n(B)} \tag{2}$$

Figure 4 depicts the results obtained using DaCapo with a %WKS of 30%. It can be seen that there is a tendency to achieve a higher accuracy when using a higher duration ratio. However, by using a Pareto ratio of 20/80, it is still possible to achieve an accuracy above 75%, which is very close to the accuracies obtained when using higher ratios (e.g., 60/40 or above). This demonstrates that it is feasible to use a lower Ph1/Ph2 duration ratio without compromising the accuracy of the WKS labeling. A slightly lower ratio appears when using 40% of ratio during Ph1, but this value is explained due to the closer delta values of the transactions in the 30% range. An additional advantage of using a ratio of 20% (in Ph1) is that it leaves more time for Ph2, hence increasing the possibility to find more performance bugs.

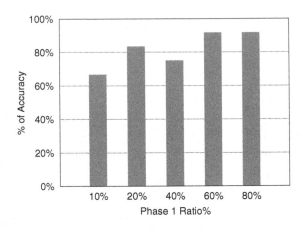

Fig. 4. Accuracy of Ph1 for DaCapo using a %WKS of 30%

We observed a similar trend with the SPECJVM results, where duration ratios from 20/80 onwards had a good accuracy (above 75%). This supports our finding that the Pareto ratio can achieve a high level of accuracy. Only when using a ratio of 10% in Ph1, the accuracy drops. This is the result of having only a short amount of time in Ph1, which makes impossible to label with high accuracy the WKS transactions. Finally, it is important to highlight that, in the cases where the accuracy did not reach 100%, the missed transactions were the ones closest to the WKS transactions (according to the baseline table). These results also reinforced the finding that DYNAMO's accuracy tends to be high and that the Pareto ratio can achieve a high accuracy without spending "too much" time in Ph1 (as it would not bring any real benefit).

To answer RQ$_2$, the focus of our analysis shifted to assess how well Ph2 could identify performance issues. With that aim in mind, we fed WAIT (i.e., our chosen diagnosis tool) with snapshots of the JVM state (i.e., Javacores [6]) sampled during the execution of the test runs. These samples were taken in intervals of 30 s, following common industrial standards [1]. WAIT provided a report with all the identified bugs sorted by their frequency of occurrence, information that was used to classify the bugs as low or high relevant. A bug was considered as high relevant if it occurred above 5% (of the test run duration). Alternatively, it was considered as low relevant. Regarding bug finding, DYNAMO's

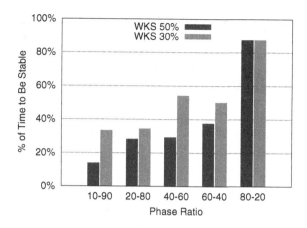

Fig. 5. Percentage of time in Ph2 to find a stable load

Ph2 enhances this process by finding a load big enough to stress, as much as possible, the AUT without reaching a point of saturation (called stable load). To define the appropriate load, DYNAMO takes samples of the response times, calculates the average of the error rates, and makes load adjustments on the fly. Figure 5 depicts the time taken to achieve a stable load per phase ratio. There, it can be noticed how an earlier stable load was found when using a ratio of 10/90. Yet, the second best result came from the load with a Pareto ratio of 20/80, where the stable load was found when the lapsed time was at 34% (for WKS of 50%) and 28.13% (for WKS of 30%) of the total time of the workload. This is in comparison with spending 87% of the time for the 80/20 ratio.

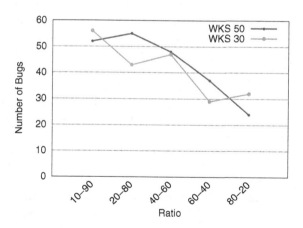

Fig. 6. DaCapo bugs per %WKS ratios

When analyzing the number of performance bugs found during Ph2 across the different duration ratios, we observed that the number of bugs decreased when the time spent in Ph2 was lower (as depicted in Fig. 6). Additionally, if the ratio in Ph2 is lower, the time required to find a stable load is longer (as shown in Fig. 5). Consequently, there is less time to find bugs. In terms of load, when a %WKS of 50% was used, a stable load was found earlier and also the number of adjustments was higher. This explains why this value of %WKS found more performance bugs during Ph2 (as shown in Fig. 6) due to the use of higher loads of users as depicted in Fig. 7.

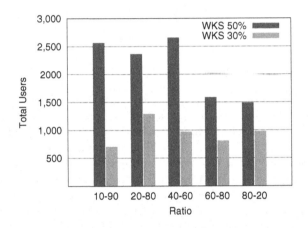

Fig. 7. Number of users during Ph2

With these results, it is possible to assert that using a higher load is better to find bugs than using a lower load for a long time. This observation denotes the importance of finding a high enough load to stress a system, but without reaching a saturation point (as that would negatively affect the bug-finding process). Also, it is crucial to consider the distribution of the WKS transactions during Ph2, as a higher %WKS ratio (e.g., 50%) will work better. This is because there will be a broader range of eligible transactions to increase the load, rather than overstressing the server with a load composed of a limited number of transactions. In summary, during Ph2 a higher %WKS is recommended to find a better workload to stress the system and find more bugs.

It is also worth mentioning that the workload adjustments during Ph2 are important because they are part of the core logic of DYNAMO. This illustrated in Fig. 8, where one can see the adjustments made according to the error rate, as well as the process of rollback. During the initial adjustments, the error passed the threshold, then other adjustments were made following the operations shown in Table 5 to define the final workload.

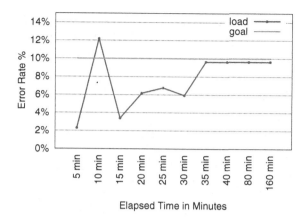

Fig. 8. Workload adjustment for ratio 20/80

Table 5. Adjustments

Operation	Transactions
Increase	[T11, T3]
Rollback	[T11, T3]
Increase	[T5, T6]
Increase	[T5, T6]
Increase	[T5, T6]
Increase	[T5, T6]
Rollback	[T5, T6]

Furthermore, the bugs considered as highly relevant (due to its frequency of occurrence) were stable in all the phase ratios while using both 50% and 30% as %WKS, as depicted in Fig. 9. However, bugs with low relevance changed depending on the ratio. This is because if less time is spent in Ph2, there is not enough time to get data samples to analyze the relevance of these bugs. With these results, the tradeoffs of changing the ratios were reflected in the finding of low relevant bugs, while the high relevant bugs kept the same regardless of the ratio. Also, the Pareto ratio generated results that were not far from the ratios that spent more time in Ph2 (e.g., 90/10). What is more important, the Pareto ratio did not compromise the accuracy in WKS labeling during Ph1.

In relation to bug accuracy, previous work [3,22] has proved that DYNAMO is better for finding bugs than traditional testing approaches. Therefore, our analysis concentrated on comparing the results from the different ratios (w.r.t. Ph2). We conclude that Ph2 was affected by two main variables: The Ph2 ratio and %WKS. As shown in Fig. 8, the Pareto ratio obtained good results (compared to the other ratios), also the %WKS of 50% found more bugs. This was also confirmed by Fig. 7, which showed that the %WKS of 50% had a big load, increasing the chances to find bugs. Lastly, lower ratios in Ph2 found a large number of bugs; yet, most of them were categorized with low relevance and were associated with a drop in accuracy caused by having less time during Ph2.

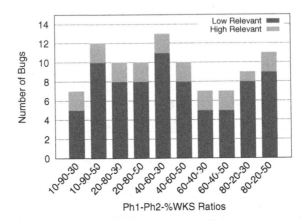

Fig. 9. DaCapo bug classification distribution

5 Conclusions and Future Work

Identifying the appropriate load to stress a system to expose performance issues is challenging. This task requires a lot of effort and experienced testers trying different static workloads. Dynamic workload adaptation approaches make possible to find an appropriate workload automatically. However, they require several configuration parameters. In this paper, we have comprehensively explored such parameters using a representative example of this type of approaches called DYNAMO, which works in 2 phases. After our evaluation, we were able to prove the accuracy of DYNAMO's Phase1 (Ph1) w.r.t. WKS labeling, where all the ratios showed an accuracy above 75% except the lowest one (i.e., 10–90). This was the consequence of the low time spent in Ph1. In DYNAMO's Phase2 (Ph2), we found that using a higher ratio of WKS transactions led to more transactions to be adjusted and thereby a generated workload closer to the saturation point. Moreover, it was possible to perceive that higher ratios during Ph2 provided more time for workload adjustment, which left more time to run the "ideal" workload. In addition, we showed that the Pareto ratio offered good results between different ratios without compromising bug finding (in Ph2) and WKS accuracy (in Ph1). Finally, we found that the bug finding accuracy during Ph2 was better when higher ratios were used, as this led to more adjustments and testing time used to discover more bugs. These results offer practitioners a valuable reference regarding the use of DYNAMO and the benefits of implementing a dynamic workload adaptation strategy for performance testing.

In future work, we plan to explore other approaches of dynamic workload adaptation to perform a comparative study and derive more guidelines for practitioners. Moreover, we intend to incorporate machine learning techniques to study the behavior of the approaches and then be able to make automatic recommendations of the configuration parameters based on the characteristics learned from the applications under test. Additionally, incorporate information about the structure and behavior of the web application to focus the testing on sensitive code that could trigger performance bugs. Finally, we plan to incorporate the approaches in easy-to-use JMeter plugins with a friendly graphical interface so it can be more easily adopted by performance engineering practitioners as many of the approaches are built as basic research prototypes running in the command line.

Acknowledgments. This work was supported, in part, by Science Foundation Ireland grant 13/RC/2094 and co-funded under the European Regional Development Fund through the Southern & Eastern Regional Operational Programme to Lero - the Irish Software Research Centre (www.lero.ie).

References

1. Altman, E., Arnold, M., Fink, S., Mitchell, N.: Performance analysis of idle programs. ACM SIGPLAN Not. **45**(10), 739–753 (2010)
2. Angelopoulos, V., Parsons, T., Murphy, J., O'Sullivan, P.: GcLite: an expert tool for analyzing garbage collection behavior. In: 2012 IEEE 36th Annual Computer Software and Applications Conference Workshops, pp. 493–502. IEEE (2012)
3. Ayala-Rivera, V., Kaczmarski, M., Murphy, J., Darisa, A., Portillo-Dominguez, A.O.: One size does not fit all. In: ICPE 2018, pp. 211–222. ACM Press, New York (2018)
4. Aziz, M.W., Shah, S.A.B.: Test-data generation for testing parallel real-time systems. In: El-Fakih, K., Barlas, G., Yevtushenko, N. (eds.) ICTSS 2015. LNCS, vol. 9447, pp. 211–223. Springer, Cham (2015). https://doi.org/10.1007/978-3-319-25945-1_13
5. Basak, J., Wadhwani, K., Voruganti, K.: Storage workload identification. ACM Trans. Storage **12**(3), 1–30 (2016)
6. Bourne, D.A., Chung, A.A., Price, D.L.: Capturing trace information using annotated trace output, 31 May 2016, US Patent 9,355,002
7. Bures, M., Miroslav: Metrics for automated testability of web applications. In: CompSysTech 2015, pp. 83–89. ACM Press, New York (2015)
8. de Camargo, A., Salvadori, I., Mello, R.d.S., Siqueira, F.: An architecture to automate performance tests on microservices. In: iiWAS 2016, pp. 422–429. ACM Press, New York (2016)
9. Carothers, C.D., et al.: Durango: scalable synthetic workload generation for extreme-scale application performance modeling and simulation. In: SIGSIM-PADS 2017, pp. 97–108. ACM Press, New York (2017)
10. Chen, T.H., et al.: Analytics-driven load testing: an industrial experience report on load testing of large-scale systems. In: ICSE-SEIP. IEEE (2017)
11. Conley, M., Vahdat, A., Porter, G.: Achieving cost-efficient, data-intensive computing in the cloud. In: SoCC 2015, pp. 302–314. ACM (2015)

12. Curiel, M., Pont, A.: Workload generators for web-based systems: characteristics, current status, and challenges. IEEE Commun. Surv. Tutor. **20**(2), 1526–1546 (2018)
13. Drave, I., et al.: Smardt modeling for automotive software testing. Softw.: Pract. Exp. **49**(2), 301–328 (2019)
14. Dulz, W.: A versatile tool environment to perform model-based testing of web applications and multilingual websites. In: ICSOFT, pp. 45–56. SciTePress (2018)
15. Ferme, V., Pautasso, C.: A declarative approach for performance tests execution in continuous software development environments. In: ICPE 2018, pp. 261–272. ACM Press, New York (2018)
16. Furda, A., Fidge, C., Barros, A., Zimmermann, O.: Reengineering data-centric information systems for the cloud-a method and architectural patterns promoting multitenancy. In: Software Architecture for Big Data and the Cloud. Elsevier (2017)
17. Grechanik, M., Luo, Q., Poshyvanyk, D., Porter, A.: Enhancing rules for cloud resource provisioning via learned software performance models. In: ICPE 2016. ACM Press, New York (2016)
18. Henein, M.M.R., Shawky, D.M., Abd-El-Hafiz, S.K.: Clustering-based Undersampling for software defect prediction. In: ICSOFT. SciTePress (2018)
19. Hooda, I., Chhillar, R.S.: Software test process, testing types and techniques. Int. J. Comput. Appl. **111**(13) (2015)
20. Huang, W., Peleska, J.: Safety-complete test suites. In: Yevtushenko, N., Cavalli, A.R., Yenigün, H. (eds.) ICTSS 2017. LNCS, vol. 10533, pp. 145–161. Springer, Cham (2017). https://doi.org/10.1007/978-3-319-67549-7_9
21. Jiang, Z.M., Ming, Z.: Automated analysis of load testing results. In: ISSTA 2010. p. 143. ACM Press, New York (2010)
22. Kaczmarski, M., Perry, P., Murphy, J., Portillo-Dominguez, A.O.: In-test adaptation of workload in enterprise application performance testing. In: ICPE 2017 (2017)
23. Krichen, M., Maâlej, A.J., Lahami, M.: A model-based approach to combine conformance and load tests: an ehealth case study. Int. J. Crit. Comput.-Based Syst. **8**(3–4), 282–310 (2018)
24. Luo, Q., Poshyvanyk, D., Nair, A., Grechanik, M.: FOREPOST: a tool for detecting performance problems with feedback-driven learning software testing. In: 38th ICSE-C, pp. 593–596. ACM (2016)
25. Maâlej, A.J., Krichen, M.: A model based approach to combine load and functional tests for service oriented architectures. In: VECoS, pp. 123–140 (2016)
26. Markthaler, M., et al.: Improving model-based testing in automotive software engineering. In: ICSE-SEIP, pp. 172–180. SciTePress (2018)
27. Meier, J.D., Farre, C., Bansode, P., Barber, S., Rea, D.: Performance testing guidance for web applications: patterns & Practices. Microsoft (2007)
28. Portillo-Dominguez, A.O., Ayala-Rivera, V.: Improving the testing of clustered systems through the effective usage of java benchmarks. In: CONISOFT (2017)
29. Portillo-Dominguez, A.O., Perry, P., Magoni, D., Murphy, J.: PHOEBE: an automation framework for the effective usage of diagnosis tools in the performance testing of clustered systems. Softw.: Pract. Exp. **47**, 1837–1874 (2017)
30. Portillo-Dominguez, A.O., Wang, M., Murphy, J., Magoni, D.: Automated WAIT for cloud-based application testing. ICSTW (2014)
31. Portillo-Domínguez, A.O., Murphy, J., O'Sullivan, P.: Leverage of extended information to enhance the performance of JEE systems. In: IT&T 2012 (2012)

32. Ramakrishnan, R., Shrawan, V., Singh, P.: Setting realistic think times in performance testing: a practitioner's approach. In: ISEC 2017, pp. 157–164. ACM (2017)
33. Reichelt, D.G., Kühne, S.: Better early than never. In: ICPE 2018. ACM Press, New York (2018)
34. Reichelt, D.G., Kühne, S.: How to detect performance changes in software history. In: ICPE 2018. ACM Press, New York (2018)
35. Sánchez, A.B., Delgado-Pérez, P., Segura, S., Medina-Bulo, I.: Performance mutation testing: hypothesis and open questions. Inf. Softw. Technol. **103**, 159–161 (2018)
36. Segura, S., Troya, J., Duran, A., Ruiz-Cortes, A.: Performance metamorphic testing: motivation and challenges. In: ICSE-NIER (2017)
37. Shams, M., Krishnamurthy, D., Far, B.: A model-based approach for testing the performance of web applications. In: SOQUA 2006, p. 54. ACM Press, New York (2006)
38. Spear, W., et al.: Making performance analysis and tuning part of the software development cycle. In: DoD High Performance Computing Modernization Program Users Group Conference (2009)
39. Tang, W., Fu, Y., Cherkasova, L., Vahdat, A.: Medisyn: a synthetic streaming media service workload generator. In: NOSSDAV 2003. p. 12. ACM Press, New York (2003)
40. Troya, J., Segura, S., Ruiz-Cortés, A.: Automated inference of likely metamorphic relations for model transformations. J. Syst. Softw. **136**, 188–208 (2018)
41. Wu, H., Tantawi, A.N., Yu, T.: A self-optimizing workload management solution for cloud applications. In: ICWS 2013, pp. 483–490. IEEE (2013)

DYNAMOJM: A JMeter Tool for Performance Testing Using Dynamic Workload Adaptation

Osvaldo Huerta-Guevara$^{(\boxtimes)}$, Vanessa Ayala-Rivera, Liam Murphy,
and A. Omar Portillo-Dominguez

Lero@UCD, School of Computer Science, University College Dublin, Dublin, Ireland
osvaldo.huertaguevara@ucdconnect.ie,
{vanessa.ayalarivera,liam.murphy,andres.portillodominguez}@ucd.ie

Abstract. Performance testing is a critical task to assure optimal experience for users, especially when there are high loads of concurrent users. JMeter is one of the most widely used tools for load and stress testing. With JMeter, it is possible to test the performance of static and dynamic resources on the web. This paper presents DYNAMOJM, a novel tool built on top of JMeter that enables testers to create a dynamic workload for performance testing. This tool implements the DYNAMO approach, which has proven useful to find performance issues more efficiently than static testing techniques.

Keywords: Software engineering · Performance testing ·
Performance bug · Workload · Web systems and applications

1 Introduction

The importance of providing stable and reliable sites for users has increased with the consumption of services throughout the internet. The performance of a service is still a major concern due to its crucial impact on applications [14]. Performance failures are not acceptable with the rising competition in the market [8]. The goal of performance testing is to assess how well a service can work under certain workloads [10]. Nevertheless, performance testing is challenging due to the multiple variables involved in enterprise-level services [16]. Nowadays, software performance continues to be tested using tools based on static workloads such as JMeter [1], HP LoadRunner [3] and RTP from IBM [4]. An inconvenience with this approach is that the tester requires to have prior knowledge of the applications to define an appropriate test workload. If this does not occur, there is a risk that the application under test (AUT) does not exhibit some performance issues and bugs are not found. DYNAMO [7] is an approach that can automatically find an adequate workload for testing without a try and

© IFIP International Federation for Information Processing 2019
Published by Springer Nature Switzerland AG 2019
C. Gaston et al. (Eds.): ICTSS 2019, LNCS 11812, pp. 234–241, 2019.
https://doi.org/10.1007/978-3-030-31280-0_14

Table 1. Configuration parameters

Phase	Parameter	Example
Initial settings	Test duration	200 min
	Phase 1 and Phase 2 ratio	40/60%
Phase 1 settings	Calibration workloads (WK1, WK2)	[2,20]
	Number of transactions considered as WKS (%WKS)	30%
Phase 2 settings	Sample interval (SI)	5 min
	Error rate threshold (ERT)	90%
	Adjustment strategy (ADS)	Min
	Workload increment (WKINC)	5 users
	WKS transactions to be increased (%WKINC)	50%

error process, hence, saving time without compromising bug detection. To generate the workload, DYNAMO relies on the analysis of performance samples to dynamically adjust the workload to the maximum allowed without reaching a saturation point in the system. However, DYNAMO is currently built as a basic research prototype that was developed to demonstrate a new testing approach. Therefore, it does not provide a graphical interface to facilitate its usage and configuration. Moreover, it has a lot of parameters that need manual configuration using the command line which hinders its usability. To tackle this, in this paper we present DYNAMOJM, a tool built on top of JMeter that incorporates all DYNAMO logic into a more usable plugin for practitioners.

The DYNAMO approach involves two main phases [11]. The objective of Phase 1 (Ph1) is to identify the workload sensitive transactions(WKS) involved in the test, that is, those transactions that are more susceptible to suffer performance degradation. Whereas Phase 2's (Ph2) goal is to exercise the WKS as much as possible while avoiding the saturation of the system. DYNAMO's configuration requirements and some example values are illustrated in Table 1.

The calibration workloads in Ph1 are used to calculate performance differences (deltas) between the runs. The adjustment strategies are used to identify the transactions that will be increased. DYNAMO supports 3 strategies: *Min*, which increases the best performance WKS transactions; *Max*, which increases the worst performance WKS transactions; and *Random*, which randomly selects a set of WKS transactions to be adjusted.

2   Background and Related Work

In spite of the increasing access to more and better computational resources (e.g., CPU, RAM), system performance remains a major concern due to its crucial impact on applications. Currently, software performance is typically tested using tools based on static workloads (e.g., Apache JMeter [1] and IBM RPT [4]).

This is usually complemented with a diagnosis tool (e.g., WAIT [5] and New Relic [6]) to monitor and analyze in real-time the performance of applications.

Some approaches to enhance performance testing include the use of static code analysis to discover performance errors. The authors of [18] determine a test plan based on code commits and the use of artificial unit tests to compare the performance between different versions. Meanwhile, the work presented on [17] describes the performance analysis of software systems as a comparison of two versions of software and their performance results to find possible (regression) bugs. Due to the complexity of running performance testing, another used technique is to analyze key performance indicators on the fly. The work of [13] proposes the use of a Timed Automata to monitor and analyze the request invocations and responses between the components of web services. This tool gathers all the information and creates a log with it. After that, the data is examined to create a report that includes the possible performance faults of the services.

The work of [12] incorporates the use of machine learning to analyze the outputs and feedback of the AUT to find bottlenecks in the system. Other methods examine the elasticity of cloud applications [9] to determine how many resources are needed to run the service without affecting the performance. Finally, other authors propose the use of metamorphic testing and mutation testing to improve the results of performance testing. The work of [20] involves the use of metamorphic testing to reduce the complexity of the system configuration by creating test cases based on the inputs and outputs of the program. Another important variable is the optimization of garbage collection [15]. On the other hand, mutation testing is used to improve the effectiveness of performance testing plans. The work presented in [19] describes how using mutation testing in combination with performance testing can lead to a fault detection enhancement.

3   DYNAMOJM's Implementation and Example

The architecture of DYNAMOJM consists of 4 main components: *Controller*, *DecisionMaker*, and the implementation of two interfaces: *WorkloadTool* and *LogAnalizer* (as shown in Fig. 1). The Controller is the main component in charge of managing the required inputs and control the flow of the plugin calling the logic for the different phases. The DecisionMaker contains DYNAMO's logic and functions to analyze the information provided by the implementation of the LogAnalyzer and functions to adjust the workload using the implementation of the WorkloadTool. The interfaces were designed to facilitate the implementation of DYNAMO using other workload tools, as depicted in Fig. 1.

To evaluate the performance of a web application, performance testers (hereinafter users) need to define an estimated workload to be tested in the AUT. The problem with this approach is that users need to have some experience or previous knowledge in the AUT to calculate an adequate workload. The other option is to estimate an ideal workload based on a try and error approach with the risk of expending more time and to overlook problems. With DYNAMOJM, the users prepare their test plan as normal using JMeter and now they have available a

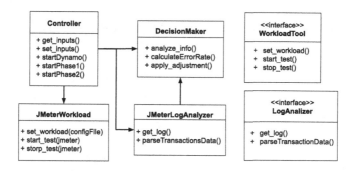

Fig. 1. DYNAMOJM interfaces

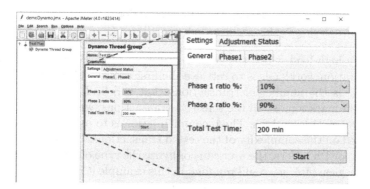

Fig. 2. General configuration

configuration panel to help them to identify the best workload with minimum knowledge of the AUT. For our evaluation study, we tested DYNAMOJM using an experimental web app built around DaCapo [2] which is a well-known Java benchmark used in the literature. DaCapo is wrapped with java servlets to emulate the transactions of a web application. DaCapo consists of 13 benchmarks who are called individually as web transactions.

The main panel of DYNAMOJM is comprised of two tabs: *Settings* and *Adjustment Status* (as shown in Fig. 2). In *Settings*, there are three tabs for the setup of DYNAMOJM (*General, Phase1*, and *Phase2*). Users start by accessing the *General* tab and entering the values of the test run (we have used some example values to illustrate our approach): 10% for the Ph1 and 90% for Ph2, considering that Ph1 plus Ph2 should be equal to 100%, we also configure the total test time. As a guideline for practitioners, to configure *General* Settings on DYNAMOJM, we recommend using values between 10% and 40% for Ph1 ratio because reducing the time of Ph2 will lead to the detection of fewer bugs. For the Total Test Time, it depends on the AUT and its requirements. In Fig. 3, the settings of Ph1 are defined: workload 1 of 500, workload 2 of 4000, and using 30% as WKS. Workload 1 indicates the initial load for the AUT; while Workload 2 is

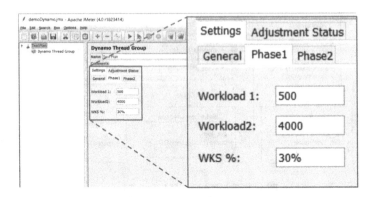

Fig. 3. Phase1 configuration

considered a high load which the AUT is still able to handle properly. The aim of the calibration workloads is to retrieve the first samples of the AUT behavior. The WKS% is the number of transactions that will be labeled as WKS, so a higher % will mark almost all the sensitive transactions, while a lower value will mark only a few transactions. The recommendation is to use a value close to the 50% or based on the complexity of the tested transactions. In Fig. 4, we configure the settings for Ph2. Here, the user can configure the type of adjustment choosing from 3 strategies: *min, max* and *random*; in this example it is set to *min* although *max* is another viable option while *random* is not recommended as this strategy was used for research purposes. The number of users that the transactions will be increased by is set to 200. This increment is based on the values of the tests runs of Ph1, because Ph2 will start adjusting the transactions using the second value of the Ph1 as a starting point. The WKS to modify is set to 50% because modifying a high number of transactions at the same time could rapidly saturate the system, this value also depends on the capacity of the system. Finally, the saturation point is set as 90%. The Saturation point is the threshold defined to make the adjustments while the sample interval configured to 5 min, is the time to collect metrics for the analysis and adjustments during Ph2.

Once the configuration is completed, the user can move to the *General* tab and start the test run. When the run is started, the user can monitor the adjustments of the workload through the *Adjustment Status* tab. For example, Fig. 5 demonstrates how the workload is adjusted during the test run until reaching the maximum load under the defined parameters. Moreover, when using the *Details* button at the bottom of the window, the user can visualize which transactions are affected during each adjustment.

An example of the type of results that can be achieved with DYNAMOJM are depicted in Figs. 5 and 6: Fig. 5 shows the behavior of the saturation point (i.e., the error rate threshold -goal- which is represented by a red line) exhibited by an AUT during a 60-min test run. It can be noticed how the gradual increases in test workload have an impact in the overall error rate (represented by the blue line). In the early stages of the test, the error rate is very close to 0% because

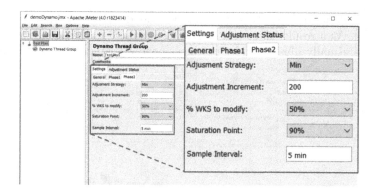

Fig. 4. Phase 2 configuration

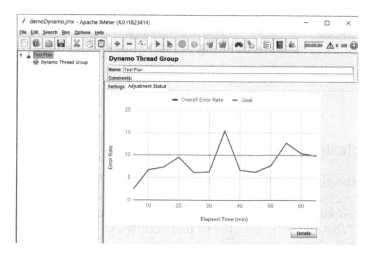

Fig. 5. Workload adjustment

the test workload is low. Nevertheless, during the test run the error rate might become relevant (as a consequence of the increments in workload) and eventually exceed the configured threshold (peaks exhibited in the figure around minutes 30–40 and 50–60 of the test duration). If this occurs, the workload gets automatically decreased in order to keep the error rate under control. Figure 6 shows the *Details* page that presents the actual workload adjustments made during the test (per functional transaction tested). This is visually depicted by the segments of some transactions (within the stacked bar chart that represent 5-minute sections of the test run) which gradually become considerable wider that others which remain very narrow. This is the result of DYNAMO gradually increasing the test workload of the most sensitive transactions (i.e., the wider segments) by following the selected adjustment strategy (e.g., *min* in our example) until the appropriate combination of workloads (i.e., the one closest to the saturation point) is found. On the contrary, the least workload-sensitive transactions never get stressed. As a result, their test workload remains low during the whole test run. This is visually illustrated by the most narrow segments in the figure.

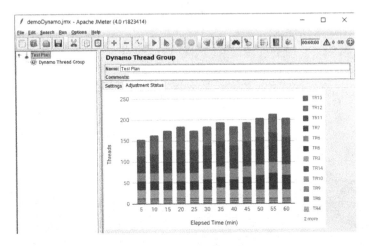

Fig. 6. Transaction details

4   Conclusions

Designing the appropriate workload for performance is challenging because it requires experienced testers to define a workload, as well as a series of trial-and-error test runs, to find the appropriate load to stress a particular system. By using DYNAMO, it is possible to find such workload automatically. However, DYNAMO itself requires several configuration parameters which have been implemented in this tool. The accuracy of DYNAMO to find bugs or potential issues has been proved using a proof of concept demo [7]. However, with the DYNAMOJM plugin presented in this paper, it is possible to use the same logic and automation with a friendly graphical interface easy to adopt by performance engineering practitioners.

Acknowledgments. This work was supported, in part, by Science Foundation Ireland grant 13/RC/2094 and co-funded under the European Regional Development Fund through the Southern & Eastern Regional Operational Programme to Lero - the Irish Software Research Centre (www.lero.ie).

References

1. Apache JMeter. http://jmeter.apache.org/
2. Dacapo benchmark suite. http://dacapobench.org/
3. HP Loadrunner. https://ssl.www8.hp.com/sg/en/ad/load-runner/load-runner.html

4. Ibm rational performance tester. https://www.ibm.com/us-en/marketplace/ibm-rational-performance-tester

5. IBM WAIT Tool. https://publib.boulder.ibm.com/httpserv/cookbook/Major_Tools-IBM_WholeSystem_Analysis_Tool_WAIT.html

6. New relic. https://newrelic.com

7. Ayala-Rivera, V., Kaczmarski, M., Murphy, J., Darisa, A., Portillo-Dominguez, A.O.: One size does not fit all. In: Proceedings of the 2018 ACM/SPEC International Conference on Performance Engineering - ICPE 2018, pp. 211–222. ACM Press, New York (2018)

8. Conley, M., Vahdat, A., Porter, G.: Achieving cost-efficient, data-intensive computing in the cloud. In: SoCC 2015, pp. 302–314. ACM (2015)

9. Grechanik, M., Luo, Q., Poshyvanyk, D., Porter, A.: Enhancing rules for cloud resource provisioning via learned software performance models. In: Proceedings of the 7th ACM/SPEC on International Conference on Performance Engineering - ICPE 2016, pp. 209–214. ACM Press, New York (2016)

10. Jiang, Z.M., Ming, Z.: Automated analysis of load testing results. In: Proceedings of the 19th International Symposium on Software Testing and Analysis - ISSTA 2010, p. 143. ACM Press, New York (2010)

11. Kaczmarski, M., Perry, P., Murphy, J., Portillo-Dominguez, A.O.: In-test adaptation of workload in enterprise application performance testing. In: 8th ACM/SPEC on ICPE 2017 Companion, pp. 69–72. ACM Press (2017)

12. Luo, Q., Poshyvanyk, D., Nair, A., Grechanik, M.: Forepost: a tool for detecting performance problems with feedback-driven learning software testing. In: Proceedings of the 38th International Conference on Software Engineering Companion, pp. 593–596. ACM (2016)

13. Maâlej, A.J., Hamza, M., Krichen, M.: WSCLT: a tool for WS-BPEL compositions load testing. In: 2013 Workshops on Enabling Technologies: Infrastructure for Collaborative Enterprises, pp. 272–277. IEEE (2013)

14. Portillo-Dominguez, A.O., Perry, P., Magoni, D., Murphy, J.: PHOEBE: an automation framework for the effective usage of diagnosis tools in the performance testing of clustered systems. Softw. Pract. Exp. **47**(11), 1837–1874 (2017)

15. Portillo-Dominguez, A.O., Wang, M., Murphy, J., Magoni, D.: Automated WAIT for cloud-based application testing. In: ICSTW (2014)

16. Portillo-Domínguez, A.O., Murphy, J., O'Sullivan, P.: Leverage of extended information to enhance the performance of JEE systems. The IT&T 11th International Conference on Information Technology and Telecommunication 2012, Cork, Ireland, 29–30 October 2012 (2012)

17. Reichelt, D.G., Kühne, S.: Better early than never. In: Companion of the 2018 ACM/SPEC International Conference on Performance Engineering - ICPE 2018, pp. 127–130. ACM Press, New York (2018)

18. Reichelt, D.G., Kühne, S.: How to detect performance changes in software history. In: Companion of the 2018 ACM/SPEC International Conference on Performance Engineering - ICPE 2018, pp. 183–188. ACM Press, New York (2018)

19. Sánchez, A.B., Delgado-Pérez, P., Segura, S., Medina-Bulo, I.: Performance mutation testing: hypothesis and open questions. Inf. Softw. Technol. **103**, 159–161 (2018)

20. Segura, S., Troya, J., Duran, A., Ruiz-Cortes, A.: Performance metamorphic testing: motivation and challenges. In: 2017 IEEE/ACM 39th International Conference on Software Engineering: New Ideas and Emerging Technologies Results Track (ICSE-NIER) (2017)

Attack Tolerance for Services-Based Applications in the Cloud

Georges Ouffoué[1]([⊠]), Fatiha Zaïdi[1], and Ana R. Cavalli[2,3]

[1] LRI, Univ. Paris-Sud, UMR 8623 CNRS, Université Paris-Saclay, Paris, France
{ouffoue,zaidi}@lri.fr
[2] IMT/TELECOM SudParis, SAMOVAR, UMR 5157 CNRS, Evry, France
ana.cavalli@it-sudparis.eu
[3] Montimage, Paris, France
ana.cavalli@montimage.com

Abstract. Web services allow the communication of heterogeneous systems and are particularly suitable for building cloud applications. Furthermore, such applications must verify some static properties, but also tolerate attacks at runtime to ensure service continuity. To achieve this, in this paper we propose an attack tolerance framework that includes the risks of attacks. After describing the foundation of this framework, we propose expressing cloud applications as choreographies of services that take into account their distributed nature. Then, we extended the framework to introduce choreography verification by incorporating monitoring (passive tests) and reaction mechanisms. These techniques are validated through relevant experiments. As a result, our framework ensures the required attack tolerance of such cloud applications.

Keywords: Attack tolerance · Runtime verification · Monitoring · Web services and cloud · Passive tests · Software reflection

1 Introduction

Computer systems are now at the heart of all business functions (accounting, customer relations, production, etc.) and, in general, in everyday life. These systems are based on heterogeneous applications and data. Service Oriented Architectures (SOA) have been proposed for this purpose. These architectures are distributed and facilitate communication between environments of heterogeneous nature. The main components of such architectures are Web services. A Web service is a collection of open protocols and standards for exchanging data between systems. These services can be internal and only concern one organization. In addition, the need to expose services to the outside world is growing due to the technological advances in communication networks, especially the Internet. Besides, security is at the heart of business concerns. Web services, since they are open and inter-operable, are privileged entry points for attacks. Moreover,

© IFIP International Federation for Information Processing 2019
Published by Springer Nature Switzerland AG 2019
C. Gaston et al. (Eds.): ICTSS 2019, LNCS 11812, pp. 242–258, 2019.
https://doi.org/10.1007/978-3-030-31280-0_15

Web services deployed in the cloud inherit their vulnerabilities. Security must then be taken into account when implementing Web services and this at all levels: design, specification, development and deployment. It is also appropriate to quantify the risks in order to clearly identify the threats and reduce the vectors of attacks.

In this paper, we adopt a new end-to-end security approach based on risk analysis, formal monitoring, software diversity and software reflection. We propose a new formal monitoring methodology that takes into account the risks that Web and cloud services may face. More precisely, the contributions of the paper are the following:

- A risk-based monitoring methodology is proposed. We claim that the detection and prevention of attacks require a good knowledge of the risks that these systems are facing.
- An instantiation of this methodology for cloud applications based on Web services is described. We propose an attack tolerance framework (offline and online), for such applications. Indeed, it is appropriate to consider tolerance during the modelling of the application and also to monitor that application at runtime for anticipating and detecting attacks $w.r.t$ to the risks. For this goal:
  - We first consider any application deployed in the cloud as a choreography of services which must be continuously monitored.
  - For the verification and monitoring of the choreography obtained, we extend a formal framework for choreography verification by incorporating our previous detection and remediation strategies [3].
  - We finally propose a new Domain Specific Language (DSL) called *ChorGen*. If choreographies written in a process algebra are formally verified and projected on the peers, skeletons of the corresponding services are generated by *ChorGen*.

The paper is then organized as follows. We propose a quick presentation of the main attack tolerance techniques in Sect. 2. Section 3 fully describes the risk-based monitoring methodology. Following the above methodology, an attack tolerance framework for cloud applications is presented in Sect. 4. In Sect. 5, we present a concrete case study: an electronic vote system. Experiments on this use-case highlight the attack tolerance capability of the whole framework. Conclusions and future enhancements of this work are given in Sect. 6.

2   Attack Tolerance: State of the Art

This section presents existing attack tolerance techniques highlighting the main issues that remain unsolved.

2.1   Intrusion and Attack Tolerance

Several solutions for attack tolerance were proposed. [8] proposed a formalism based on graphs to model an intrusion tolerant system. In this model they introduce system's response to (some of) the attacks. They call this model that incorporates attacker's actions as well as the system's response an Attack Response Graph (ARG).

Besides [18] classify ITS (Intrusion Tolerant Systems) architectures into four categories:

- **Detection-triggered** [16]: these architectures build multiple levels of defense to increase system survivability. Most of them rely on an intrusion detection that triggers reactions mechanisms.
- **Algorithm-driven** [10,17]: these systems employ algorithms such as the voting algorithm, threshold cryptography, and fragmentation redundancy scattering (FRS) to harden their resilience.
- **Recovery-based** [1,14]: these systems assume that when a system goes online, it's compromised. Periodic restoration to a former good state is necessary.
- **Hybrid** [15]: these systems combine different architectures mentioned above.

2.2   Attack Tolerance Techniques for Services-Based Application

It must be noted that Web services deployed in the cloud or used for building cloud applications inherit the vulnerabilities of the cloud platforms. Few works were conducted in order to transpose the techniques and framework cited in the previous section to web services. [5,13] presented an attack tolerant Web service architecture based on diversity techniques presented above. These solutions protect essentially against XML DoS Attacks. While these approaches are interesting, they do not address the specificity of services-based application deployed on cloud platforms. The solutions are attack-specific. Moreover, for this kind of application, it is necessary to integrate security in all the process steps *i.e.* from modeling to deployment. We need a more efficient intrusion-tolerant mechanism.

3   Risk-Based Monitoring Methodology

The supervision or monitoring of information systems is of paramount importance for any organization. It essentially consists in deploying probes in various parts of the system based on preset checkpoints. With automatic failure reporting, network agents can respond to key security risks. The disadvantage of such methods is the following. If risks or failures are discovered during operation, the attacks may have already occurred and one or more parts of the system may be non-functional. So, the detection and prevention of attacks require a good knowledge of the risks that these systems face.

As such, it is mandatory to include risk management in the monitoring strategy in order to reduce the probability of failure or uncertainty. Risk management attempts to reduce or eliminate potential vulnerabilities, or at least reduce the impact of potential threats by implementing controls and/or countermeasures. In the case, it is not possible to eliminate the risk, mitigation mechanisms should

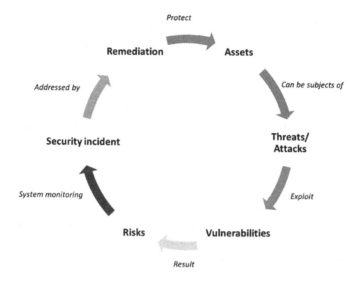

Fig. 1. Risk-based monitoring loop

be applied to mitigate their effects. We leveraged the risk management loop to build our risk-based monitoring loop depicted on the Fig. 1. Indeed, this risk-based monitoring solution can be summarized in the following objectives:

3.1 Identifying Assets

Assets are defined as proprietary resources of value to the organization and necessary for its proper functioning. We distinguish business-level assets from system assets. In terms of business assets, we mainly find information (for example credit card numbers) and processes (such as transaction management or account administration). The business assets of the organization are often entirely managed through the information system. System assets include technical elements, such as hardware, software and networks, as well as the computer system environment, such as users or buildings. System assets can also represent some attributes or properties of the system such as the data integrity and availability. This is particularly true for cloud services consumers.

3.2 Risk and Vulnerability Analysis

Risk is the possibility or likelihood that a threat will exploit a vulnerability resulting in a loss, unauthorized access or deterioration of an asset. A threat is a potential occurrence that can be caused by anything or anyone and can result in an undesirable outcome. Natural occurrences, such as floods or earthquakes, accidental acts by an employee, or intentional attacks can all be threats to an organization. A vulnerability is any type of weakness that can be exploited. The weakness can be due to, for example, a flaw, a limitation, or the absence of a security control.

3.3 Threats Identification

The first step to perform to avoid or repel the different threats that can affect an asset is to identify: affected modules/components, actions/behaviour to trigger the threat, and potential objective of the threat. This identification helps to understand the operation of the attacks and allows the creation of security mechanisms to protect, not only the assets, but also the software mechanisms that support them. The threats can be modelled by graphical representations such attack trees.

3.4 System Security Monitoring

The monitoring mechanism we propose, allows to constantly monitor activities or events occurring in the network, in the applications, and in the systems. This information will be analysed in near real-time to early detect any potential issue that may compromise the security or data privacy. If any anomalous situation is detected, the monitoring module will trigger a series of remediation mechanisms (countermeasures) oriented to notify, repel, or mitigate attacks and its effects.

3.5 Remediation

Once the risks of any system are established and the means of detection identified, it is essential to think about how to set up mechanisms that will allow to complete the risk-based monitoring loop *i.e.*, to tolerate and mitigate the effects of the potential detected attacks.

4 Risk-Based Monitoring for Services-Based Applications in the Cloud

This section presents how we have instantiated the risk-based methodology for services-based applications deployed in the cloud. As the first stages of the risk-based monitoring loop are specific to the type of the application, we will focus on the last two phases of that loop: monitoring and remediation. Two main approaches of remediation can be described:

- Anticipating the attack tolerance capability. This consists in introducing mechanisms allowing the tolerance to the attacks during the modelling of the system. The system is likely said to be tolerant-by-design or offline tolerant to attacks.
- Considering tolerance by a constant monitoring. In this type of approach, the tolerance capacity is entirely managed by the monitoring tool. The system is actively monitored for detecting malicious behaviours. The system is likely said to be online tolerant to attacks.

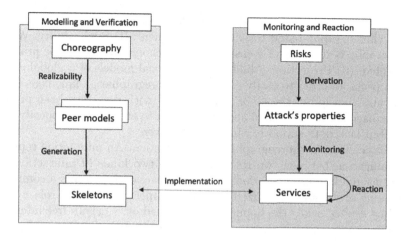

Fig. 2. Architecture and components of the framework

We believe that to have an effective attack tolerance (offline and online), it is appropriate to use these two approaches in a complementary way. We therefore propose an attack tolerance both online and offline. The resulting framework consists of two main parts (Fig. 2). The first part will present how we model services-based applications deployed in the cloud to make them attack tolerant. The second part will present how we monitor the system to detect the attacks; and how we mitigate these attacks.

4.1 Modelling of Cloud Applications

Cloud applications are distributed applications. To fully benefit from the advantages of the cloud we will consider our applications as a composition of Web services deployed in the cloud.

Generally service compositions are classified into two styles: orchestrations and choreographies. Orchestration always represents control from one participant's perspective, called the orchestrator. Unlike the orchestration, there is no privileged entities in the choreography. [6] argued that Web services composition, in particular choreography is a suitable solution used to build application and systems in the cloud. They built a middleware solution that is capable of automatically deploying and executing Web services in the cloud. We agree with them that choreography is a good approach for deploying cloud applications based on web services. The applications in the cloud will be deployed as service choreographies that integrate attack tolerance features. However, before and when deploying such choreography one should ensure that this choreography is realizable. Realizability, a fundamental issue of choreography, is whether a choreography specification can correctly be implemented. In a top-down service choreography approach, the realizability issue results in verifying whether a choreography model can be correctly projected onto role models. For this goal, we will leverage SChorA [9], a verification and testing framework for choreographies.

SChorA. SChorA[1] was proposed by [9]. This framework aims to solve the key issues in choreography-based top-down development: (i) Realizability: Whether a choreography is realizable *i.e* ensuring that a choreography can be practically implemented. (ii) Projection: Ability to derive local models of a global choreography on peers. In order to easily express the choregraphies, a language, *ChorD* which is an extension of the *Chor* language [12] with data, has been proposed. *Chor* language is expressive and abstract enough to enable one to specify collaborations but lack data support, what *ChorD* covers.

The basic event in choreography is an interaction. An interaction represents a communication between two roles. There are two kinds of interactions: free interactions and bound interactions. A free interaction represents a communication of value of variable x realized through an operation o from role a to b is denoted by $o^{[a,b]}.x$, while the bound one is denoted $o^{[a,b]}.\langle x \rangle$. In free interaction, the data exchange must be known before the interaction may occur. In bound interaction, the data exchange is bounded at the moment the interaction occurs
ChorD is described as:

$$ChorD ::= 1|\alpha|A; A|A + A|A||A|A[> A|[\phi] \rhd A|[\phi] \star A$$

A basic activity is either an inaction (*1*), or a standard basic event (α) presented above. They are structuring operators, that can be used to specify composite activities such as sequencing (*;*), non-deterministic choice (*+*), parallel activities (*//*), and interruption (*[>*).

One should note that we distinguish the global specification of the choreography called *global model* and the specification of this choreography on the different roles termed *role model*. In *role models* event are modeled as sending (!) or reception (?). For example let's express a simple Online-Shopping choreography between two roles: b (buyer) and v (vendor). The buyer first requests an article by providing an amount to be bought. If the amount is greater than 25 then the vendor aborts this transaction. Otherwise, a confirmation will be issue from the vendor to the buyer. This can be described as follows:

$$C :: Request^{[b,v]}.\langle x \rangle; ([x < 25] \rhd Ack^{[v,b]} + [x \geq 25] \rhd Abort^{[v,b]})$$

For the Buyer: $Request^{[b,v]}!.\langle y \rangle; (Ack^{[v,b]}? + Abort^{[v,b]}?)$

For the Vendor: $Request^{[b,v]}?.\langle z \rangle; ([z < 25] \rhd Ack^{[v,b]}! + [z \geq 25] \rhd Abort^{[v,b]}!)$

In fact *ChorD* is a process algebra and its semantics is given by Symbolic Transition Graphs (STGs) [7]. An STG is a transition system. Each transition of STG is labelled by a guard ϕ and a basic event α. The guard ϕ is a boolean equation which has to hold for the transition to take place. A symbolic transition from state s to state t with a guard ϕ, and an event α is denoted as $s \xrightarrow{[\phi]\alpha} t$. $\sqrt{}$ is added to denote activity termination. The representation of the simple shopping choreography using STG is the following:

---

[1] http://SChorA.lri.fr.

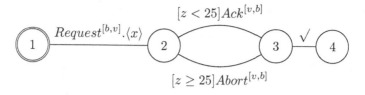

For the realizability and projection issues, STG are also used. By their formal richness, STGs are perfectly suited for verification of choreographies. STGs can be expanded to describe more operations since they support data, guard and free/bound variables. From the representation of the choreography as STG, if there are non-realizable parts, some additional interactions are incorporated to the graph to allow all the transitions to be realizable. Once the realizability is verified (*i.e* it can be directly implemented or some additional interactions are added), they are projected on the different roles or peers. By doing so, we are sure that our local models projected can actually be implemented concretely. In our case, local models are implemented as a web service. Once this step is over, it is useful to implement these projected models on the peers. The next section presents how in this framework, skeletons of the services are made possible.

Code Generation. In top-down software development approaches, an important part of the process is to reduce the costs of development by promoting modularity, reusability, and code generation. This is especially true in modeling and designing choreographies. It is therefore essential to have automatic mechanisms that perform code generation. This is why we propose a code generation strategy in this framework.

For this aim, we can leverage frameworks or tools in the literature ([11]) that take as input STGs and produce source code. Moreover, we propose a new Domain Specific Language (DSL) for our choreography called *ChorGen*.

The *ChorGen* language has the following grammar:

```
Model:
  (choreographies+= Choreography)+;

Choreography:
  'choreography' name=ID '{'
    (roles+=Roles)*
  '}'
;
Roles:
  'role' name=ID '{'
    operations+=Operation
  '}'
;
Operation:
  'operations' '{'
```

```
     (methods+=Function)*
  '}'
;
Function:
  name=ID '('(params+=Param)* ')'
;
Param:
  name=ID type=ID ',' |name =ID type=ID
;
```

We used model-driven engineering technologies Xtext[2] for the semantics and Xtend[3] for code generation to the target languages: WSDL and Python. This means that a choreography contains several roles that expose some operations to interact with the other roles. The advantage of doing such code generation is the reduction of the development costs and efforts. This allows us to be more efficient when implementing the services. This is useful, for example, for choreographies containing a very large number of peers. Another advantage is that since all interactions are taken into account, we are sure that developers will not forget to implement them since their signatures are available. Moreover, it should be noted that a single implementation is not sufficient to have a complete tolerance. It is admitted that more diversification implies more security.

4.2 Deployment, Monitoring and Reaction

We will leverage diversity as well. For implementing choreography, we had the choice between two methods. The first was to diversify for example at the level of programming languages, *i.e* having the implementations in different languages. This method has the advantage of generating few dependency between the variants of these services. However, this can create significant costs and workload for developers and can increase the time-to-market. The developer may not be able to master other languages. Moreover, since one of the members of the service choreography can be changed on the fly while the others remain intact, there could be some inconsistencies between the communication between these services. Indeed, although based on the remote procedure call (RPC), the ways to deploy web services are not the same.

The second way is to consider only one target programming language but have diversified implementation. The variants differ for example at the control flow (AST) level and use different data structures. The advantage of such an approach is that it is more flexible. The disadvantage is that we have a low diversity rate. However this rate may be improved by using different OS during the deployment of the services. For such reasons we chose the second method. So, from the global choreography, the local models are projected taking into account the interactions added to the specifications. This is the case for example

---

[2] https://www.eclipse.org/Xtext/.

[3] https://www.eclipse.org/xtend/.

when in the verification phase, interactions are added to the models to make the choreography realizable. After, there is a generation of the skeletons of the services that will implement the choreography. In particular, we generate the WSDL files (interface file of the Web services) as well as the skeletons of the implementations of these services in Python.

Besides, it is undeniable that to better tolerate attacks, it is necessary to detect them. Our approach of monitoring is based on reflection. Reflection makes it possible to dynamically get the code and even the execution trace of a method, a class and a module. One can also modify the class at run time. Using reflection all the hashes of the source code of any methods of the system are processed ([3]). An example of code using the reflection API in python is depicted in Fig. 3. In this piece of code, the source code of the running function in the call stack is retrieved and the hash of this code is computed.

```
def show_stack():
    stack = inspect.stack()
    ''' Inspect the stack '''

    for s in stack:
        a=inspect.getsource(s[0])
        ''' Get the source '''

        m=hashlib.md5()
        ''' hash that source code'''
```

Fig. 3. An example of using reflection in python language.

In fact, hash functions by their robustness are used to ensure the integrity of messages or transactions in distributed systems. This is the case in modern protocols, for example ssh and bitcoin. As such, the detection of attacks leveraging hash functions is legitimate. Any deviation at runtime of that hash value means the presence of a misbehavior. Such misbehavior could be caused by an insider attack or a virus attack. Information such as Date, Hour, Operation, hash, host are stored in the log file. Any request has then two traces in the logs: outbound(request) and inbound(response). For example, Table 1 presents a situation where there is no attack. We observe that the hashes for the Outbound and Inbound requests are the same.

Table 1. Normal entries in the log of the client application

Date	Hour	Methode	Hash	Host
31/05/2019	10:00:00 AM	! update(Outbound)	2224d35250e	a
31/05/2019	10:15:00 AM	? update(Inbound)	2224d35250e	b

If there is an attack, the hashes of both Outbound and Inbound could not correspond in the log files. This is the case depicted on Table 2. One can also get some other inconsistencies in the logs: hashes not equal, timestamps incoherence, method inconsistencies (answer before request), or combination of inconsistencies.

Table 2. Bad entries in the log of the client application

Date	Hour	Methode	Hash	Host
31/05/2019	10:00:00 AM	! update(Outbound)	2224d35250e	a
31/05/2019	10:15:00 AM	? update(Inbound)	2504d35222e...	b

For detecting attacks, log are located on the peers. We developed a new plugin for this kind of detection in the monitoring tool MMT. The MMT (Montimage Monitoring Tool) is a solution for monitoring networks and applications. MMT's Security properties are written in XML format. This has the advantage of simple and straightforward structure verification and processing by the tool. Any security property is written in XML. Each property begins with a <property> tag and ends with </property>. A MMT-Security property is an IF-THEN expression that describes constraints on network events captured in a trace T = $\{p_1, ..., p_m\}$. It has the following syntax:

$$e_1 \xrightarrow{W,n,t} e_2$$

$W \in \{$ BEFORE, AFTER $\}$, $n \in \mathbb{N}$, $t \in \mathbb{R}_{>0}$ and e_1 and e_2 two events. This property expresses that if the event e_1 is satisfied (by one or several packets p_i , $i \in \{1, ..., m\}$, then event e_2 must be satisfied (by another set of packets p_j , j $\in \{1, ..., m\}$) before or after (depending on the W value) at most n packets and t units of time. e_1 is called triggering context and e_2 is called clause verdict. When monitoring a system to detect attacks, the non respect of the MMT-Security property indicates the detection of an abnormal behaviour that might imply the occurrence of an attack. For example, if we consider a vote system (our use case deeply presented in the Sect. 5) a rule in the MMT formalism is the following.

Figure 4 describes a property for detecting the insider attack according to the formalism of MMT (Sect. 4). This means that in the log file any vote request should have hashes for its operations (outbound and inbound) in the log files and these hashes must correspond; otherwise an attack is triggered. Event 1 (e_1) expressed the reception of the inbound operation in the log file with a hash. If event 2 (e_2), the reception of the corresponding inbound operation in the log appears, there is a comparison between the hash collected of that event and the hash obtained in the previous event e_1 (the built-in C function *strcmp* was used for the comparison). If the hashes correspond, the system is attack free. Otherwise, an alert is triggered.

Then every module is monitored by extracting the program stack using reflection. We have a local database(M-DB) in which all the sources of the program functions are securely stored. If the attack is not known in the M-DB (i.e the

```
<beginning>
        <property value="THEN" delay_units="s" property_id="10"
            type_property="ATTACK"
            description="Detection of the insider attack: ">
                <event value="COMPUTE" event_id="1"
                    boolean_expression="((#strcmp(log.method,
                    'vote(inbound)') != 0)&amp;&amp;(#strcmp(log.hash, '')!=
                    0))"/>

                <event value="COMPUTE" event_id="2"
                    boolean_expression="((#strcmp(log.hash, '')!= 0)
                    &amp;&amp; (#strcmp(log.method, 'vote(outbound)') ==
                    0) &amp;&amp;(#strcmp(log.hash, log.hash.1) != 0))"/>
        </property>
</beginning>
```

Fig. 4. Security rule of the insider attack of the vote example

hash is not conform), the system checks in the own DB (M-DB). If the attack exists, countermeasures are launched else the hash is stored in the M-DB. For the mitigation of the attack, in case of attacks the current source code is replaced with one of the other variants randomly. The hash is also adapted. However, it should be noted that classic hash functions can provide the same hash for two different strings of characters. In practice, the probability of this happening is small. As a result, a more robust hash will not be foolproof either, but the probability of a collision will be higher and/or the means of generating it will be more complex and inaccessible.

5 Use Case: Vote Application

In this section, we present the implementation of the risk-based monitoring approach through a concrete case study. To illustrate our approach, we propose an electronic voting choreography for the election of the president in a certain country. This application allows citizens to register on the electoral lists and to vote electronically. The application is described by the *VoteElecService* choreography. It is composed of three basic members: *Inscription*, *Vote* and *Citizen*. The first member of that choreography allows to register a citizen on the electoral lists by providing the personal information (surname, first name, date of birth, address,...). Now, we describe the main components of the risk-based monitoring associated to this use-case.

5.1 Identifying Assets

In line with our risk-based monitoring approach the main assets remain the votes of the citizens and the availability of the platform. These citizens must be able to vote at any time of the election day.

5.2 Risk and Attack Scenarios

The main vulnerability in the vote example is an insider malicious developer or a not cautious user of the vote choreography [2,4]. Then, the following attacks (of course this is not an exhaustive list) can appear:

- Brute force: By analysing the unauthorised user's activities, user impersonation can sometimes be detected using MMT.
- Insider attacks (modification of the votes by a human being or by a virus): A member of the development team can modify the algorithm of the vote method in order to help a candidate or a political party of his choice to win the elections. We will provide some properties for such an attack.
- DoS/DDoS attacks: Making the vote service unavailable.

Brute force and DoS/DDoS attacks are classical and easy to detect and to mitigate. Using strong authentication such as 2-factors authentication and providing some classical MMT security rules can be sufficient. In addition, the reflection methodology is particularly useful for source code attacks. As such, due to space limitation, in the experiment part, we will focus on insider attacks that are more destructive.

5.3 System Security Monitoring and Reaction

Modelling and Verification. Let's first describe the choreography. Once registered, the citizen can vote electronically after verification of his registration by the member *Vote*. Subsequently, this service will provide the list of associated candidates and their identification number (1, 2,...) in addition to the number *zero* that is associated with the blank ballot. A registered citizen will vote by selecting one or more voting numbers (including the blank ballot) and submitting his/her choices. The choreography can be expressed in *ChorD* as follows:

$$inscription^{[c,i]}.\langle info \rangle; voteRequest^{[c,v]}.\langle y \rangle; resultVerifInfo^{[v,i]}.\langle x \rangle;$$
$$([x = 0] \triangleright rejection^{[v,c]} + [x! = 0] \triangleright (confirmation^{[v,c]}; liste^{[v,c]}; vote^{[c,v]})).$$

Where the Citizen member, the Inscription member, the Vote member and the result member correspond to respectively c, i and v. As one can observe on Fig. 5, the choreography is fully realizable without the need of adding new interactions since the projection is effective and doesn't include such added interactions. And from these descriptions, we generate skeletons of the roles that the developer should complete later.

Deployment, Experiments and Results. The services were deployed on the Amazon Web Services (AWS) cloud platform. We used a virtual machine for each member of the choreography. AWS is among the leaders of the cloud computing market.

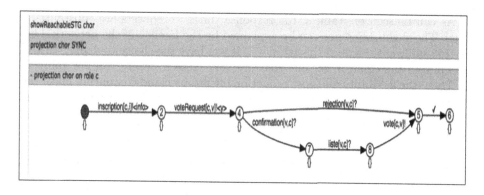

Fig. 5. Projection of the choreography on the peers

For the monitoring, Fig. 4 presents a property for detecting the insider attack. This means that in the log file any vote request should have hashes for its operations (outbound and inbound) in the log files and these hashes must correspond; otherwise an attack is triggered.

The same choreography has been deployed on a local test-bed consisting of three Dell machines having two micro processors, 3 Go RAM memory and all using the Ubuntu OS in its latest version. The same choreography has been deployed on an amazon cloud. The three different virtual machines also have 3 Go RAM memory and 2 Vcpu. Some experiments where conducted to test the attack tolerance capability of our approach.

Experiment 1: Since the approach of the framework consists of modelling and deploying cloud-based applications as distributed service choreographies, we evaluated the latency of the service to respond to some amounts of requests on premises and in the cloud.

Table 3. Latency measurement

Number of requests	On premises	In the cloud
100	0.27 s	0.34
200	0.69 s	0.87
300	1.10 s	1.40
400	1.80 s	2.56
500	2.48 s	3.24
600	3.45 s	5.13
700	4.41 s	6.35
800	5.65 s	7.24
900	6.89 s	8.68
1000	8.41 s	9.17

As can be seen on Table 3, the response times to requests are substantially equal. The slight difference can be explained by the latency of the network. One way to significantly reduce this latency is if you have the choice to deploy virtual machines in the cloud in regions that are very close to where you are going to go. Then, the flexibility and cost reduction offered by cloud computing make the overhead negligible. The following experiments were conducted for testing the detection capability of the framework. Here, we only focus on attacks consisting in modifying the source code of a method or a function deliberated (by a human being) or made by a virus. As we explained earlier, it has been proven in the literature that this kind of attacks may appear in voting systems. For the sake of demonstration, we design a relatively harmless virus. This virus modifies all the codes of the classes, methods or functions of the python modules of a given directory tree. We generated a signature of the new virus and added to the virus database.

Experiment 2: We evaluated the time elapsed to detect the insider attacks coming from both a modification of the source code and a virus. The accuracy of the detection mechanism was discussed in [3]. In this section, we only evaluate the efficiency of the monitoring *w.r.t* the two attacks above.

Table 4. Detection mean time

Virus	Modification
0.053 s	0.031 s

On Table 4 the modification seems to be easily detectable than the virus. This was predictable since the database of virus may contain a larger number of rows in comparison with the database containing the hashes of the methods. To have a fair detection time, one can have a unique database. The drawback of this solution is that we loose readability and flexibility. Along with the detection of attacks, the system reacts as mentioned in Sect. 4. This reaction is transparent for the user. Although we can detect attacks with great granularity, it is also important to consider the impact of the monitoring mechanism. That's why we will measure the overhead of the new monitoring method in the next experiment.

Experiment 3: Evaluation of the impact of the monitoring mechanism.

As one can see on Table 5, the overhead of the monitoring is not too significant. In future works, we will investigate how to reduce this overhead. The detection approach based on software reflection is suitable for the monitoring of cloud applications deployed as choreographies of services. To a certain extent, it can also be useful for detecting attacks such as buffer overflows and SQL injections. One limitation of such approach is the fact that this detection is only appropriate for attacks targeting the source code. But the main limitation is that the approach can not be applied in programs developed in programming languages that do not allow reflection or do not provide a powerful reflection API.

Table 5. Overhead of the monitoring mechanism

Number of requests	Without monitoring (s)	With monitoring (s)
100	0.38	0.46
200	0.88	0.91
300	1.39	1.4
400	2.50	2.57
500	3.26	3.27
600	5.22	5.30
700	6.31	6.35
800	7.21	7.45
900	8.89	9.12
1000	9.15	10.02

6 Conclusion

In this paper, we have proposed a new approach for attack tolerance based on formal runtime monitoring and software engineering techniques. We show that a good tolerance to attacks requires, on the one hand, to perform attack detection and continuous monitoring; and, on the other hand, reliable reaction mechanisms. In addition, we leverage the traditional risk management loop to build a risk-based approach that integrates risks into monitoring. Finally, we proposed an offline and online attack tolerance framework for Web services-based application in the cloud. With this aim, we first express any application deployed in the cloud as a choreography of services, which must be continuously monitored and tested. Then, we extend a formal framework for choreography testing by incorporating the methods for detecting and mitigating attacks presented in the previous sections. Adding mechanisms of detection and reaction on the fly to these applications, ensure optimal attack tolerance. In the future work we will evaluate the scalability of the framework for very large choreographies. Besides, we believe that in addition to detection and remediation, it would be necessary to be able to predict and anticipate future attacks. We think that diagnosis and prediction techniques would be interesting to investigate in order to improve the attack detection and tolerance of our approach.

References

1. Arsenault, D., Sood, A., Huang, Y.: Secure, resilient computing clusters: Self-cleansing intrusion tolerance with hardware enforced security (SCIT/HES). In: The Second International Conference on Availability, Reliability and Security (ARES 2007), pp. 343–350 (2007)
2. Beaucamps, P., Reynaud, D., Marion, J.Y., Filiol, E.: On the impact of malware on internet voting. In: 1st Luxembourg Day on Security and Reliability (2009)

3. Cavalli, A.R., Ortiz, A.M., Ouffoué, G., Sanchez, C.A., Zaïdi, F.: Design of a secure shield for internet and web-based services using software reflection. In: Jin, H., Wang, Q., Zhang, L.-J. (eds.) ICWS 2018. LNCS, vol. 10966, pp. 472–486. Springer, Cham (2018). https://doi.org/10.1007/978-3-319-94289-6_30

4. Estehghari, S., Desmedt, Y.: Exploiting the client vulnerabilities in internet e-voting systems: hacking helios 2.0 as an example. In: Proceedings of the 2010 International Conference on Electronic Voting Technology/Workshop on Trustworthy Elections, pp. 1–9. USENIX Association (2010)

5. Ficco, M., Rak, M.: Intrusion tolerant approach for denial of service attacks to web services. In: Proceedings of the 2011 First International Conference on Data Compression, Communications and Processing, CCP 2011, pp. 285–292. IEEE Computer Society (2011)

6. Furtado, T., Francesquini, E., Lago, N., Kon, F.: A middleware for reflective web service choreographies on the cloud. In: Proceedings of the 13th Workshop on Adaptive and Reflective Middleware, ARM 2014, pp. 9:1–9:6. ACM (2014)

7. Hennessy, M., Lin, H.: Symbolic bisimulations. Theor. Comput. Sci. **138**(2), 353–389 (1995)

8. Madan, B.B., Trivedi, K.S.: Security modeling and quantification of intrusion tolerant systems using attack-response graph. J. High Speed Netw. **13**(4), 297–308 (2004)

9. Nguyen, H.N.: Une Approche Symbolique pour la Vérification et le Test des Chorégraphies de Services. Ph.D. thesis, Université Paris-Sud (2013)

10. O'Brien, D., Smith, R., Kappel, T., Bitzer, C.: Intrusion tolerance via network layer controls. In: Proceedings DARPA Information Survivability Conference and Exposition, vol. 1, pp. 90–96 (2003)

11. Pavel, S., Noyé, J., Poizat, P., Royer, J.-C.: A java implementation of a component model with explicit symbolic protocols. In: Gschwind, T., Aßmann, U., Nierstrasz, O. (eds.) SC 2005. LNCS, vol. 3628, pp. 115–124. Springer, Heidelberg (2005). https://doi.org/10.1007/11550679_9

12. Qiu, Z., Zhao, X., Cai, C., Yang, H.: Towards the theoretical foundation of choreography. In: Proceedings of WWW 2007 (2007)

13. Sadegh, B., Azgomi, M.A.: A new architecture for intrusion-tolerant web services based on design diversity techniques. J. Inf. Syst. Telecommun. (JIST), Autumn (2015)

14. Sousa, P., Bessani, A., Neves, N.F., Obelheiro, R.: The forever service for fault-/intrusion removal. In: Proceedings of the 2nd Workshop on Recent Advances on Intrusiton-tolerant Systems, WRAITS 2008, pp. 5:1–5:6. ACM (2008)

15. Sousa, P., Bessani, A.N., Correia, M., Neves, N.F., Verissimo, P.: Resilient intrusion tolerance through proactive and reactive recovery. In: 13th Pacific Rim International Symposium on Dependable Computing (PRDC 2007), pp. 373–380 (2007)

16. Valdes, A., et al.: An architecture for an adaptive intrusion-tolerant server. In: Christianson, B., Crispo, B., Malcolm, J.A., Roe, M. (eds.) Security Protocols 2002. LNCS, vol. 2845, pp. 158–178. Springer, Heidelberg (2004). https://doi.org/10.1007/978-3-540-39871-4_14

17. Verissimo, P.E.: Intrusion-tolerant middleware: the road to automatic security. IEEE Secur. Priv. **4**(4), 54–62 (2006)

18. Wang, F., Raghavendra, U., Killian, C.: Analysis of techniques for building intrusion tolerant server systems. IEEE Mil. Commun. Conf. (MILCOM) **2**, 729–734 (2003)

Industrial Applications

Automatic Generation of Test Oracles from Component Based Software Architectures

Maxime Samson and Thomas Vergnaud[✉]

Thales, 1, Avenue Augustin Fresnel, Palaiseau, France
{maxime.samson,thomas.vergnaud}@thalesgroup.com

Abstract. In a software development process, the integration and verification of the different parts of the application under development often require a lot of effort. Component Based Software Engineering (CBSE) approaches help cut software integration costs by enabling the automatic generation of data types, method signatures and middleware configuration from a model of the application structure. Model Based Testing (MBT) techniques help cut software verification costs by enabling the automatic generation of test oracles from a model of the expected application behaviour. Models for CBSE and MBT are usually separate. This may result in discrepancies between them, especially when the application architecture is updated, which always happens.

In this paper, we describe how to rely on a single CBSE model to produce both code generation and oracles for some tests, thus ensuring consistency between them. Our work is based on existing OMG standards, mainly UCM and UML.

Keywords: Component Based Software Engineering ·
Model based testing · UCM

1 Introduction

The development cycle of a software system involves a verification phase to ensure the system meets its requirements. A typical way of verifying a system is to test it. Test are often very expensive in terms of efforts. Model Based Testing (MBT) [11] is usually considered to be an efficient approach to cut test costs by modelling the expected system properties and automatically producing the tests themselves.

Yet, the creation and maintenance of the test specification models is still a source of difficulty. In particular, system requirements are likely to change during the development cycle, especially in agile processes [2]. The test specification models must be updated to follow the requirement changes.

In this paper, we present our approach to overcome consistency issues by deducing some test specification models from architecture specifications. We use

© IFIP International Federation for Information Processing 2019
Published by Springer Nature Switzerland AG 2019
C. Gaston et al. (Eds.): ICTSS 2019, LNCS 11812, pp. 261–269, 2019.
https://doi.org/10.1007/978-3-030-31280-0_16

a Component Based Software Engineering model as a unique reference, from which code and tests are generated. Thus we ensure consistency between software and tests, while reducing development cost. We focus on testing that the implementation code of a given component conforms with the a sequence of port calls specified for this component.

The paper explains the process we are currently implementing. We illustrate it with a very simple example. First, we provide a quick overview of UCM; we explain its scope and explain how we combine it with UML to gather all the necessary information to specify expected behaviours. Then we describe Diversity, a MBT tool we use to compare execution traces with the expected behaviours. Then we provide an overview of our process. We conclude the paper by discussing our solution. Our study is done in the scope of project DisTA[1].

2   Software Component Design with UCM

Component based software engineering (CBSE) addresses middleware dependency of software applications [8,9]. It consists in isolating the business code from the middleware configuration code. The business code is encapsulated inside components. Components are connected through ports and connectors. Glue code is generated from the component declarations. This glue code provides an API to the business code; this API depends only on the component declaration, and is independent from the underlying middleware. The implementation of the glue code API is specific to a given middleware implementation; it manages the middleware configuration and control.

UCM [5] is a component model published by the Object Management Group. It is a successor of the CORBA Component Model [3]. While CCM was initially bound to CORBA, UCM is independent from any middleware technology. Also, UCM is more focused on real-time embedded systems than CCM was.

UCM defines three main entities: connectors, technical policies and components. Components are the application itself; they encapsulate the business code. Connectors and technical policies specify the execution platform that supports the execution of the application; tools generate technical code from them.

2.1   Declaration of UCM Components

Components are made of two parts: a component type and a component implementation. A component type specifies the possible interactions between the component and other components. Such interactions consist of ports. A component implementation carries the technical information related with the component realization. The UCM standard specifies how to interpret component declarations to produce the glue code between technical and business code. This part of the UCM standard is called the container model.

---

[1] https://www.linkedin.com/pulse/automated-distributed-test-platform-iot-testing-fabrice-trollet.

Figure 1a represents an example of UCM component declaration. We design a UCM component that should be connected to a thermometer and filter out erroneous temperature data. Component type `Filter` carries four ports. One is named `raw_in` and receives messages. The others are named `norm_out`, `raw_out` and `deviation`; they all emit messages. All messages carry temperature data— the details of the data binding are declared in binding `temperature_msg`, which is not represented here. The implementation `Filter_1` is implemented in C++11.

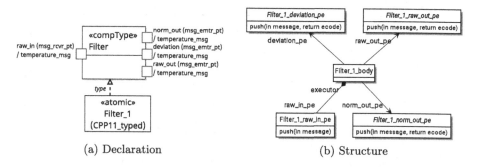

(a) Declaration   (b) Structure

Fig. 1. Declaration and structure of UCM component `Filter_1`

Components are translated into one class that stores the component states, and classes that hold the business code of each provided interface. The container model class diagram for component `Filter_1` is represented on Fig. 1b. According to the definition of message ports in the UCM standard library, message reception and message emission are realized by methods named "push".

2.2   Adding Behaviour Specifications to UCM Compponents

UCM in itself does not specify component behaviours: the standard defines atomic components as black boxes that contain business code. The component developer needs additional information in order to correctly write the C++ code for `Filter_1`. In the scope of our work, we extend UCM by adding such information.

As the container model actually corresponds to basic UML class diagrams (see Fig. 1b), it is possible to combine UCM declarations with UML sequence diagrams [4] to specify expected behaviours inside components. Such sequence diagrams specify the behaviours of the method implementation code; They consist of sequences of calls to external methods, loops and alternatives.

Let us consider the following behaviour specification for component `Filter_1`. Upon the reception of a raw temperature data on port `raw_in`, `Filter_1` shall have different behaviours, depending on the value of the input temperature. If the input temperature is similar to the previous temperature data, send it through `norm_out`. If one sample of temperature input is obviously erroneous (i.e. very different from the previous value), send the old input value through norm_out. If the input temperature is repetitively erroneous, send it through raw_out and send the deviation between the current temperature and the last correct temperature through deviation. This specification is illustrated in Fig. 2.

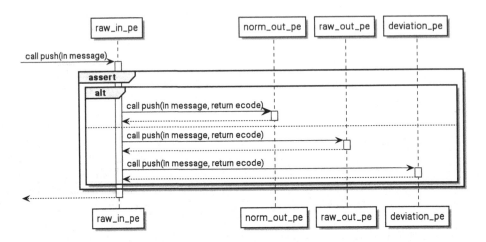

Fig. 2. Behaviour specification associated with UCM component Filter_1

The sequence diagram specifies requirements regarding relationships between calls of component port methods. In order to check if the component implementation code is correct with respect to the behaviour specification, we can trace all method invocations, execute the application and analyze the traces: the traces must *always* conform with the component behaviour specification.

In order to automate trace analysis, our solution is to create formal oracles from the sequence diagrams. From the component declaration (Fig. 1a) and the behaviour (Fig. 2) associated with the container model (Fig. 1b), we can build an oracle to check that each invocation of method push of port raw_in is either followed by a call to method push of port norm_out *or else* by a call to method push of port raw_out then a call to method push of port deviation. The remaining of the paper briefly explains how we do.

3   Coordinating Specification and Verification

Our work focuses on cutting the cost of verification in a software development process. Typical development processes, like the weel-known "V" cycle, involve three steps: specification, implementation and verification. Iterative process usually involves short development cycles that combine these three steps. In the scope of this paper, "verification" consists of checking the system properties against its requirements.

The verification steps consists of ensuring the implementation conforms to some oracles that reflect the specification. Hence, the oracles are supposed to be correct while the implementation might contain errors—that is why we perform verification. In Model Based Testing techniques, verification consists of tests. These tests are built from a model that describes the expected system behaviour. Yet, nothing ensures the test model is correct with respect to the initial specifications. This may lead to inconsistencies between specifications and tests.

Our work consists of automating as much as possible the production of both implementation and verification oracles from the specifications. This way, we reduce the risk of inconsistencies. Figure 3 illustrates the process we follow.

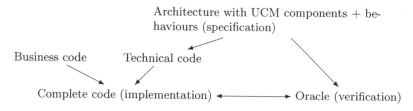

Fig. 3. Production process

It is not possible to automate the complete generation of the implementation. This would mean the specifications gather all the implementation details (data structure, architecture and algorithms); that is, the specification would be the implementation. That is why we separate the business code (written by hand or produced by a third-party tool) and the technical code, which is generated from a specification of the architecture.

It is not possible to completely specify all possible tests either: this would imply a very complex and formal specification, difficult to create, maintain and understand for humans. In our work, we focus on testing the occurence of events in execution traces.

4   Model-Based Testing with Diversity and xLIA

Since the UCM standard is dedicated to the specification of real-time and embedded systems, it can be used to specify finite-state system, allowing model checking techniques to be used to verify the correctness of their implementation. Instead of requiring the user to create multiple models for a single application, our approach to model-based testing only requires a single model from which other models can be derived.

Diversity is a formal analysis tool based on symbolic execution developped by CEA LIST institute [1]. It supports the definition and symbolic execution of models and it can be used for automated test sets generation and for evaluating execution traces' conformance to models [7]. These models are concurrent communicating systems expressed in eXecutable Language for Interaction & Assemblage (xLIA).

The xLIA language offers a variety of primitives that allows it to encode classical semantics such as UML and SDL (Specification and Description Language). In this paper, we describe how to use xLIA as a pivot language to create timed input output labelled transition systems (TIOLTS) that can be used by Diversity.

In the xLIA models we produce, the different state machines can communicate with each other through rendez-vous interactions. State machines can also communicate with the environment (i.e. what is external to the system under test).

5   Mapping from UCM to xLIA

A UCM specification can contain execution scenarios attached to methods. An execution scenario contains execution steps that will be executed upon the invocation of the method. These scenarios are what will be translated into xLIA in order to automatically generate test oracles.

The translation follows these general principles: each scenario is translated to a state machine and each step contained by that scenario is translated to a state. Since a scenario's steps are ordered, the transitions from one state to the next follow that order.

Some steps are calls to other methods, they are named "call steps". Such steps are assigned a subscenario, which is a reference to the execution scenario of the method they call. The translation of a call step adds an instruction on the exiting transition of the state. This instruction makes the state machine that represents the scenario interact with the state machine that represents the subscenario through their ports. Most call steps have to wait for their subscenario to terminate before allowing the scenario to continue its execution. This is translated to a transition into a "waiting" state that waits for a new interaction between the two state machines.

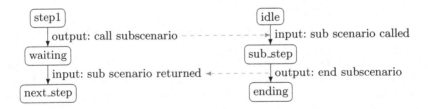

Fig. 4. Communication between state machines.

As scenarios can be executed multiple times throughout the execution of the application, the state machines that represent them have to be cyclic. Therefore, every state machine has an "idle" and an "ending" state that are respectively the first and the last step of one cycle of their execution. In the "idle" state, a state machine waits for a timed guard or an interaction from either another state machine or the environment to begin its execution. The execution traces will then be confronted to the outputs produced upon exiting both these states.

Other kinds of steps can be used to specify an application's behaviour in UCM: alternative and loop steps. The alternative step offers a set of steps among which only one will be executed without specifying the condition used to make the decision. The loop step contains a list of steps that will be executed multiple times, the minimum and maximum number of iterations have to be specified.

An alternative step is translated into a state that has multiple nondeterministic exiting transitions, one for each possible next step. A loop state is translated to a state that has two transitions: one to the first state of the loop and one to the next state. Nondeterminism can be used to translate alternative and loop steps to xLIA because Diversity's symbolic execution engine will explore every possibility. In the following example, i is initialized to 0 and the loop iterates between 2 and 5 times. This is nondeterministic for i $\in$ {2, 3, 4}.

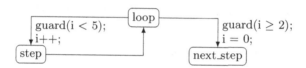

Fig. 5. Example of nondeterminism in loops.

6   Implementation and Experiments

We are currently developping a UCM code generator, Sigil-UCM [10], to demonstrate our approach. This tool is a code generator that implements the standard mapping from UCM to C++ and also the mapping from UCM to xLIA we outlined in the previous section.

Sigil-UCM produces the necessary calls to the log4cpp [6] library to trace the execution of all component port methods (method entry, method exit, method call, returning from call). Traces are compared with the xLIA test oracles by Diversity. Users get a test verdict that indicates if the execution traces conforms to the call sequences specified in the UCM components or not.

After generating the technical code with Sigil-UCM, users have to implement the methods for which they specified the behaviour in the UCM model. In our example, users have to implement method **push** whose behaviour is specified by the sequence diagram in Fig. 2.

Let us suppose users misunderstood the component specifications and wrote business code that systematically produces output to **norm_out**, even for erroneous data cases. The component execution produces the traces illustrated in listing 1.1.

Listing 1.1. Execution trace produced by an erroneous implementation

```
1  TRACE log_policy : filter.logger (raw_in__pe) entering push
2  TRACE log_policy : filter.logger (norm_out_pe) calling push
3  TRACE log_policy : filter.logger (norm_out_pe) returning from push
4  TRACE log_policy : filter.logger (raw_out_pe) calling push
5  TRACE log_policy : filter.logger (raw_out_pe) returning from push
6  TRACE log_policy : filter.logger (deviation_pe) calling push
7  TRACE log_policy : filter.logger (deviation_pe) returning from push
8  TRACE log_policy : filter.logger (raw_in_pe) exiting push
```

Users launch Diversity to compare the traces produced by the execution of the business code and the xLIA oracle generated from the specifications. The automatic analysis with Diversity produces the verdict *FAIL* because the traces do not match the test oracle. Indeed, after receiving a message, the business code implementation of **push** emits on all its outgoing ports instead of either emitting on **norm_out** or on **raw_out** and **deviation**.

The automatic analysis performed by Diversity indicates that line 4 in listing 1.1 caused the failure. This helps understand the implementation of the alternative is incorrect. After fixing the implementation of **push** and relaunching the execution, the component produces the execution trace shown in listing 1.2.

Listing 1.2. Execution trace produced by a correct implementation

```
1  TRACE log_policy : filter.logger (raw_in_pe) entering push
2  TRACE log_policy : filter.logger (raw_out_pe) calling push
3  TRACE log_policy : filter.logger (raw_out_pe) returning from push
4  TRACE log_policy : filter.logger (deviation_pe) calling push
5  TRACE log_policy : filter.logger (deviation_pe) returning from push
6  TRACE log_policy : filter.logger (raw_in_pe) exiting push
```

Now the automatic analysis with Diversity produces verdict *PASS*. This indicates the business code implementation of method **push** conforms to the specification.

7   Conclusion

In this paper, we gave the main lines of our work to ease the use of Model Based Testing in a software development process. We demonstrated Component Based software Engineering can be used to generate both technical code and test models. Having a unique, central model prevent inconsistencies between code and tests, especially for agile development processes in which application specifications are likely to evolve over time. From an industrial process point of view, it is convenient to manipulate a unique set of UML based models: it requires little additional effort for component designers to specify behaviours in order to get test oracles at almost no cost. This eases the smooth adoption of MBT techniques in industry.

References

1. Eclipse format modeling project. https://projects.eclipse.org/proposals/eclipse-formal-modeling-project
2. The agile manifesto (2001). http://agilemanifesto.org/principles.html
3. CORBA Component Model, version 4.0. OMG (2006). https://www.omg.org/spec/CCM/
4. Unified Modeling Language, version 2.5.1. OMG (2017). https://www.omg.org/spec/UML/
5. Unified Component Model for Distributed, Real-Time And Embedded Systems, version 1.1. OMG (2019). http://www.omg.org/spec/UCM
6. Bakker, B.: Log for c++ project. http://log4cpp.sourceforge.net
7. Bannour, B., Escobedo, J.P., Gaston, C., Le Gall, P.: Off-line test case generation for timed symbolic model-based conformance testing. In: Nielsen, B., Weise, C. (eds.) ICTSS 2012. LNCS, vol. 7641, pp. 119–135. Springer, Heidelberg (2012). https://doi.org/10.1007/978-3-642-34691-0_10
8. Crnkovic, I., Sentilles, S., Vulgarakis, A., Chaudron, M.R.V.: A classification framework for software component models. IEEE Trans. Softw. Eng. **37**(5), 593–615 (2011). https://doi.org/10.1109/TSE.2010.83
9. Szyperski, C.A., Gruntz, D., Murer, S.: Component Software - Beyond Object-Oriented Programming. Addison-Wesley Component Software Series, 2nd edn. Addison-Wesley, Boston (2002). http://www.worldcat.org/oclc/248041840
10. Sigil-ucm. https://www.thalesforge.thalesgroup.com/projects/sigil-ucm/
11. Utting, M., Legeard, B., Bouquet, F., Fourneret, E., Peureux, F., Vernotte, A.: Recent advances in model-based testing. Adv. Comput. **101**, 53–120 (2016)

Industrial IoT Security Monitoring and Test on Fed4Fire+ Platforms

Diego Rivera[1], Edgardo Montes de Oca[1(✉)], Wissam Mallouli[1],
Ana R. Cavalli[2], Brecht Vermeulen[3], and Matevz Vucnik[4]

[1] Montimage, 39 rue Bobillot, 75013 Paris, France
{diego.rivera,edgardo.montesdeoca,wissam.mallouli}@montimage.com
[2] Telecom SudParis, 9 rue Charles Fourier, 91011 Evry, France
ana.cavalli@telecom-sudparis.eu
[3] IMEC, Remisebosweg 1, 3001 Leuven, Belgium
brecht.vermeulen@ugent.be
[4] Jozef Stefan Institute, Jamova cesta 39, 1000 Ljubljana, Slovenia
matevz.Vucnik@ijs.si

Abstract. This paper presents the main results of the experiments conducted using the MMT-IoT security analysis solution run on a IoT Fed4Fire+ platform (Virtual Wall - w.iLab proposed by IMEC, Belgium). MMT is a monitoring framework developed by Montimage, and MMT-IoT is the tool that allows monitoring and analysing the security and performance of IoT networks. The results obtained concern two principal advancements. First, the adaptations made to deploy MMT-IoT on the IoT platform in order to run the tool on the platform's IoT devices. Second, the deployment of the software allowed us to run preliminary tests on the selected platform for performing initial validation and scalability tests on this real environment. To this end, Montimage defined and implemented three test scenarios related to security and scalability with 1 or more clients. These results will be used to prepare a new experimentation phase involving also another Fed4Fire+ platform (LOG-a-TEC proposed by IJS, Slovenia).

Keywords: Monitoring · Testing · IoT · Industrial applications · Fed4Fire · MMT

1 Introduction

Internet of things (IoT) is a concept that describes a network of interconnected devices capable of interacting with other devices, human beings and its surrounding physical world to perform a variety of tasks [1].

Modern IoT devices make use of sensors (e.g., accelerometer, gyroscope, microphone, light sensor, etc.) [6] to detect any changes in their surrounding and take necessary actions to improve any ongoing task efficiently [15]. The increasing popularity and utility of IoT devices in divergent application domains made

© IFIP International Federation for Information Processing 2019
Published by Springer Nature Switzerland AG 2019
C. Gaston et al. (Eds.): ICTSS 2019, LNCS 11812, pp. 270–278, 2019.
https://doi.org/10.1007/978-3-030-31280-0_17

the IoT industry to grow at a tremendous rate. According to a report by Business Insider [3], 30 billion devices will be connected to the Internet by 2020. These devices can provide new functionality in different domains, but can also be used as vehicles to launch attacks (examples can be found for instance in [4,7,9–11,13]).

The challenge of security monitoring on IoT network arises when trying to detect these attacks on devices that have strict resource limitations. Furthermore, existing centralised monitoring techniques (Intrusion Detection and Prevention Systems) cannot handle the large amounts of data that needs to be analysed, and have been designed to work on the edge of the networks and cannot cope with IoT networks that lack clear boundaries. In this paper, we present MMT-IoT, a security tool intended for addressing the requirements for security monitoring on IoT networks, and its application in industrial settings. MMT-IoT allows capturing IoT network traffic near the IoT devices and analyses them to detect potential attacks. In this work we take advantage of the industrial Fed4Fire testbed to deploy MMT-IoT on a near-to-real-life scenario, validate its security detection properties and perform initial scalability tests.

The rest of the paper is organized as follows. Section 2 presents the general architecture of the MMT-IoT tool. Section 3 presents the description of the Fed4Fire platforms that were used for the experimentation. Section 4 presents the methodology followed for the deployment and experiments on the Fed4Fire testbed, as well as the results obtained. Finally, Sect. 5 presents the conclusions and future work.

2   Montimage Monitoring Tool (MMT) for IoT Networks

The Montimage Monitoring Tool (MMT) [8] is a modular monitoring framework that allows detecting behavior, security and performance incidents based on a set of formal properties (written in XML) and embedded functions (written in C or any script or interpreted language). MMT allows real-time data capture, metadata extraction, correlation of data from different sources (i.e. network, applications traces and logs, operating systems), complex event processing, and distributed analysis. It uses temporal logic to detect given security properties (expected or anomalous), and statistical and machine learning-based analysis for detecting more sophisticated activities and behaviour. It is relatively easy to extend by adding new: (i) properties and embedded functions; (ii) plugins for parsing any structured message; (iii) new dashboards for visualising data, statistics and alarms; and, (iv) instructions to trigger reactions (e.g. mitigation or blocking of attacks).

In order to correctly adapt this approach – designed initially for traditional Ethernet networks – to IoT networks, it was required to split the network extractor (sniffer) in two parts: *the MMT-IoT Sniffer* (a Contiki-based IoT device), and the *MMT-IoT Bridge* (a Linux-based tool). The former is the IoT endpoint that is in charge of sniffing the packets and forwarding them – using a USB line – to a more powerful machine. The latter recovers the transferred packets from

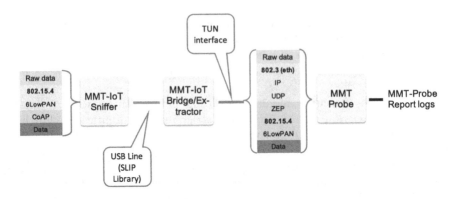

Fig. 1. General architecture of the MMT-IoT solution.

the USB line and injects them (encapsulated using the ZEP protocol) in the loopback interface of the machine, making the packets ready for analysis by the MMT-Probe and MMT-Security. Figure 1 summarises the general architecture of the solution.

Concerning the MMT-IoT Sniffer, the implementation of this architecture was achieved by introducing modifications in the network drivers to make the sniffing feature work. Such modifications were focused in three main axes:

- *Radio driver in promiscuous mode*: This modification was done to avoid dropping of packets by the Contiki kernel.
- *Avoid dropping packets with bad checksum*: By default, the radio driver reads the packet and checks the CRC to detect potential transmission failures. If this check fails, the packer is discarded to avoid processing a misformatted packet and save energy. This behaviour was changed, since a sniffing solution must extract all the packets on the medium whether they are correct or not.
- *Insertion of callbacks to redirect the received packet*: A sniffer is a passive network element, therefore, once the packet is received on the radio driver layer, it is transferred via callbacks directly to the application layer. This behaviour bypasses the Contiki network processing and redirects the packets immediately using the USB line, saving energy in the sniffer device. The structure of the inserted callbacks is depicted in Fig. 2.

Finally, the MMT-IoT Bridge is responsible for capturing the packets sent through the USB line and making them available for the security analysis performed by the MMT-Probe and MMT-Security; both part of the MMT software. This security analysis is performed by a set of security rules – previously assessed by a network security engineer – which codify the set of network events that need to be correlated for detecting security issues.

It is important to notice that computation complexity of detecting an attack is given by the rule itself; complex attacks require more complex rules which correlate a higher number of network events. Considering this, the computation complexity will be taken by MMT-Probe, and not MMT-IoT, which only

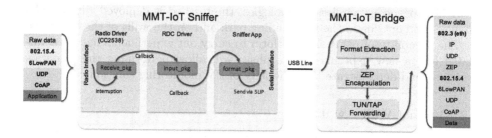

Fig. 2. Internal details of the MMT-IoT solution.

redirects the traffic to MMT-Probe. This is why neither MMT-IoT Sniffer nor MMT-IoT Bridge components contain any complex logic, since, as mentioned before, the security analysis is performed by MMT-Probe.

3   Fed4Fire+ Testbeds

Experimentally driven research is considered to be a key factor for growing the European Internet industry. In order to enable this type of RTD activities, a number of projects for building a European facility for Future Internet Research and Experimentation (FIRE) have been launched, each project targeting a specific community within the Future Internet ecosystem. Through the federation of these infrastructures, innovative experiments become possible that break the boundaries of these domains. Besides, infrastructure developers can utilize common tools of the federation, allowing them to focus on their core testbed activities.

In this sense, Fed4FIRE+ is a project under the European Union Programme Horizon 2020, offering the largest worldwide federation of Next Generation Internet (NGI) testbeds. These provide open and reliable facilities supporting a wide variety of different research and innovation communities and initiatives in Europe, including the 5G PPP projects.

The following platforms, LOG-a-TEC and Virtual Wall – w.iLab that are part of Fed4FIRE+ where considered. It must be noted that only Virtual Wall – w.iLab was used to perform the experiments described in this paper. In the case of LOG-a-TEC, only a feasibility study was made and the experiments on this platform will be performed at a later stage.

3.1   LOG-a-TEC

LOG-a-TEC is proposed by IJS, Slovenia [14]. It is composed of several different radio technologies that enable dense and heterogeneous IoT, MTC and 5G experimentation. Specially developed embedded wireless sensor nodes can host four different wireless technologies and seven types of wireless transceivers. In order to enable different experiments in combined indoor/outdoor environments using heterogeneous wireless technologies, the testbed is deployed within JSI's premises and outside in the surrounding park and on the walls of the buildings.

The feasibility of using this platform to carry out experiments has been validated and a new experimentation phase will allow performing the scenarios described and demonstrate the genericity of the monitoring solution.

3.2   Virtual Wall – w.iLab

The w.iLab platform [5] is an IoT and 5G emulation testbed that allows running experiments on nodes on real IoT deployments. This platform was designed by the IMEC, Belgium. It provides "bare metal" access to its nodes, i.e., it gives root access to physical machines that will be used to run the experiment. This allows the experimenter to have full control of the nodes on the testbed. The deployment of the MMT-IoT and MMT-Probe software and the execution of the tests are performed remotely without requiring major interventions from the operators. For this, we created credentials on the iMinds platform and performed a reservation of the Intel NUC nodes from the "Datacenter" floor of the platform. The jFED-Experimenter tool was required to design an experiment to access these nodes.

4   Experimental Evaluation

4.1   Methodology

Considering these testbeds, we used the w.iLab platform to deploy the MMT-IoT Sniffer and the MMT-Probe solutions. In this way, we were able to use the w.iLab t.1 platform to evaluate the scalability of these by overloading them. By performing the extraction of the packets from an IoT network, this experimentation pursues two principal sub-objectives: (1) perform an initial DPI-based security analysis on an IoT network traffic; and (2) determine the maximum throughput a single instance of MMT-IoT Sniffer can handle.

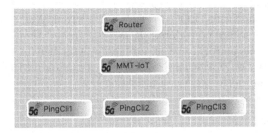

Fig. 3. Deployment of the MMT-IoT Solution of the w.iLab platform.

To achieve these objectives, we deployed a set of IoT devices as shown in Fig. 3. In this deployment we used 3 types of devices:

- Ping Client: An emulated IoT sensor programmed to attack the server. For the emulation purposes we used a client that performs a "ping" to the IoT router, however in real life a client can be any device generating some type of traffic.
- IoT Router: A gateway running a routing protocol to allow communications within the IoT network.
- MMT-IoT: A node running the Montimage software under test.

We used the deployment described above to perform initial validation and scalability tests in scenarios that contain respectively 1, 2, 3 malicious clients. We used these configurations to pursue both objectives previously mentioned: (1) the security analysis validation, by means of determining the number of detected attacks; and (2) the scalability of the MMT-IoT solution, by means of analyzing the number of extracted packets on each scenario. This latter aims to be a first test of the scalability of the MMT-IoT software, aiming to determine the amount of information an IoT sniffer is capable to handle.

To deploy the testing scenarios we used the nodes provided by the w.iLab platform, each one composed of a Linux machine with two Zolertia Re-Mote IoT nodes. On each node we used the Zolertia Re-mote nodes to install the corresponding device type (in form of an IoT firmware) and generate the test traffic. Additionally, we installed the MMT-IoT Bridge, MMT-Probe and MMT-Security software on the MMT-IoT Linux machine. This was done in order to read the packets extracted by the IoT sniffer and perform the security analysis on the same node.

The Ping Client IoT sensors were configured to trigger the attack every 10 seconds. At each triggering, the client sent a burst of 10 ICMP ping packets equally spaced within a second. Additionally, an RPL router image was deployed in the "IoT-Router" machine in order to allow packets to flow through the network. All the MMT software was deployed in the MMT-IoT machine, including the MMT-IoT sniffer (in the Zolertia remote connected to that node), the MMT-IoT Bridge (running on the same NUC machine) and the MMT-Probe (also running on the NUC machine). This latter was the component in charge of analyzing the extracted packets and performing attack detection according to a rule previously defined: "we should not allow more than 2 ICMP ping packets per second on an IoT network". This rule comes to the fact that in IPv6 network (and particularly in 6LowPAN networks) the ICMP traffic (and specifically the ping packets) is important to keep the network running. In this sense, the rule allows a fair amount of ICMP packets run through the network without raising an attack alert. This is done to reduce the number of false positives detected by MMT. Using this rule, MMT-Probe was capable of detecting the occurrence of three or more ICMP packets as an attack, generating a report in the MMT-Probe logs.

Each scenario was executed continuously during 5 minutes, in order to generate enough traffic for later analysis. The packets extracted with MMT-IoT Sniffer (using the tcpdump tool) and the MMT-Probe logs are used to check the number of detected attacks in the scenario.

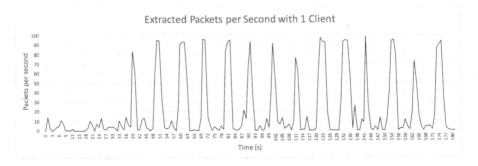

Fig. 4. Throughput extracted using MMT-IoT and 1 client.

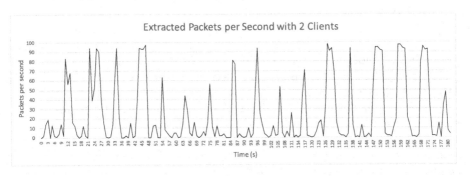

Fig. 5. Throughput extracted using MMT-IoT and 2 clients.

4.2 Results and Discussion

Figures 4, 5 and 6 show the results of the execution of the three scenarios. In this figure one can observe peaks each 10 s. These peaks correspond to the automatic triggering of the attacks, i.e. they show the moment when the clients started to send the ICMP ping packets. In these particular instances we observe a raise in the extracted traffic since there was more data available to be processed. In the 3-clients scenario we see that after 3 min of execution the peaks appear more often. We conjecture that this behaviour is due to some type of "desynchronization" between the three clients, and the different attacks appear more frequently.

An interesting observation is the limit of the extracted packets per second. Despite the fact that in the scenario we add more and more clients, and thus more traffic, the maximum number of packets extracted remained practically the same: around 95 packets per second. This opens the possibility of performing experiments to answer the following questions: "How does the packet size impact the number of packets extracted by MMT-IoT?" and "given the MTU of the IoT network, what is the upper limit of the throughput extracted by MMT-IoT?"

Finally, by analysing the logs of the MMT-Probe it was possible to count the number of attack detected. In the scenario with 1 attacking client, MMT-Probe detected 183 attacks; with 2 clients, 1046; and with 3 clients, 968. These numbers

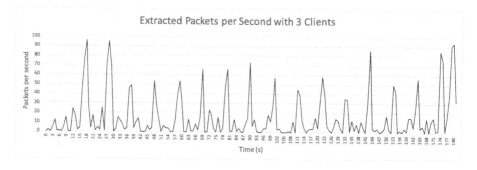

Fig. 6. Throughput extracted using MMT-IoT and 3 clients.

allow us to validate the applicability of the MMT solution in the IoT networks. In the case of a single attacker, MMT-Probe was capable of analysing the packets extracted by the MMT-IoT Sniffer and detect a simple security threat inside an IoT network.

5   Conclusions and Future Work

This paper presented the MMT-IoT tool and its deployment on the Fed4Fire+ testbed. It also presented the results of the feasibility and preliminary tests performed on the Virtual Wall–w.iLab platform. These tests allowed us to validate a proof-of-concept version of MMT-IoT on a real IoT environment. In particular, they allowed increasing the Technology Readiness Level of the tool and the added value of a future product.

It is important to note that even though this paper aimed performing initial feasibility analysis of the scalability issues, the preliminary results allowed us to draw promising conclusions about the future of the tool. In particular, Montimage will aim extending this study in order to clarify how the size of the IoT packets influences the extracted throughput and experiment other more sophisticated attacks. Our first analysis point out that these experiments would allow us to identify potential optimisations in the MMT-IoT sniffer and improve the detection algorithms, aiming to increase the value of the tool and gaining competitive advantage over other similar products such as Bastille's Enterprise IoT Security [2] that uses Bayesian statistics to identify anomalies, and Pwnie Express' Pulse IoT Security Platform [12] that performs device discovery to detect rogue devices, vulnerability scans and policy-infringing connections.

As a future work, we prepare a new experimentation phase that will involve two Fed4Fire platforms: LOG-a-TEC and w.iLab.

References

1. Bari, N., Mani, G., Berkovich, S.: Internet of things as a methodological concept. In: IEEE Fourth International Conference on Computing for Geospatial Research and Application (COM. Geo), pp. 48–55 (2013)

2. Basille: Enterprise IoT Security (2019). https://www.bastille.net/product. Accessed 12 July 2019
3. Greenough, J.: How the internet of things will impact consumers, businesses, and governments in 2016 and beyond. In: IEEE 4th International Conference on Distance Learning and Education (ICDLE) (2015). http://www.businessinsider.com/how-the-internet-of-things-market-will-grow-2014-10
4. Hasan, R., Saxena, N., Haleviz, T., et al.: Sensing-enabled channels for hard-to-detect command and control of mobile devices. In: 8th ACM SIGSAC Symposium on Information, Computer and Communications Security, pp. 469–480 (2013)
5. IMEC: w.ilab (2018). https://doc.ilabt.imec.be/ilabt/wilab/index.html. Accessed 12 July 2019
6. Lane, N.D., Miluzzo, E., Lu, H., Peebles, D., Choudhury, T., Campbell, A.T.: A survey of mobile phone sensing. IEEE Commun. Mag. **48**(9), 140–150 (2010)
7. Maiti, A., Jadliwala, M., He, J., Bilogrevic, I.: (Smart) watch your taps: side-channel keystroke inference attacks using smartwatches. In: ACM International Symposium on Wearable Computers, pp. 27–30 (2015)
8. Montimage: MMT (Montimage Monitoring Tool) (2019). https://montimage.com/products/MMT_DPI.html. Accessed 12 July 2019
9. Nahapetian, A.: Side-channel attacks on mobile and wearable systems. In: 13th IEEE Consumer Communications & Networking Conference (CCNC), pp. 243–247 (2016)
10. Petracca, G., Reineh, A.A., Sun, Y., Grossklags, J., Jaeger, T.: AWare: preventing abuse of privacy-sensitive sensors via operation bindings. In: 26th USENIX Security Symposium (2017)
11. Petracca, G., Sun, Y., Jaeger, T., Atamli, A.: AuDroid: preventing attacks on audio channels in mobile devices. In: 31st ACM Annual Computer Security Applications Conference, pp. 181–190 (2015)
12. Pwnie: Pulse IoT Security Platform (2019). https://www.pwnieexpress.com/pulse. Accessed 12 July 2019
13. Sikder, A.K., Aksu, H., Uluagac, A.S.: 6thsense: a contextaware sensor-based attack detector for smart devices. In: 26th USENIX Security Symposium, pp. 397–414 (2017)
14. Vucnik, M., Fortuna, C., Solc, T., Mohorcic, M.: Integrating research testbeds into social coding platforms. European Conference on Networks and Communications (EuCNC) (2018). https://doi.org/10.1109/EuCNC.2018.8443242
15. Yu, Y., Wang, J., Zhou, G.: The exploration in the education of professionals in applied internet of things engineering. In: IEEE 4th International Conference on Distance Learning and Education (ICDLE), pp. 74–77 (2010)

TestDCat: Catalog of Test Debt Subtypes and Management Activities

Bruno S. Aragão$^{(\boxtimes)}$, Rossana M. C. Andrade, Ismayle S. Santos,
Rute N. S. Castro, Valéria Lelli, and Ticianne G. R. Darin

Group of Computer Networks, Software Engineering, and Systems (GREat),
Federal University of Ceará (UFC), Fortaleza, Ceará, Brazil
{bruno,rossana,ismaylesantos,rute,valerialelli,
ticiannedarin}@great.ufc.br

Abstract. When deadlines and resources of software projects become scarce, testing is usually in the first row to have its activities aborted or reduced. If defects cannot be found, products quality can be affected. In a software development process, aborted or reduced activities that can bring short-term benefits, but can be harmful to the project in a long run, are considered Technical Debt (TD). When TDs impact testing activities, they are called *Test Debt*. There are several studies dealing with *Test Debt*, however, current solutions often deal with specific types of tests (*e.g.,* exploratory and automated tests) and do not address the whole software testing process. Aiming to fill these gaps, this paper proposes a *Test Debt Catalog* with subtypes of *Test Debts* and technical debt management activities. This catalog was built based on semi-structured interviews conducted with practitioners who perform testing activities in five projects from industry. With our catalog, we intend to help the management of test debts during the execution of software testing processes.

Keywords: Technical Debt · Test Debt · Testing process · TD management activity

1 Introduction

Software Testing is one of the most commonly used approaches to evaluate software quality [14]. Moreover, one way to mitigate the risk of projects failing to perform tasks related to software testing is the use of a well-defined testing process. By using a process, the software development team can monitor and control the activities, as well as adjust them as required [14].

However, when deadlines or resources become scarce, organizations tend to reduce tasks and practices related to software testing [23]. Besides this, even

B. S. Aragão—Researcher scholarship - Master student, sponsored by FCPC.
R. M. C. Andrade—Researcher scholarship - DT Level 2, sponsored by CNPq.
I. S. Santos and R. N. S. Castro—PhD student Scholarship, sponsored by CAPES.

C. Gaston et al. (Eds.): ICTSS 2019, LNCS 11812, pp. 279–295, 2019.
https://doi.org/10.1007/978-3-030-31280-0_18

using a testing process, members of a project may not perform (intentionally or unintentionally) some activities to achieve faster delivery and gain some competitive advantage [23]. In the context of a Test Factory - independent organizations that can offer high-quality testing services at a lower cost [4,17] - these decisions are even more critical as they can directly affect the quality of testing services offered to customers.

This kind of technical commitments generated in software projects that may bring short-term benefits, but which in the long-term may be detrimental to project quality, are defined as *Technical Debts* (TDs) [13]. This concept was first used by Cunningham [7], who related the characterization of TD to problems in the code and the need for refactoring to pay the debts acquired. Other studies have addressed TDs in other activities of the software development process (*e.g.,* tests, requirements, documentation) and provided solutions to manage them in software projects [1,13]. For example, *Technical Debts* that concern the software testing are known as *Test Debts*. They arise when inadequate decisions regarding testing activities (*e.g.,* lack of tests, test estimation errors) are made [16].

Our problem identification came from our experience in a successful long-term partnership with the industry [2] in Research, Development and Innovation (R&D&I) projects. In these kinds of projects, the GREat[1] test factory team has followed a testing process [4].

We have conducted an empirical study[2] to identify the main issues faced on the GREat Test Factory. The objects of the study are five tools (two mobile and three web) we have developed in a partnership with industry. The web tools deal with critical information about the company's internal processes such as schedules, activity monitoring and resource allocation. The mobile applications are based on Android technology and are continuously updated with new features and changes in the interaction flow to cover usability issues. They currently have together over 3 millions active users, so they must be tested in several Android versions running on different target devices to ensure they work as users expected. As a result of the study, we identified several problems related to incomplete test specification such as lack of test procedures to execute the test or incorrect preconditions of test cases. Also, we observed that several releases are launched without any tests in 2019. In addition, some types of tests that were initially planned were postponed.

The problems mentioned before were identified even with the GREat test factory team using a well-defined testing process. This occurred because, under delivery pressure or by decision of the customer, the team failed to perform some steps of the testing process (intentionally or unintentionally) and, with that, they

---

[1] Group of Computer Networks, Software Engineering, and Systems. The GREat Research Group works on research and development software projects, developing web and mobile tools that are constantly being tested by the GREat Test Factory team.

[2] The details of the study are available on: https://great-ufc.github.io/TestDCat/empirical/study.html.

don't do it or leave some test artifacts immature[3]. With the problem identified, we decided to formulate the problem as a test debt. Thus, the approaches and techniques used to manage this type of problem were studied in order to propose a solution to assist professionals deal with test debt. However, in spite of works dealing with *Test Debts* [16,18,20,22], they do not present in a consolidated manner the possible causes of *Test Debts* and how they can be identified and managed.

So, this work proposes a catalog, called *TestDCat*, of *Technical Debts* related to software testing as well as ways to manage them. We intend to give software engineers a broad view of subtypes of *Test Debts* that could occur in their projects and how to support their management. These subtypes were gathered from a systematic mapping study on *Technical Debts* and its management [13] and interviews with practitioners from five industry projects.

We evaluate the catalog in two steps. The first one was through a survey with the same interview participants and had the objective to identify if the catalog was in accordance with what they reported in the interviews. The second evaluation was through a focus group and the participants analyzed the entire catalog in detail and made observations and suggested improvements.

The following sections are organized as follows. Section 2 discusses related work. Section 3 presents the catalog design. Section 4 introduces our test debt catalog and Sect. 5 details its evaluation performed with experts. Section 6 discusses the results and, finally, Sect. 7 concludes the paper, presenting also perspectives of future work.

2   Related Work

The literature addresses different *Technical Debts* and their management activities. In this section, we focus the discussion on work related to *Test Debts* and management activities regarding to them.

Samarthyam et al. [16] present an overview of *Test Debts*, factors that contribute to this type of debts, and strategies for repayment of acquired *Test Debts*. These authors also classify *Test Debts* into: (i) unit testing; (ii) exploratory testing; (iii) manual testing; and (iv) automated testing. For each type of test, they present possible factors that may generate debts.

Aiming to support the repayment of TDs, Samarthyam et al. [16] propose a process with three macro activities: (i) Quantify the test debt, get the permission of the high administration, and execute the refund; (ii) Repay debts periodically; and (iii) Avoid the *Test Debts* from accumulating. They also present strategies for the payment of *Test Debts* that involve the application of good practices of test codification and in the accomplishment of the activities of software testing. Besides that, these authors describe two case studies in industry, in which they report experiences with *Test Debts*.

Although Samarthyam et al. [16] present a process with macro activities for the management of TD and identify good practices to prevent and repay TDs, this process does not detail all activities for TD management.

---

[3] Immature artifact means any artifact that is not fully developed.

de Sousa [20] presents a set of 22 TDs collected from literature review. The author describes its causes, indicators and possible solutions related to the software testing process. To evaluate the TDs, a survey was performed with test professionals. A map was also prepared to support professionals in the management of TDs that may occur during the execution of the testing process. This map was evaluated applying a questionnaire with software testing professionals, but the map was not applied in software organizations. Besides that, this work does not related, explicitly, the *Test Debts* with the TDs management activities.

Shah et al. [18] performed a systematic review to answer the following questions: (i) "Is the exploratory testing an example of a practice that induces technical debt?" and (ii) "Should the debt be repaid later in the software life cycle?". In this review, the authors present how the exploratory testing influences the test activities and the related *Technical Debts*. Thus, they conclude that: (i) The lack of definition of test cases makes it difficult to perform regression tests and may cause residual defects; (ii) High human dependence, the missing of results evaluation, and lack of test planning may cause residual defects; (iii) Lack of documentation may lead to a poor understanding of the functionalities, generating rework and causing a wrong effort planning.

Therefore, the review of Shah et al. provides an overview of *Technical Debts* regarding exploratory testing, but it does not cover TDs management nor other types of TDs that can occur during the test process.

Wiklund et al. [22] outline which factors contribute to the accumulation of *Technical Debts* in automated testing and assess the awareness of these debts in organizations that use automated testing. They identified these factors by performing semi-structured interviews with software designers.

Like the study of Shah et al., the work of Wiklund et al. is limited to one type of *Test Debts* - regarding automated testing - not addressing the wide range of debts generated during the testing process.

Based on the studies analyzed and presented in this section, we identified there is a need of presenting a consolidated view of possible causes of *Test Debts* and ways of managing them. We also identify this need from practical knowledge, inside the projects activities of the GREat Research Group.

3   Catalog Design

Information and know-how that comes from practitioners and that can be organized like a body of knowledge can be arranged in a catalog [5]. Based on this definition and the gaps identified in the literature, we decided to build a catalog to assist practitioners in managing *Test Debts*.

The design to build the catalog follows the methodology presented in Fig. 1. This methodology is partially based on the Gorschek technology transfer model [9].

The model on which our methodology is based favours mutual cooperation between academia and industry and can be beneficial to both. Researchers can study relevant industry issues and validate their results in a real environment.

In return, professionals receive knowledge about new technologies that can, for example, optimize their processes.

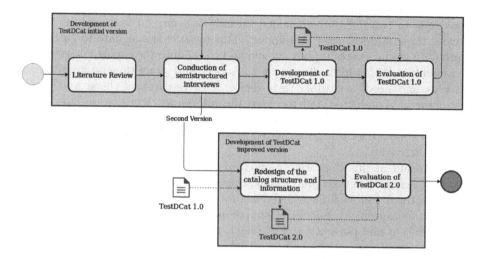

Fig. 1. Methodology used to build the *TestDCat* Catalog

The methodology is organized in two stages. At the first stage, we performed the activities: *Literature Review*; *Conduction of semistructured interviews*; *Development of TestDCat 1.0*; and *Evaluation of TestDCat 1.0*. At the second stage, we developed a new version of our catalog. Initially, we performed the *Redesign of the catalog structure and information* and evolved to the version *TestDCat 2.0*. Next, we conducted the *Evaluation of TestDCat 2.0*.

In the next sections, we detail the activities of the methodology.

3.1 Literature Review

Once problems were identified from the empirical observation[4], the first step that we conducted was a *Literature Review* in the main databases of Computer Science (*e.g.,* Scopus, IEEE Xplore Digital Library and Science Direct) to identify how these problems could be formulated and what solutions are commonly used in the literature. Based on the results of our research, we realized that these problems could be formulated using the concept of *Technical Debts* (TD), more specifically, *Test Debts*. We also identified that most of the work dealing with *Test Debts* did not provide an overview of how to manage these debts throughout the test process. Thus, we realized the need to create a catalog for managing *Test Debts*.

In order to collect the information for the creation of the catalog, we started the second stage of the methodology: *Conduction of semistructured interviews*.

---

[4] The details of the study are available on: https://great-ufc.github.io/TestDCat/empirical/study.html.

3.2   Conduction of Semistructured Interviews

Seeking to investigate practitioners' perspective about test debt, as well as to identify their strategies to deal with them, we conducted ten semi-structured interviews, in two different moments: initially focusing on test analysts' point of view, then on developers' standpoint. This method is adequate to gather in-depth data about a certain phenomenon and to tap into the expert knowledge of an individual [10], which allowed us to understand practitioners' approaches, concerns and needs regarding tests debts. Two researchers (head and auxiliary/observer) conducted and recorded the interviews, which were later transcribed and analyzed. Each session took about two hours on average and explored questions about practitioners' experience, subtypes of *Test Debts*, and TD management activities.

As a result of this step, we obtained information on which subtypes of test debt were acquired in their practical experience and actions taken to manage the debts identified. For each identified debt, we collected the actions used to: identification, measurement, prioritization, communication, monitoring, repayment, documentation and prevention of the debt. Such information was the basis for the definition of the actions to be carried out in each of the subtypes of *Test Debts*, which were later organized as a catalog.

Further details about interviews planning and conduction are explained in the remainder of this subsection, organized according to the four activities we conducted in this step: (1) Interview planning; (2) Participants selection; (3) Interviews conduction; (4) Data analysis and consolidation.

Interview Planning. Initially, we narrowed down some areas and topics to elicit conversation with the practitioners. Then, we organized the topics in a script format with an opening statement, a set of general questions to be explored by each topic, and additional questions designed to probe for information, in cases it did not come up[5]. To guide interviews, we developed a protocol which was refined with the consultation from experts in the field and also experts in qualitative research to provide us with feedback and guidance. We also piloted the interview guide to help improve its instrumentation [15]. Other than helping us to pay close attention to the relationship between the questions asked and the content produced during the interviews, the protocol also included statements of confidentiality, consent, options to withdraw, and intended use of the results. We formulated the topics and questions following the good practices presented in [10]. The protocol established the following steps to conduct the interview sessions: 1. *Profile Identification*, which included questions about the participants demographics, background, and experience in the field; 2. *Questions about Test Debts* to identify evidence of their presence in projects participants were currently working; 3. *Questions about the TDs management activities* selected from [13], these questions are intended to identify whether respondents execute any form of management among those identified *Test Debts*; and 4. *Slowdown,*

---

[5] The interview script is available on: https://bit.ly/2JPy1CD.

used for final considerations, with questions about the impact of lack of TD management activities and the possibility of using a catalog that could assist the process of managing *Test Debts*.

Participants Selection. We selected participants according to the technique classified as selective or purposeful sampling [6], since selection was according to the availability of practitioners at GREat laboratory and GREat Test Factory. All participants work in research and development projects conducted in partnership with industry at the GREat Research Group. Currently, such projects encompass the development of six web tools and two mobile applications, which are periodically tested by the GREat Test Factory. Table 1 summarizes the participants profile.

Interviews occurred in two different moments. First, we conducted five interview sessions focusing on test analysts' point of view. Hence the participants included three test analysts, a test leader, and a software testing researcher who also works on projects with industry. On average, they had about three years of experience working in software tests field, including functional and non-functional testing. Later, we conducted five more interviews to endeavor to address software developers perspective on testing. For these interviews, five more participants were selected: four system analysts and a technical leader. Besides their vast experience in software development activities, all of them also worked with functional tests.

Interviews Conduction. Each interview was conducted by two researchers. They both followed the instructions from the interview protocol detailing each procedure that must be followed during data collection. The information collected from participants was properly kept anonymous and private and was used exclusively for the analysis of test debt characteristics and actions in the scope of this investigation. Before beginning the interview session, the researcher organized a room with no distractions, and set the evaluation environment, including voice recorder so that each person's interview session could be documented. Before a participant entered the room, the recorder and all data collection instruments were already available and organized. When a participant entered the room, the researcher explained what the investigation was about and requested participants' permission to record the interviews. Then, the participant would sign a *terms of free and informed consent*, which assured data confidentiality and anonymity.

Data Analysis and Categorization. Initially, we run a brief quantitative analysis on closed ended questions including, for example, whether practitioners felt pressured to perform test activities, and the occurrence of different sub-types of *Test Debts*. Objective answers were often also followed by comments that were later analyzed in a qualitative way.

Then, a qualitative analysis was conducted on the answers recordings from each interview. Interviews were transcribed, and critical comments were iden-

Table 1. Participants profile

ID	Specialty	Expertise	Current position	TDs reported
P01	Software testion	Functional and non-functional tests	Junior Test Analyst	-Deferring testing -Lack of tests -Defects not found in tests -Expensive tests -Test estimation errors
P02			Mid-level Test Analyst/Test Leader	
P03			Junior Test Analyst	-Deferring testing -Lack of tests -Lack of tests automation -Defects not found in tests -Expensive tests -Test estimation errors
P04			Researcher	
P05			Junior Test Analyst	-Lack of tests -Expensive tests -Test estimation errors
P06	SW development and testing	SW development and functional tests	Mid-level System Analyst/Technical Leader	-Low code coverage -Deferring testing -Defects not found in tests -Expensive tests -Test estimation errors
P07			Senior Systems Analyst/Technical Leader	-Low code coverage -Deferring testing -Lack of tests -Expensive tests -Test estimation errors
P08			Mid-level System Analyst	-Deferring testing -Lack of tests -Lack of tests automation -Defects not found in tests -Expensive tests -Test estimation errors
P09			Mid-level System Analyst	-Low code coverage -Lack of tests -Defects not found in tests
P10			Researcher	-Low code coverage -Deferring testing -Lack of tests automation -Defects not found in tests -Test estimation errors

tified by using open coding approach for the categorization of transcripts and identification of goals connections among the findings they revealed [3]. Overall, the transcripts analysis took about 70 h. We used the classification tree and *Technical Debts* management activities proposed by Li et al. [13] as basis for our data categorization. Hence, we organized the transcripts into eight well-defined categories that guided data consolidation as described in the *Test Debt Catalog* section.

3.3   Development of TestDCat 1.0

For the *Development of TestDCat 1.0*, all information obtained from the first session of interviews (with five participants) was analyzed and organized in a matrix that represents the *TestDCat 1.0* catalog. The matrix was formed by test debt subtypes and, for each of them, a set of TD management activities was associated. Within each of these activities, there was information about "Approaches", "Points of attention in the test process" and "Good Practices". Figure 2 presents an example with the test debt subtype "Low code coverage" and the TD management activity "Identification".

Test Debt subtype	TD Management Activities
	Identification
Low code coverage	**Approaches:** **Code analysis:** Investigate the code to analyze its coverage. This analysis is usually done with a specifc tool (e.g., Eclema).
	Points of attention in the test process: **Test Planning:** Definition of the coverage targets. **Test Design:** Registration of test coverage **Test Execution:** feedback about the coverage to test monitoring **Test Monitoring:** Collection and analysis of measurements
	Good Practices: Use of continuous integration to automate the code coverage verification process

Fig. 2. *TestDCat 1.0* example

3.4   Evaluation of TestDCat 1.0

The goal of the first evaluation was to gather the participants perception about the catalog clarity, ease of use and completeness. So, the evaluation intended to get answers to the following: *Does the TestDCat catalog have clear and enough information to support the management of Test Debts?*

For this evaluation, we presented the whole catalog, printed on paper, to the five interviews' participants of the first moment and, after reading and analyzing the catalog, they answered the questions of the survey.

With regards to clarity, all participants agree, 60% strongly agree and 40% agree, that the catalog presents the information in a clear and objective way. Furthermore, most of the participants agrees, 40% strongly agree and 40% agree, that the catalog is easy of use. Just one of them chose a neutral response.

Regarding the completeness, most of the participants agrees, 20% strongly agree and 60% agree, that the catalog has enough information to support the management of *Test Debts*. On the other hand, one of them disagreed about the completeness of the catalog.

Regarding the usefulness of the catalog, all participants agree, 100% strongly agree, that it would certainly help users to manage their *Test Debts*.

In addition, the participants suggested improvements to the catalog in the open questions. For instance, they asked for more details on each approach presented, as well as more practical information that would make the use of the catalogue more precise.

3.5 Redesign of the Catalog Structure and Information

Based on the results of the first evaluation and new information from the second interview session, we created a new version of the catalog. This new version is described in Sect. 4.

3.6 Evaluation of TestDCat 2.0

In order to evaluate the new version of *TestDCat* produced, a new evaluation was performed. This evaluation was conducted through focus groups with five participants of different kinds of expertise in the software development process. Details about this evaluation are in Sect. 5.

4 Test Debt Catalog

Based on the results of the first evaluation carried out, as well as the new information taken from the new interview session conducted, we redesigned the catalog.

The *TestDCat* 2.0 catalog consists of TD management activities and, for each of them, a set of subtypes of *Test Debts* are associated. Within each of these subtypes, actions are presented using the 5W1H (Who, What, When, Where, Why, and How) model. This model is commonly used for the development of action plans [8].

The data is categorized according to TD management activities and subtypes of test debt, both mapped by Li et.al [13]. The test debt subtypes are the possible causes for this kind of debt. In addition to the subtypes identified by Li et.al, we identified two other subtypes: Inadequate equipment; and Inadequate allocation.

Figure 3 presents the new structure of the catalog, emphasizing with listed circles parts of the catalog. Circle number 1 emphasises the technical debt management activities: Identification, Measurement, Prioritization, Communication, Monitoring, Repayment, Documentation, and Prevention. By clicking on any of these activities, are presented subtypes of *Test Debts* and its related actions. In this example, the "Identification" activity was selected.

The circle number two presents the subtypes of *Test Debts*: Low code coverage, Deferring testing, Lack of tests, Lack of tests automation, Defects not found in tests, Expensive tests, Test effort estimation errors, Inadequate equipment, and Inadequate allocation. In this catalog, we present a set of actions for each subtype. For example, after clicking on the "Identification" activity, the user can choose which subtype he wants to handle. In this example, we choose "Low Code Coverage", which has two related actions.

The circle number three brings forward the actions identified through semistructured interviews conducted. They are following the 5W1H model. In this case, these are the suggested actions to help catalog users to identify *Test Debts* caused by "Low Code Coverage".

Actions can be used together or individually. Thus, in the circle number four we present the functionality in which the user can select which actions are most related to their context. After selecting, a custom action plan will be created. Finally, it's possible to print or download this plan.

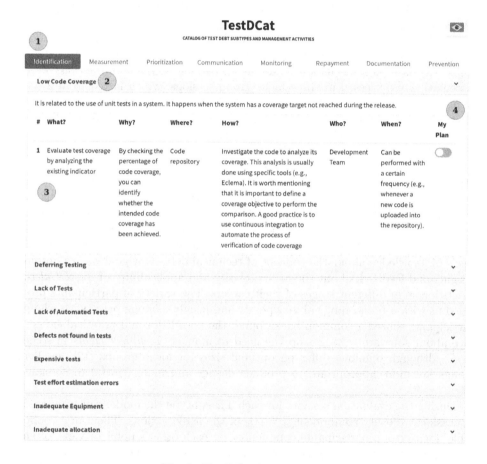

Fig. 3. *TestDCat 2.0* structure

All the catalog's information can be viewed on the *TestDCat*'s website[6]. Another aspect of this catalog website is that we inserted a form so the visitors can also suggest improvements or new actions for managing *Test Debts*.

---

[6] *TestDCat*'s website: https://great-ufc.github.io/TestDCat/index.html.

5   Catalog Evaluation

After producing *TestDCat* version 2.0, we further conducted in-depth evaluations to assess the correctness, quality, and coverage of the catalog content - including all statements, descriptions and subcategories - under the perspective of practitioners. Hence, to capture impressions of potential catalog users and elicit their suggestions, reactions, frustrations, and fears we convened three sessions of focus groups. Focus group is an inexpensive and powerful approach from the social sciences largely used in human-computer interaction experimental and empirical researches to help generating a deeper and more nuanced understanding of an issue [12,19].

The focus group was planned, piloted and conducted by an experienced moderator, together with two assistant observers who took structured notes. *TestDCat* was used as a discussion guide, as all catalog sections and actions were systematically discussed in three focus group sessions, which lasted from 2–3 h each. Each participant received a hard copy of *TestDCat*, some Post-its and pens, and was encouraged to make annotations and suggestions as the discussions progressed. Due to the long sessions, the typical question and answer style script was combined with prioritization and summary exercises. Additionally, refreshments were made available and regular comfort breaks were offered to the participants.

Five participants were carefully selected according to their expertise, background and availability. As summarized in Table 2, the focus group sessions gathered practitioners with different types of expertise within the software development process, as well as various levels of experience. They also had different levels of knowledge about the concept of technical debt. Our goal was to obtain insights and feedback about the utility, clarity and applicability of *TestDCat* to practitioners in different stages of their careers. The variety of participants provided us with a broad range of viewpoints and insights among peers with whom participants shared a common background: the knowledge and practical experience about software testing, and the need to manage *Technical Debts* in some level. Although opinions differ on optimal sizes for focus groups [12], smaller groups are more appropriate to produce deeper and more fruitful discussions [11].

During the evaluation session, for each TD subtype the moderator promoted discussions on every component (5W1H) of the listed actions. Then, in a round table, focus group participants commented on each other's point of view, often challenging each other's motives and actions, and relating their own experiences to the catalog descriptions. This procedure allowed participants to thoroughly analyze each action and its steps. In addition, a flip chart was available so that moderator could summarize the identified drawbacks and advantages, suggestions of improvements, and doubts that were common to all participants. The moderator would sum up important points at convenient times, making sure participants had understood them. After discussing an action, the mediator asked whether the participants indicated that the action should be kept in the catalog, undergo changes, or whether they felt it was not appropriate and should leave.

Table 2. Profile of focus group sessions participants

ID	Specialty	Experience in the field	Current position	Level understanding about technical debt
P01	Software testing	3 years	Junior Test Analyst	I'm familiar with the concept
P02	SW development and testing	13 years	Senior Systems Analyst/Technical Leader	
P03	SW development and testing	1,5 year	Junior Systems Analyst	I've applied strategies to manage TDs
P04	Software testing	2 years	Software testing researcher	I'm familiar with the concept
P05	Software development	4 years	Mid-level Systems Analyst	I'm not familiar with the concept

Then, when all actions of a subtype category were discussed, participants individually used a 5-point Likert rating scale to assess the following criteria: applicability to the full range of intended uses, concreteness, clarity, ease of understanding, ease of use, impartiality, and relevance to the context. Such criteria were adapted from those proposed to assess the quality of evaluation checklists in a particular area [21]. The results of participants' rating scales are summarized in Fig. 4. By the end of each session, the moderator and observers conducted a debriefing and led a summary exercise to gather key themes and check for further understanding on participants, moderation and observers' notes. Besides, they identified and categorized note themes, hunches, interpretations, and ideas. Then, they labeled, compared and contrasted information from field notes, and other materials.

A total of 63 actions were evaluated and analyzed. Overall, participants suggested to remove an action related to the "Communication" activity and add a new action to the "Identification" activity. Some relevant doubts arose regarding: "Test coverage and code coverage. Is it separate or is it the same thing?", "How to identify the ideal version?". The main improvements suggested were "Categorize separating tests of what is manual and automated", "Standardize the terms (especially for the columns "Who" and "Where")". Finally, some of the changes requested included: "Put a glossary with test area terms and technical debt (TD) for people who are not very experienced in testing and TD", "As it is dependent on some preconditions, it would be better to clearly separate what is precondition and what is the action in fact", "Use the term iteration instead of Sprint" and "Keep the term follow-up meetings in all actions that mention holding meetings".

6   Discussion

The second evaluation, in which the participants evaluated each action in the catalog, proved to be very useful, despite requiring a lot of effort. Several improve-

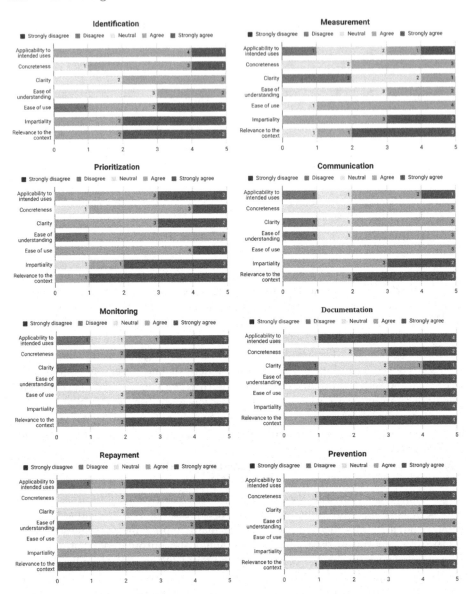

Fig. 4. Results of the evaluation

ments were suggested and only one of the actions was considered inadequate for the proper purpose. In a nutshell, the proposed catalog got good results.

All criteria had more than 50% agreement. The criteria "Applicability to all intended uses" obtained 77.5% agreement and "Relevance to the context" obtained more than 95%, which reflects that the participants believe that the catalog can indeed be used to assist in the management of *Test Debts*.

The criteria "Clarity" and "Ease of understanding" were the ones that had the highest rate of disagreement with 12.5%. In the individual analysis of the answers, we noticed that the majority of the participants who had these opinions had less work experience. However, as the use of the catalog must be made by all levels of expertise, these are points of improvement that must be addressed. It is worth mentioning that during the evaluation the participants made many observations in order to improve these criteria, so we believe that when considering these new improvements, these rates tend to decrease.

It is also worth mentioning that the interview with professionals brings the benefit of gathering information about the perception of the regarding *Test Debts*. This was useful to identify new *Test Debts*. For instance, to the best of our knowledge, the *Test Debts Inadequate equipment* and *Inadequate allocation* were not previously reported in the literature.

Threats to Validity. Regarding the threats to validity, we discuss threats related to *Internal Validity* and *External Validity*. According to [24], threats to *Internal Validity* are influences that can affect the independent variable with respect to causality, and threats to *External Validity*, in turn, are conditions that limit the ability to generalize the results to industrial practice.

In our case, the main threat regarding the *Internal Validity* is the selection of the subjects that was made based on convenience sampling [24]. In the case of *External Validity*, the small number of participants is our main threat. Despite these limitations, it is worth noting that the participants were professionals with great experience on software testing activities in industry. Furthermore, these professionals had experience of testing mobile and web software.

7   Conclusion and Future Work

Test Debts have a high impact on software quality. So, they require the use of management activities within the testing process to be monitored and controlled during the testing releases. Nevertheless, most of the studies focus on the management of *Technical Debts* in general or management of specific *Test Debts*.

Aiming to address the gap in supporting practitioners in the management of *Test Debts*, we proposed a catalog, called TestDCat, that was created based on the information gathered from semi-structured interviews performed with professionals from industry.

TestDCat presents an overview of management activities, subtypes of *Test Debts* and actions to assist in TD management activities. To get an initial evaluation, we presented the catalog to the participants of the interviews who answered a survey regarding clarity, ease of use and completeness. In the second evaluation, we made a focus group that aimed to analyze in detail the actions of the catalog and suggest changes and improvements.

The results of these two evaluations presented evidence that the information organized in the catalog can support the management of *Test Debts*. Thus, it may help the development and testing team to monitor the current debts and to take the actions according to the identified test debt.

As future work, we intend to proceed with the improvements suggested during the second evaluation and apply the actions catalogued in *TestDCat* in real projects so that it will be possible to evaluate their practical contribution.

References

1. Alves, N.S., Mendes, T.S., de Mendonça, M.G., Spínola, R.O., Shull, F., Seaman, C.: Identification and management of technical debt: a systematic mapping study. Inf. Softw. Technol. **70**, 100–121 (2016)
2. Andrade, R.M.C., Lelli, V., Castro, R.N.S., Santos, I.S.: Fifteen years of industry and academia partnership: lessons learned from a Brazilian research group. In: 2017 IEEE/ACM 4th International Workshop on Software Engineering Research and Industrial Practice (SER IP), pp. 10–16, May 2017. https://doi.org/10.1109/SER-IP.2017.2
3. Burnard, P.: A method of analysing interview transcripts in qualitative research. Nurse Educ. Today **11**(6), 461–466 (1991)
4. Andrade, R.M.C., Santos, I.S., Lelli, V., Oliveira, K.M., Rocha, A.R.C.: Software testing process in a test factory - from ad hoc activities to an organizational standard. In: ICEIS (2017)
5. Chung, L., Nixon, B.A., Yu, E., Mylopoulos, J.: Non-Functional Requirements in Software Engineering, vol. 5. Springer, Boston (2012). https://doi.org/10.1007/978-1-4615-5269-7
6. Coyne, I.: Sampling in qualitative research. Purposeful and theoretical sampling; merging or clear boundaries? J. Adv. Nurs. **26**(3), 623–630 (1997)
7. Cunningham, W.: The WyCash portfolio management system. SIGPLAN OOPS Mess. **4**(2), 29–30 (1992). https://doi.org/10.1145/157710.157715
8. Fernandes, F., Sousa, S., Lopes, I.: On the use of quality tools: a case study. In: World Congress on Engineering 2013, vol. 1, pp. 634–639. Newswood Limited Publisher (2013)
9. Gorschek, T., Garre, P., Larsson, S., Wohlin, C.: A model for technology transfer in practice. IEEE Softw. **23**(6), 88–95 (2006)
10. Hove, S.E., Anda, B.: Experiences from conducting semi-structured interviews in empirical software engineering research. In: 2005 11th IEEE International Symposium on Software Metrics, p. 10. IEEE (2005)
11. Krueger, R.A., Casey, M.A.: Designing and conducting focus group interviews (2002)
12. Lazar, J., Feng, J.H., Hochheiser, H.: Research Methods in Human-Computer Interaction. Morgan Kaufmann, Burlington (2017)
13. Li, Z., Avgeriou, P., Liang, P.: A systematic mapping study on technical debt and its management. J. Syst. Softw. **101**, 193–220 (2015)
14. Orso, A., Rothermel, G.: Software testing: a research travelogue (2000–2014). In: Proceedings of the on Future of Software Engineering, pp. 117–132. ACM (2014)
15. Rogers, Y., Sharp, H., Preece, J.: Interaction Design: Beyond Human-Computer Interaction. Wiley, Hoboken (2011)
16. Samarthyam, G., Muralidharan, M., Anna, R.K.: Understanding test debt. In: Mohanty, H., Mohanty, J.R., Balakrishnan, A. (eds.) Trends in Software Testing, pp. 1–17. Springer, Singapore (2017). https://doi.org/10.1007/978-981-10-1415-4_1

17. Sanz, A., Garcia, J., Saldana, J., Amescua, A.: A proposal of a process model to create a test factory. In: 2009 ICSE Workshop on Software Quality. WOSQ 2009, pp. 65–70. IEEE (2009)
18. Shah, S.M.A., Torchiano, M., Vetro, A., Morisio, M.: Exploratory testing as a source of technical debt. IT Prof. **16**(3), 44–51 (2014)
19. Shneiderman, B., Plaisant, C., Cohen, M., Jacobs, S., Elmqvist, N., Diakopoulos, N.: Designing the User Interface: Strategies for Effective Human-Computer Interaction. Pearson, London (2016)
20. de Sousa, C.L.: Mapa de apoio à gestão de dívida técnica no processo de teste de software. Master's thesis, Universidade Federal de Pernambuco (2016)
21. Stufflebeam, D.L.: Guidelines for Developing Evaluation Checklists: The Checklists Development Checklist (CDC). The Evaluation Center, Kalamazoo (2000)
22. Wiklund, K., Eldh, S., Sundmark, D., Lundqvist, K.: Technical debt in test automation. In: 2012 IEEE Fifth International Conference on Software Testing, Verification and Validation, pp. 887–892, April 2012. https://doi.org/10.1109/ICST.2012.192
23. Wiklund, K., Eldh, S., Sundmark, D., Lundqvist, K.: Impediments for software test automation: a systematic literature review. Softw. Test. Verif. Reliab. **27**(8), e1639 (2017)
24. Wohlin, C., Runeson, P., Hst, M., Ohlsson, M.C., Regnell, B., Wessln, A.: Experimentation in Software Engineering. Springer, Berlin (2012). https://doi.org/10.1007/978-3-642-29044-2

Author Index

Printed in the United States
By Bookmasters